G000136450

GENERAL OFFICE

To:	Select:	Then:
Start an application	Start → Programs	Open program folder containing program icon and click program icon
Save document	File → Save or 💾	Type name, select folder, and click Save
Open document	File → Open or 📂	Open folder containing document, click 🔼, use the Look in: box and double-click your file
Create new document	File → New or 📄	Select template you want to use and click OK button
Print document	File → Print or 🖨	Make any changes to print options and click OK button

POWERPOINT

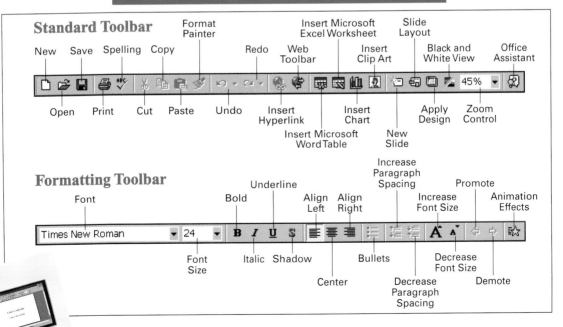

EXCEL

How to Select a Cell with the Keyboard

Press	To move...
→	Right one cell
←	Left one cell
↓	Down one cell
↑	Up one cell
Ctrl + →	To right edge of current region
Ctrl + ←	To left edge of current region
Ctrl + ↓	To bottom edge of current region
Ctrl + ↑	To top edge of current region
Ctrl + Home	First cell in worksheet
Ctrl + End	Lower right cell in worksheet
PgDn	Down one screen
PgUp	Up one screen
Alt + PgDn	Right one screen
Alt + PgUp	Left one screen
Ctrl + PgDn	Next sheet
Ctrl + PgUp	Previous sheet

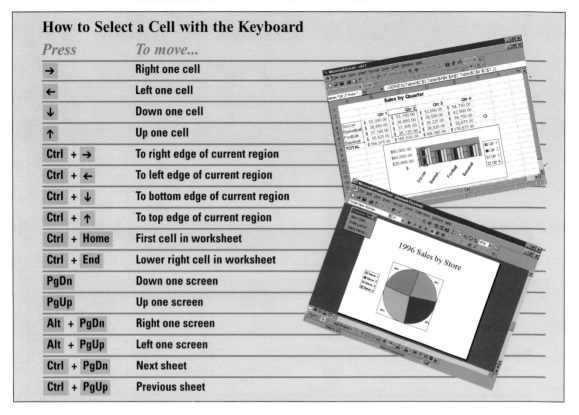

Standard Toolbar

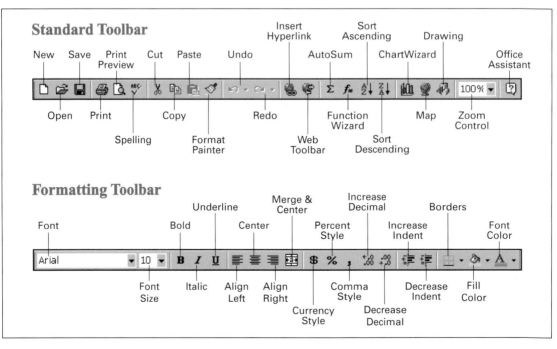

New, Open, Save, Print Preview, Print, Spelling, Cut, Copy, Paste, Format Painter, Undo, Redo, Insert Hyperlink, Web Toolbar, AutoSum, Function Wizard, Sort Ascending, Sort Descending, ChartWizard, Map, Drawing, Zoom Control, Office Assistant

Formatting Toolbar

Font, Font Size, Bold, Italic, Underline, Align Left, Center, Align Right, Merge & Center, Currency Style, Percent Style, Comma Style, Increase Decimal, Decrease Decimal, Increase Indent, Decrease Indent, Borders, Fill Color, Font Color

Arial | 10

DISCOVER
OFFICE 97

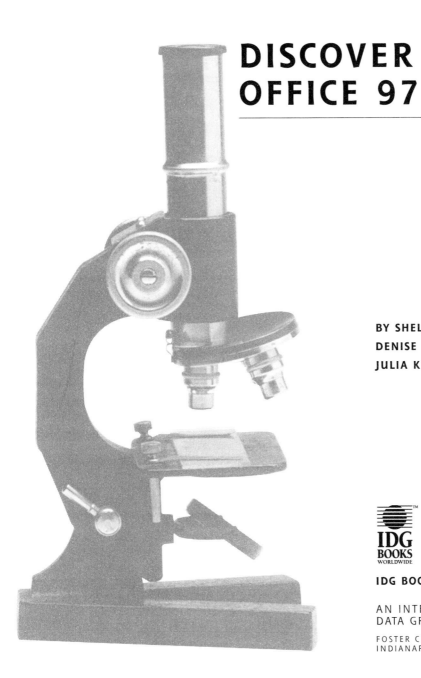

DISCOVER
OFFICE 97

BY SHELLEY O'HARA,
DENISE B. VEGA, AND
JULIA KELLY

IDG BOOKS WORLDWIDE, INC.

AN INTERNATIONAL
DATA GROUP COMPANY

FOSTER CITY, CA • CHICAGO, IL •
INDIANAPOLIS, IN • SOUTHLAKE, TX

Discover Office 97

Published by
IDG Books Worldwide, Inc.
An International Data Group Company
919 E. Hillsdale Blvd.
Suite 400
Foster City, CA 94404
www.idgbooks.com (IDG Books Worldwide Web site)
www.dummies.com (Dummies Press Web site)

Library of Congress Catalog Card No.: 96-80455

ISBN: 0-7645-3079-8

Printed in the United States of America

10 9 8 7 6 5 4

1B/SW/QZ/ZX/FC-IN

Distributed in the United States by IDG Books Worldwide, Inc.

Distributed by Macmillan Canada for Canada; by Transworld Publishers Limited in the United Kingdom; by IDG Norge Books for Norway; by IDG Sweden Books for Sweden; by Woodslane Pty. Ltd. for Australia; by Woodslane Enterprises Ltd. for New Zealand; by Longman Singapore Publishers Ltd. for Singapore, Malaysia, Thailand, and Indonesia; by Simron Pty. Ltd. for South Africa; by Toppan Company Ltd. for Japan; by Distribuidora Cuspide for Argentina; by Livraria Cultura for Brazil; by Ediciencia S.A. for Ecuador; by Addison-Wesley Publishing Company for Korea; by Ediciones ZETA S.C.R. Ltda. for Peru; by WS Computer Publishing Corporation, Inc., for the Philippines; by Unalis Corporation for Taiwan; by Contemporanea de Ediciones for Venezuela; by Computer Book & Magazine Store for Puerto Rico; by Express Computer Distributors for the Caribbean and West Indies. Authorized Sales Agent: Anthony Rudkin Associates for the Middle East and North Africa.

For general information on IDG Books Worldwide's books in the U.S., please call our Consumer Customer Service department at 800-762-2974. For reseller information, including discounts and premium sales, please call our Reseller Customer Service department at 800-434-3422.

For information on where to purchase IDG Books Worldwide's books outside the U.S., please contact our International Sales department at 415-655-3200 or fax 415-655-3295.

For information on foreign language translations, please contact our Foreign & Subsidiary Rights department at 415-655-3021 or fax 415-655-3281.

For sales inquiries and special prices for bulk quantities, please contact our Sales department at 415-655-3200 or write to the address above.

For information on using IDG Books Worldwide's books in the classroom or for ordering examination copies, please contact our Educational Sales department at 800-434-2086 or fax 817-251-8174.

For press review copies, author interviews, or other publicity information, please contact our Public Relations department at 415-655-3000 or fax 415-655-3299.

For authorization to photocopy items for corporate, personal, or educational use, please contact Copyright Clearance Center, 222 Rosewood Drive, Danvers, MA 01923, or fax 508-750-4470.

ABOUT IDG BOOKS WORLDWIDE

Welcome to the world of IDG Books Worldwide.

IDG Books Worldwide, Inc., is a subsidiary of International Data Group, the world's largest publisher of computer-related information and the leading global provider of information services on information technology. IDG was founded more than 25 years ago and now employs more than 8,500 people worldwide. IDG publishes more than 275 computer publications in over 75 countries (see listing below). More than 60 million people read one or more IDG publications each month.

Launched in 1990, IDG Books Worldwide is today the #1 publisher of best-selling computer books in the United States. We are proud to have received eight awards from the Computer Press Association in recognition of editorial excellence and three from *Computer Currents'* First Annual Readers' Choice Awards. Our best-selling *...For Dummies®* series has more than 30 million copies in print with translations in 30 languages. IDG Books Worldwide, through a joint venture with IDG's Hi-Tech Beijing, became the first U.S. publisher to publish a computer book in the People's Republic of China. In record time, IDG Books Worldwide has become the first choice for millions of readers around the world who want to learn how to better manage their businesses.

Our mission is simple: Every one of our books is designed to bring extra value and skill-building instructions to the reader. Our books are written by experts who understand and care about our readers. The knowledge base of our editorial staff comes from years of experience in publishing, education, and journalism — experience we use to produce books for the '90s. In short, we care about books, so we attract the best people. We devote special attention to details such as audience, interior design, use of icons, and illustrations. And because we use an efficient process of authoring, editing, and desktop publishing our books electronically, we can spend more time ensuring superior content and spend less time on the technicalities of making books.

You can count on our commitment to deliver high-quality books at competitive prices on topics you want to read about. At IDG Books Worldwide, we continue in the IDG tradition of delivering quality for more than 25 years. You'll find no better book on a subject than one from IDG Books Worldwide.

John Kilcullen
John Kilcullen
CEO
IDG Books Worldwide, Inc.

Steven Berkowitz
Steven Berkowitz
President and Publisher
IDG Books Worldwide, Inc.

VIII
WINNER
*Eighth Annual
Computer Press
Awards ≥1992*

IX
WINNER
*Ninth Annual
Computer Press
Awards ≥1993*

X
WINNER
*Tenth Annual
Computer Press
Awards ≥1994*

XI
WINNER
*Eleventh Annual
Computer Press
Awards ≥1995*

Welcome to the Discover Series

Do you want to discover the best and most efficient ways to use your computer and learn about technology? Books in the Discover series teach you the essentials of technology with a friendly, confident approach. You'll find a Discover book on almost any subject — from the Internet to intranets, from Web design and programming to the business programs that make your life easier.

We've provided valuable, real-world examples that help you relate to topics faster. Discover books begin by introducing you to the main features of programs, so you start by doing something *immediately*. The focus is to teach you how to perform tasks that are useful and meaningful in your day-to-day work. You might create a document or graphic, explore your computer, surf the Web, or write a program. Whatever the task, you learn the most commonly used features, and focus on the best tips and techniques for doing your work. You'll get results quickly, and discover the best ways to use software and technology in your everyday life.

You may find the following elements and features in this book:

Discovery Central: This tearout card is a handy quick reference to important tasks or ideas covered in the book.

Quick Tour: The Quick Tour gets you started working with the book right away.

Real-Life Vignettes: Throughout the book you'll see one-page scenarios illustrating a real-life application of a topic covered.

Goals: Each chapter opens with a list of goals you can achieve by reading the chapter.

Side Trips: These asides include additional information about alternative or advanced ways to approach the topic covered.

Bonuses: Timesaving tips and more advanced techniques are covered in each chapter.

Discovery Center: This guide illustrates key procedures covered throughout the book.

Visual Index: You'll find real-world documents in the Visual Index, with page numbers pointing you to where you should turn to achieve the effects shown.

Throughout the book, you'll also notice some special icons and formatting:

 A Feature Focus icon highlights new features in the software's latest release, and points out significant differences between it and the previous version.

 Web Paths refer you to Web sites that provide additional information about the topic.

 Tips offer timesaving shortcuts, expert advice, quick techniques, or brief reminders.

 The X-Ref icon refers you to other chapters or sections for more information.

Pull Quotes emphasize important ideas that are covered in the chapter.

 Notes provide additional information or highlight special points of interest about a topic.

 The Caution icon alerts you to potential problems you should watch out for.

The Discover series delivers interesting, insightful, and inspiring information about technology to help you learn faster and retain more. So the next time you want to find answers to your technology questions, reach for a Discover book. We hope the entertaining, easy-to-read style puts you at ease and makes learning fun.

Credits

ACQUISITIONS EDITOR
Ellen Camm

DEVELOPMENT EDITOR
Susannah Davidson

TECHNICAL EDITOR
Constantine Mengason

COPY EDITORS
Robert Campbell
Michael Welch

PROJECT COORDINATOR
Ben Schroeter

GRAPHICS AND PRODUCTION SPECIALISTS
Elizabeth Cárdenas-Nelson
Tom Debolski
Renée Dunn
Stephen Noetzel
Ed Penslien
Christopher Pimentel
Dina F Quan
Andreas F. Schueller
Elsie Yim

QUALITY CONTROL SPECIALIST
Mick Arellano

PROOFREADERS
Desne Border
Andrew Davis
Stacey Lynn
Candace Ward
Anne Weinberger

INDEXER
Sharon Hilgenberg

BOOK DESIGN
Seventeenth Street Studios
Phyllis Beaty
Kurt Krames

About the Authors

Shelley O'Hara is a freelance writer based in Indianapolis. She has written over 50 computer books, including *Discover Office 97*. In addition to writing, she is a trainer of computer programs for the Division of Continuing Studies for Indiana University and Purdue University at Indianapolis. O'Hara has a BA in English from the University of South Carolina and an MA in English from the University of Maryland. She has also penned *101 Ways to Drive Your Husband Insane* and *The Marriage Trifecta*, her yet-to-be-discovered fiction work.

Denise Vega received her Master's in Education from Harvard University. She works as a freelance writer and trainer in Denver, training on and writing about a variety of applications. She is the author of two books on WordPerfect 6.1 for Windows, as well as a series of courseware on the Microsoft Office suite for a Denver client. Her computer articles have appeared in a number of national magazines, and she is a regular contributing editor to *WordPerfect for the Law Office* magazine. She enjoys camping, fishing, and snow fun and is currently working on a children's novel.

Julia Kelly is a freelance writer and a former U.S. Air Force pilot (the first female member of the Caterpillar Club, having had to eject from a disabled aircraft and return to earth via parachute). She is also a former biotechnology laboratory scientist. Among the books she has written are *Discover Outlook 97* and *Microsoft Excel 97 Step by Step*. Kelly lives in Idaho.

TO THE JOY OF MY LIFE, MY SON MICHAEL

—*Shelley O'Hara*

PREFACE

Think about a typical desk 15 or 20 years ago. Perhaps you had some paper and a pen to do your writing. If you were somewhat high-tech, perhaps you even had a typewriter. For calculations, most people probably had some type of calculator. If you had extensive accounting and financial information to take care of, you might have had special ledger paper. And your friends, colleagues, coworkers, clients? How did most keep track of people? With a simple Rolodex. And appointments? Probably a little date book. Simple tools for simple tasks.

What's changed isn't *what* we do, but *how* we do it. That's why you shouldn't be intimidated when you think of all of this computer stuff. You aren't really doing anything different than you ever did. You're still typing letters, totaling numbers, keeping track of addresses, remembering appointments. What's changed isn't the basic task, but how you complete that task. All these tasks are made easier with computers and computer programs such as Office 97.

What Is Office 97?

Office 97 is a suite of computer programs, each designed to help you with a set of common tasks:

* **Word 97** is a word processing program. This program replaces pen and paper, or typewriters. You can use it to create anything from simple documents such as a letter to complex documents such as an entire manuscript.

* **Excel 97** is a spreadsheet program. This program replaces a calculator. You can use it to work with numbers and calculations — figure budgets, total sales, calculate commissions, and so on.

* **Access 9**7 is a database program and replaces your old Rolodex. You can use Access to keep track of names and addresses, events, products, inventory, sales orders, and more.

* **Outlook 97** is a desktop information management program — that's a fancy name for a program to keep track of appointments, contacts, and tasks, and also to handle your e-mail. This program is a replacement for your handy date book.

* Office 97 also includes a program for creating slide presentations, called **PowerPoint**.

You can use these programs to do the same routine, everyday tasks you used the old stuff for, but you can do them much more easily. In this book, you learn how to accomplish the basic tasks using each program.

Keep in mind, though, that these programs also are much more than their simple counterparts. You can do much more with Word 97, for instance, than you could ever do with pen and paper or even a typewriter. The same is true for Excel, Access, Outlook, and PowerPoint. This book also explains how to get the most from each program — ways you can save time, features you can use to improve accuracy, ways to enhance the look of your work, and more.

Basically, this book explains how you can use these same tools to do the same tasks you always did but better, faster, and more accurately.

Is This Book for You?

If you are new to Office 97, then this book is for you. This book can help you learn the basics of using each program. You learn what each program does and what types of documents you can create with each program. All the basics are covered so that you can get to work quickly.

If you are upgrading to Office 97, this book is for you. This book can help you learn about new features to try and improvements that will help you work smarter. You can use this book to get up to speed with the new version quickly.

If you are familiar with some programs in Office or another package, but not all, then this book is for you, too. You may have started with a single program and moved to the entire Office suite. Or perhaps you have used another suite and have changed to Office. In either case, you can use this book to learn all about the features of Office. You can build on what you already know to add more skills to your repertoire.

If you have used Office but don't feel you are getting the most from it, then this book is for you. This book explains the most helpful features and covers shortcuts to improve efficiency. You can learn more about how to take advantage of the many, many features and commands in each program.

What's in This Book?

This book is divided into several parts, and each part is divided into several chapters. Read the following list of contents to see what's covered.

Part One: Getting Started

Part One, "Getting Started," covers all the skills you need to begin using any of the Office programs. You learn how to start a program, work with the program window, create and save documents, get help, and more. The skills you learn in this part carry over to all the applications covered in the rest of the book.

Part Two: Creating Word Documents

Part Two, "Creating Word Documents," covers the word processing program, Word 97, included with Office. You learn all you need to create any type of Word document in this part.

Part Three: Creating Worksheets with Excel

Part Three, "Creating Excel Worksheets," discusses the spreadsheet program, Excel 97, included with Office. Here you learn all the skills for creating most types of worksheets.

Part Four: Creating Presentations with PowerPoint

Part Four, "Creating PowerPoint Presentations," covers how to use the presentation program, PowerPoint, to create slide shows and other presentations.

Part Five: Creating Databases with Access

Part Five, "Creating Databases with Access," covers how to use this powerful database program to create simple or complex databases. If you need to manage a list of clients, products, sales, inventory, or something similar, try Access.

Part Six: Using Outlook

Part Six, "Using Outlook," covers how to use the desktop information management program. That's a big term for a program that does a lot of little, helpful stuff such as keeping track of names and addresses, handling e-mail, and maintaining your schedule.

Part Seven: Using Office in Concert

Part Seven, "Using Office in Concert," explains how to expand your skills to create more complex documents, including documents with data from more than one source and Web documents.

The book also includes four reference sections: a Discovery Center section, a Visual Index, a troubleshooting guide, and a glossary. The Visual Index is something you should definitely turn to. It includes a number of document examples for all of the Office programs. You can not only see some neat things you can do with Office but also see which features were used to set up the document.

You can think of any learning as an adventure, a journey, a path to discovery. That's the theme of this book. Have a great journey!

Acknowledgments

A friend once said that "there's a fine line between too much and too little salad dressing." The same is true with editing. Susannah Davidson, our development editor, manages the line between too much and too little editing to perfection. There's nothing an author enjoys more than working with a good editor. Thanks, Susannah.

Thanks also to Ellen Camm, Acquisitions Editor, for her many, many ideas and suggestions. This series is more hers than anyone's. We also appreciate the wisdom and guidance of Walt Bruce, Publishing Director.

Finally, we would like to thank Constantine Mengason, the technical editor, and Bob Campbell and Michael Welch, the copy editors.

—*Shelley O'Hara, Denise B. Vega, and Julia Kelly*

CONTENTS AT A GLANCE

CONTENTS

PART SEVEN—SHARING DATA AND WEB PUBLISHING, 471

29 SHARING DATA AMONG APPLICATIONS, 473

30 USING INTERNET EXPLORER, 499

OFFICE 97 QUICK TOUR

Office is a package of several programs, all designed to make your working and home life easier. To get an idea of what each program looks like, try this Quick Tour. This tour introduces you to each program and helps you learn a little about what each program can do.

Trying Out Word

Word processing is the most popular program type, and Word for Windows is the most highly rated word-processing program. You can use Word to create any type of document — a memo, a letter, a résumé, a newsletter, a flyer, a brochure, a report, a manuscript, or whatever.

Follow these steps to take a peek at Word:

1. Start Word for Windows by clicking the Start button on the Windows desktop. Select Programs and then Microsoft Word. You see a blank document on-screen (see Figure QT-1).

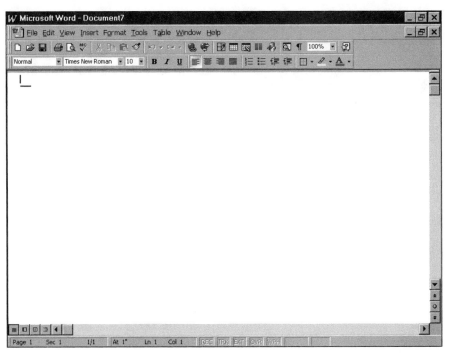

Figure QT-1   You can start typing in the blank document.

2. Take a look at the top few lines of the screen. The top line, the title bar, lists the name of the program and that of the document. The next line, the menu bar, contains the names of the menus. You can click each of the menu names to see the various commands available in Word. To close a menu, click outside the menu or press Esc.

3. Take a look at the two lines of buttons under the menu bar. These toolbars include buttons for frequently used commands. For example, the button with the "B" is the Bold button. You can use this button to make text bold. Word makes it easy to make editing and formatting changes.

4. Go ahead and type some text. You can type anything you want. The blank document is like a blank piece of paper. You don't need to save this document, but you can get a feel for typing by just experimenting. Now you can close the document and the program.

5. Click **File** in the menu bar and then click **Exit**. You are prompted to save your document. Normally, you would save and name your document, but this is just a test document, so you don't need to.

6. Click the No button. Your document and the Word program are closed.

You'll learn all about the many features of Word in Part Two of this book.

Trying Out Excel

Another popular program is Excel, a spreadsheet program. You use this program to work with numbers; you can create documents such as budgets, expense reports, sales charts, income statements, and more. *To get an idea of how this program is set up, follow these steps:*

1. Start Excel by clicking the Start button on the Windows desktop. Select Programs and then Microsoft Excel. You see a blank worksheet (see Figure QT-2). Notice that the worksheet is a grid of rows and columns. The intersection of a row and a column is a cell; that's where you enter data.

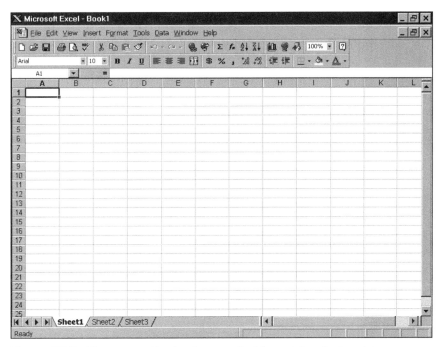

Figure QT-2 You can use Excel to keep track of financial and other data.

2. Use the arrow keys to move around. Pressing the arrow key moves you one cell in that direction. For example, if you press →, you move one cell right. If you press ↓, you move one cell down. You can also use the mouse pointer to move around.

3. Move to any cell in the worksheet and type an entry. Press Enter. Making entries is that simple: You move to the cell, type, and press Enter. You learn more about the different types of data — including formulas — that you can enter in Part Three of this book.

4. Take a look at the top of the program window; it's similar to Word. You have a title bar, a menu bar, and toolbars. These perform the same

things in Excel that they do in Word. One thing that's great about Office is that so many of the features work the same way in different programs, so, for instance, once you learn how to select a menu command in one program, you know how to select menu commands in all programs.

5. Click `File` in the menu bar and then click `Exit`. You are prompted to save your document. Again, for your documents, you will save before you exit. But you can simply close this document without saving.

6. Click the No button. Your document and the Excel program are closed.

Taking PowerPoint for a Test Drive

I f you ever need to create a presentation to give to an audience, you can use PowerPoint. In your work, you may have to give presentations often. Or you may have to give one just every blue moon or so. PowerPoint provides some tools that make it simple to create a presentation. *Try starting PowerPoint by following these steps:*

1. Click the Start button on the Windows desktop. Select `Programs` and then `Microsoft PowerPoint`. Your see the PowerPoint dialog box, which prompts you to select a method for creating a new presentation (see Figure QT-3). Part Four of this book covers each of these methods.

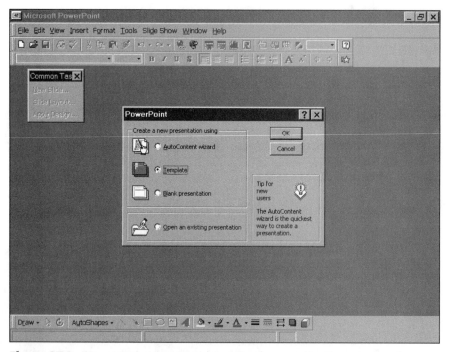

Figure QT-3 You can create a new presentation from an AutoContent wizard, a template, or a blank presentation.

2. Select Template and click the OK button. You see the New Presentation dialog box. A template controls the look of the slides in a presentation. You can select a design you like in this dialog box.

3. Select Dad's Tie and click the OK button. You are prompted to select a slide layout. A presentation is a collection of slides, and you can select different types of slides — ones that contain just text, ones with text and a picture, ones with a chart, ones with a table, and so on. Figure QT-4 gives you some idea of the types of slide layouts you can select.

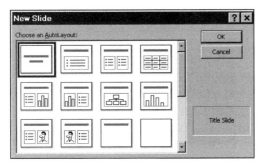

Figure QT-4   Try out some of the available templates to select a design you like.

To create a presentation, you select the slide type and then create that slide. Next you add another slide, create it, and so on until you complete the presentation. Here you will exit the program without adding any slides.

4. Click the Cancel button.

5. Click File in the menu bar and then click Exit . Because the presentation is empty, you aren't prompted to save. Instead, the program is exited.

You can learn more about the many features of PowerPoint in Part Four of this book.

Checking Out Access

I f you have to keep track of things — inventory, clients, products, orders, and so on — you should check out Access, the database program included with Office. You can use this program to create simple to highly complex databases. *Take a quick look at this program by following these steps:*

1. Click the Start button on the Windows desktop. Select Programs and then Microsoft Access . Your see the Microsoft Access dialog box, which

prompts you to select a method for creating a new database (see Figure QT-5). Part Five of this book covers each of these methods.

Figure QT-5 You can use a database wizard or create a blank database.

2. Select <u>D</u>atabase wizard and click the OK button. You see the New dialog box, shown in Figure QT-6. Notice the many different types of databases Access already has set up. Each of these has database tables, forms, and reports applicable to that type of database. You can select, for instance, address book, asset tracking, expenses, membership, music collection, video collection, and more.

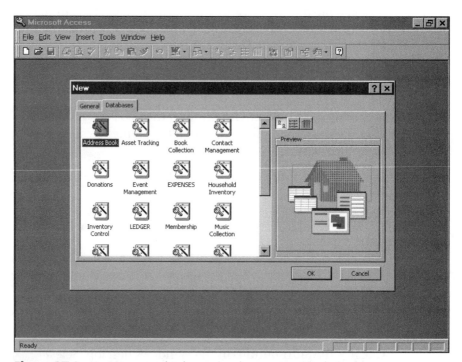

Figure QT-6 You can use a database wizard or create a blank database.

3. Scroll through the list and select some of the different databases available. Because creating a database is a somewhat involved process, this quick tour does not have you create one. Instead, you can cancel and exit the program.

4. Click the Cancel button.

5. Click **File** in the menu bar and then click **Exit**. Because you did not create anything, you aren't prompted to save. Instead, the program is exited.

Looking at Outlook

Microsoft describes Outlook as a "desktop information management program." You can use this program to send and handle e-mail, keep track of contacts, manage your schedule, and more.

Note that if you have not yet set up Outlook, you can turn to Part Six of this book for instructions on setting up Outlook. Initially, you have to do some work to get the program set up for your equipment, but after that, to use the program you simply start it.

Take a quick look at Outlook by following these steps:

1. On the desktop, double-click the Microsoft Outlook icon. When you installed Outlook, this icon should have been added to the desktop. You see the Outlook program window. In Figure QT-7, you see the messages in the Inbox.

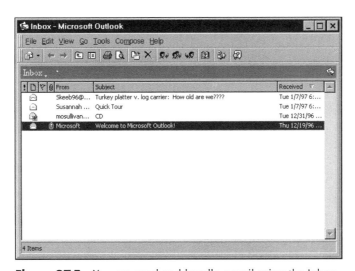

Figure QT-7 You can send and handle e-mail using the Inbox.

2. Click the down arrow next to Inbox. You see a list of other types of things you can do with Outlook, as shown in Figure QT-8. You can create a calendar, keep track of contacts, make journal entries, keep notes, and make a to-do list of tasks.

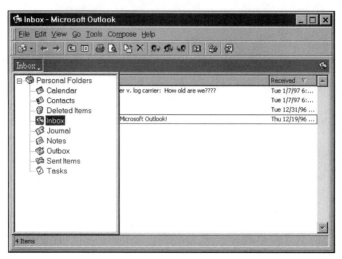

Figure QT-8 You can use Outlook to keep track of schedules, to-do lists, and more.

3. Try out some of the different views to see how they are set up.

4. When you are finished trying out the different views, click File in the menu bar and then click Exit . Outlook is exited.

LEARNING THE BASICS

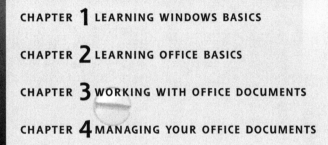

THIS PART CONTAINS THE FOLLOWING CHAPTERS:

CHAPTER **1** LEARNING WINDOWS BASICS

CHAPTER **2** LEARNING OFFICE BASICS

CHAPTER **3** WORKING WITH OFFICE DOCUMENTS

CHAPTER **4** MANAGING YOUR OFFICE DOCUMENTS

This part teaches you all the basics you need to know to use Office. These are the skills you will use over and over and over again when you are using any of the Office programs. You learn how to start and exit a program, get help, and save and open documents. The information you learn here applies not only to Office applications but to most Windows 95 programs. So learning these skills is well worth your time.

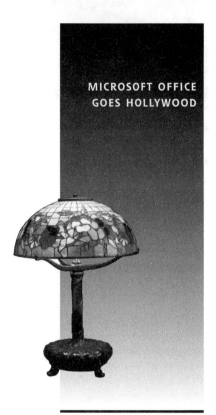

It all began on November 8, 1972, in Wilkes-Barre, Pennsylvania. Home Box Office introduced subscriber TV to a select group of 365. It broadcast the National Hockey League game between the Vancouver Canucks and the New York Rangers from Madison Square Garden and then played the film *Sometimes a Great Notion* starring Paul Newman, Henry Fonda, and Lee Remick. In 1975 HBO became the first network to distribute its signal nationwide via satellite; it currently has over 29 million subscribers (1995 numbers) throughout the United States, Puerto Rico, Guam, and the U.S. Virgin Islands.

In 1980, Cinemax hit the small screen. With its different slant and scheduling, it complemented HBO's current offerings. In May 1983, Cinemax moved from a "movies only" format and began producing *SCTV*, its first original entertainment program. From there, HBO brought us *Comic Relief*. The first program of the series aired in March 1986, hosted by Whoopi Goldberg, Billy Crystal, and Robin Williams. The show, which benefited the homeless in America, went on to become an annual HBO event.

How does Microsoft Office fit into the Home Box Office television service? "We use Microsoft Office in a variety of ways," explains Bill Baykan, supervisor of production, original programming for the West Coast. HBO uses the software on both Macintosh and PC machines and creates most of its day-to-day business documents with it. Memos, written in Microsoft Word, pass across Baykan's desk detailing meetings with directors, producers, and actors. A variety of departments use Excel and PowerPoint to produce financial information and create presentations. "We also receive programming reports that provide us with up-to-date information regarding HBO original programming," says Baykan. "The reports list the title of the program, the executives, staff, and talent involved, and its status, which tells us if the program is in preproduction, production, or postproduction, or if it has been delivered to us."

HBO continues to expand its entertainment reach with its Web site. Included on the site is a list of current shows and events, as well as a program created and maintained exclusively for the World Wide Web. Called *III:am*, this program provides a peek into the lives of people who work, play, or hang out at 3:00 in the morning. You can choose to view the guests for recent weeks or go into the archives of past shows. *III:am* provides interviews and photos of the "guests" and sometimes contains adult content.

You can check out HBO's Web site at http://www.hbo.com.

C H A P T E R   O N E

GETTING STARTED WITH WINDOWS 95

LEARN THESE KEY SKILLS:

HOW TO START WINDOWS 95 AND TAKE A LOOK
AT THE DESKTOP   PAGE   11

HOW TO OPEN AND WORK WITH WINDOWS   PAGE   14

HOW TO GET HELP FOR WINDOWS 95   PAGE   19

HOW TO SHUT DOWN WINDOWS 95   PAGE   24

Before you dive right into Office and its different applications, you need to know a few key things for working with Windows 95. Windows 95 is what you see when you start your computer. Whenever you are not within an application, you are in Windows 95. You can think of Windows 95 as the manager behind the scenes. Nothing gets done without Windows 95. Without Windows, you couldn't add new hardware, install a new program, start a program, copy a file. That's why it's important to know at least a few key things about Windows 95 first. This chapter explains what you see on the desktop, explains how to work with windows (any type of window), and covers how to get help for Windows 95.

Ladies and Gentlemen, Start Your Windows!

Before you had a PC, you had a simple desk, and on that desk, you probably kept handy the tools you used most often in your work. Maybe you had a pencil holder with pens, a stapler, a calculator, a picture of your bulldog Jelly Roll. Windows 95 uses this same metaphor for its screen. The

Windows screen is called the *desktop*, and like your desktop, the Windows desktop has handy tools available for your use. These tools are represented by little pictures called *icons*. This section explains how to start Windows and get familiar with the desktop.

Starting Windows

To start Windows 95 and view the desktop, turn on your PC and monitor. Windows 95 starts automatically. You don't have to type a special command or press a key combination. When you turn on your PC, you see the startup routine of your computer and then you see Windows 95 (see Figure 1-1).

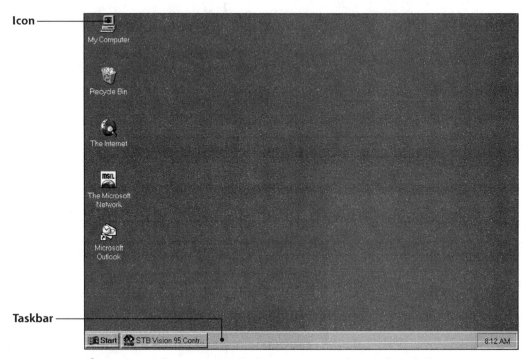

Figure 1-1   When you start Windows 95, you see the Windows desktop.

Taking a Look at Desktop Icons

What you have on your desk is different than what your coworker Darlene has, and what Darlene has is probably different than what Raymond has. Likewise, what you see when you start Windows depends on how your system is set up. But at the minimum you should see the following two icons, shown in Figure 1-1:

* *My Computer.* Use this icon to browse through the contents of your system. You can view what files, folders, and programs are stored on your hard disk(s), floppy disk(s), or CD-ROM.

✳ *Recycle Bin*. Use this "trash can" to delete files, programs, and icons that you no longer need.

You may also have icons for Microsoft Network and the Internet. If you have a modem, you can use these to get connected to Microsoft's online service and to the Internet. If you are hooked up to a network, you may see an icon for Network Neighborhood. You can use this icon to browse through your network.

If you used the default installation for Office 97, you should also see an icon for Microsoft Outlook (covered in Part 5 of this book). You may also see icons for any other programs you have added to the desktop.

Using the Start Button and the Taskbar

You can't put everything on the desktop, so you need a way to access the other programs on your system. You also need commands to work with Windows. You do these tasks through the Start button. To display the available commands in the Start menu, click the Start button. As you can see, you use this button to start programs, open documents, get help, customize Windows, run a command, find files, or shut down Windows (see Figure 1-2).

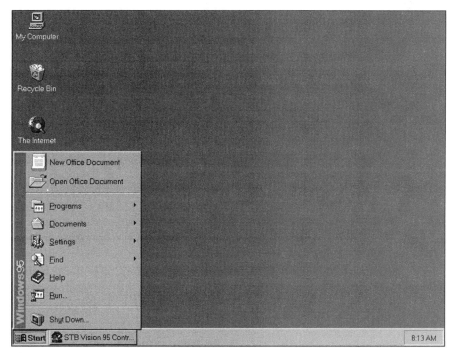

Figure 1-2 Use the Start menu to start programs and perform other key tasks such as customizing Windows.

The Start button is part of the taskbar, the bar along the bottom of the Windows desktop. In addition to including the Start button, the taskbar also displays a button for each program that is running or window that is open. In Figure 1-2, for instance, you see a button for STB Vision 95 (a program that manages my monitor). You can use the taskbar to switch quickly to any of the other programs or windows. The taskbar also displays other information, such as the time.

 TIP **To see the current date, put the pointer on the time. The date pops up.**

I Do Windows

To see what any icon does, you double-click it. If that icon is a program, the program is started (that's covered in the next chapter) and you see the program window. If that icon is a "container" icon like the Recycle Bin or My Computer, you see the contents of the icon in a window.

You are probably starting to understand the significance of the name Windows. Anything you do in Windows is displayed in a window. If you start a program, that program is displayed in a window. If you browse the contents of My Computer, the contents are displayed in a window. For example, Figure 1-3 shows the contents of My Computer.

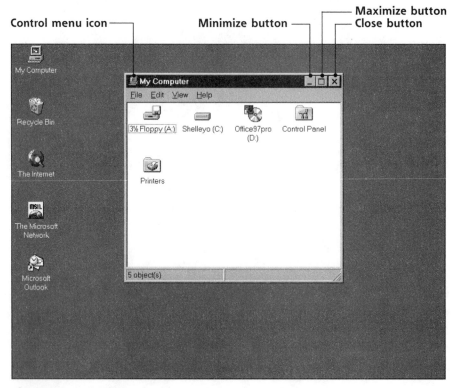

Figure 1-3 All windows have the same set of controls (buttons).

The great thing about windows is that they all work the same way; they all have the same set of controls, as shown in Figure 1-3. You open, close, move, resize, and scroll all windows the same way using these buttons. That means once you pick up the basics of working with one window, you can use these same skills in any other program in Windows 95. This section explains the basics of working with a window.

TIP **You can use the Control menu to close and make other changes to the window placement. To display this menu, click the Control menu icon in the upper-left corner of the window. You see a drop-down list of commands. Click the command you want.**

Resizing the Window

You can resize a window so that it takes up more or less space on the desktop. For example, if you are working in a program, you probably want to make the window as big as possible (*maximize* the window) so that you have as much working room as possible. If the window has just a few contents, you don't need to make the window that big. You can adjust the size so that you can see what you need.

You can change the size of the window in either of two basic ways. First, you can use the buttons in the upper-right corner of the window. Using these buttons, you can minimize the window (turn it back into an icon) or maximize the window (make it fill the entire screen). Second, you can resize the window by dragging one of its borders.

To change the size of a window, do any of the following:

* To resize a window, put the pointer on a window edge and drag.

* To minimize a window, click the Minimize button. The window is displayed as a taskbar button.

* To maximize a window, click the Maximize button. The window is enlarged to fill the entire screen. Figure 1-4 shows a program window maximized. When a window is maximized, the Maximize button changes to the Restore button. You can click this button to restore the window to its original size.

When you maximize a window, it fills the entire screen and does not have any borders. Because the window is as big as it can get, you can't resize a maximized window by dragging its borders.

* To restore a window, click the Restore button. Figure 1-5 shows a program window restored.

The Maximize button becomes the Restore button ───────

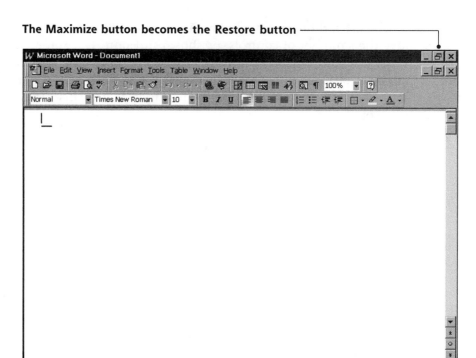

Figure 1-4   Maximize a window to make it as big as possible.

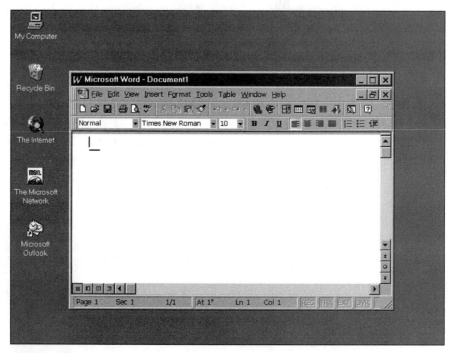

Figure 1-5   A restored window has borders so that you can resize it.

Arranging Windows

Do you always work with one thing at a time? Probably not. You might, for instance, be looking at a sales report and a price list at the same time. The same is true with Windows. You might want to take a look at two windows (say a worksheet in Excel and a document in Word) at the same time.

You can arrange and move the windows so that they are situated just so, just as you can arrange the physical items. You can arrange windows manually by dragging them to the spots you want. Or you can have Windows arrange all open windows for you.

If you have several windows open on the desktop and none of them is maximized, you can simply move the windows around until you get them as you want them. *To move a window, follow these steps*:

1. Put the pointer within the title bar of the window you want to move.

2. Drag the window to the spot you want.

To have Windows arrange all your open windows, follow these steps:

1. Right-click a blank area of the taskbar. You see a pop-up menu.

2. Select the arrangement you want:

   <u>Cascade</u> — The windows are arranged on top of each other in a cascading pattern; you can see the title bars of all open windows.

   <u>Tile Horizontally</u> — The windows are arranged top to bottom in panes, as shown for the program windows in Figure 1-6.

SIDE TRIP

ARRANGING ICONS

Just as you can move the windows around on the desktop, you can also move the icons. The icons will initially be placed in a vertical row along the left edge of the desktop. If you don't like this placement, you can move them around.

You can easily drag the icons to any place on the screen. Or you can have Windows arrange the icons for you. Follow these steps:

1. Right-click the desktop. You see a pop-up menu.

2. To line up the icons, select <u>Line up Icons</u>. To arrange them in a particular order, select <u>Arrange Icons</u> and select the type of arrangement you want: by <u>N</u>ame, by <u>T</u>ype, by <u>S</u>ize, or by <u>D</u>ate. Windows aligns the icons.

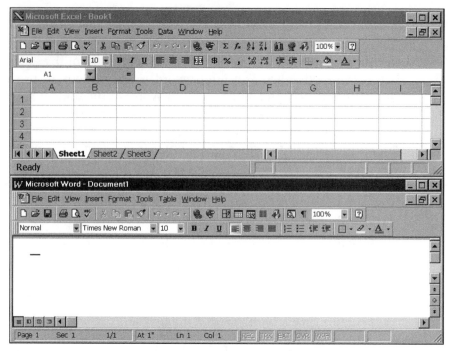

Figure 1-6 In this figure, the windows are tiled horizontally.

Tile Vertically — The windows are arranged side by side in panes.

Minimize All Windows — All windows are minimized to icons.

Switching Windows (Programs Too)

To remind you of what you have open, the taskbar includes a button for any window that is open and any program that is running. Not only is this a handy reminder of what's going on in your PC, but you can also use the taskbar to switch to a different program or window. To switch to a different program, you simply click the program button in the taskbar.

The taskbar is a handy reminder about which programs are running; you can also use it to switch between programs.

Closing a Window

When you don't want to work in a window anymore, you can close it. Remember that when you close a program window, you in effect exit the program.

To close a window, click the Close button.

Questions Answered Here

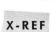

You have this book to help you with questions about Office, but what about Windows questions? You may not really feel that you need to expend a lot of time and energy learning every little thing about Windows. But when you have a question or problem, you may wish you had a handy resource. You do. You can use the online help system to look up information.

X-REF **The next chapter explains how to get help within an Office 97 application. The help system works similarly, but Office 97 also includes the Office Assistant.**

Think of online help as a big book with all the information you need about Windows. You can look up information in the help system just as you look up information in a book: using the table of contents or using the index. You can also search for a particular word or phrase and find matching topics using the help system.

Using the Table of Contents

If you are just browsing through the topics and want to learn something about Windows, you may choose to use the table of contents. The contents screen is organized like a book, and topics are broken into categories. You select the category you want and then the subtopic until you find the information you need. *Follow these steps*:

1. Click the Start button and then select ⬛ **Help** . You see the Contents tab of the Help Topics dialog box, shown in Figure 1-7. Each main topic is represented by a book icon. You can select Introducing Windows, How To, Tips and Tricks, and Troubleshooting.

2. Double-click the topic you want. Windows 95 lists additional subtopics.

3. Continue to double-click on subtopics until you see a help topic. Help topics are indicated with a question mark icon (see Figure 1-8). You can think of these as "pages" in the help system.

4. After you display the help topic you want, double-click it. Windows displays a help window listing information about the selected topic (see Figure 1-9).

5. Close the window by clicking the Close button.

TIP **For more information on navigating in the help system, see the later section, "More Stuff to Know about Help."**

Figure 1-7   Select the book topic you want.

Figure 1-8   Double-click the help topic.

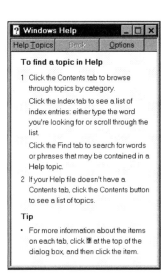

Figure 1-9 Review the information in the help window.

Using the Index

If you want to look up help on a particular feature and don't want to have to figure out how that feature might be categorized in the table of contents, try another method. Use the index. To use the index, you type the first few letters of the topic; Windows then displays matching topics. You can then select the topic you want. *Follow these steps*:

1. Click the Start button and then select Help.

2. Click the Index tab. You see the Index tab of the Help Topics dialog box.

3. In the first text box, type the first few letters of the topic you want help on. For example, to find help on the desktop, type **desk**. You see a list of matching topics (see Figure 1-10).

4. Double-click the topic you want. (You can also click the topic and then click the Display button.) Windows displays the help information for the selected topic.

5. Click the Close button to close the help window.

Searching for a Topic

If you can't find help using the contents or index, you can try searching for the word or phrase. When you use this method, Windows will display all topics that include the word or phrase you type.

Note that the first time you use the Find tab, you are prompted to set up the word list. Follow the instructions in the Setup wizard.

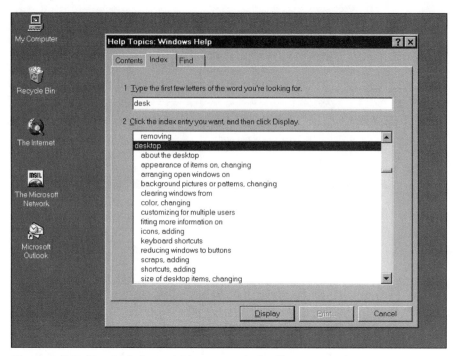

Figure 1-10 Use the index to look up a particular feature or topic.

Follow these steps to search for help on a particular topic:

1. Click the Start button and then select **Help** .

2. Click the Find tab. You see the Find tab of the Help Topics dialog box.

3. In the first text box, type the word or words that you want to find. Windows displays matching topics in the list box.

4. To narrow the search, click the matching topic that is closest to what you are looking for. For example, Figure 1-11 shows the search for the word "find." The matches are narrowed to those that include the text "Finding."

5. Double-click the topic you want. Windows displays the help information for the selected topic.

6. Close the window by clicking the Close button.

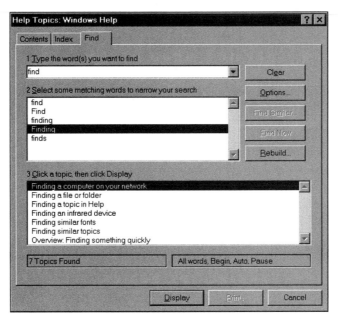

Figure 1-11   You can search for a word or phrase in online help.

More Stuff to Know about Help

If you find what you want, you will most likely review that information and then close the window. If you don't find what you want, you may need to go back a step or two. You can do that and other things using the buttons in the help window. You can do any of the following things:

* To go back to the table of contents and select a different topic, click the Help Topics button.
* If the topic has any related topics, you can go to them by clicking the Related Topics link (usually found at the end of the help entry).
* To go back to a previous topic, click the Back button.
* Some terms are underlined. This means you can click the term to display a pop-up definition.
* To print the help topic, click the Options button and select Print Topic. Click the OK button in the Print dialog box.
* To change the font, click the Options button, select the Font command, and then select Small, Normal, or Large.

Shutting Down Windows

At the end of the workday, don't just turn off your PC and take off. First, you need to take care of some housekeeping — simple stuff. Before you exit any program, save all the documents you are working on. Saving a document is covered in Chapter 3. (If you forget to save, most applications will remind you when you exit the program.) Then exit any programs that are running. The next chapter covers how to exit a program.

Finally, use the Shut Down command to exit Windows. This command makes sure that everything is as it should be before the power is turned off. *To use this command to exit, follow these steps*:

1. Click the Start button.

2. Select **Shut Down**. You are prompted to confirm you want to shut down windows. (You can also simply restart Windows or restart in MS-DOS mode).

3. Click the Yes button. Windows 95 goes through its shutdown procedures and displays a message telling you it is safe to turn off the PC.

BONUS

Customizing the Desktop

What do you like on your pizza? Pepperoni? Anchovies? Just cheese? How do you keep your desk arranged? Neat and tidy? Tornado City? And how do you handle your work assignments? Get started right away? Wait until the last moment?

Each person is different — in what they like, how they work, what they think, and so on. If Windows forced you to work like everyone else, it wouldn't be all that useful. Instead, you can customize Windows so it works the way you do.

This section focuses on some cosmetic changes you can make — changes to express your own style. You can also add shortcut icons for programs as covered in the next chapter's bonus section.

Changing the Desktop

Does your coworker Michael have a fancy desktop that looks like a cloudy sky? Wonder how he made his desktop look like this? He used a desktop wallpaper.

You can wallpaper your desktop too, using an image for the background. Or if you prefer, you can use one of the selected repeating patterns: bricks, cargo net, circuit, and so on.

You can select either a pattern or wallpaper, but not both. If you select both, the wallpaper takes precedence.

Follow these steps to use a pattern or wallpaper:

1. Right-click the desktop. From the pop-up menu that appears, select Properties . You see the Display Properties dialog box, with the Background tab selected.

2. In the Pattern list, select the pattern you want to use.

   Or

   In the Wallpaper list, select the wallpaper you want to use.

TIP **In addition to the wallpaper that comes with Windows, you can create and use your own wallpaper. For example, you can create an image using Paint, save the image as a .bmp file, and then use this image as your wallpaper. To change to another folder and select a different wallpaper file, use the Browse button.**

   Windows displays a sample of how the desktop will look in the dialog box.

3. Click the OK button. Windows uses the new pattern or wallpaper for the desktop.

Changing the Screen Colors

Green has never been a color for me. I like something brighter. How about you? If you don't like the default set of colors used not only for the desktop but for other window elements (title bar, dialog box, window borders, and so on) as well, you can change them. You can also use a different font for on-screen text. The easiest way is to use a different scheme. *Follow these steps:*

1. Right-click the desktop. From the pop-up menu that appears, select Properties . You see the Display Properties dialog box.

2. Click the Appearance tab.

3. Display the Scheme drop-down list and select the scheme you want to use. If you aren't sure what each one does, experiment. Windows shows you how each window element will look using this scheme.

4. Click the OK button. Windows uses the new scheme.

CHAPTER TWO

WORKING WITH OFFICE PROGRAMS

LEARN THESE KEY SKILLS:

W hen you start using any program, you need to learn some key skills first. For example, you need to learn how to start the program, to get familiar with what the screen looks like, to learn how to use such on-screen items as menus and toolbars, and to learn to get help. You also need to figure out how to call it quits and turn off or exit the program. This chapter covers these skills. The great thing about the stuff you learn here is that the information applies to all Office applications — in fact, all Windows 95 programs. So you will use what you learn here again and again.

Ready, Set, Go!

T he first step in using any program is to get it started. Starting is pretty simple: you just click a few commands. What can be confusing is that everyone's system can be set up differently. The programs you have on your system may be different than your neighbor Ed's. The place you put your Word program icon, for instance, may be different than where your coworker Camille puts it. It's kind of like finding your car keys. Once you find those keys — that is, the program icon — you are set.

Follow these steps to start an application:

1. Click the Start menu. You see the Start menu options.

2. Click Programs. You see the programs and program folders you have set up on your system.

3. If necessary, click the folder that contains the program icon. If you have not made a change since installing Office, you can skip this step. The program items are added to the Programs folder, and you should see program icons for each Office application (see Figure 2-1). If you have made a change, select the folder you used to store this program icon.

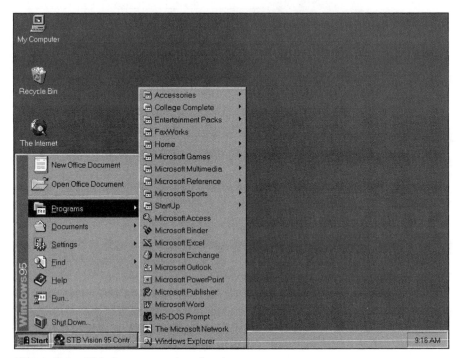

Figure 2-1   Click the program icon for the program you want to start.

4. Click the program icon to start that program. For example, to start Word, click the Microsoft Word program icon. The program starts, and you see a blank document on screen.

What's All This Stuff?

When you start most Office programs, you see a blank document on screen. For PowerPoint and Access, the startup is a little different. What happens when you start these programs is covered in their respective parts of this book. Still, all program windows look about the same and have the same set of items you use to create something.

At first, you may look at the screens and wonder "What is all the other stuff? What are the little hieroglyphics at the top of the screen? Modern cave drawings?" But you will quickly become familiar with the on-screen tools. To begin doing so, take a look at Figure 2-2, which identifies some key parts of the screen. This figure uses Word as the screen, but other Office applications include the same elements.

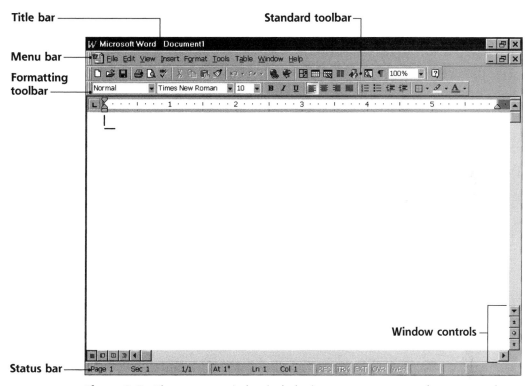

Figure 2-2 The program window includes items you can use to select commands, get information, move around, and more.

You may also see a little window with a paper clip icon. This is the Office Assistant, which you can use to get help. See the section "I'm Stumped. Help!" later in this chapter.

The Title Bar and the Status Bar

The top and bottom lines of the screen display helpful information. The top bar, called the title bar, displays the name of the program and the name of the document. If you have not yet saved the document, you see some generic name such as Document1.

The status bar displays helpful information about the current document. For instance, in Word, you see the page number, the section number, and the position of the insertion point.

The Menu Bar and Toolbars

The bar under the title bar is the menu bar; it contains the names of the different menus: File, Edit, View, and so on. You'll notice as you use other Office applications that some of the menu names and even commands remain the same from application to application. For instance, you can expect to find a File menu in Word, Excel, PowerPoint, and Access. These programs also all have an Edit menu with Cut, Copy, and Paste commands. A section later in this chapter explains how to select a menu command.

Under the menu bar, you see toolbars. These toolbars again vary from program to program but will contain some buttons that are the same. For instance, most Office applications include a toolbar with the Save button. Formatting buttons such as Bold, Italic, and Underline are common in Office toolbars. (The first chapter in each part includes a table with the buttons for that particular program.)

To use a button, click it. Some buttons have arrows next to them, which means you can select from a list of items. For instance, click the down arrow next to the Font button to display and select from a list of fonts.

TIP   Not sure what a button does? If you can't tell from the picture on a button what the button does, you can display the button name (called a ScreenTip). Put the mouse pointer on the bottom edge of the button, and the name should pop up.

The Window Controls

The program window also includes buttons for manipulating the windows; some of these appear in the title bar and the menu bar. Keep in mind that when you are working in a document, you actually have two windows open: one for the program and one for the document. Each window has its own set of controls, which you can use to work with that window. For instance, you can click the Close button in the document window to close the document but keep the program open. Click the Close button in the program window to exit the program.

X-REF   For more information on working with windows, see Chapter 1.

Do This Now!

One day you will be able to say aloud "Open this document. Make this text bold." And the program will. This day will probably come sooner than you expect. For now, though, when you want a program to do something, you have to select the command you want. Each program organizes its many commands into different menu categories, which appear in the menu bar. Selecting a command is easy. You can use the mouse or the keyboard.

To select a command with the mouse, follow these steps:

1. Click the name of the menu you want to open. For example, click the **File** menu. The menu drops down, and you see a list of commands (see Figure 2-3).

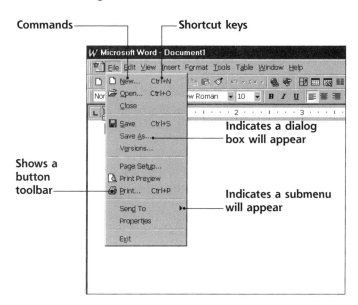

Figure 2-3 When you open a menu, you see a list of commands.

2. Click the command you want to execute. Some commands are executed right away. Other commands display a submenu or a dialog box. Submenus are indicated on the menu with an arrow. If a command is followed by an ellipsis, it means a dialog box will appear.

3. If you see a submenu, select the command you want from this menu. If you see a dialog box, select the dialog box options you want and then click the OK button. For more help on dialog boxes, see the next section.

To select a command with the keyboard, follow these steps:

1. Press the Alt key. This step activates the menu bar.

2. Press the key letter of the menu name. The key letter appears underlined in the menu bar. For instance, to open the File menu, press F. The menu drops down, and you see a list of commands (refer to Figure 2-3).

3. Press the key letter for the command you want. Again, the key letter is underlined.

Making Selections in a Dialog Box

To execute some commands, the program may need some additional information. For example, if you print a document, the program needs to know how many copies you want, the printer to use, and other options you may want to change. When there are other options for carrying out a command, the program displays a dialog box. It's kind of like ordering a meal. If you order some things — say a steak dinner — the waitress bombards you with questions. "How do you want your steak cooked? Do you want baked potato or french fries? What kind of salad dressing?" A dialog box is like this questioning waitress. When you see one, you make your selections and then click the OK button to carry out the command.

You'll encounter dialog boxes quite a bit when you use any program, and even though the options are different, they all work the same way. Figure 2-4 shows the Options dialog box. (If you want to follow along and display this dialog box yourself, in Word, open the Tools menu and select the Options command. Click the Save tab.) Table 2-1 explains the different types of options you can find in a dialog box.

TABLE 2-1 Dialog Box Options

Item	Description
TAB	Some dialog boxes have more than one set of options, indicated with tabs at the top of the dialog box. Click the tab name to display the options for that tab.
CHECK BOX	Click in the check box to check (turn on) or uncheck (turn off) the option. If a dialog box has more than one check box, you can check as many as you want.
OPTION BUTTON	Click in the option button to turn on (appears darkened) or off (blank). You can select only one option button in each group of option buttons. (Figure 2-4 does not show an option button.)
TEXT BOX	Click in the text box and then type the entry. If the text box already contains an entry, drag across it to select the entry and then press Delete.

Item	Description
SPIN BOX	A spin box is a type of text box with spin arrows next to it. You can type an entry in the spin box. Or you can click the spin arrows to scroll through the text box values.
LIST BOX	A list box displays a list of selections. Click the item you want in the list. (Figure 2-4 does not show a list box.)
DROP-DOWN LIST BOX	This type of list box displays only the first selection in a list. Click the down arrow next to the item to display other selections. Then click the item you want.
COMMAND BUTTON	Click the OK command button to confirm and carry out the command. Click the Cancel button to cancel the command. Some dialog boxes also have other buttons that display other options. Click a button to display these options.

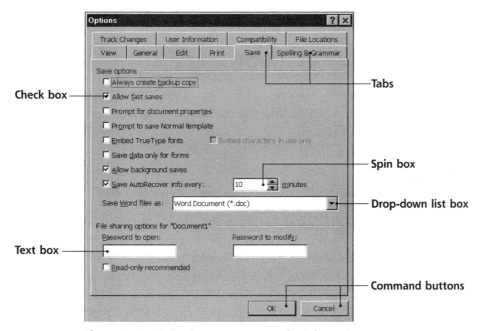

Figure 2-4 Dialog boxes prompt you for information about how to carry out a command.

TIP If you don't know what a dialog box option does, you can get help on an option. Right-click the option. From the pop-up menu that appears, select What's This? You see a pop-up explanation of the dialog box option.

Tips on Commands

You'll select commands again and again and again. So it's a good idea to learn a few tips about them:

* The command you will probably value the most is the Undo command. You can use this command to undo the action you just performed. For instance, if you've deleted text accidentally, you can undo the command. To use this command, select Edit → Undo or click [↺▾].

You can use the Undo command to undo the action you just performed.

---

* Sometimes you may undo a command and then think "Why did I undo that? Now I want to undo the undo." In that case, click [↻▾]. What you just undid is undone. Think of it as going back two steps.

* If you want to execute the same command again, you can select it again or simply use the Edit → Repeat command.

* You can also use shortcut menus to select commands. To display a shortcut menu, click the right mouse button on the item you want to modify. For instance, to modify the toolbar, right-click this item. To display a shortcut menu for selected text, right-click the selected text. A shortcut menu pops up. Click the command you want.

* Another way to select commands is to use the shortcut keys. Shortcut keys appear in the menus next to the command names. The tips in this book point out some of the most common shortcut keys.

I'm Stumped. Help!

Each program included in Office includes many, many features. For the most part, you'll quickly learn the features and commands you use day after day and won't need much help remembering how to perform these common tasks. For less often used features, you may need a little reminder, though. If this book isn't handy, you can use the Office Assistant to get help.

In addition, you can also look up help in the online help "books." For these help pages, you can look up something in the table of contents or the index, or you can search for help.

Using the Office Assistant

See that winking paper clip in the little window at the lower-right corner of the window? That's one of the new features of Office 97, called the Office Assistant. You can use this animated icon to get help. You can type a question in "natural" language (how you talk and think rather than in some formatted query language), and the Office Assistant can display pertinent help topics. The Office Assistant will also appear during some tasks and ask whether you want advice on how to use the feature.

To ask a question of the Assistant, follow these steps:

1. Click the Office Assistant. If the Office Assistant is not displayed, click [?]. You see a cartoon caption for the Assistant, which you can use to get help (see Figure 2-5).

Figure 2-5 Tell the Office Assistant what you want to do.

2. Type what you want to do and then click the Search button. You see all the matches in the caption (see Figure 2-6).

Figure 2-6 The Office Assistant lists the things you can do that match your query.

3. Click the topic you want. You see a help window with information about the selected topic (see Figure 2-7).

4. After you review the information, click the Close button to close the help window.

Using the Help Window

When you display help, you see a help window (refer to Figure 2-7) with appropriate information. This window also includes buttons and references that you can use to navigate through the help system.

✳ To display the Help Topics dialog box, click the Help Topics button.

✳ Click the Back button to go back to the previous topic.

✳ To print the information, click the Options button and then select the Print Topic command.

✳ If you see other topics indicated with a chevron, you can display these topics by clicking the reference.

✳ If you see a dotted line under a word or phrase, it means that you can display a pop-up definition for the term. Point to the term and click the mouse button. A definition appears. Click back in the help window to close the definition.

✳ To close the window, click the Close button.

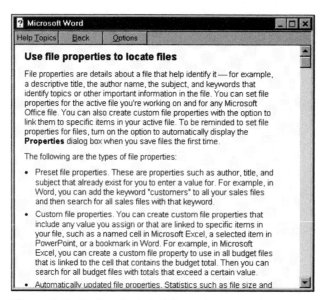

Figure 2-7 Review the help information.

Using Help Topics or Index

If you aren't partial to animated paper clips, you can use the more traditional help window to get help. This help system works a lot like a book. You can look up topics in the table of contents or in the index. Unlike a book, though, you can also use the help system to search for a topic. This help system works the same as the Windows 95 help system you learned about in Chapter 1.

To get help using the online help "manual," follow these steps:

1. Open the **Help** menu and select the **Contents and Index** command. You see the Help Topics dialog box.

2. To look up a topic in the table of contents, click the Contents tab. You see a table of contents of help topics. Top-level topics are indicated with book icons. Double-click the "book" you want until you see the help page you want. Help pages are indicated with question mark icons. Figure 2-8 shows both book icons and help page icons. Double-click the help page icon to display a window with specific information on the selected topic.

Book topic ⎯

Help page topic ⎯

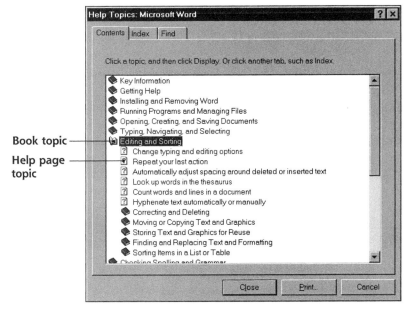

Figure 2-8 Use the Contents tab to display the topic on which you want help.

To look up a topic in the index, click the Index tab. Then type the first few letters of the topic you want. Word displays matching topics in the lower part of the dialog box (see Figure 2-9). Double-click the topic you want.

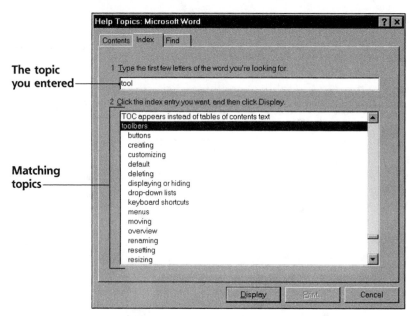

The topic you entered ─ (points to "tool" in the text field)

Matching topics ─ (points to the list of topics)

Figure 2-9 Use the Index tab to move quickly to a topic of interest.

To search for help, click the Find tab. (The first time you use this command, you have to set up the word list. Follow the on-screen instructions.) Type the topic on which you want help. Word displays matches in the middle of the dialog box. Narrow the search by selecting the topics of interest. Then, double-click the topic you want.

I'm Outta Here

When you are finished working in an application, you can exit it. You shouldn't just turn off your PC with any programs still running because that could mess up your document and program files. Instead, be sure to save all documents that you have created. If you try to exit without saving, most programs will remind you. (You can get more information on saving in the next chapter.) After all the documents are saved, you can exit the program.

Follow these steps to exit a program:

1. Save all open documents.

2. Select File → Exit . You return to the Windows desktop.

TIP You can also press Alt+F4 or click the Close button in the program window to exit the application.

BONUS

Shortcuts for Starting an Application

Y ou may use one program all the time. For example, you may start your workday by starting Word. Rather than use the Start menu, you can use some shortcuts for starting the program:

✳ If you want to be able to start a program from the desktop, you can create a shortcut icon. That's how I start my favorite programs.

✳ If you use a program all the time or most of the time, you may want to start the program each time you start Windows. This method is OK if you exit Windows each time you quit. I don't use it because I keep Windows and my PC running all the time.

✳ If you want to work on a particular document, you can open that document and start a program at the same time. I also use this method a lot when I want to edit a document I've recently worked on.

This Bonus section discusses these three shortcuts for starting a program.

Creating a Shortcut Icon

If you look around your "real" desk, you may see that you have everything you need close at hand. You can just reach across the desk, for instance, and pick up your pen. (Maybe you have to crawl under the desk to find the pen. You get the idea, though. Stuff you use often is right there on your desk.)

If you have one program you use often, you can create an icon on your Windows desktop. *To do so, follow these steps*:

1. Right-click the Start button and then select **Open** .

2. Double-click the Programs folder. You see the program folders and program icons in this folder. If you have not changed the location of the Office program icons, you should see them in this window.

3. Point to the program icon and click and hold down the right mouse button. Be sure to use the right button.

4. Drag the program icon to the desktop and release the mouse button. When you release the mouse button, you see a menu.

5. Select **Create Shortcut(s) Here** . Windows creates the shortcut and places it on your desktop. You can use the shortcut icon to start that program. To do so, double-click it.

Starting a Program Automatically

Maybe even double-clicking a shortcut icon is too much work for you. Why not just start the program you want when you start Windows? If you use one program a lot, you can add a copy of the program icon to your Startup folder. The Startup folder is a special program folder created automatically by Windows. Each time you start Windows, it starts all the programs placed in the Startup folder. *Follow these steps to add a program icon to the Startup folder:*

1. Right-click the Start button and select **Open**. You see the folders on your Start menu.

2. Double-click the Programs folder. You see the program folders and program icons in this folder. If you have not changed the location of the Office program icons, you should see them in this window.

3. Double-click the Startup folder. You see a window with any program icons already in this folder.

4. If necessary arrange the windows so that you can see both the Programs window and the Startup window. You can move a window by dragging the title bar.

5. Use the right mouse button to drag the program icon from the Programs folder to the StartUp folder. When you release the mouse button, you see a menu.

6. Select **Create Shortcut(s) Here**. Windows creates the shortcut and places it on your Startup folder. Each time you start Windows, the program will be started as well.

If you change your mind and decide you no longer want to start Word each time you start Windows, delete the program icon from the Startup folder. Open this folder, right-click the icon, and then select the Delete command.

Starting a Program and Opening a Document

Often you will start work by going back to a document that you just worked on. Windows keeps track of the last 15 documents you worked on. You can select any of these documents from the Documents menu and both start the program and open that document. *Follow these steps to start a program and open a document:*

1. Click the Start button.

2. Select **Documents**. You see a list of documents you have recently worked on.

3. Click the document you want. Windows starts that program and then opens the document. All in one fell swoop!

CHAPTER THREE

WORKING WITH OFFICE DOCUMENTS

LEARN THESE KEY SKILLS:

No matter what you create — memo, letter, budget worksheet, client database, presentation, whatever — you are basically creating the same thing, a document. One thing that is great about most Windows 95 applications is you save, open, and print documents in a single way. Thus, once you figure out how to save a document, you can use these same skills in any Windows 95 application, including all of the Office programs.

This chapter covers how to save, close, open, and create a new document. You also learn how to preview and print a document.

Avoid $#%@ by Saving

When you used the old paper method of creating a document, you never had to worry about saving. For example, you never had to worry that after typing page after page of a manuscript, your document could mysteriously vanish out the window.

With computer documents, you do — and must — remember to save your document. Why do you have to save? Because the data are stored in a temporary spot, the computer's memory. If something happens to the computer — someone accidentally turns it off or you have a power failure — all that information is lost. To make a permanent copy of the on-screen document, you need to save the document to a file on your hard disk.

You must remember to save your document.

You shouldn't wait until you finish the document to save, and don't think that saving just once is enough. There's nothing more frustrating than spending several hours getting the content just perfect and then losing all that hard work because you forgot to save. If you wait until you are finished with the document, you run the risk of losing all your work if something happens before you finish.

You should also save periodically as you work on the document. The disk version reflects all the changes you made before you saved. As you continue to work and make changes, you need to update the disk file with the changes on screen.

Saving and Naming the Document

The first time you save a document, you are prompted for a name. Naming the file enables you to find and open that file again. You also select the drive and folder where the file will be stored. Basically, then, you select a name and location each time you save a new document.

TIP When you save a document, the program will suggest a default folder. You can put the document in that or any other folder on your system. In fact, it's a good idea to spend some time thinking about how you want to organize your documents. See Chapter 4 for some advice on setting up folders.

To save a document for the first time, follow these steps:

1. Select File → Save or click 🖫. You see the Save As dialog box. Figure 3-1 shows the Save As dialog box for Word, but keep in mind that this dialog box is the same in Excel, PowerPoint, and Access. The suggested file types, of course, are different.

2. To select another drive, display the Save in drop-down list and select the drive you want.

3. To select another folder, double-click it in the folder list. You may have to move up a level in the folder structure using the Up One Level button to find the folder you want.

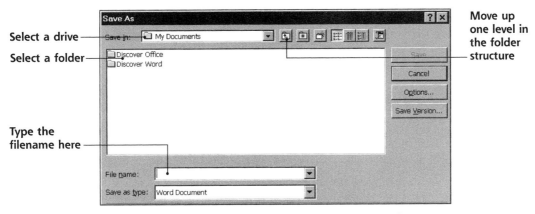

Select a drive ——— Save in:

Select a folder ———

Type the
filename here ———

Move up
one level in
the folder
structure

Figure 3-1 Select a folder for the document and enter a filename.

4. In the File name text box, type a name for the document. You used to be limited to 8 characters before Windows 95. Now you can type up to 255 characters and include spaces in the filename. Use a descriptive name that will remind you of the contents.

If you share files with someone who uses an earlier version of Windows or a Windows program, the long filenames won't convert. The filename gets cut off and end up looking something like "win95~1.doc."

5. Click the Save button. Word saves the document. The filename appears in the title bar.

Saving a Document Again

Once you save and name a file, you don't need to enter the name again. You can save the file again by simply selecting the File → Save command or clicking the Save button. If you like keyboard shortcuts, use Ctrl+S to save a document.

Using Save As

If you use Windows 95, you know that you can use it for file management tasks such as copying, renaming, or moving a document. You can also accomplish the same thing using the Save As command. For instance, suppose that you type your annual Christmas letter to your old roommate and save it as MARY.DOC. Now you also have to write another letter to your other roommate, Maureen, saying practically the same thing. You can retype the document. You can copy the text to a new document. Or you can use the Save As command and save a copy of the file. For example, you can save MARY.DOC as MAUREEN.DOC. Then you can edit MAUREEN.DOC and have two separate letters.

You can also use Save As to change the folder where you place the document or to change the name of a document. In both cases, remember that the original file remains in the same spot, with the same name.

Follow these steps to use the Save As command:

1. Select File → Save As . You see the Save As dialog box, the same dialog box you see when you save a document for the first time. The original name is listed.

2. To save the document to another drive or folder, select the drive from the Save in drop-down list or select the folder from the folder list. You can use the Up One Level button to move up through the folder structure.

3. Type a new filename.

4. Click OK.

The document is saved with the new name and remains on screen. The original file is closed and is kept intact on disk.

A Few Tips on Saving

Keep these concepts in mind when you are saving a document:

* When you save a document, all the contents of that document are saved together in one file. For instance, all worksheets in an Excel workbook are saved together, and all slides in a PowerPoint presentation are saved together as one file.

* If you close a document or exit the program without saving, the program will prompt you to save. You can click Yes to save the document.

* If you don't want to save, close the document and when prompted to save, click the No button.

* Some applications, such as Word 97, are set up to automatically save a document at certain intervals. You may see a message in the status bar when this feature is on. For more information on Autosave, check out the Save tab in the Options dialog box (select Tools → Options).

Closing a Document

After you save a document, it is not closed. It remains open so that you can continue working. When you are finished, you should save and then close the document. You can have several documents on screen at once, but closing documents you no longer need will save memory. You can close a document by clicking the Close button in the document window or by using the File → Close command.

TIP When all documents are closed, you see a blank, gray area. You can create a new document or open a document you have created before, as covered in the next two sections.

Open Says-a-Me

The whole purpose of saving a document is to make it available again for editing, printing, or reusing. To display a document you have previously saved, you use the <u>O</u>pen command. *Follow these steps:*

1. Select **File** → **Open** or click 🗁. You see the Open dialog box. Figure 3-2 shows the Open dialog box from Word, but this dialog box looks the same in Excel, Access, and PowerPoint. When you select this command in one of these other programs, however, you see its particular type of file listed.

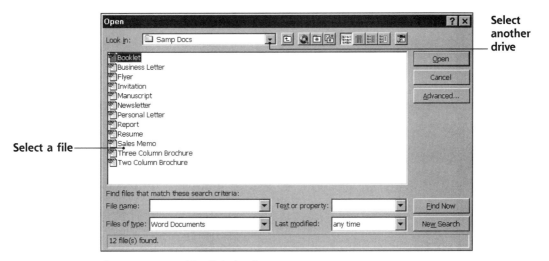

Figure 3-2 Double-click the document you want to open.

2. If you see the file listed, skip to step 3. If the file is stored on another drive, display the Look <u>i</u>n drop-down list and select the drive you want. If the file is stored in another folder, open that folder. If you see the folder listed, double-click it. You can also use the Up One Level button to move up through the folder structure.

3. Click the file you want and then click the <u>O</u>pen button. As a shortcut, you can double-click the filename. The document is displayed on screen.

SHORTCUTS FOR OPENING A DOCUMENT

If you are in an application and want to open a document you've worked on recently, open the File menu. Notice that the last four files opened are listed at the bottom of the menu. Simply click the file you want to open.

If you are at the desktop and want a quick method for opening a document, follow these steps:

1. Click the Start button.

2. Select Open Office Document. You see the Open Office Document dialog box. This is similar to the regular Open dialog box, except that all Office file types are listed.

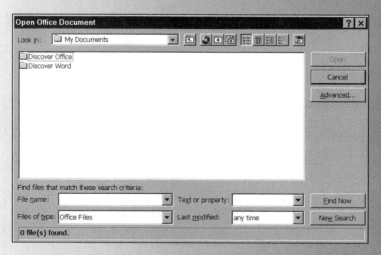

3. Change to the drive and folder that contain the document.

4. Double-click the document to open it.

A New Sheet of Paper

When you start Word or Excel, you see a blank document or worksheet on screen. To create a new document, you can start typing away or entering data.

When you start PowerPoint or Access, you can choose to create a new presentation or database (and you can select the method you want to use), or you can choose to open an existing presentation or database.

In all Office programs, it's easy to get started creating that first document. But what about the next document? How do you get another "sheet" of workbook paper? How do you start a new presentation? *To create a new document, follow these steps*:

1. Select **File** → **New** . (In Access, you select **File** → **New Database** .)

   You see the New dialog box. Figure 3-3 shows the New dialog box for Word. For all programs, you can use the default (blank document) template or select from some predesigned documents (also called templates).

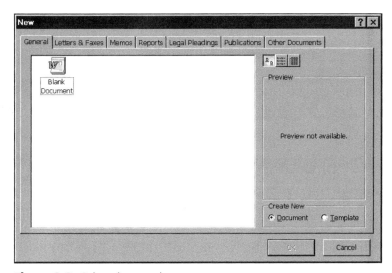

Figure 3-3 Select the template you want to use.

2. Select the template you want to use.

3. Click the OK button. A new document is displayed on screen.

TIP To create a document based on the default template, click the New button.

The Eyeball View

The rest of this book covers how to create different types of documents. As you work on your masterpiece, you may want to step back and take a peek at how your document looks. Is it long enough? How does it look on the page? Does it look professional? Taking a look at a document before you print is especially important when you make formatting changes. You can make sure the document looks acceptable before you print it.

To preview a document, select **File** → **Print Preview** or click ![icon]. You see a full-page preview. Figure 3-4 shows a preview of a Word document.

TIP The preview window also includes toolbar buttons for working with the preview. For example in Word, you can print the document, zoom in, view multiple pages, and more. In Excel, you can zoom in, display the Page Setup dialog box, check page breaks, and more. If you aren't sure what a button does, put the mouse pointer on the button border to display a pop-up name.

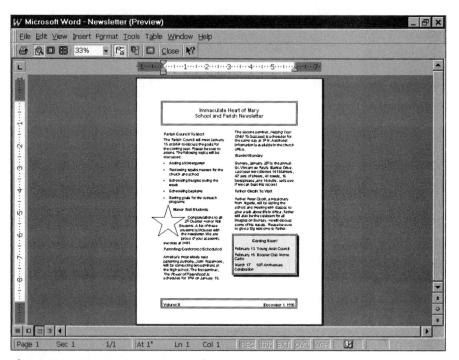

Figure 3-4 You can view a preview of your document.

Putting It to Paper

Most documents are created for someone else to look at. You type reports for your boss. You type memos for your staff. You create a worksheet with sales projections for your sales reps. You enter addresses for clients so that you can print a client list. Most documents are intended to be printed and distributed. *Printing is easy. You just follow these steps*:

1. Open the document you want to print.

2. Select **File** → **Print** or click ![icon]. You see the Print dialog box shown in Figure 3-5.

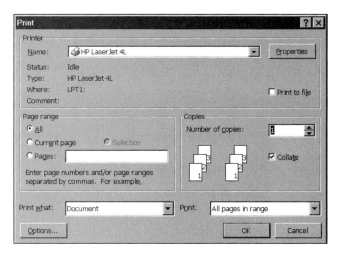

Figure 3-5 Use this dialog box to print your document.

3. Make any desired changes to the print options. You can specify what is printed (a page range, for instance), select the number of copies to print, and so on.

4. Click the OK button.

BONUS

Faxing a Document

If you have a modem, you may want to send a document via fax rather than print and snail-mail it. You can use Word's Fax Wizard to create and send a fax. This wizard leads you step-by-step through the process of setting up a fax. *Follow these steps*:

1. Select **File** → **Send To** → **Fax Recipient** . You see the first step of the Fax Wizard. The left side of the dialog box lists the steps you go through to set up and send a fax.

2. Click the Next button. You are prompted to select the document you want to fax (see Figure 3-6). You can choose to send the current document with or without a cover sheet. Or you can send just a cover sheet with a note.

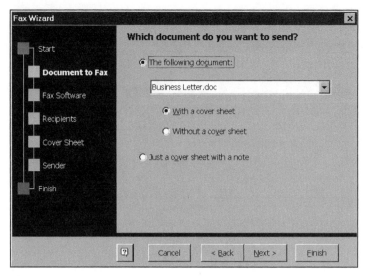

Figure 3-6 Select which document you want to fax.

3. Select what you want to fax and then click the Next button. You are prompted to select the fax program to use. You can use Microsoft Fax or your own fax program. Or you can simply print the document and then fax it on a "regular" fax machine.

4. Select which fax program to use and click the Next button. You are prompted to enter the recipient(s) for the fax.

5. In the Name text box, enter the name of the person. In the Fax Number text box, enter the fax number. You can send the fax to more than one person by completing a box for each recipient.

TIP If you have previously entered names and numbers, you can display the drop-down list and select from it. You can also select names from an address book if you have one.

6. Click the Next button. If you are sending a cover sheet, you are prompted to select a style.

7. Select a style — Professional, Contemporary, or Elegant—and then click the Next button. You are enter your fax information, including your name, company, mailing address, phone, and fax number. If you are not sending a cover sheet, skip to step 9.

8. Enter your name, company, mailing address, phone, and fax number.

9. Click the Finish button. Word sends the fax.

MANAGING YOUR OFFICE DOCUMENTS

W hen you first start using Office, you'll probably have just a few documents. You'll easily recognize each one, and you'll know exactly where each one resides. Think of this as moving into a nice new office and having about four or five sheets of paper to keep track of.

Now fast-forward a few months. Now you have about 50 or so documents to keep track of — maybe more — and your nice new office isn't so nice and new anymore. Where is everything? What the heck is this file named MXTOFF97? Why can't you find anything?

As you create more documents, you will want to learn some skills for organizing and keeping track of these documents. That's the topic of this chapter. Here you learn some additional ways to save documents as well as how to organize your documents into folders. You learn how to move, copy, rename, and delete documents you have saved. This is your file housekeeping chapter.

For Those Special Circumstances

Chapter 3 covered the basics of saving a document — how to name it and assign a folder the first time, how to save it again, and how to save it with a new name or in a different folder. These skills are critical to using any application. These are the core skills.

But what about special cases? For instance, you may want to save other key information to remind you of the contents of the file. Or you may have a different word processing program at home and want to save a Word document as a different file type. This section discusses these and other save and open options.

Saving File Summaries

When you have a gazillion files on your computer, sometimes telling what a file contains by the name — even if it is descriptive — is difficult. You may want to keep and review other information about the document, such as a title or keyword. *If so, you can save summary information by following these steps*:

1. Display the document for which you want to add summary information.

2. Select File → Properties .

3. If necessary, click the Summary tab. You see the Properties dialog box for the document (see Figure 4-1). You see the various other bits of information you can save (and then review) for the document, including a title, a subject, the author, the manager, the company name, a category, a keyword, and a comment. Notice that the program automatically completes some fields, such as the Author. The program may also suggest entries for other text boxes. You can change any of the entries.

4. Type or edit the entries in any of the text boxes.

5. Click the OK button.

TIP You can also use this dialog box to display other information about the document — such as document statistics, general file information, and so on. To do so, click the appropriate tab.

Saving a Document as Another File Type

If you work in an office, you may not use the same word processing program at home. Or perhaps you have an older version. Or you may need to share a document with a friend or coworker who uses a different program. If so, you can save the document as another file type. You can select from many different formats. For example, you can save a Word document as just plain text, Word 2, WordPerfect, Windows Write, Word for DOS, Works, and several others. You can

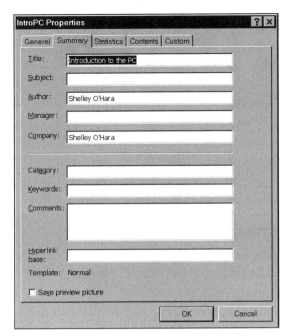

Figure 4-1 Use this dialog box to save key information about a document.

save an Excel workbook as a 1-2-3 file, a database file, or as text (tab delimited, space delimited, or comma delimited). Just find out what file format is needed first. *Then follow these steps to save the document as that type of file*:

1. Open the document you want to save as another file type.

2. Select the ⟨ **File** ⟩ → ⟨ **Save As** ⟩ command. You see the Save As dialog box.

3. Display the Save as type drop-down list. You see a list of the different file formats. Figure 4-2 shows the file types for Excel. You may see a different list depending on the application you are using.

4. Click the type of file format you want.

5. If necessary, select the drive and folder where you want to save the new file. Also, you can type a new name in the File Name text box.

6. Click the OK button. The document is saved in the new format.

If you need to share a Word document with someone who uses a different word processing program, you can save the document as another file type.

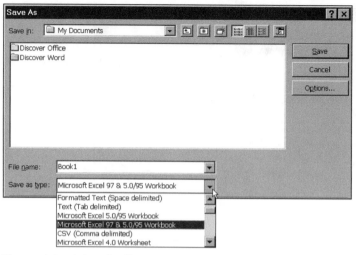

Figure 4-2   Select the file type you want from this list.

Changing How Files Are Listed

As you go to open a document in the Open dialog box, you can change how the files are listed to help identify the file you want. To do so, use these buttons in the dialog box:

LIST   Displays a list of folders and files (the default view).

DETAILS   Displays a detailed list, including file size, type, modify dates, and so on. Figure 4-3 shows a detailed view of the files in an Open dialog box from Excel.

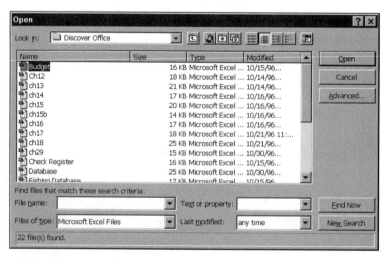

Figure 4-3   Use this view when you want more information about the listed files.

	PROPERTIES	Displays file summary information about the selected document.
	PREVIEW	Displays a preview of the selected document. Figure 4-4 shows a preview of a Word document in the Open dialog box.

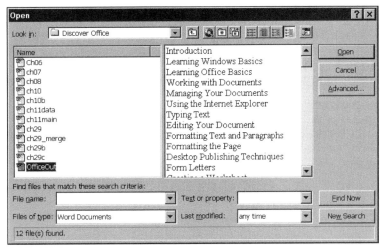

Figure 4-4   If you aren't sure what a file contains, preview it in the Open dialog box.

Organizing Your Documents into Folders: Neat and Tidy

You'd be surprised at how many people just save all their documents in one folder. That's the equivalent of having one big filing cabinet and just throwing all the papers into it without any organization. Are you guilty of this sin? If so, take a look at this section for help on keeping those documents organized.

Creating a New Folder

To better manage your documents, you should consider setting up folders and storing similar documents together. You can use any organizational scheme you want. For instance, you may want to set up different folders for each type of document you create. For Word, for instance, you may have folders for memos, letters, reports, and so on. Then when you create a memo, you can save it in the memo folder. And when you want to find a memo, you know to look in the memo folder. Or you may want to set up folders for projects or use some other organizational scheme that makes sense to you and works for your situation.

You can use Windows to create and manage folders, but you may not think to set up a folder until you are ready to save. In that case, you can use the Office program to create a new folder. *Follow these steps*:

1. If you are saving a new document, select $\boxed{\text{File}} \rightarrow \boxed{\text{Save}}$. If you are resaving a document, select $\boxed{\text{File}} \rightarrow \boxed{\text{Save As}}$. You see the Save As dialog box.

2. Change to the folder where you want the new one placed. You can place folders within other folders. You can use the Up One Level button to move up to a higher folder. You can double-click any folder listed to open and select that folder. And you can use the Save in drop-down list to change to a different drive.

3. To create a new folder, click the New Folder button. You see the New Folder dialog box shown in Figure 4-5.

Figure 4-5 Type the name for the new folder.

4. Type a name for the folder and click the OK button. The new folder is created, and you should see it listed in the Save As dialog box.

5. To change to this folder, double-click it in the folder list. You can then use the Save button to save the current document in this folder. If you want to close the dialog box without saving, click the Cancel button.

Using "Favorite" Folders

If you are a "good" saver, you probably have several folders that you use. These may be scattered all over your system — on different drives, within different folders. Rather than navigate through your drives and folders to change to these folders, you can set up a list of your favorite folders and then quickly change to these folders to save or open a document. *To add a favorite folder to the list, follow these steps:*

1. Select File → Open . You see the Open dialog box, shown in Figure 4-7. (The Add to Favorites button is not available in the Save dialog box.)

Look in Favorites button ——— ┌— **Add to Favorites button**

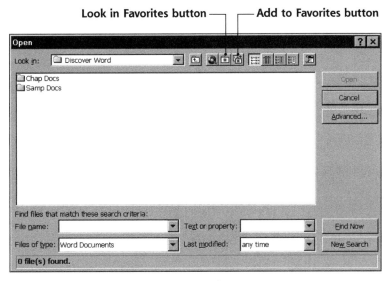

Figure 4-6 Add a folder to your list of favorites.

2. Display the folder you want to add to your favorites list. You can use the Up One Level button to move to a higher folder. You can double-click any folders listed to open and select that folder. And you can use the Look in drop-down list to change to a different drive.

3. Select the folder.

4. Click the Add to Favorites button. This folder is added to your list of favorites.

5. If you want to open a document, change to its folder and double-click the document. To close the dialog box without opening a document, click the Cancel button.

When you want to save a document to one of your favorite folders or open a document in one of these folders, you can use the Look in Favorites button to quickly display the folders and files in the favorites list. *To open a favorite folder on file, follow these steps:*

1. To open a document, select File → Open . To save a document, select File → Save . You see the Open or Save As dialog box.

2. Click the Look in Favorites button. You see the folders in your favorites list (see Figure 4-7).

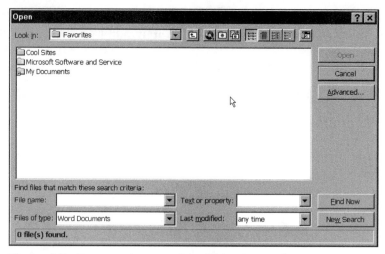

Figure 4-7   You can select any of the folders in your favorites list.

3. Double-click the folder you want to open.

4. If you are opening a file, double-click the file you want to open. To save a file, type a file name and click the Save button.

Deleting and Undeleting Files

When Windows 95 was revamped, the programs created for Windows 95 also went through some changes. One thing that's different is that you no longer have to use a separate file management program to work with files. All Microsoft programs enable you to work with files within the Open and Save dialog boxes. Say you wanted to delete a document. With previous versions, you would have to know the document name and location. You could then exit Word and use a program like File Manager or File Find to find and then delete that document. Then go back to Word. Ugh!

With Office 95 and Office 97, you can make changes to the file right from within an application. For example, you can delete files you no longer need, as covered here.

Deleting a Document

Do you save every scrap of paper no matter what its significance or importance? Do you have every magazine you've ever received starting with that *Highlights* kid's magazine? If so, you are probably a pack rat on your PC too. You probably have every document you've ever created. Sooner or later, though, you are going to run out of room. And you are going to need to do a little housekeeping. You should periodically go through your documents and delete ones you don't need.

It's a good idea to make periodic backups of your work. Then if something goes wrong, you can use these backup files. You also don't have to worry so much when you delete something because you can always use your backup copy.

Keep in mind that Murphy's Law is always in effect. The minute you think you don't need a document is the minute you do. The next section tells you how to undelete files. You might also consider backing up document(s) before you delete it.

To delete a document from within an application, follow these steps:

1. Display the Open or Save As dialog box. You can do so by selecting **File** → **Open** or **File** → **Save As**. Either dialog box is OK.

2. Right-click the document you want to delete. You see a pop-up menu with commands for working with files (see Figure 4-8).

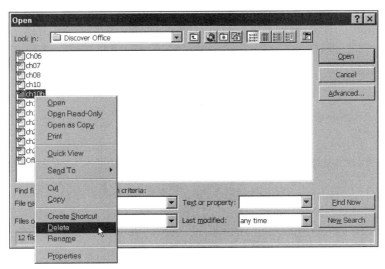

Figure 4-8 You can use these commands to delete, copy, move, and rename your documents.

3. Select **Delete**. You are prompted to confirm the deletion.

4. Click the Yes button to delete the document.

Undeleting a Document

Make a mistake? Delete a file by accident? Don't panic. Windows doesn't really delete documents; it simply moves them to a temporary holding spot called the Recycle Bin. As long as the Recycle Bin has not been emptied, you can retrieve your document from the "trash." *To do so, follow these steps:*

1. Go to the Windows desktop. You can minimize the program window by clicking the Minimize button. You may also need to minimize other open programs. You should see an icon named the Recycle Bin.

2. Double-click the Recycle Bin icon. You see the contents of this bin — any program, document, file, shortcut, and such that you have deleted recently.

3. Right-click the file you want to undelete. You see a pop-up menu (see Figure 4-9).

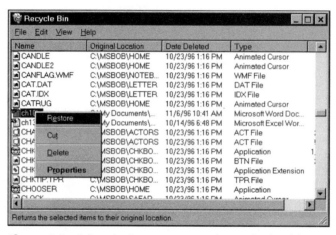

Figure 4-9   Select the Restore command to undo the deletion.

4. Select [**Restore**]. The document is removed from the Recycle Bin and put back in its original spot.

5. Click the Close button to close the Recycle Bin window.

Identity Changes

Windows 95 brought a lot of changes to file management. First, with Windows 95 you are no longer restricted to the eight-character file-name. You can type up to 255 characters, including spaces. No more decoding names like DECEXREP. You can use something descriptive, such as December Expense Report. If you need to, you can change the filename, as covered here.

Windows 95 also makes it easy to work with files. For example, you can move and copy files from within an Office application, just as you can delete them (as I explained earlier). No more switching to a separate program to do your file housekeeping. This section also covers how to move and copy files.

Renaming a Document

I can't always decide what I want to name a document. Because I have been using a computer for so long, I have a hard time *not* limiting my file names to those eight characters. Either I use a name that isn't descriptive enough like "RPTMTTOM" or I go overboard and use a name like "Report on Tuesday's Meeting with Tom about the IUPUI Project." Luckily for me (and you too), you can easily rename a document. *Simply follow these steps:*

1. Display the Open or Save As dialog box. You can do so by selecting **File** → **Open** or **File** → **Save As** . Either dialog box is OK.

2. Right-click the document you want to rename. You see a pop-up menu with commands for working with files (refer to Figure 4-8).

3. Select **Rename** . The name is highlighted with a box around it (see Figure 4-10).

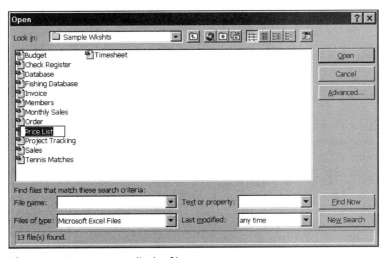

Figure 4-10   Type or edit the filename.

4. Type a new name and press Enter. The file is renamed.

Copying a Document

As mentioned in Chapter 3, you can use the Save As command to make a copy of a document. You can also use the Copy and Paste commands to copy a document. Use this method when you are reorganizing files and moving them from folder to folder. As another option, you can use the Send To command. Use this command when you are copying the document to a floppy disk to take with you or to keep as a backup copy.

COPYING AND PASTING A DOCUMENT

Just as you can use the Copy and Paste commands to copy and paste text, you can use them to copy a document. *Follow these steps*:

1. Display the Open or Save As dialog box. You can do so by selecting **File** → **Open** or **File** → **Save As** . Either dialog box is OK.

2. Right-click the document you want to copy. You may need to change to another folder to find the document you want. You see a pop-up menu with commands for working with files (refer to Figure 4-8).

3. Select **Copy** .

4. Change to the folder where you want to place the copy of the document.

5. Right-click a blank area of the dialog box and select **Paste** . The document is copied to that folder.

 Be sure to right-click a blank area of the folder list. If you right-click a document, you see the pop-up menu for working with that file.

SIDE TRIP

WORKING WITH SEVERAL FILES

For most commands, you can work with several files at once. For instance, you can select several files and copy them or move them at once. You can also print or delete several files. You cannot rename more than one file at a time, however.

To select several files that are next to each other, click the first file you want to select and then hold down the Shift key and click the last file. The first and last file and all files in between are selected.

To select files that are not next to each other, click the first file. Then hold down the Ctrl key and click the next file you want to select. Do this for each file you want to select.

Once the files are selected, you can then right-click any of the selected files and select the command you want.

SENDING A DOCUMENT TO A FLOPPY DISK

You may want to keep extra copies of important documents on a floppy disk for safekeeping. Or you may need to put a document on disk to take with you to your home or to another business site. The fastest way to copy a document to a floppy disk is to use the Send To command. *Follow these steps*:

1. Display the Open or Save As dialog box. You can do so by selecting **File** → **Open** or **File** → **Save As** . Either dialog box is OK.

2. Right-click the document you want to copy. You may need to change to another folder to find the document you want. You see a pop-up menu with commands for working with files (refer to Figure 4-8).

3. Select `Send To`.

Be sure to insert a floppy disk in the drive before you select this command.

4. From the submenu, select your floppy disk drive. The document is copied to the disk.

Moving a Document

When you save a document, you may accidentally save it in the wrong folder and then decide you want to move it to the right one. Or you may decide to change how you are organizing your documents and need to move them to another folder. Whatever the reason, you can use the Cut and Paste commands to move a document from one location to another. *Follow these steps*:

1. Display the Open or Save As dialog box. You can do so by selecting `File` → `Open` or `File` → `Save As`. Either dialog box is OK.

2. Right-click the document you want to move. You may need to change to another folder to find the document you want. You see a pop-up menu with commands for working with files (refer to Figure 4-8).

3. Select `Cut`.

4. Change to the folder where you want to place the document.

5. Right-click a blank area of the dialog box and select the `Paste` command. The document is moved to the new folder.

BONUS

Finding a Document

There's nothing more frustrating than *knowing* that you saved a document but not being able to find it. Where is that document hiding? Did that gremlin inside the PC move your file again? Are you losing your mind? You can try looking through folders on a scavenger hunt, or you can search for the document, a much better prospect.

You can search using any of several methods. This section covers the most common way. You can try some of the others on your own or consult online help for information.

I Know the Filename...

If you know part or all of the filename but just can't remember which folder you saved the file in, you can search by filename. *Follow these steps*:

1. Select File → Open . You see the Open dialog box.

2. In the File name text box, type the name of the file you want to find. You can type all or part of the filename. For example, if you know you named the file something that started with "ch," you can type **ch***. Use the asterisk (*) wildcard to indicate any number of characters in that spot. Use the question mark (?) wildcard to indicate a single wildcard character in that spot. For instance, You could use ch0? to find ch01, ch02, and so on.

   If you have a lot of files in the current folder, you may want to simply search it. But you probably could find the file if it was in the current folder, so most of the time, you will want to search through the subfolders too. If so, follow the next step.

3. If you want to search this folder and any other folders within this folder, click the Commands and Settings button and select Search Subfolders.

   Keep in mind that the search moves down — not up — through the folders. If you think the folder might be somewhere outside the current folder branch, select a higher folder. Here's an example. Suppose that you have three main folders for your Word documents: LETTERS, MEMOS, and REPORTS. Within each of these folders, you may also have several subfolders. For instance, within REPORTS, you may have a folder for SALES and one for MARKETING. If you start within REPORTS, Word searches that folder as well as SALES and MARKETING, but *not* MEMOS and LETTERS. If you want to search MEMOS and LETTERS as well as REPORTS, you have to start at the top-level folder, the one that includes MEMOS, LETTERS, and REPORTS as subfolders.

4. If necessary, click the Find Now button. (If you decided to search subfolders, you don't need to click this button.) You see the results of the search. In Figure 4-11 you see the results of searching for a filename that starts with "ch" in the Discover Office folder and all its subfolders.

Commands and Settings button

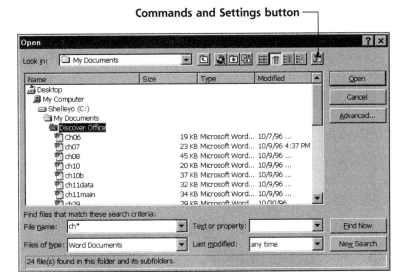

Figure 4-11 You can search for a file by its name.

5. If you want to open a found file, double-click it. To close the dialog box without opening a file, click the Cancel button.

I Know What's In the File...

OK. Say you can't even remember the filename, but you do remember what the document said. In that case, you can search for the file based on its contents. *To do so, follow these steps*:

1. Select **File** → **Open**. You see the Open dialog box.

2. Leave the File name text box empty. If it contains an entry, delete it.

3. If you want to search this folder and any other folders within this folder, click the Commands and Settings button. If you don't see a checkmark next to the Search Subfolders command, select this command.

TIP The Search Subfolders command remains on until you turn it off. You can tell whether this command is on by clicking the Commands and Settings button and looking at the command. If there's a checkmark next to it, it's on. (You can turn it off by selecting the command again.)

4. In the Text or property text box, type the text that's in the file you want to find. Type a unique word or phrase. If you type something too common, you'll get too many matches and will have a more difficult time finding the file.

5. If necessary, click the Find Now button. You see the results of the search.

In Figure 4-12 you see the results of searching for a file with the text **Michael** in the Discover Office folder and all its subfolders.

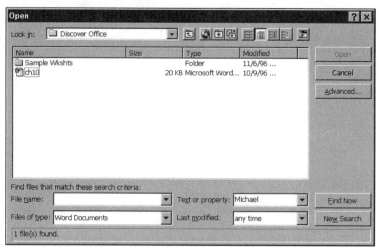

Figure 4-12   You can search for a file according to its contents.

6. If you want to open a found file, double-click it. To close the dialog box without opening a file, click the Cancel button.

I Know When I Last Worked on the File...

If you still can't find the file, but you *know* that you worked on it sometime last week, you can try searching according to when the file was last modified. *Follow these steps*:

1. Select File → Open . You see the Open dialog box.

2. Leave the File name text box empty. If it contains an entry, delete it.

3. If you want to search this folder and any other folders within this folder, click the Commands and Settings button. If you don't see a checkmark next to the Search Subfolders command, select this command.

4. Display the Last modified drop-down list and select the date range you want to search: yesterday, today, last week, this week, last month, this month, or any time.

5. If necessary, click the Find Now button. You see the results of the search.

6. If you want to open a found file, double-click it. To close the dialog box without opening a file, click the Cancel button.

Word processors are the most commonly used computer programs, and Word is the most popular Windows word processing program. You can use Word to create many different types of documents including memos, reports, letters, brochures, and more. Typing and creating documents with Word is pretty simple, and this part introduces you to Word and explains all the key skills you need to know.

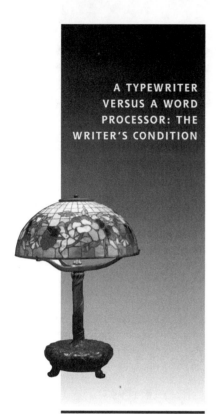

"I don't see how anyone can write without a computer these days. I really don't. I couldn't go back to retyping everything three or four times."

Eva Segar, freelance travel writer, photographer, and cryptography puzzle designer, began her writing career in 1965 with a series of hints published in *Capper's Weekly*. By an interesting coincidence, one of these first hints was how to clean a typewriter.

Three children, travels from the Arctic Ocean to the Yucatan Peninsula in everything from a pop-up camper to a thirty-foot fifth-wheel trailer, and thirty-two years later, Eva has progressed far beyond her uncle's dilapidated Remington. Eva has written articles for a major Midwestern newspaper about her extensive travels around North and Central America. In those travels she has also left her uncle's Remington behind for a Toshiba laptop.

Her computer experience is almost as varied as her travel experience. "Don't get my husband started telling you how many computers I've had," she said as she described her first computer, a Radio Shack Model 3 with two floppy disk drives. Her first laptop, also a Radio Shack with a floppy drive, was taken to Mexico in that pop-up camper to write one of her early travel articles.

Eva appreciates her Microsoft word processing software, especially the spelling and grammar checkers. She says that she often just clicks the Suggest button and follows the rules. "I can see my mistakes before I make them," says Eva.

Word 97 enables you to change your mind. Eva feels that's important for a writer. Another important aspect of being a writer, according to Eva, is the ability to try new things. "Learn how to follow instructions," she says. "You have to want to do it!"

Currently, Eva is traveling with her husband and their dog in their RV and finishing her book *Yellow Britches*, a story of growing up in Northeast Missouri in the 1920s and 1930s. She says, "During the depression, Mom made our clothes out of feedsacks. She used soft flour sacks for baby clothes for my new sister. She made most of my clothes from yellow, tightly woven meal sacks. The meal sacks had black letters on them, most of which Mom was able to scrub out." Eva is currently looking for a publisher for her book.

Oh, and for those of you using a typewriter, Eva offers a cleaning hint. "Use the reverse switch on your vacuum cleaner and blow rather than suck the dust out of your typewriter." Word 97 doesn't require the use of your vacuum cleaner.

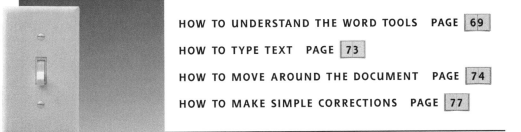

CREATING A WORD DOCUMENT

LEARN THESE KEY SKILLS:

HOW TO UNDERSTAND THE WORD TOOLS   PAGE 69

HOW TO TYPE TEXT   PAGE 73

HOW TO MOVE AROUND THE DOCUMENT   PAGE 74

HOW TO MAKE SIMPLE CORRECTIONS   PAGE 77

I f you think of Word as just a sophisticated typewriter, you are missing out on all the power of a word processing program. Word is much more than a typewriter. This chapter introduces you to the Word screen and available tools and tells you how to use Word to create a document.

Getting Familiar with Word

Y ou start Word just as you start any other Windows 95 program. *Follow these steps:*

1. Click the Start menu. You see the Start menu options.

2. Click the **Programs** command. You see the programs and program folders you have set up on your system.

3. If necessary, click the folder that contains the Word program icon. If you have not made a change since installing Word, you can skip this step.

The program item is added to the Programs folder, and you should see the Word program icon after step 2. If you have made a change, select the folder you used to store this program icon.

4. When you see the program icon, click it to start Word.

The program starts, and you see a blank document on screen (see Figure 5-1). You can probably figure out what the big blank area of the screen is. It's like a blank piece of paper. That area is where you type the text of your document. You also see the other application window items: menu bar, toolbar, scroll bars, status bar. (These are covered in Chapter 1.)

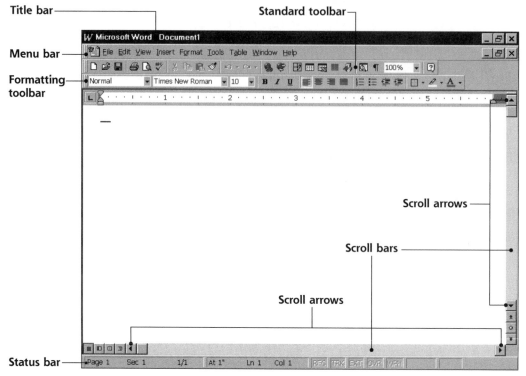

Figure 5-1 You can start typing in the blank document.

You may want to take some time to get familiar with the toolbars. The toolbars, as you know, contain buttons for frequently used commands. Tables 5-1 and 5-2 identify and describe each button in the Standard and Formatting toolbars.

TABLE 5-1 The Standard Toolbar

Button	Name	Description
	NEW	Creates a new document.
	OPEN	Displays the Open dialog box.
	SAVE	Saves the document.
	PRINT	Prints the document on screen.
	PRINT PREVIEW	Displays a preview of the document.
	SPELLING AND GRAMMAR	Checks your spelling and grammar.
	CUT	Cuts selected text.
	COPY	Copies selected text.
	PASTE	Pastes cut or copied text.
	FORMAT PAINTER	Copies and pastes formatting.
	UNDO	Undoes the last command or commands.
	REDO	Redoes the last command or commands.
	INSERT HYPERLINK	Inserts a link to a file or a Web address.
	WEB TOOLBAR	Displays a toolbar with buttons for creating Web documents.
	TABLES AND BORDERS	Displays a toolbar with buttons for formatting and working with tables and paragraph borders.
	INSERT TABLE	Inserts a table.
	INSERT MICROSOFT EXCEL WORKSHEET	Inserts a Microsoft Excel Worksheet.
	COLUMNS	Formats the selected section into columns.
	DRAWING	Displays the Drawing toolbar.
	DOCUMENT MAP	Displays a separate pane with an outline of your document headings. You can use this document map to navigate through your document.
	SHOW/HIDE ¶	Displays or hides paragraph marks (¶).
100%	ZOOM CONTROL	Zooms the document.
	OFFICE ASSISTANT	Displays the Office Assistant so that you can get help.

TABLE 5-2 The Formatting Toolbar

Button	Name	Description
Normal ▾	STYLE	Displays a style list. Click the style you want.
Times New Roman ▾	FONT	Displays a font list. Click the font you want.
10 ▾	FONT SIZE	Displays a size list. Click the size you want.
B	BOLD	Makes selected text bold.
I	ITALIC	Makes selected text italic.
U	UNDERLINE	Turns on underlining.
▤	ALIGN LEFT	Aligns selected paragraph(s) left.
▤	CENTER	Centers selected paragraph(s).
▤	ALIGN RIGHT	Aligns selected paragraph(s) right.
▤	JUSTIFY	Justifies selected paragraph(s).
▤	NUMBERING	Creates a numbered list.
▤	BULLETS	Creates a bulleted list.
▤	DECREASE INDENT	Decreases the indent of the selected paragraph(s).
▤	INCREASE INDENT	Increases the indent of the selected paragraph(s).
▢ ▾	OUTSIDE BORDER	Adds a border around the current paragraph. You can select a different type of border from the drop-down list.
▨	HIGHLIGHT	Highlights the selected text. The default color is yellow. You can select another color from the drop-down list.
A	FONT COLOR	Changes the color of the selected text. The default color is red. You can select another color by clicking the down arrow next to the button and then clicking the color you want.

 FEATURE FOCUS Insert Hyperlink and Web Toolbar buttons are new in Office 97.

Putting Words to Paper

As mentioned, when you start Word, you see a blank document on screen. Yes, a blank area just waiting for your words of wisdom. Waiting for you to commit to paper your grand scheme, your ideas for changing the world, or at least your ideas for next month's pitch-in party. To create a document, you can just start typing away.

As you type, the characters appear on screen, and the flashing vertical bar, called the insertion point, moves to the right (see Figure 5-2). This insertion point always indicates where new text will appear when you start typing. Keep typing until you reach the end of the line. Then type some more. Notice that Word will automatically wrap text to the next line.

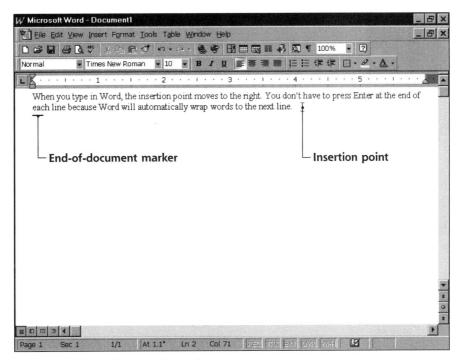

Figure 5-2 Type the text of your document.

One mistake a lot of new users make is to press Enter at the end of each line. Let Word wrap the words automatically.

In fact, one mistake a lot of new users make is to press Enter at the end of each line. You shouldn't do this because if you have to add or delete text, your lines won't automatically readjust. You should press Enter only at the end of a paragraph or when you want to insert a blank line.

Word also automatically inserts page breaks, as necessary. When a page fills up, Word inserts a break and creates a new page. If you add or delete text, Word adjusts the page breaks. This means that you don't have to worry about text running off the page.

TIP **Word inserts a hidden paragraph mark when you press Enter. If you want to see where the breaks occur, click the Show/Hide ¶ button in the Standard toolbar. You see marks for paragraphs, spaces, tabs, and other hidden characters.**

When you are typing a document, keep these tips in mind:

* If you want to insert a tab, simply press the Tab key on the keyboard. By default, Word has tabs set up every 1/2 inch. Word inserts the tab and moves the insertion point over. You can then type your text. You can change the tab settings using means covered in the Chapter 8.

A common mistake for beginners is to use the space bar to tab over in a document or press Enter until a page break occurs. These are typing no-nos. Spaces don't always align entries exactly, so instead be sure to use the Tab key. Pressing Enter to create a page break will mess you up if you add or delete text later. Instead, insert a hard page break.

* The easiest way to insert a hard page break is using the keyboard shortcut: press Ctrl+Enter. You can also select the Insert → Break command. In the Break dialog box, be sure the Page break option is selected. Click OK.

* To delete a hard page break, move the insertion point right after the page break and press Backspace.

Moving Around the Document

The insertion point is the "You Are Here" arrow. When you want to add or delete text, you start by moving the insertion point to where you want to make the change. When you want to select text, you move the insertion point to the start of the text. You can use either the mouse or the keyboard to move the insertion point.

The thick horizontal line in the page area is called the end-of-document marker; as its name suggests, it indicates the end of the document. You cannot move the insertion point past this indicator. If you click beyond this line, nothing happens. Word doesn't permit the insertion point to move where nothing exists. Only after you enter text or spaces on screen can you move the insertion point.

Using the Mouse

To move the insertion point with the mouse, move the pointer to the spot you want and click the mouse button. The insertion point jumps to that spot. Remember that the insertion point (the vertical flashing line) and the mouse pointer (the I-beam) are two separate items. You can't just point to the spot you want. You have to point and click to place the insertion point.

Using the Keyboard

If you prefer to keep your hands on the keyboard, you can use the arrow keys and other key combinations to move the insertion point. Table 5-3 lists the common movement keys. Note that if the key combination is joined with a plus sign, you must press and hold the first key and then press the second key.

TABLE 5-3 Keyboard Movement Keys

To Move	Press
One character right	→
One character left	←
One line up	↑
One line down	↓
To the beginning of the line	Home
To the end of line	End
To the beginning of the document	Ctrl + Home
To the end of the document	Ctrl + End
One word left	Ctrl + ←
One word right	Ctrl + →
One paragraph down	Ctrl + ↓
One paragraph up	Ctrl + ↑
One screen up	PgUp
One screen down	PgDn
Bottom of screen	Ctrl + PgDn
Top of screen	Ctrl + PgUp

Scrolling the Document

In a long document, you may simply want to scroll through the text without moving the insertion point. To scroll the document using the mouse, do any of the following:

* To scroll left, click the left scroll arrow. To scroll right, click the right scroll arrow.

* To scroll up through the document, click the up scroll arrow. To scroll down through the document, click the down scroll arrow.

* To scroll a relative distance in the document, drag the scroll box up or down. If you have several pages in the document, you can tell which page you are on by looking at the pop-up page number that appears next to the scroll bar. If that page includes a style heading, the heading name also appears. When you get to the page you want, release the mouse button.

* To scroll to a relative location without dragging, click within the scroll bar to move to that location.

 Keep in mind that when you use the scroll arrows, you are *not* moving the insertion point. The insertion point remains in the original spot. If you scroll to a different location and want to make a change, be sure to click the I-beam to place the insertion point before you making a change.

Navigating Using Your Document Map

If you have assigned heading styles to the headings in your document, you can use the Document Map to navigate through your document. (For information on using these heading styles, review Chapter 8.)

 The Document Map is a new feature in Word 97.

To display a document map, click the Document Map button. You see two separate panes. The leftmost pane shows all the level-1 and level-2 headings in your document. The current section is highlighted. The rightmost pane shows the text of the document (see Figure 5-3).

 Not only is the Document Map a good way to navigate, it's also a good way to see an overview of your document and keep the document organization in mind as you write and edit.

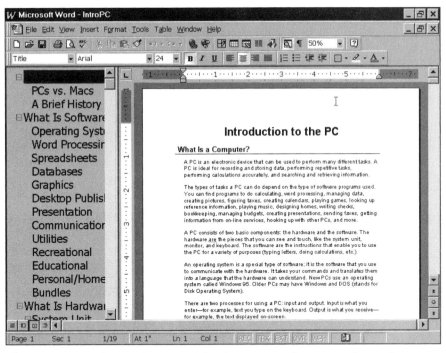

Figure 5-3 Use the new Document Map feature to navigate around your document.

To move to another section, simply click the heading in the leftmost pane. Word moves you to that section.

Oops! Making Simple Corrections

I think the hardest part of writing is that first sentence. You don't know how many times I start a sentence and then backspace, backspace, backspace to erase what I just typed. I start another sentence that sounds good in my head but looks ridiculous in the cold glare of the PC screen. Backspace, backspace!

The biggest thrill of using a word processing program comes of the ease with which you can make changes. As you type, you can make some simple corrections. (For more detailed information on editing a document, see the next chapter.) You can delete characters and insert new text with ease.

Correcting Mistakes

As you type, you see the characters on screen. If you notice a mistake, you can correct it using either the Backspace key or the Delete key. Press the Backspace key to delete characters to the left of the insertion point. (Think *back*, *Back*space.) Press the Delete key to delete characters to the right of the insertion point. (Think forward for the Delete key.) When you delete character(s), Word moves existing text up to fill in the gap.

Adding Text

If you are fairly young, you may have never had the privilege of using a type-writer. You won't even appreciate how *easy* it is to add and delete text. You won't remember having to retype an *entire document* just to add an idea you forgot (or your boss thought was critical).

Yes, Word makes it easy to add text, adjusting the text you have to make room. To add text, place the insertion point where you want the new text. Then type the text. New text is inserted, and existing text moves over to make room.

If you ever start typing and text disappears, you are in Typeover mode (rather than Insert mode). You can use Typeover mode to type over text, although I can't think of a good reason why you would. You usually want to stay in Insert mode, where new text is inserted in the document. You toggle between Typeover and Insert mode using the Insert key. So if text disappears, check the status bar. If you see OVR, press the Insert key to return to Insert mode.

The next chapter covers additional editing changes you can make to your document including copying, moving, finding, replacing, and checking the text in your document.

Important! Saving Your Document

As you work, you should save your document periodically. Remember that the words on screen are stored in a temporary spot, the computer's memory. If something happens to the computer, all that information is lost. To make a permanent copy of the on-screen document, you need to save the document to a file on your hard disk.

You must remember to save your document.

You shouldn't wait until you finish the document to save, and don't think that saving just once is enough. You should save often. Chapter 3 covers how to save a document. The first time you save, you must assign a name and folder for the document. After that, you can simply use the File → Save command to save the file with its original name and in the original location.

BONUS

Saving Time Typing Text

The thing you most when you create a document is type. Unfortunately, the ideas have to come from you. Word can't help you there. But Word can help you save time typing text that you often use. A new feature called AutoText is one of Word's greatest little features. You can use this feature to avoid retyping words, phrases, even entire paragraphs that you type over and over. This section gives complete information on this feature.

Using One of Word's AutoText Entries

Word includes some AutoText entries commonly used in memos and letters. You can select an attention line, a closing, a header or footer, mailing instructions, reference initials, a reference line, a salutation, a signature company, or a subject line. Some entries have different versions, such as "Attention:" or "ATTN." *To view or use one of these AutoText entries, follow these steps:*

1. Select `Insert` → `AutoText`. You see a list of different entries you can use.

2. Click the type of entry you want to insert. You see a submenu with additional choices for this entry.

3. Click the entry you want. Word inserts the text.

You can also start typing the AutoText entry; Word displays a ScreenTip with the entry. If you want this entry, press Enter. For example, try typing **Sept**. Word displays a ScreenTip that says "September." Press Enter to complete the entry.

Creating Your Own AutoText Entries

Word's AutoText entries are handy for memo and letters, but you'll find, in your work, text that you type again and again. To save time, you can also create AutoText entries of your own. For instance, suppose that you have a complex company name like "Yabadabadoo, A Division of Fred & Barney Enterprises." You can quickly tire of typing that over and over again.

Instead of typing the text, you can create an AutoText entry and have Word enter it for you. All you have to do is first create the entry. You only have to do this once. Then you can easily insert the entry.

CREATING AN AUTOTEXT ENTRY

Follow these steps to create an AutoText entry:

1. Select the text you want to save as an AutoText entry — a word, a phrase, or an entire paragraph or more. You can either select the text from a document you have already created or type the text in a blank document.

2. Select `Insert` → `AutoText`. From the submenu that appears, select `New`. You see the Create AutoText dialog box (see Figure 5-4).

Figure 5-4 Create an AutoText entry using this dialog box.

3. Type the name you want to assign to this entry. The best names are the shortest — even just one character. Use a name that is easy to remember.

4. Click the OK button.

 TIP **Type a short name to save time. Most of my AutoText entries are just one character, usually the first letter of the entry — for instance, w for Word for Windows.**

INSERTING AN AUTOTEXT ENTRY

Once you created the entry, you can insert it quickly and easily. *Follow these steps:*

1. Select `Insert` → `AutoText`. You see a list of AutoText categories.

2. Select the category you want. Your AutoText entry is probably placed in the category "Normal."

3. Select the AutoText entry. Word inserts the text.

 TIP **To delete an entry, select Insert → AutoText → AutoText. Then select the entry you want to delete in the AutoText dialog box and click Delete.**

The keyboard shortcut is the fastest way to insert an AutoText entry. You don't have to take your hands from the keyboard. But you do have to remember the shortcut. *To insert an AutoText entry using the keyboard, follow these steps:*

1. Move to where you want to insert the entry.

2. Type the name you assigned to the entry.

3. Press F3. Word inserts the entire entry.

EDITING A WORD DOCUMENT

One of the greatest things about using a word processing program such as Word is how easily you can make changes. Forget a word, phrase, or entire paragraph? You can add text. Decide you don't like a word, phrase, or entire paragraph? You can delete text. When you add or delete text, Word adjusts the text accordingly — moving text over to make room for additions or moving text up to fill in the gaps from deletions.

This chapter covers the most common editing changes you make to a document. You learn how to work with text: how to select, add, delete, move, copy, find, and replace text. You also learn how to check your document for errors.

Always Step One

You type one character at a time, but when you edit and format, you often want to work with whole words, lines, paragraphs, even the whole document. The most important editing and formatting skill you can learn is how to select text. Most tasks you perform start with this basic step: select the text you want to work with. Select text, select text, select text — you'll get tired of reading that step.

Once the text is selected, you can make changes to that text. You can delete it, move it, copy it, make it bold, change the font, change the color, frappé it, and so on. Selecting text is similar to highlighting, and you will find it's simple to select text. You can use either the mouse or the keyboard.

Selecting Text with the Mouse

You may prefer to use the mouse to move around and make selections. If so, you'll probably be most comfortable selecting text with the mouse. *Follow these steps:*

1. Move the insertion point to the start of the text you want to select.

2. Click and hold down the left mouse button and drag across the text you want to select.

3. When all the text is selected, release the mouse button. The text appears in reverse video (see Figure 6-1).

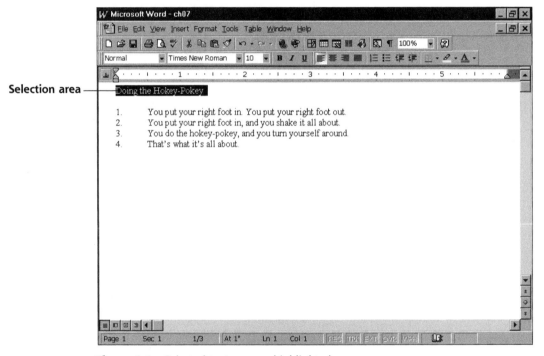

Figure 6-1   Selected text appears highlighted on screen.

 TIP Sometimes you may select text by mistake. To unselect text, simply click outside of the selected text or press an arrow key. Presto. The text is not selected.

It's easy to select some text, release the mouse button, and then try to continue selecting text. When you do this, you end up moving the text. If text mysteriously moves, this is probably what happened. Simply undo the move by clicking the Undo button.

Selecting Text with the Keyboard

If you are a fast typist, you may prefer to keep your fingers on the keyboard. In this case, let your fingers do the selecting. *Follow these steps to select text using the keyboard:*

1. Move the insertion point to the start of the text you want to select.

2. Hold down the Shift key and use the movement keys (← , ↓ , and so on) to highlight the text you want.

3. Release the Shift key. The text is selected.

Selection Shortcuts

Because selecting text is so common, Word provides several shortcuts for selecting text. You can double-click within a word to select it. Click three times within a paragraph to select it.

Feeling pretty fancy with the mouse? You can also click with the selection bar (the blank area along the left side of the Word document) to select text. Click once next to the line you want to select the entire line. Click twice next to the paragraph you want, to select that entire paragraph. Click three times to select the entire document. Click 45 times to select every document you've ever typed. (Just kidding on that last one.)

And for keyboard fans, you can press Ctrl+A to select the entire document.

Text Go Bye-Bye

Have you ever said something and then wished you could swallow your words? Told your boss that his toupee didn't look *that* bad. Asked a woman "When is your baby due?" when the baby was born two months ago? Unfortunately Word can't help you with the spoken word, but can help you get rid of words, phrases, and sentences that just don't make sense in your document.

To delete text, follow these steps:

1. Select the text you want to delete. You can select a word, a phrase, a sentence, a paragraph, part of a paragraph, part of a document, the entire document — you get the idea.

2. Press the Delete key. Word deletes the text and fills in the gap.

TIP **Make a mistake? If you delete text by mistake, use the Edit → Undo command to undo the deletion. You can also click the Undo button.**

Doing Some Rearranging

In prehistoric times (that is, BPC, or **B**efore **PC**s), you had to create a document by writing it out longhand on paper. When you wanted to edit it, you had to scribble out, write over, and add little notes to yourself. If you wanted to use a different order for the text, you had to use some scheme. Maybe you used numbers like 1, 2, or 3 to indicate the new order. Or maybe you literally cut and pasted the text in the order you wanted (that's what I used to do, little bits of handwritten "wisdom" cut into strips and scattered around my room). After all this work, you then had the arduous process of committing these scribbles to the typewriter. Good luck getting it right!

If you wanted to say the same thing twice (or something similar), you had to retype it. Not so with Word. You can easily move text to a new location or copy text to use it again in the same document or another document.

Moving Text

You can move text with Word without scissors and paste! Word does use the same metaphor of cutting and pasting. You cut the text from its original location and then paste it in its new location. *Follow these steps to move text:*

1. Select the text you want to move (see Figure 6-2).

2. Select Edit → Cut or click ✄. The text is removed from the document and placed in a temporary holding spot called the Clipboard.

3. Move to where you want to place the text. You can move to another location in a document, to another document, or even to another type of document. (For information on cutting and pasting from one program to another, see Chapter 29.)

4. Select Edit → Paste or click 📋 in the toolbar. The text is pasted into its new location (see Figure 6-3).

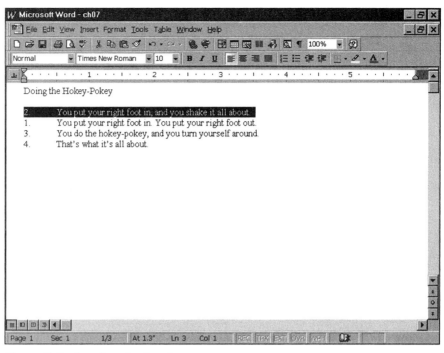

Figure 6-2   Start by selecting the text you want to move.

Pasted text ———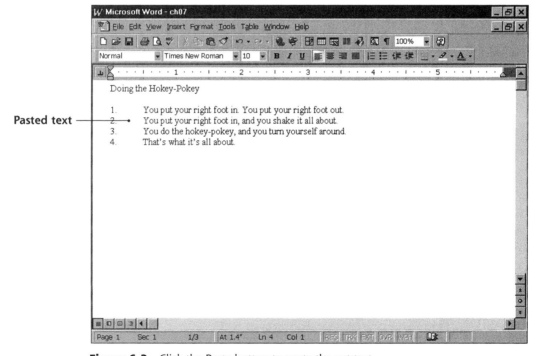

Figure 6-3   Click the Paste button to paste the cut text.

Working with More Than One Document

Just as you can have several papers on your desk, you can have several documents open on your "electronic" desk. You may want to review information in another document, or you may want to copy or move information from one document to another.

To work with more than one document, just use the <u>O</u>pen command to open the documents you want. You always see the last document you opened. You can think of this active document as the one on top of the pile. To move to another document, open the <u>W</u>indow menu and select the document you want. Each open document is listed at the bottom of this menu.

You can also display several documents at once. To do so, open the <u>W</u>indow menu and select the <u>A</u>rrange All command. Each document is displayed in a separate window. The current window has a colored title bar. You can switch to another document by clicking within its window.

To return a document to a full-screen display, move to the document window you want to expand and then click the Maximize button.

Copying Text

Copying text is a lot like moving, but instead the selected text appears in both places — the original location and the spot to which you copy it. Copying is handy when you want to use the same or similar text again. Like moving, copying text involves two processes: copying the text and pasting the text. When you copy the text, it is placed in the Clipboard, a temporary holding spot. You can paste more than one copy because the text remains in the Clipboard until you copy or cut something else.

When you cut or copy something, you must paste the selection before you cut or copy something else. The Clipboard always holds the last selection you cut or copy. So if you copy something and then copy something else, the Clipboard stores only the second thing you copied.

Follow these steps to copy text:

1. Select the text you want to copy.

2. Select <u>Edit</u> → <u>Copy</u> or click 📋.

3. Place the insertion point where you want the copy of the text to appear. You can copy the text to another location in a document, to another document, or even to another type of document. (For information on copying and pasting from one program to another, see Chapter 29.)

4. Select <u>Edit</u> → <u>Paste</u> or click . The text is copied.

TIP　**You can also use these keyboard shortcuts: press Ctrl+X for Cut, Ctrl+C for Copy, and Ctrl+V for Paste.**

If you decide you don't want the copy, you can undo it. Select the <u>E</u>dit → <u>U</u>ndo command, or just delete the copied text.

Where Is That Word?

When you are editing a short document, it's easy to find the spot you want. In a long document, though, scanning to find a word or phrase is more difficult. A way to move quickly to a particular part of your document is to use the <u>F</u>ind command.

The <u>F</u>ind command helps you move to a particular spot in the document. Its counterpart, <u>R</u>eplace, helps you make replacements. For instance, suppose that you are typing up a proposal for a new product called Ralph's Canned Chili, but decide that "Ralph's" really isn't the best name. You like "Earl's" better. You could find each time you used "Ralph" and replace it manually with "Earl." Or you can have Word make the replacements. This section covers both how to find text and how to find and replace text.

Understanding How the Search Works

When you search, Word starts at the location of the insertion point and searches through your text to the end of the document. When Word finds a match, it highlights it, and the dialog box remains open. You can continue to search until you find the match you want. If Word can't find a match, you see an error message telling you so.

Word, by default, finds the text you enter, no matter what the case and no matter if what you enter is part of another word. For instance, if you search for "ten," Word will stop on "ten," "Ten," "tennis," "often." Anyplace those characters appear. You can set options that tell Word to match the case as you type it and to find whole words only. The section "Search and Replace Tips" covers using these options.

Searching for Text

To find text, follow these steps:

1. Select <u>Edit</u> → <u>Find</u>. You see the Find and Replace dialog box (see Figure 6-4).

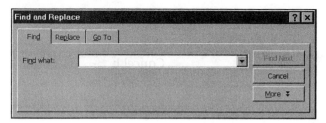

Figure 6-4 Enter the text you want to find and then click the Find Next button.

2. In the Find what text box, enter the text you want to find. You can enter a word or a phrase. Try to think of something unique. If you search for something common, you'll have to wade through a lot of matches before you find the one you want.

 TIP **Word keeps track of what you have searched for in the document. If you see an entry in the Find what text box, it means you have already done a search. If you don't want to use this text, drag across it and then type the text you do want to find. You can also click the down arrow next to the Find what text box and select an entry that you have previously searched for.**

3. Click the Find Next button. Word highlights the first match (see Figure 6-5). The dialog box remains open so that you can search again.

Found text —

Click to
search again —

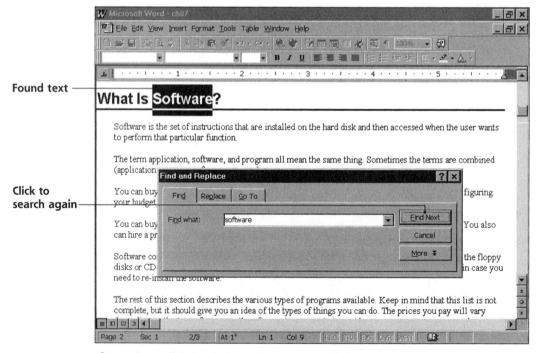

Figure 6-5 Click the Find Next button to search for the next occurrence.

4. To search again, click the Find Next button. Continue to do so until you find the match you want.

To close the dialog box, click the Cancel button.

Replacing Text

Replacing text is similar to finding text. First you tell Word the text you want to find and replace. Then you tell Word what text to use as the replacement. *Follow these steps:*

1. Select **Edit** → **Replace** . You see the Find and Replace dialog box (see Figure 6-6).

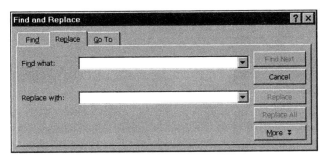

Figure 6-6 Enter the text you want to find and the text you want to use as the replacement.

TIP **If you want to search and replace just part of the document, select the text first. Then select the Edit → Replace command.**

2. In Find what text box, type the text you want to find. For instance, type **disk** here. If you see an entry already, it means you have searched and/or replaced something already. You can drag across the entry and type the new one to replace it.

3. In the Replace with text box, type the text you want to use as the replacement. For instance, type **disc**.

4. Click the Find Next button to start the search. Word moves to the first match and highlights the found word or phrase. The dialog box remains open (see Figure 6-7).

5. To make the replacement, click the Replace button.

To leave this text as is and move to the next match, click the Find Next button.

To make all the replacements without confirmation, click the Replace All button.

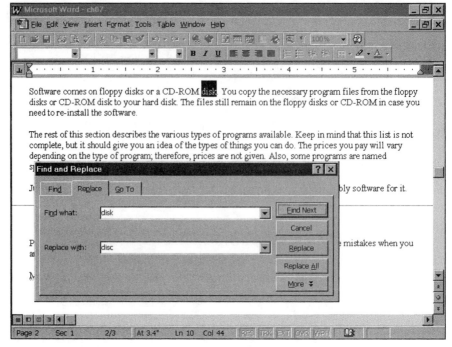

Figure 6-7   You can select whether you want the replacement made.

It's usually a good idea to go through a few replacements before you replace them all. Doing so ensures the replace operation is working as you intended. It's easy to make replacements that you didn't intend. For instance, if you replace all occurrences of "man" with "person," you can end up with some weird words like "personager" (replacement for "man"ager).

When Word is done searching the document, you see an alert message.

6. Click the OK button to close the alert box. Then click the Close button to close the dialog box.

Search and Replace Tips

If you don't find what you want or if you find too much of what you want, you can try some tips to fine-tune your search. In the Find and Replace dialog box, click the More button to expand the dialog box and show additional options (see Figure 6-8).

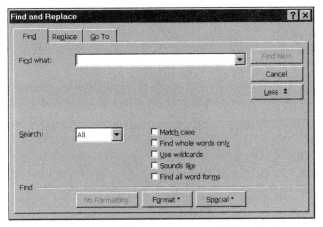

Figure 6-8 You can fine-tune your search by selecting some of these options.

The following list explains which options to try in the dialog box as well as some other strategies:

✱ Word isn't picky about matching the case of your entry. If you enter **Foreman**, it will stop on "foreman," "FOREMAN," or "Foreman." You can have Word match the case as you've entered it. To do so, check the Match case check box.

✱ Word also isn't picky about where your entry appears. It can be a whole word or part of a word. If you search for **bat**, Word will stop on "bat," "Batman," "combat," and so on. If you want to stop only on whole words, check the Find whole word only check box.

✱ The same word can appear in different forms. For instance, you can have "carry," "carries," "carrying," and so on. If you want Word to find all forms of the word, check the Find all word forms check box.

✱ By default, Word searches down through the document. You can change the search direction, by clicking the Search drop-down list and selecting Up.

✱ In addition to searching for text, you can also search for formatting. For instance, you can search for bold. To search for formatting, click the Format button and then select the appropriate formatting command. In the dialog box that appears, select the formatting you want to find. For more information on formatting options, see the next chapter.

✱ You can also search for special characters such as tabs, paragraph marks, page breaks, and so on. To do so, click the Special button and then select the item you want to find.

✱ The two other options, Use wildcards and Sounds like, can also help you fine-tune a search. To me, they aren't worth the time. I've never used them. You can more easily try searching for another word or phrase. If you want more information on these options, right-click them and then select the What's This? command.

✴ If you can't find a match, try one of two things. First, try searching for something else. Maybe you thought you used the word "peccadillo" in your document, but really used "petty sin." Try another word or phrase in the section you want to find. Second, be sure that your previous entries aren't restricting your search. Word does not clear the search options with each search. So you may have options set that you don't know about. Be sure to check the expanded dialog box (click the More button) for options you may not know were set.

Mistake-Proof Documents

You can spend all the time in the world getting your document to sound good and look good, but if your document includes a glaring mistake such as a spelling error or a grammatical mistake, it ain't going to be good.

To help you avoid embarrassing mistakes, Word includes a spell-check and grammar check program. In fact, Word flags spelling mistakes and grammar problems as you type. You can choose to make corrections as you type, or you can wait until the document is complete and then check the spelling and grammar.

Proofread Your Document!

Remember that the spelling program does not replace a careful proofreading of your work. Word does not know the difference between "there," "their," and "they're." Word doesn't know when you mean "weather" and when you mean "whether." The program just knows when a word is misspelled. You can have perfect spelling and still look like an ignoramus. Proofread your document!

The spell-checker for Word does not replace a careful proofreading of your work.

The same is true for grammatical mistakes. Just because you got an A+ according to the grammar checker doesn't mean your document doesn't include errors. You still must proofread. You'd be surprised at how many problems Word doesn't flag.

Checking Your Spelling and Grammar As You Type

As you type, you may notice that Word puts a squiggly red line under some words, and some sentences are flagged with a green squiggly line. These squiggly lines are Word's red flags alerting to you to possible misspellings (red) or grammar mistakes (green). You can ignore these flags and continue working, or you can make corrections as you create the document, as covered in this section.

If you don't see these squiggly lines, this feature may have been turned off. Select the Tools → Options command and click the Spelling & Grammar tab. Be sure the Check spelling as you type and Check grammar as you type check boxes are checked.

CORRECTING SPELLING ERRORS

You can think of Word's automatic spell-check as a nagging English teacher standing by with her red pen. Everyone had one memorable English teacher. Usually had those half glasses on a chain around her neck. Wore her hair in a bun. Enunciated each and every word. Mine's name was Mrs. Pickard. Make one little mistake and boom! she's there with that pen.

When Word's Mrs. Pickard flags a mistake, you can ignore it and check your spelling when you are done (covered later). Or you can make a correction. You can do any of the following:

* If you made a typo or know the right spelling, you can press Backspace to delete the misspelled word. Then retype the word.

* If only a few characters are wrong, you don't have to retype the entire word. You can also edit the word to correct the misspelling.

* If you don't know the right spelling, you can have Word display some choices. To do so, right-click the misspelled word. You see a pop-up menu (see Figure 6-9). If you see the correct spelling, click it. Word makes the replacement. You can also choose to ignore the misspelling, add the misspelled word to the dictionary, or start the Spelling program by selecting the appropriate command. (These commands are covered in the section on checking the entire document.)

You can continue typing words and correcting mistakes until you complete the document. If this method interrupts your writing concentration, you can just ignore the lines and check the spelling later, as covered in the next section.

CORRECTING GRAMMAR ERRORS

In addition to spelling errors, Word 97 also flags grammatical errors. Or at least what it thinks are grammatical errors. I have never been fond of the grammar feature of this or any word processing program — probably because I was an English teacher. English 101. College Composition. (No. I don't have half-glasses, a bun, or a ruler. At least not handy.) The mistakes I see flagged aren't always mistakes. Plus, I've seen the grammar checker skip over some really obvious grammatical mistakes. If you want to use the grammar checker, just remember that it's not foolproof.

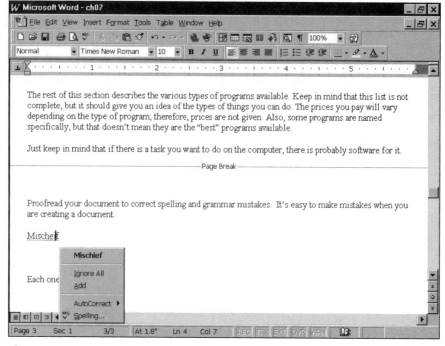

Figure 6-9 Use the shortcut menu to select an alternative spelling.

Word underlines what it considers questionable phrases and sentences. You can spot these grammatical errors by the green squiggly underline. As with the on-the-fly spell-check, you can choose to ignore the errors and check your grammar later. Or you can make corrections as you go.

You can retype the word, phrase, or sentence to fix the problem. Or you can edit it. You can also display grammatical suggestions by right-clicking the green underlined word(s). You see a pop-up menu that lists suggestions. If one of the suggestions is correct, click it to replace your original text with the new suggested revision. You can also choose to ignore the sentence (select Ignore Sentence) or start the grammar checker (Grammar).

You can make all the corrections as you type. Or you can wait until you complete the document and then check the grammar, as covered later in the section "Checking Your Document."

AUTOMATIC SPELLING CORRECTIONS

In addition to flagging some words or phrases, Word will automatically correct some mistakes. For example, try typing **teh**. You can't. Word automatically replaces this common typo with the correct word "the." Word recognizes some common misspellings and typographical mistakes and makes the replacement automatically. In addition to the ones Word already "knows," you can add other words to the list. For instance, I commonly mistype "chapter" as "chatper." Rather than correct this mistake in each document, I added an AutoCorrect entry so that Word makes the replacement for me.

You learn how to add an AutoCorrect entry during a spell-check later in the next section.

Checking Your Spelling and Grammar Later

When you are trying to concentrate on your writing, you may not want to be bothered with spelling or grammar mistakes. You might want to keep your train of thought going and worry about corrections later. If so, you can run the spell-check program to check the words in your document. By default, Word also checks the grammar in your document.

HOW THE SPELL-CHECK WORKS

The spell-check program works by comparing words in the document to words in its dictionary. When the speller cannot find a word, it flags it as misspelled and displays a dialog box. Keep in mind that just because a word is flagged doesn't necessarily mean it is misspelled. It just means Word cannot find the word in its dictionary. Proper names and some terminology, for instance, may be flagged although they are spelled correctly.

When Word flags a word and displays the dialog box, you have the option of replacing the word with a suggested spelling, correcting the word yourself, skipping the word, creating an AutoCorrect entry, or adding the word to a custom dictionary. After you select an option, Word moves to the next word and continues in this way until it has checked all words in the document.

Word will also flag double words such as "the the." You can choose to delete the second occurrence or to skip it.

HOW THE GRAMMAR CHECKER WORKS

The grammar checker knows and checks for certain grammatical rules such as subject-verb agreement. When the grammar checker finds a word, a phrase, or a sentence that breaks one of these rules, it flags the error and makes suggestions on how to correct the problem.

When Word flags a grammatical error, it displays the Spelling and Grammar dialog box, with suggested corrections. You can choose to change to one of the suggestions, manually edit the sentence, or ignore the sentence. You can also use the Office Assistant to display help on the grammatical problem.

CHECKING YOUR DOCUMENT

To start a spell and grammar check, follow this step:

1. Select `Tools` → `Spelling and Grammar` or click 🔤.

TIP To check just part of the document, select the part you want to check. You can also press F7 to select the <u>S</u>pelling and Grammar command.

For spelling errors, Word highlights the word and displays the Spelling and Grammar dialog box (see Figure 6-10). The Not in Dictionary list displays the misspelled word, and the Suggestions list displays any alternative spellings. You can do any of the following:

* To skip this occurrence but stop on the next one, click the Ignore button. To skip all occurrences of this word, click the Ignore All button. Use this option for names or terms that are spelled correctly but that Word just doesn't include in its dictionary.

* To replace the word with one of the suggested spellings, click the spelling in the Suggestions list. Click the Change button to change this occurrence. Click the Change All button to replace all occurrences of the word.

* If none of the replacements are correct, you can correct the error manually. The insertion point is in the Not in Dictionary: list box. Move the insertion point and edit the text or delete and retype the correct spelling. Then click the Change button.

* Click the Add button to add the word to the dictionary. This word will then no longer be flagged as misspelled. Do this for words, such as common names or terms, that you don't want to continually have to check. For instance, I add my first and last name to the dictionary so that they are no longer flagged.

* If Word flags a repeated word, click the Ignore button to ignore and keep the repeated word. Or click the Delete button to delete one of the words.

* If you want to add the error and its correction to the AutoCorrect list, click the AutoCorrect button. When you make this same mistake, Word will automatically replace the misspelled word with the correct spelling.

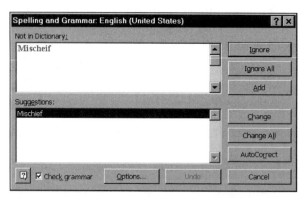

Figure 6-10 Select how to handle the misspelled word.

For grammar errors, Word highlights the word, phrase, or sentence and also displays the Spelling and Grammar dialog box. This dialog box lists the problem as well as suggestions (see Figure 6-11).

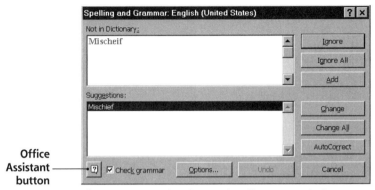

Office Assistant button

Figure 6-11 Select how to handle grammatical errors.

You can do any of the following:

✳ If you don't quite understand why the sentence was flagged, click the Office Assistant button. You see a pop-up explanation of the problem as well as some examples. To turn off this feature, click the Office Assistant button again.

✳ To use one of the suggested changes, click the one you want in the Suggestions list. Then click the Change button.

✳ To make a correction manually, edit the existing sentence or type a new sentence in the text box. Then click the Change button. Word moves on to the next questionable sentence.

✳ To ignore the flagged sentence and move to the next one, click the Ignore button. To ignore this same error throughout the document, click the Ignore All button.

✳ To skip to the next sentence and leave this sentence flagged, click the Next Sentence button.

✳ To undo a change you made, click the Undo button.

Continue making corrections until you go through the entire document. When you see the message that the spelling and grammar check is complete, click the OK button.

BONUS

Looking Up a Synonym Using the Thesaurus

Finding the right word can make the difference between a mediocre writer and true talent. As you write, you may want to tinker carefully with your word selection. There's nothing more frustrating than having a word right on the tip of your tongue. It means "fabulous," but it's not *that* word. What is it?

Rather than go insane (crazy, mad, bonkers, and so on), you can have Word display a list of synonyms. You can replace the word you looked up with the new, *improved* word. If you find a word that's close, you can look up that word, until you find the word you want. Antonyms or related words are sometimes displayed, as well. *To look up a word in the thesaurus, follow these steps:*

1. Click before or within the word you want to look up.

2. Select `Tools` → `Language` → `Thesaurus`. Word displays a list of synonyms for the selected word. Additional meanings are listed on the left half of the dialog box. The Meanings list displays Antonyms and Related Words, if available.

3. Do any of the following:

   To use one of the listed synonyms, click the word you want to use and then click the Replace button.

   To look up synonyms for another meaning, click the meaning you want in the Meanings list. Word displays synonyms for the selected meaning.

   To look up synonyms for another listed synonym, click the word you want in the Replace with Synonym list. Then click the Lookup button. Word displays synonyms for the selected word.

   If you look up other words and want to go back to a word you previously looked up, click the down arrow next to Looked Up drop-down list. Then click the word you want. Word returns to that list of synonyms.

   To close the dialog box without making a replacement, click Cancel.

If Word cannot find the word you are looking up, the dialog box displays Not Found and the selected word. An alphabetical list appears in the dialog box. If you see the word you want in this list, click it and then click the Look Up button.

FORMATTING YOUR TEXT

LEARN THESE KEY SKILLS:

You can have the most perfect content in the world for your document, but if the document is ugly, it most likely won't get notice. What's an ugly document? And how do you make a document pretty? You can learn a little lesson by taking a look at the three documents in Figures 7-1, 7-2, and 7-3. The document in Figure 7-1 doesn't have any formatting. Notice that it's hard to tell what the document is about and to tell what's important. The document in Figure 7-2, on the other hand, has way too much formatting. The page screams for attention! The document in Figure 7-3 shows a document with just the right amount of formatting.

This chapter covers some of the formatting changes you can make to improve the appearance of your document. You can change how the text appears and how paragraphs look. All the best formatting options are covered here. Remember, moderation is the key!

7

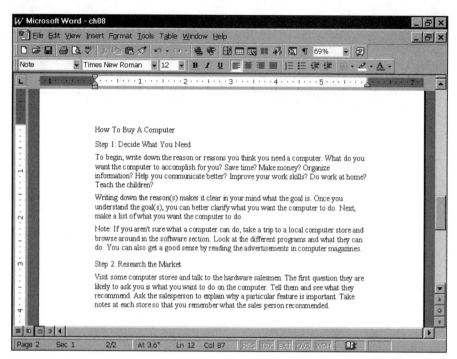

Figure 7-1 A document without formatting is hard to read and understand at a glance.

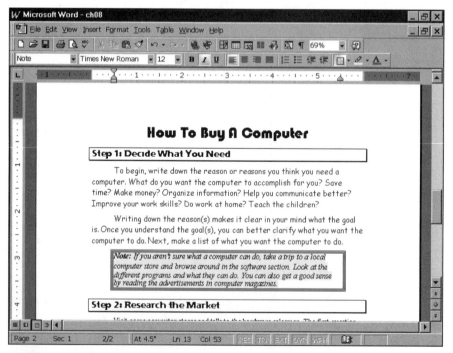

Figure 7-2 A document with too much formatting overwhelms the reader so that your message is lost.

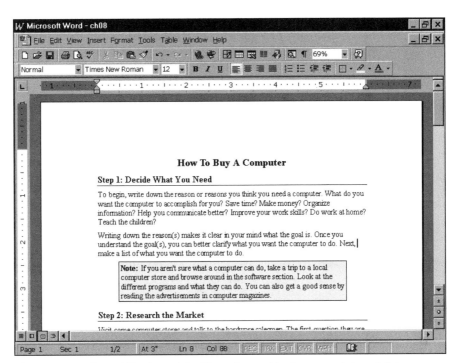

Figure 7-3 Like Goldilocks and the Three Bears, this document is just right!

 For information on formatting the overall page — such as changing margins, adding page numbers, and so on — turn to the next chapter.

Fanc-i-fied Text

The most common formatting change you are likely to make to a document is to change the look of the text. You may think that changing the text is simply frivolous, but the look does modify the meaning. Take a look at the following sentences:

The book wasn't that bad.

The book wasn't *that* bad.

If you read these sentences aloud, I'm guessing, the second one would sound different. The use of italics helps clarify what to emphasize in the sentence. Now take a look at the following sentences:

You are invited

YOU ARE INVITED

What would you wear to the first party? What would you wear to the second one? As you can see, text changes can help convey the nuances of a particular message.

What Changes Can You Make?

You can apply emphasis to text — making it bold, italic, or underline — to call attention to a word, phrase, heading. This type of change is the most common type of text formatting.

You can also change the font. A *font* is a set of characters and numbers in a certain style. Each font looks different than another font. Some fonts, like **Times New Roman**, look professional and are suited for business documents. Some fonts, like **Fajita**, are decorative or even goofy. Some fonts, like Symbol and Wingdings, are actually sets of symbols. You can use such a font to insert special characters in your document.

Part of selecting a font is choosing one appropriate for the document. You can change your text and use any of the fonts available on your system. Some fonts (called TrueType) are included with Windows 95 and with Word 97. TrueType fonts are indicated with a TT next to their name in the font list. Your printer also includes fonts, indicated with a printer icon in the font list. You can also purchase font packages to add other font choices to your system.

The size of the text is also important. Think of legal contracts. What size font do you think of? Think of advertisements. What size font would you select? Think of a document title. What size font would you select? Think of a footnote. What font size do you envision? As you can see, you can select an appropriate size for all the text in your document and also for selected text such as headings. The size of a font is measured in points, and there are 72 points to an inch. The larger the point size, the larger the type.

You can also use a different color for selected text. Color printers are becoming more and more popular. If you have one, you can add some splash to your documents by changing the color of text. If you don't have a color printer but the document will be displayed on screen, you can also make color changes. These changes do appear on screen but will print as shades of gray on your black-and-white printer.

You can use highlighting to call attention to key ideas or points in a document. When you read something important in a a book, a magazine, a report, or any document, you may take a yellow highlighter pen and drag across it. You can then use these highlighted sections to review or find the key points in the document. You can do the same in your document, selecting the words to highlight and the color to use.

The fastest way to make any of these changes is to use the toolbar buttons. Use this method when you want to make a change and you know the change you want to make — that is, you don't need to see a preview. You can also use the Font dialog box. Use this method when you want to make several changes at once or when you want to preview the changes before applying them.

Fast Text Formatting: Toolbar

Word conveniently provides buttons for the most common text formatting changes. To make a change, select the text you want to format and then do any of the following:

* Click **B** to make text bold.
* Click *I* to make text italic.
* Click <u>U</u> to make text underlined.
* Click the down arrow next to . From the list of available fonts, click the one you want. Word lists the most recently used fonts at the top of the list, separated from the main list by a double line. Printer fonts are indicated with a printer icon; TrueType fonts are indicated with TT. Depending on your printer and font files, you may see different fonts listed.
* Click the down arrow next to `10 ▼` and then click the size you want.

TIP To undo the change, click the Undo button.

* To use a different text color, click the down arrow next to **A** and select the color you want.
* To highlight text, select the text, click the down arrow next to ` ✎ ▾ `, and then click the color you want. Word applies the highlighting. To remove the highlighting, select the text, click the down arrow next to ` ✎ ▾ `, and select None.

Figure 7-4 shows some different font selections so that you can get an idea of the variety of available fonts. Remember that your system may have different font selections.

 TIP If you like keyboard shortcuts, you can use these to format text: Ctrl+B for Bold, Ctrl+I for Italic, and Ctrl+U for underlining.

More Options: The Font Dialog Box

Sure, the toolbar is quick, but it is not so quick if you have to select five or six fonts until you find one you want. If you aren't sure which font you want to use, you may want to use the Font dialog box. The dialog box displays a sample of the selected font so that you can see the change and then make up your mind. This dialog box also is more convenient when you want to make several changes at once. Besides, the dialog box lets you select some additional text formats that are not available from the toolbar.

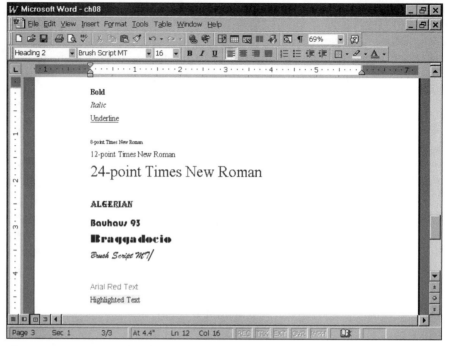

Figure 7-4 You can select from a variety of font styles.

To change the font using the dialog box, follow these steps:

1. Select the text you want to change.

2. Select **Format** → **Font** .

3. If necessary, click the Font tab to display the Font options, shown in Figure 7-5.

4. In the Font list, click the font you want. Notice that you see a sample of the text in this font in the Preview area.

5. In the Font style list, click the style you want.

6. In the Size list, click the font size you want.

7. To change the font color, select the color you want from the Color drop-down list.

8. To underline text, display the Underline drop-down list and select the style of underline that you want.

9. Click the OK button. Word makes the change. Figure 7-6 shows some of the special effects available from this dialog box.

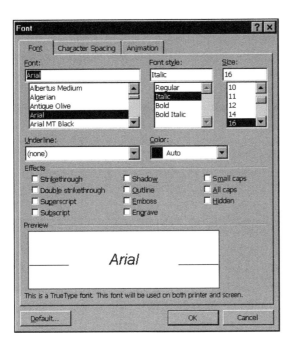

Figure 7-5 Select the font, style, and size you want from this dialog box.

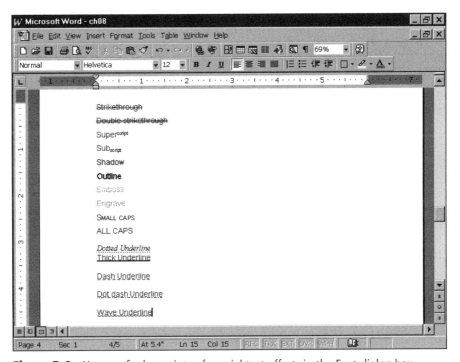

Figure 7-6 You can find a variety of special text effects in the Font dialog box.

Changing the Default Font

The default font used in all new documents is Times New Roman, 10 point type. If you don't like this font, you don't have to change each new document you create. Instead, you can change the default font. Word will then use the new font for all new documents. For instance, I like to use Arial 12-point type because I think it is more readable. You may prefer a different font and font size.

To change the default font, follow these steps:

1. Select `Format` → `Font`. If necessary, click the Font tab.

2. In the Font list, click the font you want to use as the default.

3. In the Font style area, click the default style you want.

4. In the Size list, click the default font size you want.

5. Click the Default button. You are warned that this change will affect all documents based on the NORMAL template.

6. Click the Yes button.

Text to the Left, Text to the Right

In addition to formatting individual chunks of text, you can also format the paragraphs. One of the most common changes is to change the alignment of a paragraph.

Keep in mind that a paragraph is any text followed by a hard return. (A hard return is inserted every time you press Enter. Soft returns are inserted as line breaks by Word and are adjusted when you add or delete text.) A single line, for instance, can be a paragraph. You can apply the paragraph formatting options to a single paragraph or to several paragraphs. Each paragraph, for example, can have different tab settings.

Also, each time you press Enter, the paragraph options for that paragraph are carried down to the next paragraph. And if you delete the paragraph marker, the paragraph takes on the formatting of the following paragraph. If you type a line, center it, and press Enter, the next line is centered as well. If you have a double-spaced paragraph followed by a single-spaced paragraph and delete the paragraph mark at the end of the first paragraph, the paragraph will then be single-spaced. This is confusing for beginners who wonder how a paragraph got formatted without anyone making a change. You can think of the paragraph marker as the storehouse for all formatting options for that paragraph.

If something bizarre happens, try undoing the change using Edit → Undo. If you have trouble visualizing where the paragraph marks appear, you can display them by clicking the Show/Hide ¶ button.

When you type in Word, all text is left aligned, and the right margin is ragged or uneven. For most text, this alignment works great. For other paragraphs, you may want to make a change. For instance, you can center the document title. Or you might right-align text like a newspaper banner. You can justify the text in the paragraphs to keep both margins even.

You can select four types of alignment, and the best way to make a change is to use the Formatting toolbar.

Follow these steps:

1. To change the alignment of one paragraph, first click within that paragraph. To change the alignment of several paragraphs, select the ones you want to change.

2. Do one of the following:

   Click ☐ to left align text.

   Click ☐ to center text.

   Click ☐ to right align text.

   Click ☐ to justify text.

   Figure 7-7 shows an example of each type of alignment.

TIP To undo the change, click the Undo button or select the Edit → Undo command. If you realize later you want to use a different alignment, select the paragraph(s) and then click another alignment button.

You can also use these keyboard shortcuts to change the alignment:

To make text...	*Press...*
Centered	Ctrl+E
Left-aligned	Ctrl+L
Right-aligned	Ctrl+R
Justified	Ctrl+J

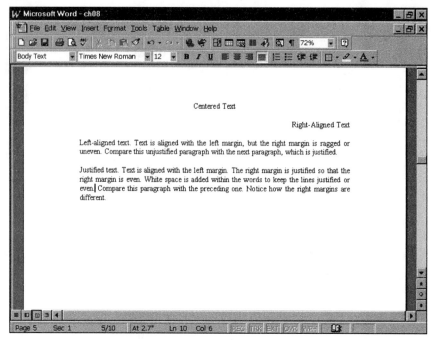

Figure 7-7 You can select from four types of paragraph alignments: left, center, right, or justified.

Indenting Text

A lignment changes are most appropriate for headings or other special paragraphs in your document. But what about the main body of the document? What types of changes are appropriate? Glad you asked.

Think about one long unending page of text. Like say an article on existentialism or some other l-o-n-g article you had to read in school. Were you excited about reading it? Nope. Nobody likes a long, never-ending treatise. Just looking at this type of document makes you yawn.

To make your document easy and inviting to read, you can use some of the paragraph formatting features described in this chapter, including indents. You might, for instance, indent the first line of each paragraph. This visual clue helps your reader see how the document is divided into paragraphs. You might also indent paragraphs, such as quotations, that you want to set apart from the main document text. As another option, you may want to use a special kind of indent, called a hanging indent, for numbered lists.

To make your document easy and inviting to read, you should use paragraph formatting features.

You can indent text the amount you want, and you can use either the Formatting toolbar or the Paragraph dialog box to make a change, as covered in this section.

Indenting Text with the Toolbar

If you want a left indent — useful for setting off a paragraph from the main body text — you can use the toolbar to set the indent. Click the Increase Indent button; the paragraph is indented ½ inch from the left margin. You can click the button again to increase the indent. Each time you click the button, the paragraph is indented another ½ inch.

If you indent too much or if you want to undo the indent, click the Decrease Indent button to decrease or undo the indents.

Indenting Text with the Paragraph Dialog Box

The Increase Indent and Decrease Indent buttons are useful if you want to indent text from the left. If you want to indent from the left and right or if you want to create a special kind of indent, you need to use a different method. You must use the Paragraph dialog box.

Follow these steps to indent text using the Paragraph dialog box:

1. Move the insertion point to the beginning of the paragraph you want to indent. To indent several paragraphs, select those paragraphs.

2. Select Format → Paragraph .

3. If necessary, click the Indents and Spacing tab. You see the Indents and Spacing tab of the Paragraph dialog box (see Figure 7-8).

4. Do any of the following:

   To indent from the left, type the amount you want to indent the text in the Left spin box or use the spin arrows to select a value.

   To indent text from the right, type the amount or use the spin arrows to enter the amount you want in the Right spin box.

   To create a first-line or hanging indent, display the Special drop-down list and select the type of indent you want. In the By spin box, enter the amount you want to indent.

5. Click the OK button.

   Word indents the paragraph(s). Figure 7-9 shows examples of different types of indents.

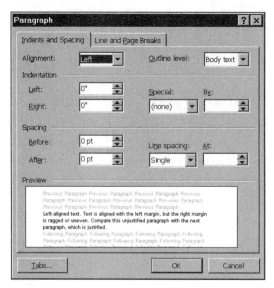

Figure 7-8 Use this dialog box to select paragraph formatting options such as indents.

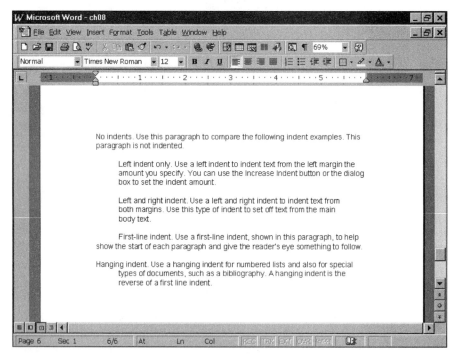

Figure 7-9 You can use different types of indents to format your paragraphs.

TIP Press Ctrl+1 for single-spacing, Ctrl+5 for 1.5 spacing, or Ctrl+2 for double-spacing.

Double-Spacing a Document

A lot of formatting options in this chapter call to mind long, boring documents. Think again of that article on existentialism or something else yawn-inducing. (Sorry to all you existentialists out there.) Was there any room between the lines? Any break at all for you the reader? Most likely it was single-spaced, crammed full of text, all swimming around on the page like one big long sentence. At least they could have double-spaced the document to make it a *little* easier to read.

By default, Word single-spaces the text in your document. This spacing works well for short documents such as letters and memos, but in longer documents, such as a manuscript, you may want to use a different spacing increment. You can choose single, 1¹/₂, and double-spacing. Or you can enter an exact amount, a minimum amount, or an amount to multiply by (for instance, add 20 percent).

To change line spacing, follow these steps:

1. Select the paragraph(s) that you want to change.

2. Select **Format** → **Paragraph** .

3. If necessary, click the Indents and Spacing tab. You see the Indents and Spacing tab of the Paragraph dialog box (refer to Figure 7-8).

4. Display the Line spacing drop-down list box.

5. Select one of the following:

   ✳ To single-space the document, select Single. Word adjusts the line to accommodate the largest font and adds a small amount of space. The amount depends on the font size in the selected paragraph.

   ✳ To add 1¹/₂ lines, select 1.5 Lines.

   ✳ To double-space the document, select Double.

   ✳ To specify the minimum amount of spacing, select At Least and then enter the spacing interval you want in the At box.

   ✳ To specify an exact amount of spacing, select Exactly and enter the spacing value you want. If characters are chopped off, you need to enter a larger value.

   ✳ To specify a multiply amount, select Multiple and enter the value you want. For instance, the value 1 is single-spacing; 1.2 would increase the spacing 20 percent. The value 2 would double-space the paragraph.

6. Click the OK button.

Tab-o-Matic

In your documents, you may want to include a list of columnar data. For instance, you may create a price list. One column for the product, one for the price. Or you may create a list of names and phone numbers. One column for the name, one for the phone number. The best way to set up this type of data is to create a table, as covered in Chapter 9. Tables are much easier to work with than tabbed lists, and Word includes several features for changing the look of a table. Tables have pretty much replaced plain old tabs. Still, you may find that you want to set tabs for some types of lists — for instance, when you want to align a column of numbers, use dot leaders, or just create a simple tabbed list.

You can use the Ruler or the Tab dialog box to set tabs, and you can select from four different tab types (left, right, center, and decimal), as covered in this section.

Setting Tabs with the Ruler

The Ruler is an on-screen formatting tool that is most useful, I think, for setting tabs. If you use the dialog box (covered next), you have to enter a precise measurement for the tabs, which you figure out by simply guessing. "How about the 4-inch mark?" you may say. "Sounds good," that voice in your head may answer. After you take a stab at the right location and close the dialog box, you see that four inches was *way* off. So you try another measurement. This process continues until you guess right or give up.

Instead, you can set tabs by just clicking about where you want them on the Ruler.

Follow these steps to use the Ruler:

1. Display the Ruler by selecting **View** → **Ruler** . You see the Ruler on screen.

2. Select the paragraph(s) for which you want to set tabs.

 Remember that each paragraph can have individual tab settings. If you don't select all the paragraphs, your changes will just apply to the current paragraph (the one with the insertion point). Be sure to select all the paragraphs you want to format.

3. Click the Tab Alignment button until the tab type you want is selected:

L	Left tab	Text starts on the marker and moves left.
⌐	Right tab	Text starts on the marker and moves right.
⊥	Center tab	Text is centered on the marker.

Decimal tab   Text is aligned on the decimal point.

Figure 7-10 shows examples of left, right, and center tabs all aligned at the same tab mark (2").

4. Click the Ruler at the spot you want to place the tab. The tab marker appears on the Ruler, and the text is formatted with the new tab settings.

5. Follow steps 3 and 4 for each tab you want to set.

TIP **To delete a tab from the Ruler, click it and drag it off the Ruler. To change the tab position, click it on the Ruler and drag it to a new location.**

Tab →
Alignment
button

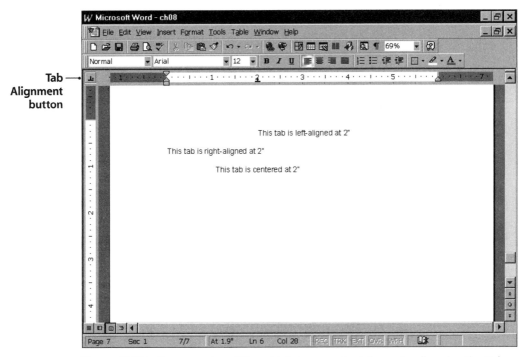

Figure 7-10 You can select different tab types and set them visually using the Ruler.

Setting Tabs with the Tabs Dialog Box

The Ruler is easy to use because it is visual, but if you can't remember which tab button to use or if you want to set a tab at a precise measurement, you can set tabs using the Tabs dialog box.

To set tabs with the Tabs dialog box, follow these steps:

1. Select the paragraph(s) for which you want to set tabs.

2. Select **Format** → **Tabs**. You see the Tabs dialog box (see Figure 7-11).

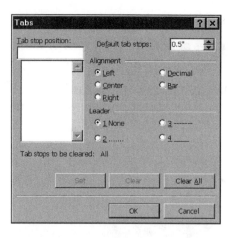

Figure 7-11 Use this dialog box to set tabs for the selected paragraphs.

3. In the Tab stop position text box, type the position for the tab. This position is measured in inches and is measured from the left margin.

4. In the Alignment area, click the type of alignment you want: Left, Center, Right, Decimal, or Bar.

5. If you want to use a dot leader for the tab, click the leader style you want in the Leader area. You can select a dotted line, a dashed line, or a regular line.

6. Click the Set button.

7. Follow steps 3 through 6 for each tab stop you want to create.

8. Click the OK button.

Fancy, Fancy!

Remember when you wanted to try something fancy with a typewriter. Maybe you went back over a line and typed an underscore to create an underline. Or maybe you created borders by typing dashes or asterisks. These style flourishes are way out of date.

Now you can not only add a border, but you can also add a gray shaded pattern to a paragraph. For example, you may want to add borders to your document headings to make them easy to scan. Or you may want to add sidebars and both shade and border these paragraphs. With the combination of borders and shading, you can create some unique effects. You can add borders to the top, the sides, the bottom, or completely around a single paragraph or a group of paragraphs. You can specify the thickness and style of the border.

For a quick border, use the toolbar. For more control over the line style and placement for the border, use the Borders and Shading dialog box. To add a paragraph shading, you must use the dialog box. This section covers each method.

Adding a Border Using the Toolbar

You can select different border placements using the Border button in the Formatting toolbar. You can select to place a line above the paragraph, on all sides, on the bottom, in between two paragraphs, and so on. *Follow these steps to add a border using the toolbar:*

1. Select the paragraph(s) to which you want to add a border.

2. Click the down arrow next to ⬚▾. You see a palette of border selections.

3. Click the border placement you want. Word adds the border and/or shading to the selected paragraph(s).

Adding a Border Using the Borders and Shading Dialog Box

If you want more control over the style of line, you can use a different method to add the border: the Borders and Shading dialog box. You can select from special border effects such as box, shadow, and 3D, plus you can select different line styles.

To add a border, follow these steps:

1. Select the paragraphs you want to border.

2. Select Format → Borders and Shading .

3. If necessary, click the Borders tab. You see the Borders tab options (see Figure 7-12).

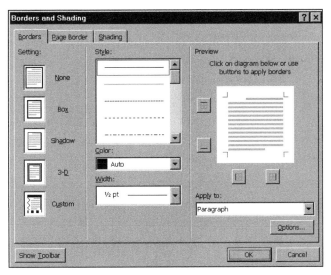

Figure 7-12 Use this dialog box to select a border style and placement.

4. In the Setting area, select the type of border you want to add: None, Box, Shadow, Three-D, or Custom.

5. In the Style list, select the line style you want.

6. To change the border color, display the Color drop-down list and then click the color you want.

7. To change the thickness of the line, display the Width drop-down list and select the width you want. (The width is measured in points.) You see a preview of your selections in the Preview area.

8. If you selected one of the predefined borders, the line you selected is added to all sides of the paragraph. Skip to the next step.

   If you selected Custom, click in the preview area on the side where you want to place the border. For example, click the top of the diagram to add the border to the top. Word adds the selected border to that side. Do this for each border you want to add.

9. Click the OK button. Word applies the border.

Adding Shading

Another way to add some flash to your paragraphs is to apply shading. You may want to combine a border with shading (although you don't have to add a border to use shading). If you have a color printer, you can select a color for the shading, and that color will be printed. If you don't have a color printer, you can select a gray pattern. *Follow these steps to shade a paragraph:*

1. Select the paragraphs you want to shade.

2. Select   Format → Borders and Shading .

3. If necessary, click the Shading tab. You see the Shading tab options (see Figure 7-13).

4. Do one of the following:

   To select a gray fill pattern, click it in the Fill area. Or display the Style drop-down list and select the pattern you want.

   To use a color, click the color in the Fill area.

   To use a color and a fill, click the color you want in the Fill area. Then display the Style drop-down list and select the pattern you want.

   Understanding how the fills and colors work together can take some time. Just experiment in the dialog box and check the Preview, which shows you how your selection will appear.

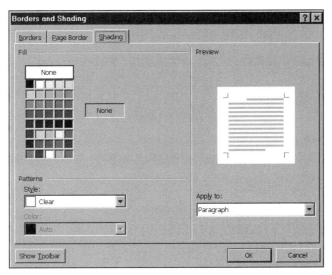

Figure 7-13 Use this dialog box to shade a paragraph.

5. Click the OK button. Word adds the shading to the selected paragraph(s).

For Lists and Steps

D o you ever feel as if you are overwhelmed with information? In the information age, you are constantly bombarded with messages from all different media. You may have an office mail box, an e-mail box, and a mail box at your home. And all those may be crammed with some type of message. How can you tell what's important and what's not?

When you are distributing your document, you won't want your reader to struggle with finding the main message. Instead, you can highlight key points to make the document easy to scan and assimilate. A well-organized document is more likely to get noticed than one that is a mish-mash of ideas.

One way to set off a list of points or topics in a document is to create a bulleted list. Each item in the list is preceded by a bullet, and the text is indented. You can also create a numbered list. Numbered lists work well for directions or other points you want to present in sequence. Word automatically numbers all the items in a list, and the text is indented.

Creating a Bulleted List

The fastest way to create a bulleted list is to use the Bullets button on the Formatting toolbar. When you use this method, you get a round bullet and a $1/2$-inch indent. Perfect for most cases. *Simply follow these steps*:

1. Select the text that you want to add bullets to. Word will add the bullet to each paragraph within the selection, not each line. Word will not add bullets to any blank lines within the selection.

2. Click 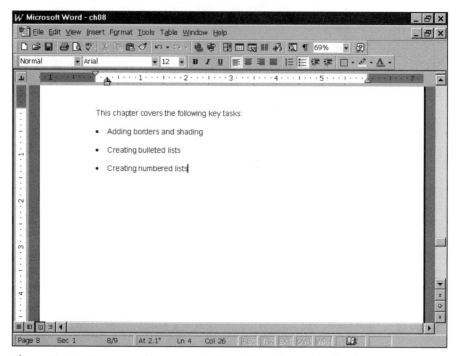. Word creates a bulleted list, as shown in Figure 7-14.

This chapter covers the following key tasks:

- Adding borders and shading
- Creating bulleted lists
- Creating numbered lists

Figure 7-14   You can easily create a bulleted list using the Bullets button.

Creating a Numbered List

For items that appear in a specific order, such as a series of steps, you can create a numbered list. Word will add the numbers automatically and also handle indenting the paragraphs so that the text is aligned properly. All you have to do is click the button. Another great thing about a numbered list is that if you add or delete an item within the list, Word renumbers the other paragraphs.

Follow these steps to create a numbered list:

1. Select the text you want to number. Word will number each paragraph. Blank lines within the selection will not be numbered.

2. Click . Word creates a numbered list.

Removing the Bullets or Numbers

To remove bullets from a list, select the list and click the Bullets button again. To remove numbers for a list, select the list and click the Numbering button. You can also use the Edit → Undo command or the Undo button.

BONUS

Using Styles

When you format a document, you may find yourself selecting the same commands over and over. For example, for your section headings, you may change the font and make them boldface. You may also add a border. If your document had 10 heads, you'd select 30 commands (3 commands, 10 times). Ugh!

Are you thinking there's got to be a better way? There is. You can create and use a style. A *style* is a collection of character (font, size, style, color, and so on) and paragraph (alignment, indents, borders, and so on) formatting. You can apply the style to other text, and Word applies all the associated formatting options. Styles offer a lot of benefits:

* Styles save time. Rather than select the same set of commands to make the formatting changes over and over, you can create a style and then apply that style with one command.

* If you use styles, you are assured your document is formatted consistently. You don't have to worry about which font size or border to use for the headings. You simply select the style heading, and Word applies all the formatting options for you.

* If you decide to modify a style, Word updates all the paragraphs tagged with that style automatically. For example, suppose that you decide that the Woodstock font is a little much for the headings in your business report. If you format the document manually, you'll have to go through and modify each heading. If you use a style for the headings, you modify the style once, and Word updates all paragraphs formatted with that style.

Using Word's Styles

Word provides some predefined styles that you can use without going to the trouble of creating your own. Trying these styles is a good way to see how styles work. You can practice applying styles and also see what types of formatting options a style can include.

The styles that are available depend on the *template* you are using. You select the template when you choose the File → New command. For the most part, you will use the Normal template. (Templates are covered in the next chapter.)

You can display the available styles by clicking the down arrow next to the Style drop-down list. You not only see the names of the styles but also get an idea of what each style looks like (see Figure 7-15).

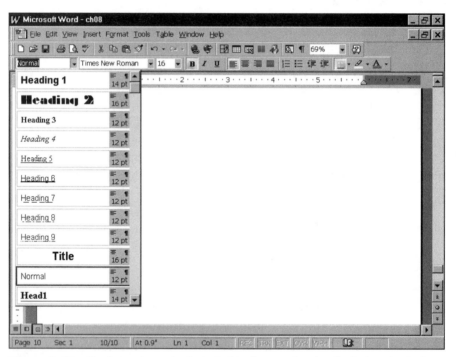

Figure 7-15   Check out the styles included in the template by displaying the Style drop-down list.

To use one of these styles, select the text you want to format, display the Style drop-down list, and then select the style you want. You can find out more about applying styles in the section "Applying Styles."

Creating Styles

If the predefined styles work OK for you, great! You don't need to worry about creating other styles. You may not be the picky type. On the other hand...

If you don't like the predefined styles or if you want to add additional styles, you can do so. The easiest way to create a style is to format a paragraph with the formats you want and base the new style on this paragraph. *Follow these steps to create a new style:*

1. Format the text and/or paragraph with the options you want. You can use any formatting features on the toolbar or within the F<u>o</u>rmat menu.

2. Click in the Style list box and highlight the current name.

3. Type a new name and press Enter. Word creates the style based on the selected paragraph.

Applying Styles

You only have to create a style once. Then you can apply it to any text in the document. The styles will also be available in other documents you create that are based on the same template.

The fastest way to apply a style is to use the Style drop-down list. Follow these steps:

1. Select the paragraph(s) or text you want to format. If you are formatting a single paragraph, you can just place the insertion point within the paragraph. To format several paragraphs, select them. If you are applying a character style, select the text you want to format.

2. Click the down arrow next to Normal. Word displays a list of available styles.

3. Click the style you want. Word applies the style to the selected paragraph(s).

FORMATTING YOUR DOCUMENT PAGES

The last chapter taught you how to change the appearance of the words, sentences, and paragraphs in a document. After you get these set, you can take a step back and look at the overall page. You may want to make some changes to the document page — for instance, change the margins, add page numbers, and so on. That's the topic of this chapter.

Here you also learn how to use a document that is already formatted and ready for you to simply enter the text. This chapter also covers templates.

Perfect Pages

Once you get the paragraphs flowing well on the page, you can step back and take a look at the overall page. Does the text fit? Is it balanced? Do you need to make some changes? If so, you can change how the page is set up. You can change the margins, the orientation, or other page options, as covered here.

Changing the Margins

Margins control how close Word prints to the edge of the page. If you have a big top margin, for instance, Word leaves much white space at the top of the document. If you have a small top margin, Word prints closer to the top of the page.

The default margins are 1-inch top and bottom margins and 1.25-inch left and right margins. These settings — like most of Word's defaults — work fine for a lot of documents. If need be, you can change the margins to add more or less space around any edges of the page (top, bottom, left, or right). For instance, if you print on letterhead, you may need to make the top margin larger and move the text down. As another example, you may want a bigger top margin for a short document so that the text is not crammed at the top of the page.

You can change margins using one of two methods. To figure out which is best for you, think about how you hang a picture on the wall. Do you eyeball it and then just hammer in a nail or two? If so, skip to the section "Changing Margins in Print Preview." Or do you get out the level and tape measure to precisely select the wall position and only then hammer in the nail? If so, read the next section.

USING THE PAGE SETUP DIALOG BOX

If you know the amount (or approximate amount) you want for each margin, you can use the Page Setup dialog box to make a change. *Follow these steps:*

1. Select **File** → **Page Setup**. You see the Page Setup dialog box.

2. If necessary, click the Margins tab. You see the Margin settings for the page (see Figure 8-1).

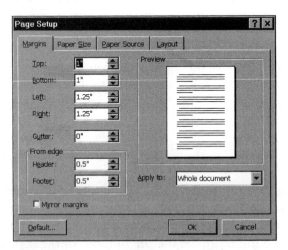

Figure 8-1 Use the Margins tab to set the page margins.

3. Press Tab to move to and highlight the margin you want to change.

4. Type the new margin setting. Or use the spin arrows to enter a new value. Notice that the Preview shows how these new margins affect the page.

5. Follow steps 3 and 4 for each margin you want to change.

6. Click the OK button. In Normal view, the text will be adjusted for the new margins, but you won't see the overall effect on the page. You can switch to Page Layout view or preview the document to see the change.

CHANGING MARGINS IN PRINT PREVIEW

If you aren't the precise sort, you can use Print Preview to change the margins. This method gives you an overall picture of the document and visually shows you how the change will affect the document. *Follow these steps:*

1. Select **File** → **Print Preview** . You see a preview of the document. (For more information on previewing a document, see Chapter 3.)

2. If the Ruler is not displayed, click the View Ruler button (see Figure 8-2).

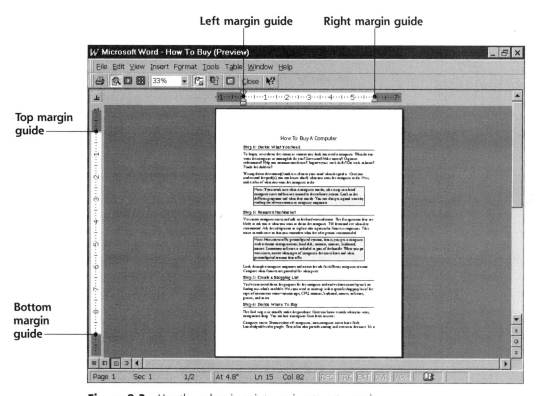

Figure 8-2 Use the rulers in print preview to set margins.

3. Put the mouse pointer on the margin you want to change — right between the gray and white areas of the ruler. When the pointer is in the right spot, it looks like a two-headed arrow and the ScreenTip says the margin name.

4. Drag the margin guide to a new location.

5. Click the Close button to return to Normal view.

Centering a Page

When you don't have a lot of text on the page, the page may look funny. You can try tinkering with the margins to get the text aligned on the page. Or you can simply center the page. For instance, centering a page works well for title pages.

To center a page, follow these steps:

1. Select **File** → **Page Setup**. You see the Page Setup dialog box.

2. Click the Layout tab. You see the Layout tab options (see Figure 8-3).

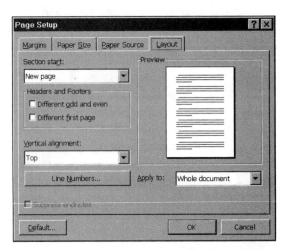

Figure 8-3 Center a page using this dialog box.

3. Display the Vertical alignment drop-down list and select Center.

4. Click the OK button. Word centers the page. In Normal view, you won't see this change. Preview the document to see the page.

Changing the Page Orientation

Think of a portrait. What dimensions do you think of? Usually the portrait is longer than it is wide, right? Now think of a landscape picture. What are the dimensions? Wider than long? These two terms carry over to Word's page orientation. You can print left to right across the short side (8½") and down the long edge (11"). This orientation is called *portrait*. Or you can print left to right across the long side (11") and down the short side (8½"). This orientation is called *landscape*. If your document is wider than it is long — if, for instance, you have a table with many columns — print in landscape.

Most documents are printed on 8½" × 11" paper. You can also select other paper sizes. For instance, you may have a printer with a bin for legal paper. You can then select and print on this paper size.

To change the orientation or paper size, follow these steps:

1. Select **File** → **Page Setup** . You see the Page Setup dialog box.

2. Click the Paper Size tab to display these options, shown in Figure 8-4.

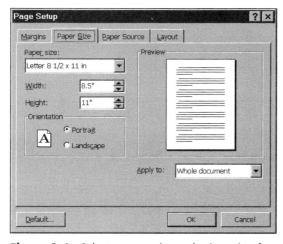

Figure 8-4   Select a paper size and orientation from this dialog box.

3. To change the paper size, display the Paper Size drop-down list and select the size you want. Or enter the width and height in the spin boxes.

4. In the Orientation, click Portrait or Landscape.

5. Click the OK button.

Keeping Track of Pages

Imagine a 20-page document without page numbers. How would you keep the pages in order? Even if the pages were stapled or bound, how would you refer to a particular page? Count out each page until you got to the one you want? In a long document, page numbers are a necessity.

In a long document, page numbers are a necessity.

Word makes it easy to insert page numbers. And when you use Word to number the pages, you don't have to worry about renumbering when you add or delete a page. The page numbers are updated automatically.

If all you want to do is insert a page number, you can do so using the Insert → Page Numbers command. This command automatically creates a footer or header, depending on where you elect to place the page numbers. If you want to include additional information in the header or footer, such as the date or document name, go to the next section. You can set up the headers and footers with page numbers and any other text you want to include.

When you insert page numbers, you can select whether they appear at the top or the bottom of the page. You can also choose to align the page number right, center, left, inside, or outside. *Follow these steps:*

1. Select Insert → Page Numbers . You see the Page Numbers dialog box (see Figure 8-5).

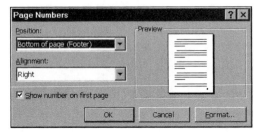

Figure 8-5 Select a position and alignment for the page numbers.

2. Display the Position drop-down list box and select Top of Page (Header) or Bottom of Page (Footer).

   If you select Top of Page (Header), Word creates a header and inserts the page number at the top of each page in the document. If you select Bottom of Page (Footer), Word creates a footer and inserts the page number at the bottom of each page.

3. Display the <u>A</u>lignment drop-down list and select the alignment of the page number:

Left	Numbers print aligned with the left margin.
Center	Numbers are centered on the page.
Right	Numbers print flush with the right margin.
Inside	Numbers print on the inside of facing pages (right-aligned on left pages and left-aligned on right pages).
Outside	Numbers print on the outside of facing pages (left-aligned on left pages and right-aligned on right pages).

If you aren't sure what an option does, select it and then check the preview, which shows the placement of the page number.

4. To skip a page number on the first page, uncheck the <u>S</u>how number on first page check box. For instance, you may not want to include a page number on a title page.

5. Click the OK button. Word creates a header or footer and inserts the page number. In Normal view, you don't see the page numbers. Switch to Page Layout view or preview the document.

From Top to Bottom

When you start creating documents that are longer than one page, you will most likely want to include some type of reference number on the page. For instance, page numbers are practically a must. In addition, you may want to include other text that helps the reader identify the document. For example, you can include the document title or a date or your last name. You might include the section name to help the reader navigate through a long document. Rather than type this information on each page, create a header and a footer. Word will insert the text on each page automatically.

Just as your head is at the top of your body (or should be), a header is printed at the top of each page of the document. And where are your feet? At the bottom. Likewise, a footer is printed at the bottom of each page. (Those of you standing on your head while reading this should ignore this paragraph.)

Which one — header or footer — is preferable? Whichever one your little heart likes best. Are there any specific situations where a header is preferable to a footer, or vice versa? Not really. You can even include both a header and a footer. This section covers how to set up headers and footers.

Creating a Header

To create a header, follow these steps:

1. Select **View** → **Header and Footer**. (I know that **View** seems a weird place for this command.)

   You see a dotted header area at the top of the page, with the insertion point. You also see the Header and Footer toolbar on screen (see Figure 8-6).

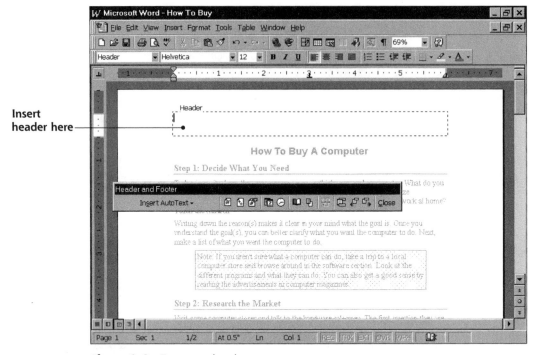

Insert
header here

Figure 8-6   Type your header.

2. Type the text for the header. You can use the toolbar to insert special text such as the page number or the date. See the section on the Header and Footer toolbar.

   By default, the header includes three predefined tabs: left-aligned, center, and right-aligned. You can include text in each of these three "areas" by pressing Tab and then typing the text you want to include.

3. Make any formatting changes to the text. You can make text italic, change the font, use a different font size, add a border — just about everything you've learned so far up to this chapter.

4. Click the Close button. Word adds the header (which you won't see in Normal view) to the document. To see the header, switch to Page Layout view or Print Preview.

Creating a Footer

You create a footer in just about the same way you do a header. You just need to use a toolbar button to move to the footer area.

Follow these steps:

1. Select ⌈ **View** ⌉ → ⌈ **Header and Footer** ⌉. You see the header area and the Header and Footer toolbar.

2. Click . You see a dotted footer area at the bottom of the page; the insertion point is within this area. The Header and Footer toolbar also appears on screen. This area is identical to the header area, apart from the fact that it appears at the bottom of the page.

3. Type the text for the footer. You can use the toolbar to insert special text such as the page number or the date. See the next section, entitled "Using the Header and Footer Toolbar."

   By default, the footer also includes three predefined tabs: left-aligned, center, and right-aligned. You can include text in each of these three "areas" by pressing Tab and then typing the text you want to include.

4. Make any formatting changes to the text. You can make text italic, change the font, use a different font size, add a border, and so on.

5. Click the Close button. Word adds the footer to the document. To see the footer, preview the document or change to Page Layout view.

Using the Header and Footer Toolbar

You can use the buttons on the Header and Footer toolbar to insert special information in the header or footer. For instance, you can insert the page number or the date by simply clicking the appropriate button. You can also use the buttons to move among different headers and footers in the document. Table 8-1 identifies each button and includes a description.

TABLE 8-1 The Header and Footer Toolbar

Button	Name	Description
Insert AutoText ▾	AUTOTEXT	Word sets up some AutoText entries that are commonly used in headers and footers. Some examples include Author, Created by, Last printed, Page X of Y, and so on. To use one of these predefined headers/footers, display the list and select the one you want.
	INSERT PAGE NUMBER	Inserts a page number that will be updated automatically.
	INSERT NUMBER OF PAGES	Inserts the number of pages. You can combine the Insert Page Number button and this button to create a header or footer that says something like "Page 5 of 10."
	FORMAT PAGE NUMBER	Use this to select a format for the page numbers. See the section on page numbers for information on using this dialog box.
	INSERT DATE	Inserts a date field that will be updated automatically.
	INSERT TIME	Inserts a time field that will be updated automatically.
	PAGE SETUP	Displays the Page Setup dialog box so that you can make changes to the margins, paper size, and other options.
	SHOW/HIDE DOCUMENT TEXT	Hides (or shows) the document text.
	SAME AS PREVIOUS	In a document with different headers and footers, click this button to use the same header or footer as in the previous section.
	SWITCH BETWEEN HEADER AND FOOTER	Moves you from the header area to the footer area.
	SHOW PREVIOUS	In a document with different headers and footers, click this button to display the previous header or footer.
	SHOW NEXT	Click to display the next header or footer. (Used with documents with different headers/footers for different pages.)

Deleting a Header or Footer

If you want to get rid of a header or footer, all you need to do is delete the text. *Follow these steps:*

1. Select View → Header and Footer .

2. If you are deleting a header, skip this step. To delete a footer, click the Switch between Header and Footer button.

3. Drag across the text and press Delete.

4. Click the Close button.

Instant Documents

As you can see, Word includes a wealth of formatting features. Deciding which features to use can be daunting. Rather than mess with the formatting yourself, you may want to try some of Word's templates. A *template* is a document that includes text and formatting already set up. You simply open the template and then add the text you want to include to complete the document. You can think of a template as a fill-in-the-blank document. Word includes templates for some common document types including memo, letter, report, fax, and so on.

Word provides two types of predesigned documents: wizards and templates. The difference is in how they work. A *wizard* is an automated document. When you use a wizard, Word leads you through the process step by step, prompting you to make selections and enter text. You follow each step and when you are finished, you have a completed document.

When you use a template, you select the template you want. You then see a new document based on the template, basically a document skeleton, which includes the text and formatting appropriate for that document type. You fill in the content to create your new document. In addition to several wizards, Word provides many templates that you can use to create professional-looking documents.

 TIP You can tell the difference between a template and a wizard because a wizard always includes "Wizard" in the name.

Using a Wizard

If you like the step-by-step approach to creating a document, try one of the many wizards provided with Word. Here are just a few of them: Envelope Wizard, Fax Wizard, Letter Wizard, Mailing Label Wizard, Resume Wizard, Memo Wizard, Newsletter Wizard, Pleading Wizard, and Web Page Wizard.

To use a wizard, follow these steps:

1. Select **File** → **New**. You see the New dialog box. The default tab, General, is selected.

2. Click the tab for the document type you want to create. You see the available templates and wizards for that document category (see Figure 8-7).

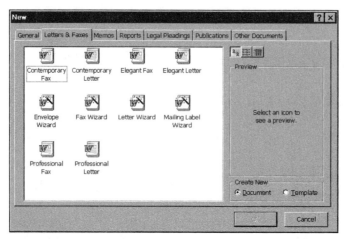

Figure 8-7 Select the wizard you want to use.

3. Click the wizard you want and then click the OK button.

Depending on what wizard you select, you see a different series of dialog boxes. The first dialog box gives you an overview of the process and steps you follow. For instance, Figure 8-8 shows the opening dialog box for the Memo Wizard.

Figure 8-8 The first dialog box for the wizard gives you an overview of all the steps.

4. Follow the instructions in the dialog box. After you complete the step, click the <u>N</u>ext button to display the next step (dialog box).

TIP **If you make a mistake or change your mind, click the <u>B</u>ack button to go back through your selections and make changes. To get help, click the Help button.**

For some steps, you are prompted to enter or select the text to include, as shown in Figure 8-9. For some steps, you are prompted to select a style for the document, as shown in Figure 8-10.

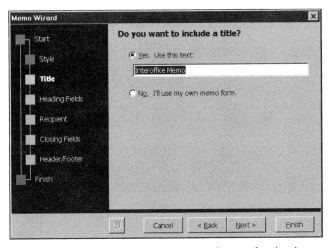

Figure 8-9 For some steps, you enter the text for the document.

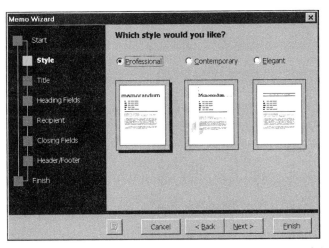

Figure 8-10 For some steps, you select the style or look of the document.

5. Continue moving through the dialog boxes, making selections, until the final one appears.

6. Click the Finish button to complete the document. You see your finished document on screen. Figure 8-11 shows a document created using the Memo Wizard. As you can see, some text is already entered, and the document is pretty much formatted for you.

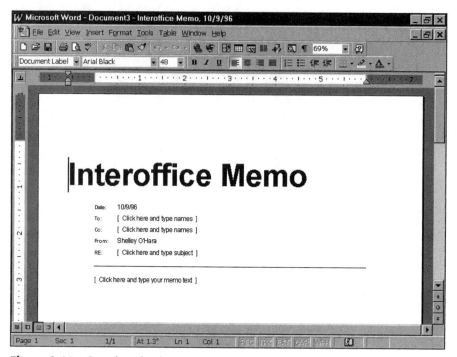

Figure 8-11 Complete the document.

7. Enter the text for the document. You can also make any changes to the text and formatting already included in the document.

8. Save and print the document. When you use `File` → `Save` to save the document, the document is saved as a separate file, with the name you assign. You can open and edit this document as needed. The original template remains on disk untouched so that you can use it again.

Using a Template

As mentioned, a template is like a fill-in-the-blank document. The document skeleton includes the text and formatting, and you fill out this skeleton to complete the document. Word includes many different templates, including Blank Document (the default); Fax, Letter, Resume, and Report in three styles (contemporary, elegant, and professional); and Blank Web Page.

To use a template, follow these steps:

1. Select **File** → **New** . You see the New dialog box.

2. Click the tab for the document type you want to create. You see the available templates and wizards for that document category.

3. Click the template you want to use. You see a preview of the selected template. Figure 8-12 shows a preview of the Professional Fax template.

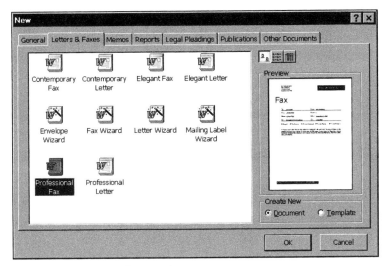

Figure 8-12   Select the template you want to use.

4. Click the OK button. Word displays the document on screen. Some text is included, such as the document title, subject fields, and date for the fax. Other text is in brackets, indicating that you need to replace this "filler" text with your "real" text.

5. Click the text you need to replace and type the actual text. Do this for each section of text that needs to be completed.

   You can make any editing and formatting changes to the document, as needed.

6. Save and print the document. This new document is saved as a separate file; the template remains unchanged.

BONUS

Creating Your Own Templates

Each person and business is different. For instance, you have your own flair and style. You may not like the formatting and text of the "canned" templates. Also, you may have other documents pertinent to your work or home life that aren't included in any of the templates. For instance, you may have forms that you want to set up as templates. If so, you can create and save your own templates and make them available for you (or others) to use.

Creating a Template

It's easy to create a template. You just create the document as you would normally do and then use a special procedure to save the document as a template. *Follow these steps:*

1. Start with a blank document and then type the text you want and format the template document as you want.

   All new documents based on this template will include all the formatting and text you include. Therefore, include in the template only the elements you want in all documents based on this template. For example, if you are creating a letterhead, you might include your company name in the header and the address in the footer. You might include a field to insert the date. You might also set up the margins you want for the page and any other formatting you want to include.

   You wouldn't, on the other hand, include any specific text like "Dear John" in the letter. You will add this text for the actual document when you use the template.

TIP **You can start with a document you have already created and formatted. If you do so, be sure to delete any text that you don't want included in the template.**

2. When you have completed the template, select File → Save As . You see the Save As dialog box.

3. Display the Save file as type drop-down list and click Document Template as the type. Word automatically selects the Templates folder — where you must place your templates to make them available. Notice that you can select the folder (tab) where you want the template to appear (see Figure 8-13).

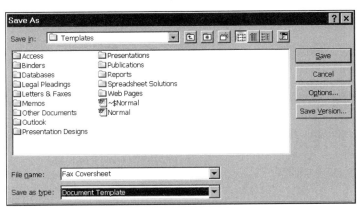

Figure 8-13   Select the folder where you want to place the template.

4. Select the folder where you want to place this template. You can place it within any of the existing folders.

5. In the File name text box, type a name for the template. Use something descriptive that will remind you of the contents and purpose of the template.

6. Click the Save button. Word saves the document as a template.

Using Your Template

When you want to use a template you have saved, you simply select it from the New dialog box.

Follow these steps:

1. Open the File menu and select the New command.

2. Click the tab for the template. This is the folder where you placed the template when you saved it. You should see your template listed.

3. Click the template name.

4. Click the OK button.

CHAPTER NINE

DESKTOP PUBLISHING WITH WORD

LEARN THESE KEY SKILLS:

The previous two chapters covered most of the commands and features you will use in Word. If you know just how to type, edit, and format, you can create most any kind of document. You're set.

When you want to get a little more creative — add a little more flair or complexity to your document — you can try some of the other formatting features. I've called them desktop publishing features, but don't let that term scare you off. Like most Word features, the commands and options covered here are easy to learn. You just need to investigate what's possible. That's the goal of this chapter: to introduce you to some features you can use to create more varied and complex documents. You learn how to set up and revise tables, divide a document into columns, and insert graphics.

Forget Those Ol' Tabs

Another time-saving feature, like styles, you can use in Word is creating tables. Forget the old-fashioned method of creating a table — setting up tabs, typing a few words, pressing Enter, typing the next line, and hoping when you get to the end that the table is somewhat aligned. If you have to add or delete something, even the somewhat alignment goes out the window.

Word makes creating a table much easier. You select the number of columns and rows you want, and Word creates the table. You move to and type your entry within each little cubbyhole (called a *cell*) in the table. You can enter a single word, a line, a paragraph, several paragraphs in the cell, and Word keeps the text aligned.

Setting Up a Table

As you might have guessed, you can set up a table using one of several methods. The simplest way to create a table is to use the Insert Table button. This method works when you want a table with equal column widths and the default border. You can also draw a table, drawing the outside border and then each column and row. Use this method to set up a table with different row and column sizes.

Which method is best? Take a look at the two tables in Figure 9-1. The first table shows what you get when you use the Insert Table button. You can change how this table looks, as covered in the section "Changing How Your Table Looks," but this is the starting point. The second table demonstrates what you can do when you draw a table. With this method, you basically do the formatting as you create the table. As for which one is the best, you can select whichever method appeals to you.

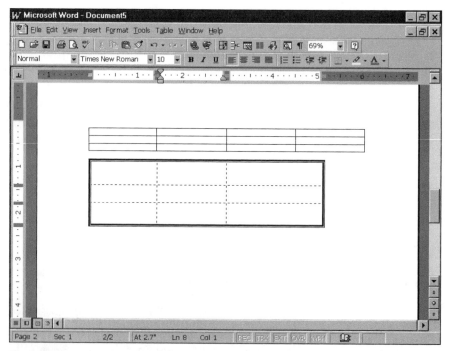

Figure 9-1   You can create a table using the default style or draw one in the style and size you want.

CREATING A SIMPLE TABLE

Follow these steps to set up a simple, default-style table:

1. Click ⊞. You see a drop-down palette of cells.

2. Drag across the number of columns and rows you want to include. For example, to create a table with three columns and two rows, drag across three columns and down two rows. Word displays the dimensions at the bottom of the palette.

3. Release the mouse button. Word displays the table, a grid of columns and rows (refer to the first table in Figure 9-1). By default, each cell includes a border. You can change the look of this border or delete it, as covered later in this chapter.

DRAWING A TABLE

If you are more of a visual sort, you can draw a table in your document. *Follow these steps:*

1. Click ⊞. You see the Tables and Borders toolbar (see Figure 9-2).

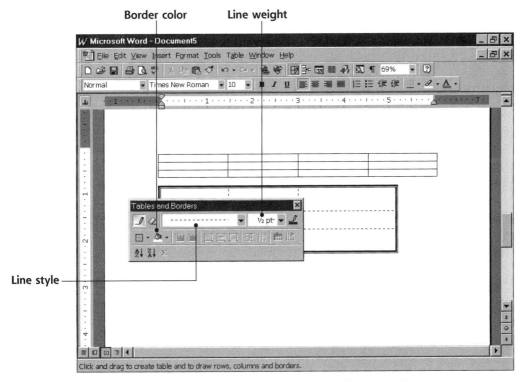

Figure 9-2 Use this toolbar to select a border and draw the table.

2. Display the Line Style drop-down list and select the style of border you want to use for the table.

3. Display the Line Weight drop-down list and select the thickness of the line. You can also display the Border Color drop-down palette and select a different color.

4. Move the insertion point into the document area. Notice that it looks like a pencil.

5. Click and drag to draw the outside border of the table.

6. Draw each column and row you want to add. You can draw columns down the table and rows across. You can make them any size you want. Word uses the selected line style, width, and color displayed in the toolbar. You can use a different line by selecting the options you want before you draw the line.

Word draws the table on screen. Figure 9-1, shown previously in the chapter, shows an example of a table created with this method.

FEATURE FOCUS Drawing tables is a new feature in Office 97.

The Meat of the Table: Entering Data

No matter how you create your table, you follow the same method for entering text in the table. Basically, the table is a grid of columns and rows, and the intersection of a row and a column is a *cell*. Word places the insertion point in the first cell in the table.

To type something in the table, move to the cell you want and type. You can click in the cell or use the arrow keys to move to the cell you want. You can also press Tab to move forward through the cells or Shift+Tab to move backward through the cells.

You can type any amount of text you want. If you type a long entry, you don't have to worry about pressing Enter to keep the text within the cell. When you reach the cell border, Word will wrap the text to the next line and expand the cell (making it taller, not wider). You can press Enter if you want to create a new paragraph within the cell.

You can use any of the editing and formatting features you learned in the preceding chapters. For instance, you can make the headings bold, use Cut or Copy to rearrange table entries, shade cells, and so on. Each cell is a paragraph, so you can also use paragraph formatting options, such as setting tabs, indenting text, or changing the alignment.

Selecting Part of the Table

As when formatting or editing text, you often need to select part of a table — a cell, a column, a row, even the entire table. For example, to delete a row, you select it. To add a column, you select the column where you want the new one to appear. The following check list explains how to select different table elements:

* To select text within a table, drag across the text as you would in a normal document.

* To select a row, put the insertion point within the row and then select the **Table** → **Select Row** command. Or click in the selection bar next to the row you want to select.

* To select a column, put the insertion point within the column and then select the **Table** → **Select Column** command. Or click right at the top of the column.

* To select the entire table, put the insertion point within the table and then select the **Table** → **Select Table** command or press Alt+Num 5

Don't see these commands? If most of the commands in the Table menu are dimmed, it probably means your insertion point is not within the table. The commands are available only when the insertion point is within the table. Put the insertion point somewhere in the table and try again.

Adding or Deleting Rows and Columns

It's sometimes hard to tell how many rows and columns you need for your table. You may need to add a row or even a column. If you set up tabs, you're stuck with the format you started with. If you set up a table using either method, you can easily add rows or columns. You can also delete rows or columns you don't need. Keep in mind that when you delete a column or row, you also delete any data contained in that column or row.

ADDING A ROW OR COLUMN

You don't have to worry about guessing the exact number of rows you'll need, because it is easy to add a row. The simplest way to add a row is to press Tab in the last row and last column of the table. Word adds a new row. You can also add a row or column within the table. *To do so, follow these steps*:

1. To insert a row, put the cursor in a row in the table. The new row will be inserted above this row.

   To insert a column, select the column using $\boxed{\text{Table}} \rightarrow \boxed{\text{Select Column}}$. The new column will be inserted to the left of this column.

2. To insert a row, select $\boxed{\text{Table}} \rightarrow \boxed{\text{Insert Rows}}$. To insert a column, select $\boxed{\text{Table}} \rightarrow \boxed{\text{Insert Column}}$.

If the Tables and Borders toolbar button is displayed, you can also use it to draw a new row or column. To do so, select the line style you want and then draw the new row or column within the table.

DELETING ROWS AND COLUMNS

Just as you can add rows and columns, you can also delete them. *Follow these steps:*

1. Select the row or column by selecting $\boxed{\text{Table}} \rightarrow \boxed{\text{Select Row}}$ or $\boxed{\text{Table}} \rightarrow \boxed{\text{Select Column}}$. If you just put the insertion point in the row or column, you can delete only the cell, not the entire row. Be sure to highlight the entire row or column.

2. To delete a row, select $\boxed{\text{Table}} \rightarrow \boxed{\text{Delete Rows}}$. To delete a column, select $\boxed{\text{Table}} \rightarrow \boxed{\text{Delete Columns}}$.

TIP **If you want to keep the row but simply clear the contents of that row, select the row by dragging across it. Then press the Delete key.**

DELETING THE ENTIRE TABLE

Deleting a table is tricky. You might think that you just drag across it and press Delete. This deletes all the entries in the table but leaves the table structure. Arg! How do you get rid of the entries and the table? *Do so by following these steps:*

1. Select the table by selecting $\boxed{\text{Table}} \rightarrow \boxed{\text{Select Table}}$.

2. Select $\boxed{\text{Table}} \rightarrow \boxed{\text{Delete Rows}}$. Word deletes the entire table.

Changing the Look of the Table

You have a lot of control over how the table looks. One common change is to resize the columns. When you create a table, it's unlikely that you will want each column to be the same size. Some may contain just a word or two. Some may contain longer entries. To balance out the table, you can adjust the column widths.

You may also want to use different borders for the table. And you can change the alignment of the text within a cell. You can make these changes and more, as covered in this section.

CHANGING THE COLUMN WIDTH

When you create a table using the Insert Table button, Word bases the column width on the sizes of the page margins and the number of columns you have. Each column is the same size. You can adjust the column widths if necessary. *Follow these steps:*

1. Place the mouse pointer on the right border of the column you want to change. The pointer should look like two vertical lines with arrows on either side (see Figure 9-3).

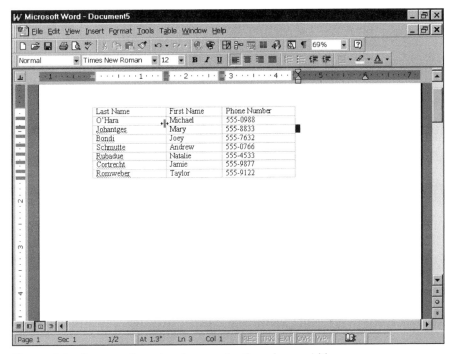

Figure 9-3 Drag a column border to resize the column width.

2. Drag the border to resize the column width. Drag to the left to make the column narrower. Drag to the right to make the column wider.

Note that you can also use the Table → Cell Height and Width command to set the column width. Use this method when you want to enter precise measurements for each column.

MAKE THEM ALL THE SAME SIZE

Another table size option is to have Word make selected rows or columns the same size. *To make this change, follow these steps:*

1. Select the rows or columns you want to resize. To resize all rows or columns in the table, select the entire table.

2. To make all columns even, click the Distribute Columns Evenly button in the Tables and Borders toolbar or select [Table] → [**Distribute Columns Evenly**] .

To make all rows even, click the Distribute Rows Evenly button in the Tables and Borders toolbar or select [Table] → [**Distribute Rows Evenly**] .

LAZY MAN FORMATTING

You can take the time to format a table — aligning the headings, adding borders, possibly shading certain rows or columns. Manual formatting is covered in the next section. Before you take the long route, try the short one. Word provides several predefined table formats. You can use these formats to quickly create a professional looking table. If none of these work, you can then use the other method.

To try one of the AutoFormats for a table, follow these steps:

1. Click within the table you want to format.

2. Select [Table] → [**Table AutoFormat**] . You see the Table AutoFormat dialog box, shown in Figure 9-4.

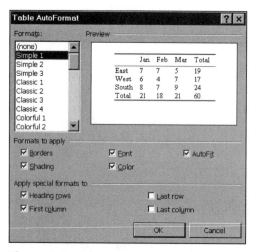

Figure 9-4 Select an AutoFormat for the table.

3. In the Formats list, click the format you want to use. You see a preview of a sample table formatted with this style.

4. If you want to use some but not all of the format options, uncheck the options you don't want in the Formats to apply area: Borders, Shading, Font, Color, AutoFit.

5. Check which rows and columns you want specially formatted: Heading rows, First column, Last row, Last column.

6. Click the OK button. Word formats the table with the selected AutoFormat.

HARD WORKING FORMATTING: DO IT YOURSELF

If the AutoFormats don't give you exactly what you want, you can also format the table yourself. You can use any of the formatting toolbar buttons and commands to make text bold, change the font, use a different alignment, and so on. The Tables and Borders toolbar also includes some buttons for formatting the table. You can do any of the following:

* To change how the text is aligned vertically (top to bottom), click the Align Top, Center Vertically, or Align Bottom button.

* To change how the text reads in a cell (across, down, up), click the Change Text Direction button until you get the direction you want.

* To use a different line style, thickness, or color, select the style, thickness, and color you want using the Line Style, Line Weight, and Border Color drop-down lists. Then use the pencil to draw across the border you want to change. You can also select where the line appears by using the Outside Border button.

* To apply shading to a cell, a row, or a column, select what you want to shade. Then click the Shading Color button and select the color or pattern you want.

Dividing a Document into Columns

For certain documents, you may want to vary the look of the page by using columns. You can create two, three, four, or more columns of the same size or different sizes. You can set up the columns first and then type the document. Or you can format an existing document into columns.

If you want columns all the same size, the fastest method is to use the toolbar. If you want to set up different sizes from the start, use the menu command. (You can always modify the columns you have set up with the toolbar, changing the size, for instance.)

Setting Up Columns

Follow these steps to divide a document into equal columns:

1. Switch to Page Layout view using **View** → **Page Layout** . If you forget this step, Word prompts you to change to this view. Click the OK button in the alert box.

2. If you want to create columns for just part of the document, select the text you want to format into columns. Word will divide the document into sections automatically. If you want to use columns for all the text, don't select anything.

3. Click 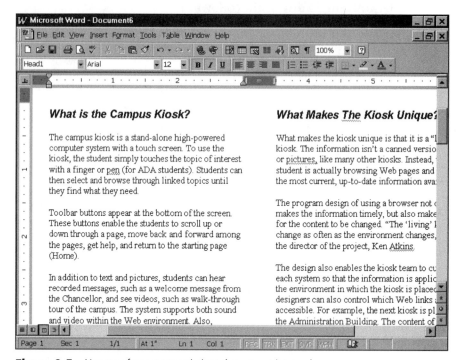. You see a drop-down palette of columns.

4. Click the number of columns you want.

If you are formatting a document you have already created, you see the text formatted into columns. Figure 9-5 shows a two-column document.

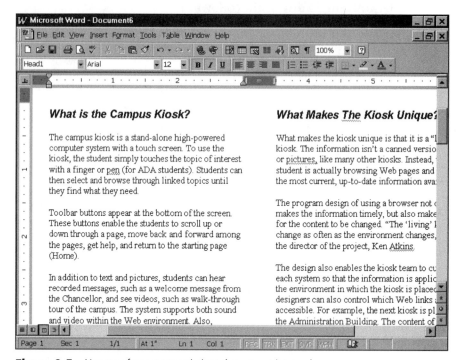

Figure 9-5   You can format an existing document into columns.

If you have not typed text, you may have a hard time telling that the document is now formatted into columns. Notice that the Col indicator appears in the status bar.

Typing in Columns

If you set up columns in a blank document, you can simply start typing to create the document. Word keeps the text aligned within the columns. If you fill up one column, Word automatically moves you to the next column. Continue typing until you complete the document. You can use any of the editing and formatting features covered in this book. You can copy, move, delete, or add text. You can change the font, apply styles, make text bold, add borders, insert graphics, and so on.

To make an editing change, use the mouse to position the insertion point and then edit as you normally do. You can also use the keyboard to move through the document, but keep in mind that pressing the right-arrow key will *not* move you to the next column. You have to go to the end of that column and then up to the top to move through the document. It's faster to use the mouse.

I don't see my columns! In Normal view, the columns are shown in one single column down the page. Normal view works well when you are typing because Word doesn't have to constantly adjust the columns and redisplay the screen. When you are formatting the document and want to see the columns side by side, change to Page Layout view using the <u>V</u>iew → <u>P</u>age Layout command.

Inserting a Column Break

If you want to move to the next column, you may be tempted to press Enter until you jump to the column. But you shouldn't do this, because these blank returns will mess up the breaks if you add or delete text. Instead, insert a column break when you want to force a column break. *Follow these steps:*

1. Select **Insert** → **Break**. You see the Break dialog box.

2. Click the <u>C</u>olumn break option button.

3. Click the OK button.

Word inserts the column break and moves the insertion point to the next column. In Normal view, you see a dotted line with the words "Column Break" in the center. In Page Layout view, you see the actual break.

Changing the Column Layout

If you want to use more than four columns or if you want to use columns of unequal widths, use the <u>C</u>olumns command to format a document into columns. You can also use this command when you want to change the columns you have created with the toolbar.

Follow these steps to set up or modify columns with the <u>C</u>olumns command:

1. Select **Format** → **Columns**. You see the Columns dialog box (see Figure 9-6).

2. To use one of the preset column formats, click the one you want in the Preset area: <u>O</u>ne, T<u>w</u>o, <u>T</u>hree, <u>L</u>eft, <u>R</u>ight. Skip to step 5.

   To set the number of columns manually, enter the number of columns you want in the <u>N</u>umber of columns spin box. Follow the remaining steps.

TIP If you aren't sure how the columns will affect the document, check the preview in the dialog box. It gives you an idea of how the selected options will look when used in your document.

3. To use the same width for all columns, check the <u>E</u>qual column width check box and then enter the width you want in the W<u>i</u>dth spin box. Word uses this width for all columns.

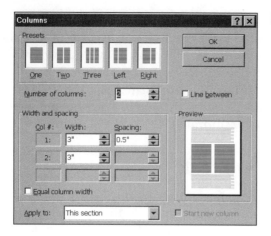

Figure 9-6 Use this dialog box to select the number and sizes of the columns.

To create columns of unequal widths, uncheck the Equal column width check box. Click in the Width spin box for the column you want to change and enter a new width. Do this for each column width you want to change.

4. To change the spacing between columns, click in the Spacing text box for the column you want to change. Enter a new width or use the spin arrows to select the value you want. Do this for each column you want to change.

5. To include a line between the columns, check the Line between check box.

6. Click the OK button.

Word reformats the document into the number of columns you have selected with the column width and spacing as you entered them.

A Picture Is Worth...

Tables and columns are a good way to break up text in a document and make a document have some visual impact. Another way is to use a well-placed graphic. Notice I say "well-placed." Have you ever gotten a memo from someone about, say, your 401K plan and found that it's decorated with little cats everywhere? Or maybe you've gotten a newsletter with each little article illustrated with some kind of clip art image — even if that image has nothing to do with the article. You're reading about the annual fund drive, and there's a picture of a mouse driving a car next to the article. Clip art makes it easy to add images to your document, and you probably remember all the *bad* examples of pictures in a document.

Adding a well-placed clip art graphic can enhance your document.

9

But you have better sense than that, don't you? You know that adding a well-placed graphic can enhance a document. This section tells you how to do just that.

Inserting a Picture

Word enables you to insert several types of pictures. You can use one of the many clip art images provided with Word. (A *clip art* image is a canned drawing that anyone can use.) If you have other clip art images or picture files (such as bitmap or PCX files), you can insert them. You can also insert an AutoShape, such a circle, a smiley face, or a lightning bolt. These types of pictures are for all the nonartists (like me!) out there.

Inserting a Clip Art Image

If you're like me... I can draw a pretty good stick man, but that's about it. If I want to include any sort of artwork in my document, you can guarantee it isn't something I drew myself. I prefer predrawn clip art images to dress up my documents. Word provides quite a nice collection of images in several categories, including animals, buildings, electronics, flags, food, maps, nature, people, plants, signs, sports, travel, and more.

To use one of these images, follow these steps:

1. Place the insertion point where you want the picture. You can always move the picture around if necessary, but at least start in the general area.

2. Select **Insert** → **Picture**. From the submenu that appears, select **Clip Art**. You see the Microsoft Clip Gallery.

3. In the category list, click the category you want to view. Word displays the images in that category in the middle of the dialog box. Figure 9-7 shows the clip art images for the Places category on the Microsoft Office CD.

4. Click the image you want to insert.

5. Click the Insert button. Word inserts the image in the document. It is sized to its "ideal" dimensions, but you can also change the size (see Figure 9-8).

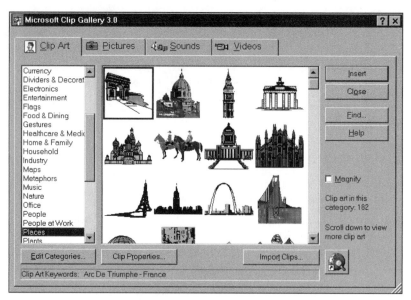

Figure 9-7 Select the category you want to view, and then select the image you want to insert.

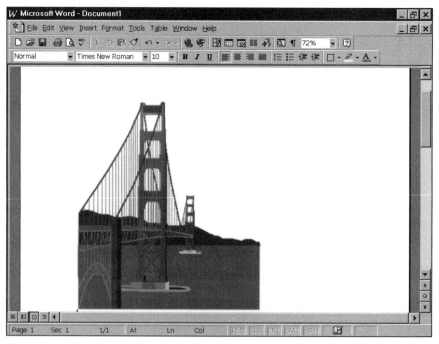

Figure 9-8 You can insert a clip art image into your document.

Inserting Your Own Pictures

In addition to the clip art images that come with Word, you can insert other images that you may have. You can insert other image types, such as TIFF files, PCX files, BMP files — any type of image file you may have available. For instance, you can purchase additional clip art packages, or you can scan in photos or other illustrations to include in your document.

To insert a picture from a file that you have, follow these steps:

1. Place the insertion point where you want the picture.

2. Select **Insert** → **Picture** . From the submenu that appears, select **From File** . You see the Insert Picture dialog box (see Figure 9-9). This dialog box lists the available picture files in the current folder.

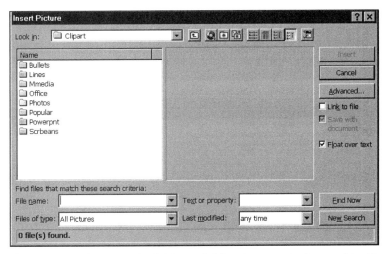

Figure 9-9 Change to the folder and drive that contain the graphics file you want to insert.

3. To change to another drive, display the Look in list and select the drive you want. To change to another folder, double-click it in the Name list. If you don't see the folder listed, use the Up One Level button to move up through the folder structure until you find the folder you want. Then double-click it.

4. When you see the picture file you want, click it. Word displays a preview of the selected file. You can also type the name in the File name text box as an alternative to clicking it.

TIP By default, all picture file types are listed. If you want to view just a particular file type, you can do so. To change the types of files that are displayed in the dialog box, display the Files of type drop-down list and select the file type you want. You can select from Windows Enhanced Metafile, Windows Metafile, JPEG, Bitmap, PC Paintbrush, Kodak Photo CD, TIFF, GIF, and several other popular graphics file formats.

5. Click the Insert button. Word inserts the image in the document. It is sized to its "ideal" size, but you can also change the size, as covered later in this chapter.

Adding an AutoShape

If what you want to insert in your document is a basic shape (square, rectangle, triangle, or such), an arrow, a flowchart symbol, a star, a banner, or a callout, try AutoShape. This feature includes several styles of commonly used shapes. You can use any of the shapes in your document.

To insert an AutoShape, follow these steps:

1. Select Insert → Picture . From the submenu that appears, select AutoShapes . You see the AutoShapes toolbar, which you can use to insert a shape. The Drawing toolbar is also displayed.

2. Click the shape type that you want. You see a drop-down palette of available choices, as shown in Figure 9-10.

Figure 9-10 Select the AutoShape that you want to insert.

3. When you find a shape you want, click it.

4. Click and drag within the document area to draw the shape. Word adds this shape to your document.

Hanging Your Artwork

The great thing about adding a graphic is that you aren't stuck with its size and location. Making a change is as simple as dragging it around. You can also delete an image that you don't think works or is no longer need. The procedures in this section work for any type of graphic you have added: clip art images, pictures inserted from a file, AutoShapes, and shapes you've drawn yourself (covered in the Bonus section).

Moving, Resizing, and Deleting a Graphic

When you first draw the object, you may not get it in the exact spot you want or the right size. You may even decide you don't want the graphic. If so, you can make a change. To start, click the object to select it. You should see selection handles along the edges of the object, as shown in Figure 9-11.

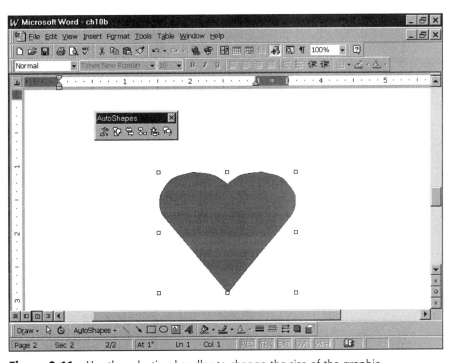

Figure 9-11   Use the selection handles to change the size of the graphic.

Once it is selected, do any of the following:

✳ To move the object, point to the center of the object — anywhere but on one of the selection handles. When the mouse pointer is in the right spot, it changes into a four-headed arrow. Drag the object to a new location.

* To resize the object, put the mouse pointer on one of the selection handles. Drag the selection handle to resize the object.

* To delete a graphic, press Delete.

Copying a Graphic

If you want to use the same shape or image again in the document, don't go to the trouble of inserting or drawing it again. *Instead, simply copy it by following these steps:*

1. Click the object to select it. You should see selection handles around the graphic.

2. Click 🗐 or select **Edit** → **Copy** .

3. Click 🗐 or select **Edit** → **Paste** .

4. Drag the copy to the location where you want it to appear.

You can also hold down the Ctrl key and drag a copy off of the original one.

Controlling How Text Flows around the Picture

How the text and image flow together varies depending on the type of image you insert. When you insert a clip art image, the image is inserted above the text. The text does not flow around the object. When you draw a shape, the shape is placed above the text; the text doesn't flow around the object. You can change how the text flows, selecting from several different options.

To control how the text flows around the picture, follow these steps:

1. Click the object you want to change.

2. Select **Format** → **AutoShape** for shapes you've drawn or **Object** for clip art images. You see the Format Object (or AutoShape) dialog box.

3. Select the Wrapping tab. You see the different options you can use for text wrapping (see Figure 9-12). The one currently in use is highlighted.

4. Select the wrapping style you want. You can select Square, Tight, Through, None, or Top & Bottom. The picture for each option is pretty self-explanatory.

5. For Square, Tight, and Through, select where you want to wrap to: Both sides, Left, Right, or Largest side. Again, the picture in the dialog box give you a good idea of the effects of each option.

6. Click the OK button. Word wraps the text accordingly.

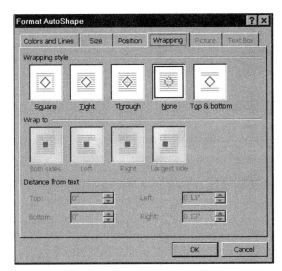

Figure 9-12 Select how you want text to wrap
around the graphic.

BONUS

Playing Picasso: Drawing Stuff Yourself

The easiest way for me, an artistic simpleton, to add artwork is to use someone else's handiwork. You, on the other hand, may have more talent. You may want to try your hand at drawing your own shapes and squiggles. If so, you can read this section to find out all about the drawing tools available in Word.

Getting Out Your Palette, the Drawing Toolbar

Your palette of tools is called the Drawing toolbar, and you display this palette of tools by clicking the Drawing button on the Standard toolbar. Word displays the toolbar on screen, usually along the bottom of the screen. Table 9-1 identifies the tools you use to draw and format objects.

TABLE 9-1 The Tools for Drawing Objects

Button	Name	Description
Draw ▾	DRAW	Display a menu with commands for working with the object.
	SELECT OBJECTS	Select the object you want to work with.
	FREE ROTATE	Rotate an object.
AutoShapes ▾	AUTOSHAPES	Display the AutoShapes toolbar for drawing an AutoShape.
	LINE	Draw a line.
	ARROW	Draw an arrow.
	RECTANGLE	Draw a rectangle or a square.
	OVAL	Draw an oval or a circle.
	TEXT BOX	Draw a text box.
	FILL COLOR	Fill an object with a color or pattern. Click the color you want from the palette that appears.
	LINE COLOR	Select a line color. Click the color you want from the palette that appears.
	FONT COLOR	Select a font color (available only for objects, such as text boxes, that have text). Click the color you want from the palette that appears.
	LINE STYLE	Select a line style. Click the style you want.
	DASH STYLE	Select a dash style. Click the style you want.
	ARROW STYLE	Select a style and placement for arrows. Click the style and arrow placement.
	SHADOW	Add a shadow. Click the shadow effect.
	3-D	Select a 3D effect. Click the 3D effect.

Drawing a Shape

When you want to draw something, you follow the same basic steps:

1. Click the button for the shape you want to draw. The mouse pointer changes to a small cross hair.

2. Click within the document and drag to draw the object.

When you draw objects, keep these pointers in mind:

* To draw a straight line, hold down the Shift key as you drag.

* You can change the line style, color, thickness, and so on. To do so, use the appropriate toolbar button (see the preceding table).

* To draw a square, use the Rectangle button, but hold down the Shift key as you drag.

* To draw a circle, use the Oval tool, but hold down the Shift key as you drag.

* In addition to changing the line style, color, and thickness for the outside of a rectangle or circle, you can also add a fill or color, use a shadow, or apply a 3D effect. Select the object and then click the appropriate toolbar button, as described in Table 9-1.

Drawing a Text Box

Sometimes you may want to insert text in a certain spot in a document. Perhaps you want to include a pull quote or a note or something in the document's margin. You can try to set up this element within the main document and then use the paragraph and other formatting options to get it positioned just right, but you'll probably struggle a lot to get it to work. Instead, create a text box. Text boxes are flexible: you can draw them anywhere within the document and also move them if needed.

To draw a text box, follow these steps:

1. Click the Text Box button in the Drawing toolbar or select `Insert` → `Text Box`.

2. Point to the spot in the document where you want to add the text box.

3. Click and drag to draw the text box. After you draw the box, Word displays the insertion point within the text box.

4. Type the text you want to include. You can also make any formatting changes to the text. Figure 9-13 shows a text box with text added.

5. Click outside the box to return to the document.

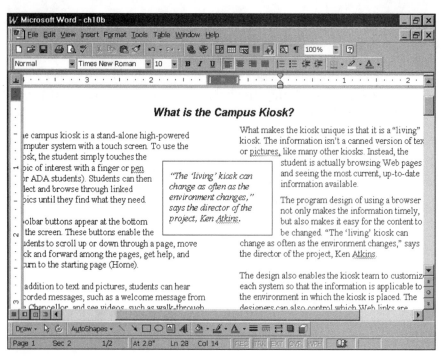

Figure 9-13 Type the text you want to include in your text box.

 WEB PATH For links to other sites with clip art, visit this Yahoo! page:

`http://www.yahoo.com/Computers/Multimedia/Pictures/Clip_Art`

CREATING FORM LETTERS

10

'm willing to venture that everyone at sometime or another has received a form letter. You know, the letter that reads at least a little like the following:

Dear Bob:

Guess what, Bob! You may already be a winner. Yes, Bob, you might already have won one of the 1,000 fabulous prizes in our grand prize drawing. You may have won a trip to Hawaii or a new car. Isn't that great, Bob?

All you need to do is attend this really, really boring presentation where I or one of my many salespersons will try to pressure you into buying something you don't need, like the world's lightest vacuum cleaner or a timeshare in downtown Burbank. Then you will receive some really lame prize like a box of Rice-o-Roni and a jar of Turtle Wax. If you're lucky.

And Bob, don't think about throwing this away. Because, Bob, we know where you live, and you can expect to receive this same letter next week. Every week, Bob, for the rest of your life. How do you like that, Bob?

Maybe this letter is a little untrue (or maybe a little too true). Form letters, or *mail merges,* are a way to send the same letter to many people. And even though you may think "junk" mail, these types of letters can come in handy to you or your business.

For instance, if you have a small business, you may want to send a letter to your clients announcing a new product or service. Or you may want to thank a customer for an order. If you are a real estate agent, you may want to send out a letter introducing yourself to your neighbors. If you mainly use Word for family functions, you may want to send a holiday letter to all your friends and family. Or you may be in charge of one of your children's sports teams and need to send the same information to several people. The types of letters you may want to create are endless.

Word provides a convenient way to send the same letter — but personalized — to several people. This chapter starts by giving you an overview of the process and then tells you how to set up the two documents you need and then perform the merge.

Merging: Two Documents Into One

Two files make up a basic merge procedure: the data source and the main document. And you follow three basic steps to create a merge:

* Set up the main document
* Create the data source
* Merge the two

This section gives you an overview of the process and explains what each document contains. The remaining sections tell you specifically how to create each document and then do the merge.

Setting Up the Main Document

The main document contains the text of the letter. This is the boilerplate letter that you want to send to everyone. That's the text of your yearly Christmas letter that tells all your friends and family about Jimmy Junior getting released from jail and Little Suzie winning the Little Miss Okra Pageant. You type this text as you do for any other letter.

What's special about the letter is that you insert codes for the fields you want to include. For example, a last name field code tells Word to take the specific last name and insert it in that spot in the main document.

You start this document first, then create the data source, and then go back to complete the main document.

Creating the Data Source

The data source is the list of variable information (usually names and addresses) that you want to use to personalize the main document. You can use an existing data source (such as an address book or a database file), or you can set up a data source.

If you create the data source, you basically create a table. The first row of the table contains the name of the *fields* or variable information you want to insert in the main document. For example, you may have fields for the first name, last name, address, city, state, zip, and so on. Each field has a name and appears in its own column. Word provides several predefined fields that you can use in the data source. Or you can create your own.

After you set up the data source, you then enter the specific information for each field. One set of fields (or a row) is called a *record.* For instance, in one row you would have the name and address of a specific person. You next enter the records using a data form. You enter a record for each person that you want to send the letter to.

Merging the Two

After you've created both documents, you merge the two. Word creates one big document, with a personalized letter for each record in the data source. You can then print or save the resulting document.

Starting the Mail Merge Helper

To lead you through the process of performing a mail merge, Word provides the Mail Merge Helper, which outlines the three steps you follow. *To display this helper and start the main document, follow these steps:*

1. Start with a blank document on screen. Word makes a connection between the two documents (the main document and the data source). You will create the main document using this blank document later.

2. Select **Tools** → **Mail Merge** . You see the Mail Merge Helper dialog box (see Figure 10-1). Notice that the dialog box outlines the three key steps you follow.

   To start, you select the type of main document you want to create, but you don't create this document until later. (The steps are kind of misleading.)

3. Under Main document, click the Create button. You see a drop-down list of the different types of main documents you can set up. You can create form letters, mailing labels (covered later), envelopes, or a catalog.

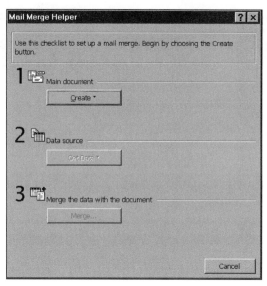

Figure 10-1 The Mail Merge Helper shows you the three steps to performing a merge.

4. Click Form <u>L</u>etters. You are prompted to use the current window or a new window for the main document.

5. Click the <u>N</u>ew Main Document button. Word records the document type (form letters) and document window you are using for the main document. This information is listed in the Mail Merge Helper dialog box, which remains open. The next step is to create the data source, as described in the next section.

Names and Addresses Here

Your next task is to create the data source. Remember that the data source contains the header row with field names for each piece of information you want to include. The data source also includes individual records for each person (or item or event). When you create the data source, you start by defining the fields to include. Then you enter the data.

Setting Up the Fields

To start, you set up the fields you want to include. Word includes some commonly used fields such as FirstName, LastName, Company, Title, City, State, HomePhone, and so on. You can use any of these fields. Plus, you can add your own fields.

Which fields do you need? To come up with your list of fields, think about each individual piece of data you want to include. Which of the predefined fields are appropriate? Which additional fields do you need to include? For instance, suppose that you are in charge of organizing the community services program for your company. Part of that task involves setting up committees for each activity. You could create a form letter to send to each volunteer. For this data source, you would include all the name and address information for each person, as well as a field for the committee to which that person was assigned.

TIP **You may want to think through the contents of the letter and write down a list of fields you need to include. Remember that you can include other variable information, such as a committee name, project, sales representative, class, and so on, relating to each person. And you can include more than one "added" field.**

To select the fields you want to include in the form letter, follow these steps:

1. Click Get Data in the Mail Merge Helper dialog box. You see a submenu of choices. You can choose to create the data source, open a data source, use the address book, or set header options. Here you will create a data source.

X-REF **For information on using other data sources — such as an Access database — see Chapter 29.**

2. Click Create Data Source. You see the Create Data Source dialog box (see Figure 10-2). Word sets up some common fields which are listed in the Field names in header row list. You can delete any of these fields that you don't want to include and add any additional fields.

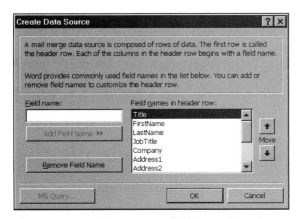

Figure 10-2 Add or remove fields to or from the data source using this dialog box.

3. To remove a field, select it in the Field names in header row list. Then click the Remove Field Name button. Do this for each field you want to remove from the predefined list.

4. To add a field, type the name of the field in the Field name text box and then click the Add Field Name button. Do this for each field you want to add.

5. When you are finished adding or removing fields, click the OK button. Word displays the Save Data Source dialog box. Before you enter records, save the data source.

6. Use the Save in drop-down list to change to the drive or folder you want. You can also double-click folders listed in the file and folder list. To move up through the folder structure, click the Up One Level button.

7. In the File name text box, type the file name. Use a name that will remind you that this is a data source document and of that data source's purpose.

8. Click the Save button. Word next prompts you to decide whether you want to edit the main document or data source. You want to edit the data source, adding the records to your data table. This is the topic of the next section.

Entering the Data for the Data Source

After you've set up the fields, you next enter the specific information for each person that you want to receive a letter. For instance, if you wanted to send out ten letters, you would next enter the specific name and address information for those ten people. *Follow these steps:*

1. Click the Edit Data Source button. You see the Data Form, shown in Figure 10-3. You see an entry box for each of the fields you added in the preceding section. Here you type the information for each of those fields for each person you want to receive the letter.

2. Type the information for the first field and press Tab.

TIP   **If you somehow get off track when completing the data source, you can always go back to setting up the data source or adding records. You can also edit records. See the section "I Got Lost" later in this chapter.**

3. Continue entering information for all the fields until you complete the record.

4. When you are finished, click the Add New button.

5. Follow steps 2–4 for each record you want to add.

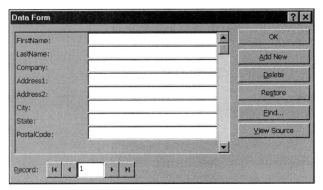

Figure 10-3 Enter the data for each person.

6. When you have completed all the records, click the OK button. You see the main document on screen. The next section describes how to complete this document.

Creating the Main Document

Congratulations! You've completed the first step of the mail merge. Now you are onto step 2 — creating the main document. When you finish adding records, Word displays the main document. You can then type the text of the document as well as insert the merge fields. *Follow these steps:*

1. Type the text of the letter.

2. When you get to a spot where you want to insert variable information (such as the name and address), click the Insert Merge Field button. You see a list of fields you have set up in the data source (see Figure 10-4).

Figure 10-4 Select the field you want to insert.

3. Click the field you want to insert. Word inserts the merge code into the document. You can tell that this is a code rather than regular text because it is appears within little brackets.

Be sure to include appropriate spaces and punctuation in between each of the merge fields. Otherwise, the fields will run together. Instead of "John Smith," you'll get "JohnSmith."

4. Continue typing and inserting fields until you complete the document. Figure 10-5 shows a document with text for the letter as well as merge codes to merge the information from the data source. Once the main document is complete, you need to save it.

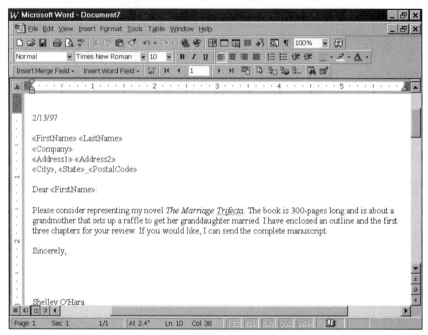

Figure 10-5 This form letter includes text as well as merge codes for the fields you want to include.

5. To save the main document, select **File** → **Save** or click 🖫 in the toolbar. You see the Save As dialog box.

6. Type the filename and click the <u>S</u>ave button.

Now that both documents are completed, you can merge the two.

Abracadabra

T he final step is the easiest. You select a few commands, and Word performs the merge. Word takes your main document and pulls the specific information from each record in the data source, creating a custom letter for each record in the data source.

To perform the merge, follow these steps:

1. Select **Tools** → **Mail Merge**. You see the Mail Merge Helper dialog box. All the selections you made and filenames for each file is listed, as shown in Figure 10-6.

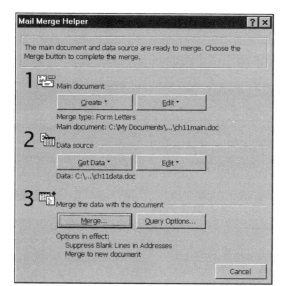

Figure 10-6 The Mail Merge Helper dialog box keeps track of your progress.

2. Click the <u>M</u>erge button. You see the Merge dialog box, shown in Figure 10-7.

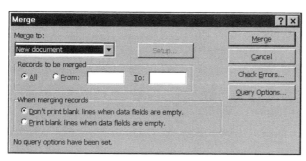

Figure 10-7 Select how to perform the merge.

TIP **To merge directly to a new document, click the Merge to New Document button on the Merge toolbar. To merge directly to the printer, click the Merge to Printer button on the Merge toolbar.**

3. To merge to the printer, display the Mer<u>g</u>e to drop-down list and select Printer. You can also select Electronic mail.

4. To merge only selected records, select the <u>F</u>rom option button and then enter the record numbers you want to use in the merge.

5. If Word encounters a blank field or line, it does not print the line. If you want to print this line, select the button to <u>P</u>rint blank lines when data fields are empty.

6. Click the <u>M</u>erge button. Word merges the letters and displays each one on a separate page (if you merged to a new document). Figure 10-8 shows the first page of the merge example used throughout this chapter.

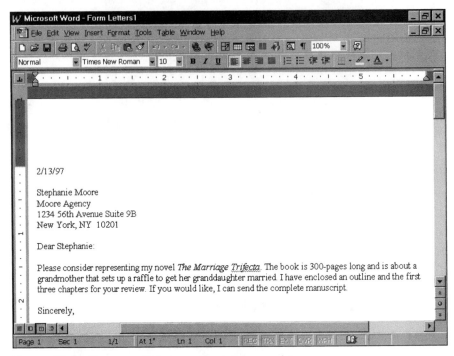

2/13/97

Stephanie Moore
Moore Agency
1234 56th Avenue Suite 9B
New York, NY 10201

Dear Stephanie:

Please consider representing my novel *The Marriage Trifecta*. The book is 300-pages long and is about a grandmother that sets up a raffle to get her granddaughter married. I have enclosed an outline and the first three chapters for your review. If you would like, I can send the complete manuscript.

Sincerely,

Figure 10-8 The merged document is shown complete.

7. Print the letters by selecting `File` → `Print`.

I Got Lost

A merge is really one long process. You need to follow each step in each section in order to get the merge to work. But some steps can go wrong, and you may get off track. If that happens, use this section to figure out where you are and how you can get back on the 1-2-3 step of the merge.

Forget Where You Are?

If you forget where you are in the merge process, you can always display the Mail Merge Helper, which keeps track of your progress. You can tell a lot from the dialog box, including the names of the main document and data source (refer to Figure 10-6). You can also use this dialog box to switch to and work on another file.

If you forget where you are in the merge process, you can always display the Mail Merge Helper, which keeps track of your progress.

For instance, suppose that somehow you got sidetracked and did not complete your main document. To return to the main document, display the Mail Merge Helper dialog box by selecting `Tools` → `Mail Merge`. Then click the Edit button under Main document.

TIP You can also switch between the main document and the data source using the Window menu. Open this menu and then, at the bottom of the menu, click the document you want to switch to.

Need to Find or Add Records?

When you are creating the data source, you have a wealth of options for working with the records. For instance, you may want to add another field. Or perhaps you prefer a different view of the data. Or maybe you need to edit a record.

To edit the data source, display the Mail Merge Helper dialog box, click the Edit button under Data source, and then click the file name for the data source. You should see the data form displayed (see Figure 10-9).

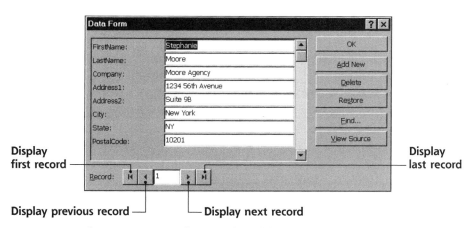

Display first record

Display last record

Display previous record

Display next record

Figure 10-9 Use the Record scroll buttons to move among the records.

You can then do any of the following:

✴ To edit a record, use the Record scroll arrows to display the record. Make changes to any field in the record. When you move to another record, the changes are saved.

✴ To delete a record, use the Record scroll arrows to display the record you want. Then click the Delete button.

✴ If you have a lot of records, you may not want to scroll through them individually. Instead, you can search for a record. To do so, click the Find button. In the Find in Field dialog box, enter the text you want to find in the Find what text box. Select which field to search from the In field drop-down list. Then click the Find First button.

* If you would rather work in a table view than in the data form, click the View Source button to see the data source in a table layout. You can use the toolbar buttons to work with the records or change to the main document. To redisplay the data form, click the Data Form button.

I'm Not Done with the Main Document!

If you somehow got out of the main document when you weren't finished, you can switch back to it from the Mail Merge Helper dialog box or from the Window menu. Then you can make any changes. When creating or editing the main document, keep these tips in mind:

* If you make any mistakes while typing, just correct them as you would in any regular document.

* If you insert a field incorrectly, select it and press the Delete key.

* You can use the same field more than once in the document. Also, you don't have to use all the fields you've included in the data source.

* Be sure to include spaces after the merge fields. Otherwise, when you do the merge, the text won't be spaced properly.

* To check on your progress and see how the data will be merged, click the View Merged Data button in the toolbar. You can then use the record scroll buttons next to the View Merged Data button to move through the records, displaying the letter for each record.

* To edit the data source, click the Edit Data Source button in the Merge toolbar.

BONUS

Printing Mailing Labels

You've saved all that time creating the letters, but what about addressing them? Word can save you time there, too. You can set up mailing labels, using the names and addresses in the data source, as covered here.

To print mailing labels for your form letters, follow these steps:

1. Start with a blank document on screen. You will use this document to set up your labels.

2. Select [**Tools**]→[**Mail Merge**]. You see the Mail Merge Helper dialog box (refer to Figure 10-1).

3. Under Main document, click the Create button and select Mailing Labels.

4. When prompted to use the current window or a new one, click the Active Window button. You next open the data source, which you have already created.

5. Click the Get Data button and select Open Data Source. You see Open Data Source dialog box. Change to the drive and folder that contain the data source. Use the Look in drop-down list to change to a drive. If you see the folder listed, double-click it to open it. You can use the Up One Level button to move up through the folder structure until you find the folder you want.

6. When you see the file listed, double-click it. Word prompts you to set up the main document.

7. Click the Set Up Main Document button. You see the Label Options dialog box.

8. Display the Label products drop-down list and select the brand of label you are using. The most common types of labels are made by Avery. Many other labels are compatible with the Avery labels, too.

9. In the Product number list, select the name of the labels you are using. Check the label box for the product number.

10. If necessary, make any changes to the printer information. Select the type of printer as well as the tray that contains the labels (for laser and inkjet printers).

11. Click the OK button. You see the Create Labels dialog box. Here you use the merge labels to set up an address.

12. Click the Insert Merge Field button and select the merge field to include in the address label. Do this for each part of the address.

13. When you have finished setting up the sample label, click the OK button. You are returned to the Mail Merge Helper dialog box. You can now merge your mailing label document with the data source.

14. Click the <u>M</u>erge button and then, in the Merge dialog box that appears, click the <u>M</u>erge button again. Word creates a document based on the label size and includes an address for each label.

15. Insert the labels into the printer, select ` File ` → ` Print `, and click the OK button to print the labels.

I f you need to work with any type of financial data — budgets, sales reports, income or expense tracking — you will want to use Excel. This spreadsheet program includes many tools for working with numbers. To learn all you need to know about Excel, read this part's chapters.

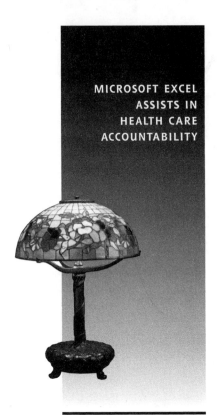

"Although there are a variety of views on health care in America, few would argue with one of the Foundation for Accountability's (FACCT) prime tenets: "...the health care system — encompassing all providers of care — is accountable to consumers and purchasers to demonstrate quality through meaningful information."

Because consumers and providers deserve to be informed, FACCT, based in Portland, Oregon, works to get useful information to consumers by evaluating the quality of health care from their point of view. FACCT's goal is to "equip consumers to evaluate the quality of health care they are receiving and to make apples-to-apples comparisons among health care provider services."

In operation since only January 1996, FACCT has already succeeded in raising awareness of the consumer's right to quality health care. An extensive article in the *New York Times* in July 1996 had the headline "Assessing H.M.O.s by New Standard: A Patient's Progress." The article detailed FACCT's role in developing new standards, including a list of questions for health plans to answer.

How does Microsoft Excel play a role in all this? "I use Excel to determine sample sizes," explains Christina Bethell, director of accountability measurement. "I need an appropriate sample size to detect meaningful differences in the measures of quality across health care systems." Because she must specify how to collect information, Bethell has developed a formula in Excel that helps her determine what sample size to recommend when studies are performed.

"For example," says Bethell, "If you have a health care provider with 1,000 people who are diabetics, how many of those 1,000 must we study to provide accurate findings and get statistically meaningful results?" Bethell has devised her formula so that she can plug in various assumptions about her sample group and then come up with the appropriate number as her result. Because conditions and assumptions change with each study, Bethell must use this formula frequently. "Excel has been great for this type of calculation. If I have to do more complex statistical calculations, I'll use my statistical software, but for this, I like Excel."

Microsoft Excel also plays a big role in developing FACCT's budget. Louise Dunn, director of special projects, uses Excel to develop marketing and grant budgets. "I also use it for estimated and actual projections, determining things like FACCT's break-even point." This includes utilizing Excel's graphic feature to provide a visual representation of the data.

You can contact FACCT at 503-223-2228.

CREATING AN EXCEL WORKSHEET

LEARN THESE KEY SKILLS:

N ext to a word processor, the next most commonly used type of program is a spreadsheet. You can use this type of program to create financial worksheets to figure your budget, keep track of sales, list and total your expenses, calculate your net worth, and more. When you want to work with numbers, think Excel, the spreadsheet program included with Microsoft Office.

This chapter introduces you to the Excel program and its worksheet area and tools. You learn how to plan and set up a worksheet. Soon you will be excelling with Excel!

Finding Your Way around the Neighborhood

Y ou start Excel as you start any other Windows 95 program. *Follow these steps:*

1. Click the Start menu. You see the Start menu options.

2. Click the [**Programs**] command. You see the programs and program folders you have set up on your system (see Figure 11-1).

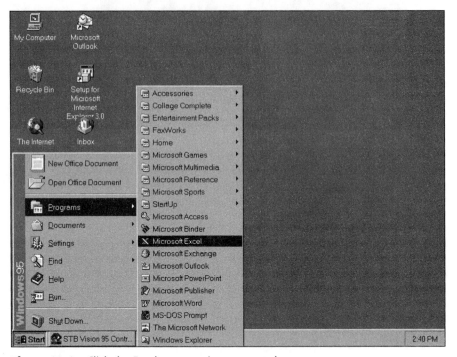

Figure 11-1   Click the Excel program icon to start the program.

3. If necessary, click the folder that contains the Excel program icon. If you have not made a change since installing Excel, you can skip this step. The program item is added to the Programs folder, and you should see the Excel program icon after step 2. If you have made a change, select the folder you used to store this program icon.

4. When you see the program icon, click it to start Excel.

The program starts, and you see a blank worksheet on screen (see Figure 11-2). You should already be familiar with most of the program window elements (menu bar, status bar, scroll bars, and so on). The next two sections discuss the worksheet area and the toolbars so that you can quickly learn all the vital areas of the program window.

 X-REF   Unfamiliar with the menu bars, toolbars, and other window elements? See Chapter 1, which discusses the different elements you can expect to find in a window.

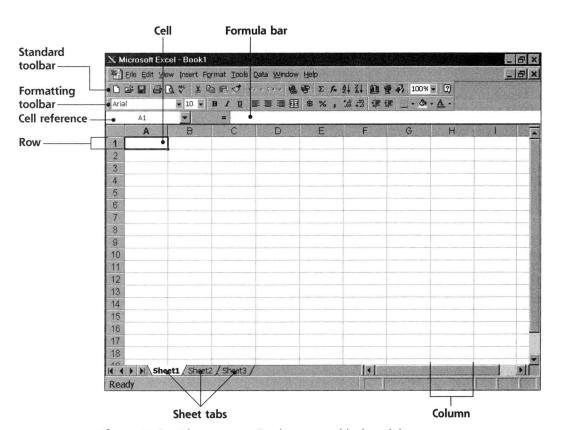

Figure 11-2 When you start Excel, you see a blank worksheet.

The Worksheet

The main part of the Excel screen is the worksheet area — a grid of rows and columns. Notice that rows are numbered and columns are lettered. The intersection of a column and row is called a *cell,* and that's where you enter your data — into one of these little cubbyholes.

FEATURE FOCUS The new version of Excel allows more than 655,536 rows — four times as many rows as the previous version.

To help you keep track of which cell you are in, each cell has a name or *cell reference*. The name consists of the column letter and row number. For instance, A1 is the first cell (column A, row 1). The active cell is indicated by a thick black border. The name of the active cell appears in the reference area next to the formula bar (under the toolbars).

You can think of this worksheet as a "sheet" of ledger paper. Notice the sheet tabs along the bottom of the window. Excel provides more than one "sheet" of paper. By default, you can work in three different worksheets. All these worksheets are stored together in one file called a *workbook*. You can switch among sheets, add sheets, rename sheets. You can have as many sheets as memory allows in a workbook. This chapter and Chapter 12 cover how to move around and work with the different sheets.

Click for Shortcuts

As you learn Excel, consider the two toolbars. Toolbars, as you probably know by now, provide fast access to commonly used features and commands. Rather than open a menu and select the command, you can use the toolbar shortcut.

The Standard toolbar includes buttons for working with files, cutting and copying text, undoing and redoing commands, and more. The Formatting toolbar includes buttons for changing how your entries appear. Table 11-1 identifies each of the Standard toolbar buttons. Table 11-2 identifies each of the Formatting toolbar buttons.

FEATURE FOCUS The Insert Hyperlink, Web Toolbar, Decrease Indent, and Increase Indent buttons are new features in Office 97.

Don't see Map? If you performed a standard install, you may not see this button. You must install the Map features. See the online help for information on installing additional Excel features.

SIDE TRIP

DISPLAYING AND HIDING A TOOLBAR

If you don't use the toolbars, you may want to turn them off so that you have more room on screen for the worksheet. You can also display other toolbars. Follow these steps:

1. Select View → Toolbars .

2. From the list of toolbars that appear, check the ones you want displayed. Uncheck the ones you want to hide.

TABLE 11-1 Standard Toolbar Buttons

Button	Name	Description
NEW	NEW	Create a new workbook.
OPEN	OPEN	Open a previously saved file.
SAVE	SAVE	Save the workbook.
PRINT	PRINT	Print the workbook currently on screen.
PRINT PREVIEW	PRINT PREVIEW	Display a preview of the entire worksheet page.
SPELLING	SPELLING	Check your spelling.
CUT	CUT	Cut selected range. (You use Cut and Paste to move data from one location to another.)
COPY	COPY	Copy selected range.
PASTE	PASTE	Paste data.
FORMAT PAINTER	FORMAT PAINTER	Copy formatting.
UNDO	UNDO	Undo the last command.
REDO	REDO	Redo the last command.
INSERT HYPERLINK	INSERT HYPERLINK	Insert a link to a file or a Web address.
WEB TOOLBAR	WEB TOOLBAR	Display a toolbar with buttons for creating Web documents.
AUTOSUM	AUTOSUM	Create a sum function. (The next chapter explains what a sum function is.)
FUNCTIONWIZARD	FUNCTIONWIZARD	Insert a function. (The next chapter describes functions.)
SORT ASCENDING	SORT ASCENDING	Sort selections in ascending order.
SORT DESCENDING	SORT DESCENDING	Sort selections in descending order.
CHARTWIZARD	CHARTWIZARD	Create a chart. (See Chapter 16.)
MAP	MAP	Create a map showing geographic data.
DRAWING	DRAWING	Display the Drawing toolbar.
100%	ZOOM	Zoom in or out on the worksheet data.
OFFICE ASSISTANT	OFFICE ASSISTANT	Display the Office Assistant so that you can ask a question and get online help.

TABLE 11-2   Formatting Toolbar Buttons

Button	Name	Description
Arial · 10 ·	FONT	Select a different font.
10 ·	FONT SIZE	Select a different font size.
B	BOLD	Make selected data bold.
I	ITALIC	Make selected data italic.
U	UNDERLINE	Underline selected data.
≡	ALIGN LEFT	Align selected data to the left edges of cells.
≡	CENTER	Center selected data within cells.
≡	ALIGN RIGHT	Align selected data to the right edges of cells.
⊞	MERGE AND CENTER	Center text across the selected range.
$	CURRENCY STYLE	Apply the currency style ($0.00) to the selected range.
%	PERCENT STYLE	Apply the percent style (00%) to the selected range.
,	COMMA STYLE	Apply the comma style (0,000.00) to the selected range.
+.0 .00	INCREASE DECIMAL	Increase the number of decimal points displayed in the selected range.
.00 +.0	DECREASE DECIMAL	Decrease the number of decimal points displayed in the selected range.
≣	DECREASE INDENT	Decrease the indent for data.
≣	INCREASE INDENT	Increase the indent for data.
⊟	BORDERS	Select and apply borders to the selected range.
⬧	FILL COLOR	Select and apply color to the selected range.
A	FONT COLOR	Select and apply color to text in the selected range.

The Big Picture

Now that you know the terrain of Excel, you can start exploring and creating your own worksheet. This entire part covers how to work with Excel. This section gives you an overview of the steps you follow to create a worksheet. Read this section to get a general idea of the process. Then read the rest of this chapter and this part for the specifics.

Step 1: Plan Your Worksheet

Just as you wouldn't start building a house by starting to hammer some nails into wood, you shouldn't create a worksheet by just plugging in numbers. Save yourself some headaches by first thinking about what you want your worksheet to do.

Knowing what you want to do will help you set up a worksheet that is best designed for your goal. You can also figure out the best and fastest way to set up this worksheet. Excel has a lot of time-saving features, but if you don't take time to figure out when they come in handy, you are like a one-tool carpenter. Use all your tools!

Knowing what you want to accomplish will help you set up a worksheet that is best designed for your goal.

Ask yourself, "What do I want this worksheet to do? Show how much money I spend? Show how much money I save? Keep track of travel? Total sales?" Once you know what you want to accomplish, ask yourself, "What data do I need to get to my goal? Monthly expenses? Weekly sales amounts? Mileage for each month?" Then ask yourself, "What do I need to enter and what will be calculated?" Some data you will enter; other data will be a total or average or some other calculation. Finally ask yourself, "Why am I talking to myself?"

Step 2: Enter Your Data

You've got your road map outlined — you know what you want to get from the worksheet and what you need to enter to get the data. Now you can create the worksheet. This chapter and the next cover how to enter data including text, dates, formulas, and so on. As you review this information, keep these tips in mind:

* When you start entering data, you usually start with the column and row headings, the worksheet titles, and any other text information. This text information provides the framework for the values. This chapter covers how to enter text.

* Excel includes some time-saving features for entering data. Check out the section on AutoComplete and filling data in the bonus section in this chapter.

* When you enter the numeric values, don't worry about formatting the numbers. It's easier to format after you enter all the numbers. Chapter 14 covers formatting numbers.

* For calculations, use a formula or a function. The next chapter covers how to enter formulas and functions. If you want to use the same formula in several places (for instance, a row that totals each column), don't recreate the formula. Fill it or copy it instead.

* As you build your worksheet, be sure to save it. Chapter 3 covers all you need to know about saving, closing, opening, and creating new documents.

* After you complete the worksheet, it's a good idea to check the formulas. Excel won't make a calculation mistake, but you need to be sure that you haven't made a mistake when creating the formulas. If you refer to a wrong cell or enter a wrong value, the formula may not be calculated correctly. Cross-checking helps avoid any errors. Chapter 12 covers some features for checking a worksheet.

Step 3: Make the Worksheet Look Nice

Once the guts of the worksheet are complete, you can make them look nice. Chapters 12 and 13 cover all you need to know about formatting. Here are some things you can do:

* Change how numbers appear. For instance, you can display numbers as "9,999," "$9,999.99," "99%," or in other formats.

* Make cell contents bold, italic, or underline.

* Outline key data or points.

* Format your headings so that they stand out.

* Create a chart or add other graphics to the worksheet. (This topic is covered in Chapter 16.)

Once the worksheet is set up how you want, you can print it, as described in Chapter 3.

Point and Click

When you want to enter data in your worksheet, you start by selecting the cell where you want the data to appear. You can easily move from cell to cell using either the keyboard or the mouse, and you can also move to and enter data in the other worksheets in the workbook. This section tells you how to do just that.

Moving to a Cell

As mentioned, the active cell is indicated by a thick black border. When you type data or enter a formula, that entry will be placed in the active cell. If you want the entry to go into another cell, you need to move to that cell first. To move around the worksheet, you can use the mouse or the keyboard.

To select a cell with the mouse, follow these steps:

1. Point to the cell that you want to select. The pointer should look like a big ol' fat cross.

2. Click that cell. That cell becomes active.

You can also use the keyboard. To move with the keyboard, use the keys listed in Table 11-3.

TABLE 11-3   Key Combinations for Moving around the Worksheet

Press	To move...
→	Right one cell
←	Left one cell
↓	Down one cell
↑	Up one cell
Ctrl + →	To the right edge of the current region
Ctrl + ←	To the left edge of the current region
Ctrl + ↓	To the bottom edge of the current region
Ctrl + ↑	To the top edge of the current region
Home	To the first cell in the row
Ctrl + Home	To the first cell in the worksheet
Ctrl + End	To the lower-right cell in the worksheet
PgDn	Down one screen
PgUp	Up one screen
Alt + PgDn	Right one screen

(continued)

TABLE 11-3 Key Combinations for Moving around the Worksheet *(continued)*

Press	To move...
Alt + **PgUp**	Left one screen
Ctrl + **PgDn**	Next sheet
Ctrl + **PgUp**	To the previous sheet

Scrolling the Worksheet

If you want to keep the active cell where it is but view another part of the work-sheet, use the scroll arrows along the right and bottom sides of the workbook window. Click the arrow in the direction you want to move. Or drag the scroll box. As you drag, you see a ScreenTip that shows the current row so that you can get a sense of how far you are scrolling.

 If you scroll the worksheet, keep in mind that the active cell doesn't change. If you type an entry, it will be entered in the active cell, which has not changed. If you scroll and then want to select a cell, be sure to point to the cell you want and click the mouse button.

Moving to a Specific Cell

Moving from cell to cell with the mouse, keyboard, or scroll bars is fine when you want to move a short distance. But if you want to move farther, you may want to try another method: use the Go To command. You can use this com-mand to move quickly to any cell in the worksheet.

To go directly to a cell, follow these steps:

1. Select **Edit** → **Go To**. You see the Go To dialog box.

2. Type the cell reference in the Reference text box (see Figure 11-3).

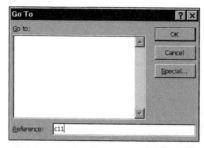

Figure 11-3 Use this dialog box to go directly to a cell.

3. Click the OK button. Excel moves to the selected cell.

Moving to a Different Sheet

The top worksheet is the active one — where data are entered. In many cases, you will use just this "sheet" of paper. If you are creating more complex workbooks, you may also want to use and enter data in the other worksheets. For instance, you may track sales by quarter. You might have a worksheet for each quarter, plus one for the totals, for a total of five worksheets.

When you start, Excel has three sheets available. To move to one of these other sheets, click the sheet tab at the bottom of the workbook window. The active tab appears in white. You'll learn more about sheets — such as how to insert sheets, change the sheet names, delete sheets, and so on — in Chapter 13.

Grabbing a Bunch of Cells

I f you have read or reviewed the Word part of this book, you know how important selecting is. When you want to edit or format something, you select that text first. The same is true for Excel. When you want to work on your cell entries — edit, make bold, change the font, move data, or whatever — you select them. You already know how to select a single cell, but often you will want to work on a group of cells at once.

In Excel, a group of cells is called a *range*, which can be a set of cells next to each other, an entire row, an entire column, a group of cells in one area and another group of cells in another area (called a *noncontiguous range*), or the entire worksheet.

Just as a cell has a cell reference, a range is indicated by a range reference. This reference includes the upper-leftmost cell, a colon, and the lower-rightmost cell. The range A2:C2, for instance, includes cells A1, B1, C1, A2, B2, and C2.

You can use either the mouse or the keyboard to select a range, as described in this section.

Selecting a Range Using the Mouse

The easiest way to select a range is to use the mouse. Most often, the ranges you select will be next to each other, so selecting a range is as simple as dragging across the cells you want. *Follow these steps:*

1. Click the first cell in the range.

2. Hold down the mouse button and drag across the cells you want to include. Then release the mouse button. The range appears highlighted on screen (see Figure 11-4). Also, the row and column letters of the range are in bold.

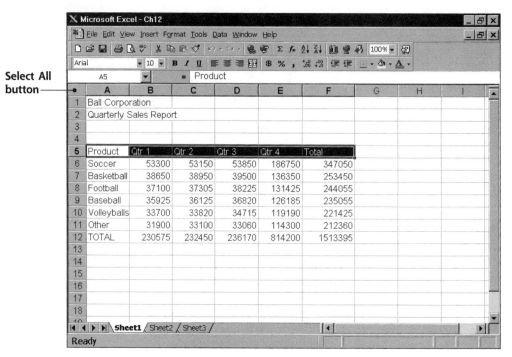

Figure 11-4 A selected range appears highlighted.

TIP   To deselect a range, click outside of the selected range.

Selecting a Range Using the Keyboard

If you prefer to keep your hands on the keyboard, you can use it to select a range. *Follow these steps:*

1. Use the arrow keys to move to the first cell in the range.

2. Press and hold down the Shift key.

3. Use any of the arrow or movement keys to highlight the range. Table 11-3 lists some of the movement keys you can use.

Selection Shortcuts

In many cases, you will want to select more than a set of cells. You may want to select an entire row or column or perhaps even the entire worksheet. Excel provides shortcuts for selecting these areas:

＊ To select a column, click the column letter or press Ctrl+Spacebar.

＊ To select a row, click the row number or press Shift+Spacebar.

* To select the entire worksheet, click the Select All button (the blank spot above the row numbers and to the left of the column letters) or press Ctrl+Shift+Spacebar.

The Value of Values

Basically, you can make two types of entries in a worksheet: values and formulas. *Values* are the things you enter: quantities, dates, times, part names, budget categories, and so on. You can enter text or numerals for the values. These are the unchanging part of the worksheet. This section explains how to enter these values.

Formulas, covered in the next chapter, use the values you enter to perform calculations. Find the average response time for a customer service call. Total your expenses for January. Count the number of absences. And so on. The cool thing about formulas, as you learn in the next chapter, is that their results can change. For instance, suppose that you total your expenses for January and find that you spent $3,400. But then you notice that your entry for Chinese Takeout was $150, not $170! You can change the incorrect entry, and the formula cell is updated!

Entering Text

You might think a worksheet is all about numbers, but without text, those numbers are meaningless. Your worksheet will include plenty of text entries, for column headings, row labels, worksheet titles, and more.

To enter text in a worksheet, follow these steps:

1. Select the cell you want.

2. Type the text. You can type up to 32,000 characters in a cell. (That's a much bigger limit than the 255-character limit of the previous version.) As you type, Excel displays an X and a checkmark next to the entry, in the formula bar (see Figure 11-5).

3. Press Enter or click the checkmark to accept the entry. Excel enters the text and moves to the next cell. You can also press any arrow key to make the entry and move the cell pointer to the next cell in that direction.

TIP Click the X or press Esc to cancel the entry.

By default, text is left aligned. Also, if the text entry is too long, it spills over to the cells next to it, unless those cells contain data, in which case the displayed entry is truncated or shortened — the whole entry is still intact, you just can't see it. You need to widen the column or wrap the text, as covered in Chapter 14.

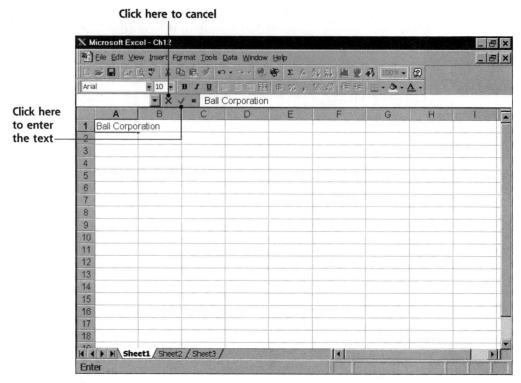

Click here to cancel

Click here to enter the text

Figure 11-5 As you type, you see the entry in the formula bar.

 TIP If you have a large worksheet with lots of columns or rows, you may want to freeze the column and/or row headings so that they always remain on-screen. For information on freezing row and column headings, see Chapter 17.

Entering Numbers

Numbers are the backbone of most worksheets. Once you enter the numeric values you need, you can use formulas to make the values dance and sing.

To enter a number, follow these steps:

1. Select the cell where you want the number.

2. Type the number. To type a negative number, precede the number with a minus sign or enclose the number in parentheses. As you type the entry, Excel displays an X and a checkmark next to the entry, in the formula bar.

3. Press Enter or click the checkmark to enter the number. (To cancel the entry, click the X or press Esc.) Excel enters the number and moves to the next cell. You can also press any arrow key to make the entry and move the cell pointer to the next cell in that direction.

By default, numbers are right-aligned and displayed in the General number format. If the number is too big to fit within the cell, Excel displays the number using scientific notation. You can change the number format, change the alignment, or widen the column. Figure 11-6 shows a worksheet with several numeric entries.

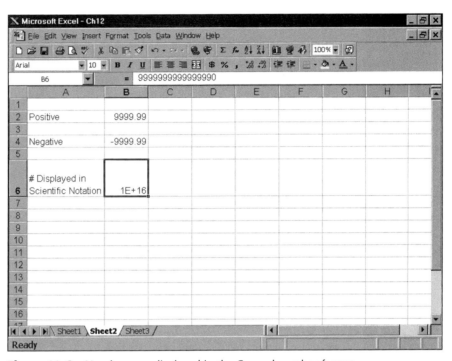

Figure 11-6 Numbers are displayed in the General number format.

 TIP You can type a comma, percent sign, dollar sign, and a period (to indicate decimal places) as you type the entry. Excel will use the appropriate format — for instance, comma format when you type a comma.

Entering Dates and Times

You can use dates to keep track of when an expense was incurred, when a project was completed, when a bill was sent, when a payment was received, and so on. Not only do dates provide information, but you can also use them in calculations. You can, for example, create a report on past due bills.

Times are similarly worthwhile. You can use times to track when a project started and ended, when a call was made and how long it took, and so on.

ENTERING A DATE

To enter a date, follow these steps:

1. Select the cell you want.

2. Type the date using one of these formats:

1/4 (assumes the current year and will be displayed as 1-Apr)

1/4/97 or 01/04/97

1-Apr (assumes the current year)

1-Apr-97 or 01-Apr-97

Apr-97 or April-97 (assumes the first of the month)

April 1, 1997

3. Press Enter. No matter how you enter the date, you should see the date in the format "1/4/97" in the formula bar. The date appears in the cell as you typed it.

ENTERING A TIME

To enter a time, follow these steps:

1. Select the cell you want.

2. Type the time using one of these formats:

13:30

1:30 PM

13:30:55

1:30:55 PM

30:55.7

3. Press Enter.

Figure 11-7 shows some date and time entries in a worksheet.

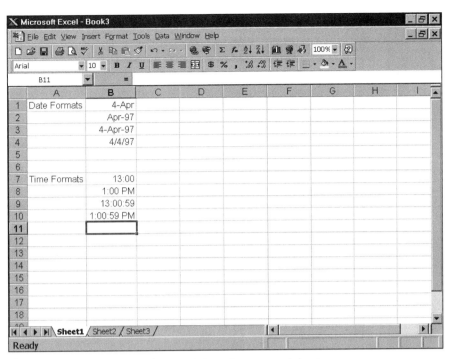

Figure 11-7   You can use dates and times in your worksheet.

 TIP   To enter the current date, press Ctrl+;. To enter the current time, press Ctrl+Shift+:.

BONUS

Shortcuts for Entering Data

Once you get the data entered, it's easy to manipulate them — perform calculations, create charts, tinker with projections, and so on. But getting the data entered can take some time. Luckily, Excel provides some shortcuts for entering data. Two are covered in this section: using AutoComplete and filling data. You can also copy data as a shortcut. Copying data is covered in Chapter 13.

Using AutoComplete

Excel tries to be just one step ahead of you. Because you often enter the same text again in a worksheet, it remembers all the entries you have made in a column.

If you want to use an entry more than once in a column, you don't have to type the entire entry. You can type just part of it.

For example, suppose that you are tracking orders and you enter the salesperson's name in one column. Suppose you have someone named Krycievski, and he's quite the salesman. If you had to enter that name 50 times in the worksheet, you'd probably go bonkers. Instead, you only have to enter it once. Then type **Kr** in the same column in a different cell . Excel guesses that you want to enter "Krycievski" and displays it. You can simply press Enter, and voilà, the text is entered for you. If you don't want that entry, you can simply keep typing.

Filling Data

As another shortcut, you can use Excel to fill in a series of numbers or dates. For example, think about how many worksheets include a sequence of months, days, or years. Or how many use a series of numbers. Instead of entering these, let Excel do the work for you. You can use Excel to fill in a series of numbers, text, dates, or formulas.

To get fills to work how you want them to, you have to know what to start with. Basically, you have to enter the first two cells. These two cells set the pattern that's used. Here are some examples:

* If you want to enter a series of numbers, enter the first number in one cell and the second number in the next cell. To enter a series of numbers incremented by 100, for example, you would enter **100** and **200** in two cells next to each other.

* To fill dates, enter the first date. Excel will increment the date by one. If you want to increment by a different value, enter a second date into an adjoining cell.

* If you fill text, the text is simply copied or repeated.

* If you fill a text entry containing a number, Excel will increment the number. For instance, if you enter **Qtr 1** and then fill a range, Excel will enter "Qtr 2," "Qtr 3," and so on.

* If you enter a formula and then fill the entry across a range, Excel will copy the formula. Any relative references are adjusted; absolute references remain the same. See Chapter 12 for more information on references.

The easiest way to fill a range is to use the fill handle. *Follow these steps:*

1. Type the entry into the first cell.

2. Type the entry in the second cell. Remember that these two cells define the pattern you want for the fill. If you are filling dates incremented by one or text with numbers incremented by one, you can skip this step and the next one.

3. Select these two cells.

Be sure to select both cells, not just one. If you don't select them both, Excel won't pick up the pattern you want to use.

4. Click and hold down the left mouse button on the fill handle in the lower-right corner of the second cell. The pointer appears as a small cross (see Figure 11-8).

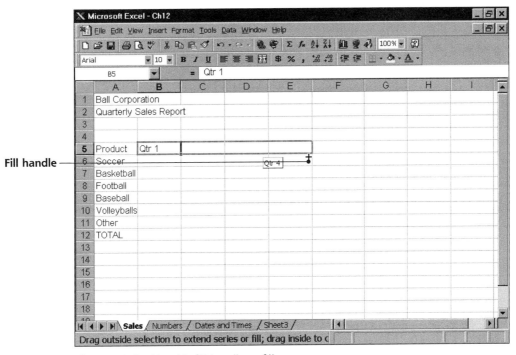

Figure 11-8   Use this fill handle to fill a range.

5. Drag across the range you want to fill. As you drag you see an outline. Also, a ScreenTip shows you the current value of the entry as you drag.

6. Release the mouse button. Excel fills the selected cells.

Creating a Custom List

The preceding section covers how to fill numbers and dates, but if you fill text, all you get is the same entry over and over. For text entries that you use over and over, you can create a custom list. For instance, you might have a list of product names, or sales reps, or budget categories — basically any list of text items that you often enter as a series into a worksheet. You can create a custom list and then use the fill handle to fill these entries rather than type them. Start by setting up the list.

SETTING UP THE LIST

To set up the custom list, you can use entries you have already typed, or you can type the list entries manually. *Follow these steps:*

1. If you've already typed the list in a worksheet, select it.

2. Select $\boxed{\text{Tools}} \rightarrow \boxed{\text{Options}}$.

3. Click the Custom Lists tab. You see the Custom Lists tab of the Options dialog box (see Figure 11-9).

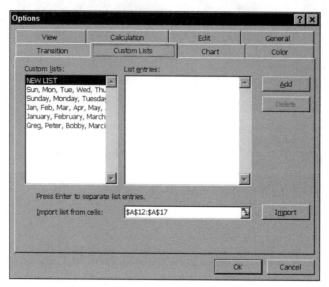

Figure 11-9 Use this dialog box to set up your custom list.

4. If you selected text in step 1, click the Import button. Excel displays the list in the List entries list in the dialog box.

   If you didn't select text for step 1, type the list items in the List entries text box. Press Enter after each entry.

5. Click the OK button to add the list and close the dialog box.

INSERTING A LIST

Once you set up the list, you can use it in any worksheet in Excel. *Follow these steps:*

1. Type the first item in the list. Excel will mimic the case of the first value you enter, so if you enter a list item in lowercase, Excel will fill the other values, using lowercase.

2. Drag the fill handle to fill the range with the custom list entries.

USING FORMULAS AND FUNCTIONS

LEARN THESE KEY SKILLS:

12

You spend a lot of time entering numbers so that you can use those numbers to do something. Perhaps you want to find out the value of all your possessions. Or maybe you want to calculate your interest on a certificate of deposit. Maybe you want to average your bowling scores. Or total how much you spent on Christmas presents (too much!).

When you want to perform some magic on your numbers, you create a formula. And this chapter tells you how to do that as well as how to use functions. Functions are fancy formulas that Excel creates for you.

Number Magic

Most of the time, you enter numbers in a worksheet so that you can perform some calculation on them — total annual sales, figure a sales commission, subtract expenses from income, and so on. To perform calculations, you create a formula. And to create a formula, you type the equation. For instance, here's a simple equation:

$$1 + 1$$

Notice that this formula uses absolute values — that is, exact numbers. You can type the exact values you want to work on, but that makes Excel nothing more than an expensive calculator. What makes Excel powerful is being able to *reference* a value in a cell. Instead of retyping an exact value, you point to the cell that contains the value. Excel includes the cell reference in the formula. Then if you change the referenced cell, Excel updates the formula. Here's a better formula:

```
=A1+A2
```

This formula takes the value in cell A1 and adds it to that in A2. If A1 and A2 both contain 1, the total is 2. If you change A1 to 2, the total is recalculated to 3. This simple equation shows you the benefits of using a reference.

Pieces and Parts of a Formula

An Excel formula is made up of an equal sign, cell references, and an operator. The equal sign is what tells Excel that the entry is a formula as opposed to a text or number entry. The cell references tell Excel where to find the data to use in the formula. And the operator tells Excel what to do with the numbers.

You can include more than two cell references, and you can use other operators than just addition (+). Table 12-1 explains the most common operators.

TABLE 12-1 Formula Operators

Operator	Description
+	Addition
-	Subtraction or negation
*	Multiplication
/	Division
%	Percentage
^	Exponentiation
=	Equal
<	Less than
<=	Less than or equal to
>	Greater than
>=	Greater than or equal to
<>	Not

HOW EXCEL CALCULATES A COMPLEX FORMULA

If you don't use parentheses to break up a complex formula, Excel just does the calculation using the default order, shown from first to last:

-	Negation
%	Percentage
^	Exponentiation
* and /	Multiplication and division
+ and -	Addition and subtraction

Creating Complex Formulas

You aren't limited to just simple calculations. As mentioned, you can include more than one cell reference, and you can include more than one calculation. For instance, you may want to add increase your prices by 10 percent. To get the new price, you multiply the current price by .1 (10 percent) and then add this amount to the price:

```
Old Price * 10% + Old Price = New Price
```

When you build complex formulas, you need to be sure that the calculations are performed in the order you want. For instance, take a look at the following formula:

```
5 + 5 * 10
```

You can calculate this one of two ways:

```
(5 + 5) * 10 = 100
5 + (5 * 10) = 55
```

As you see, you can get two results. To make sure Excel does the calculation you want, use parentheses to set what you want to do first.

Understanding Cell References

One final concept to know about formulas is cell referencing. When you point to a cell in a formula, Excel notes the relative relationship of that cell to the cell that contains the formula. For instance, if you sum the two cells above a formula cell, Excel thinks of this as "Take the two cells above this one and total them." This concept is known as *relative addressing*.

Relative addressing enables you to copy and move cells and have the references adjust according to location.

This type of referencing makes it easy to copy and move formulas. Suppose that you want to create a similar formula in the next column. Rather than retype it, you can copy the formula. Since the formula doesn't refer to specific cells — it refers to cells by relative location — the same formula will work in the next column over. Excel will adjust the cell references. Relative addressing enables you to copy and move cells and have the references adjust according to location. For instance, take a look at the worksheet in Figure 12-1. All of the formulas in row 10 use relative addressing. You start with the original formula in B10,

=B6+B7+B8+B9

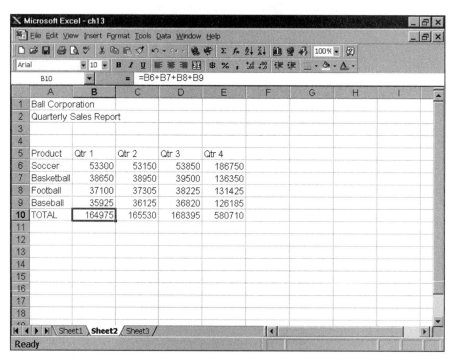

Figure 12-1   Excel uses relative addresses in formulas so that the references are adjusted when you move or copy a cell with a formula.

You can copy this same formula to C10, and it adjusts to

```
=C6+C7+C8+C9
```

If you copy the same formula to D10, it adjusts to

```
=D6+D7+D8+D9
```

 X-REF For more information on copying formulas, see the section "The Quick Way to Enter Formulas" later in this chapter. The next chapter also covers copying and moving in more detail.

You get the idea. This type of referencing helps you when you are building a worksheet.

In some formulas, you may want to refer to a specific cell. That is, you don't want the formula to adjust. In this case, you use a different type of cell reference: a mixed reference or an absolute reference. In a *mixed reference,* you can tell Excel to adjust the column but keep the row reference the same, or to adjust the row but keep the column reference the same. In an *absolute reference,* you tell Excel use a certain cell no matter what.

To change a reference from relative to absolute, type a dollar sign ($) before the part you want to make absolute. Press F4 to cycle through the various reference combinations until you get the one you want. Here are some examples:

$A1 Refers always to row A, column will vary.

A$1 Refers always to column 1, row will vary.

A1 Refers always to cell A1.

Figure 12-2 shows an example of an absolute reference. In this worksheet, you always want to refer to cell B1, which contains the commission percentage. You don't want to adjust this reference if you move or copy formulas that refer to it. The formulas in Column C use an absolute reference:

```
B4*$B$1
B5*$B$1
B6*$B$1
```

and so on down the column.

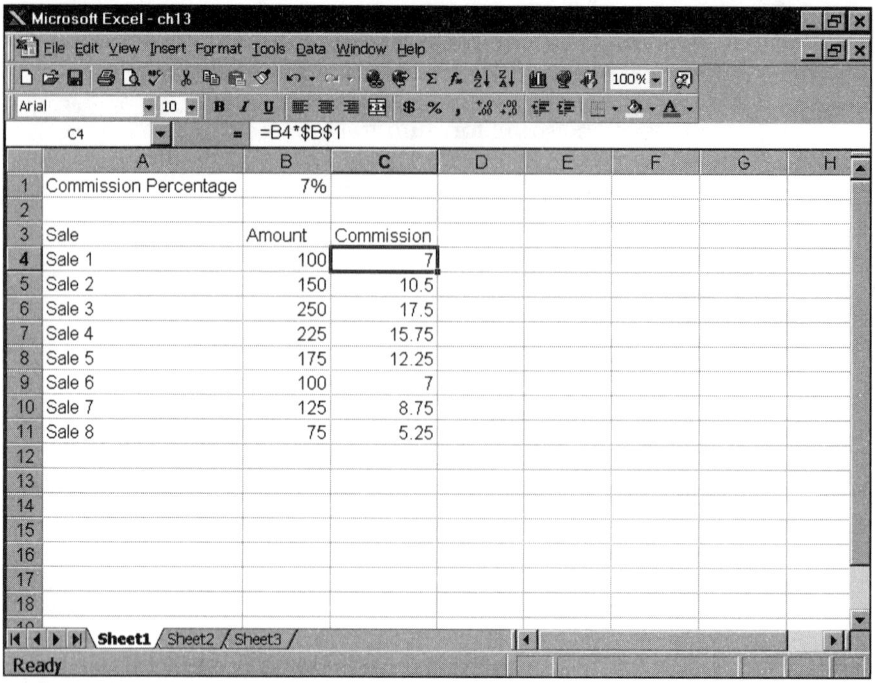

Figure 12-2 Use an absolute reference when you want to freeze the cell reference.

1 + 1 Is 2

Now that you understand the basics of formula, you can use them in your worksheets. To create a formula, you just put together the various pieces — the equal sign, the cell references, and the operators — in the order you want.

Follow these steps:

1. Select the cell that will contain the formula.

2. Type an = sign.

3. Point to the first cell you want to include in the formula. Excel displays a moving marquee as you move to the selected cell, and the cell reference appears in the active cell and in the formula bar (see Figure 12-3). You can also type the cell reference.

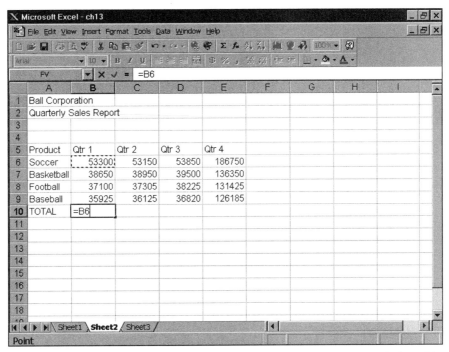

Figure 12-3 You build a formula by pointing to the cells you want to include and by typing the operator(s) you want to use.

4. Type an operator. Excel moves back to the cell that contains the formula.

5. Point to the next cell you want.

6. Continue typing operators and selecting cells until the formula is complete.

7. When the formula is complete, press Enter. You see the actual formula in the formula bar. The cell displays the results of the formula (see Figure 12-4).

TIP Rather than build a long string of addition formulas, use the SUM function, covered later in this chapter.

Excel won't make a mistake in calculating the formula, but it's possible *you* might make a mistake. If you refer to the wrong cell, enter the wrong operator, or type the wrong value, the formula may not be accurate in your estimation. It's a good idea to audit (check the accuracy of) your worksheet and check that you've set up the formulas correctly. See the bonus section for help on auditing a worksheet.

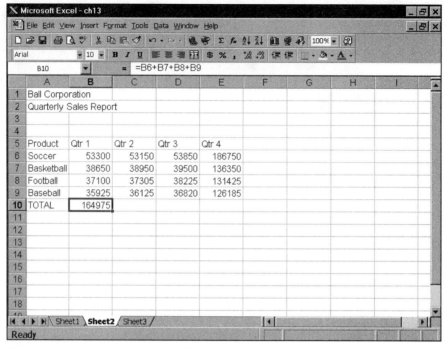

Figure 12-4 You see the results of the formula in the cell and the actual formula in the formula bar.

If you get an error message when you press Enter, review the message, click the OK button, and then make the suggested change. If you don't know what to do, try pressing F1 to get help.

No-Hassle Formulas

With Excel, you don't have to be a mathematician to create and use complex formulas. Instead, you can use a predefined formula, called a *function*. Functions are a shorthand way for entering complex formulas. For example, one of the simplest functions, SUM, condenses a longer formula into a shorthand version. Rather than have this formula:

    =A1+A2+A3+A4+A5

You can use this function:

    =SUM(A1:A5)

Functions also enable you to perform complex calculations, such as figuring a loan amount or determining your rate of return on an investment. This section explains how to use functions.

Using AutoSum

Guess what's the most popular calculation of all? If you guessed summation (or addition or totaling), you're right. That makes SUM the king of all functions. Because totaling numbers is so common, Excel includes an AutoSum button that automatically creates a SUM function, using a best guess for the range you want to sum. Here's how Excel figures which range to use. First, Excel looks up and suggests the range above the selected cell, if those cells contain values. If the cells above the formula cell do not contain values, Excel looks to the left and suggests the range to the left of the selected cell. If no cells above or to the left of the selected cell contain values, Excel enters =SUM(). You can then select the range you want to sum.

Follow these steps to use AutoSum:

1. Select the cell that you want to contain the sum formula.

2. Click $\boxed{\Sigma}$. Excel guesses which cells you want to sum and surrounds them with a marquee (see Figure 12-5).

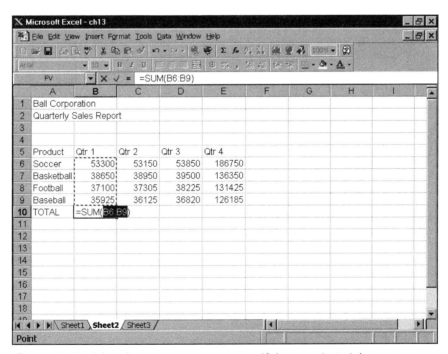

Figure 12-5 Select the range you want to sum if the guess isn't right.

3. Check that the correct range is selected. If it is not, select the range you want to sum.

4. Press Enter. Excel enters the function into the cell. In the cell, you see the results of the function. When the cell is selected, you see the actual function in the formula bar (see Figure 12-6).

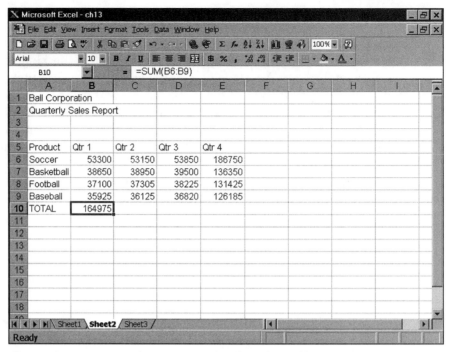

Figure 12-6   Use AutoSum to create a sum formula quickly.

Using AutoCalculate

Sometimes you want to see a quick total or average or count. If so, you can use AutoCalculate. Select the range you want to calculate. By default, Excel displays the sum in the status bar.

You can change the function that is used by right-clicking the AutoCalculate area and then selecting the function you want.

Decoding a Function

The AutoSum function is simple to use; you don't even really have to know how it is constructed. But Excel includes lots and lots of other useful functions, and to use these, you do need an idea of how to create the function.

Here's a sample function:

```
=AVERAGE(A1:A4)
```

This function averages the contents of the range A1:A4. Take a look at how it is constructed. Like a formula, the function starts with an equal sign. The next part is the function name, usually a short, abbreviated word that indicates what the function does. (Or in this case, the entire name!) After the function name, you see a set of parentheses. Inside the parentheses, you see the *arguments* — the values used in the calculation. Different functions require different arguments.

Before you get into a tizzy about all this formatting, just take a deep breath. Excel includes a function wizard that displays all the functions so that you can pick the one you want. The wizard also includes blanks for each of the arguments as well as a description so that you know what you have to enter and what you don't. The next section tells you how to use this handy tool to build a function.

Using the Function Wizard

To build a function more easily, you can use Excel's Function Wizard. This wizard leads you step by step through the process of entering the different parts of a function. *Follow these steps:*

1. Select the cell you want to contain the function.

2. Select **Insert** → **Function** or click **fx**. You see the Paste Function dialog box, which lists the most recently used functions. Other categories are listed in the Function category list (see Figure 12-7).

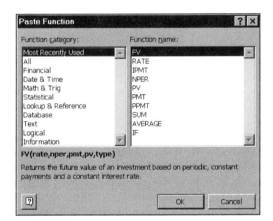

Figure 12-7 Select the function you want to use.

3. In the Function category list, click the function category you want. The Function name list shows the functions in that category.

 TIP **To see a description of what a function does, simply click it in the dialog box and then review the short description at the bottom of the dialog box.**

4. In the Function name list, click the function you want.

5. Click the OK button. Excel displays the Formula Palette below the formula bar. This palette that shows the arguments for the function (see Figure 12-8). Basically, arguments can be a single value, a single cell reference, a series of cell references or values, or a range. Some arguments are

mandatory; these appear in boldface in the palette. Others are optional; these are not in boldface. Excel also tries to guess the appropriate values for some functions. If it does, it selects the best guess and includes the reference in the palette.

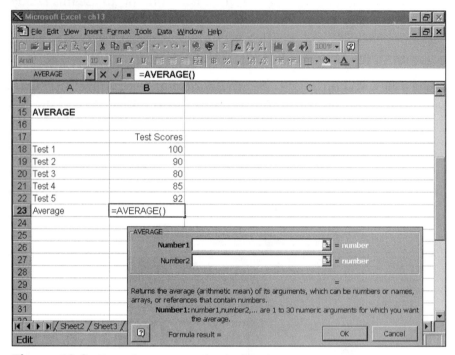

Figure 12-8 Enter the arguments for the function.

TIP If you can't see the worksheet area where you're inserting the function, drag the palette to another part of the screen.

6. Enter values for each of the arguments. You can click a cell in the worksheet or drag across a range. You can also type the cell reference, range, or value directly in the argument text box.

7. Press Enter or click the OK button. Excel creates the function (see Figure 12-9).

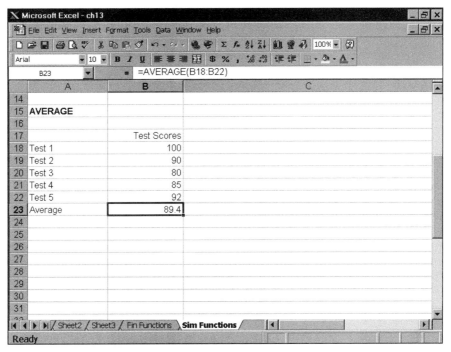

Figure 12-9 The results of the function are displayed in the cell.

If you know the appropriate format for the function, you can type it directly into the worksheet cell — just as if you were creating a formula.

These Are a Few of My Favorite Functions

Excel provides many, many functions that you can use to perform complex calculations. This reference lists the commonly used functions (or at least the ones I like the best). Keep in mind that there are lookup functions, reference functions, math and trig functions, information functions, statistical functions, engineering functions, and database functions. Let this list just get you familiar with the functions. Then use the online help to get information about the many other available functions included with Excel.

Statistical Functions

`=AVERAGE(`*number 1*`,`*number 2*`...)`

Average the numbers in parentheses. The numbers can be specific values, cells, or a range.

```
=COUNT(value 1,value 2...)
```

Count the values in parentheses. The values can be specific values, cells, or a range. Excel will count only values (numbers, dates, and times). It will not count text entries.

```
=MAX(value 1,value 2...)
```

Return the largest value in a range.

```
=MIN(value 1,value 2...)
```

Return the lowest value in a range.

Figure 12-10 shows examples of MAX and MIN functions.

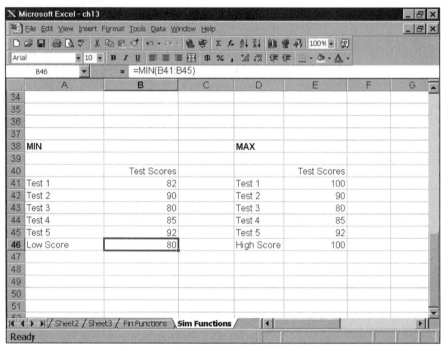

Figure 12-10 Use MAX and MIN to find the highest and lowest values, respectively.

```
=ROUND(number,num_digits)
```

Round a number to the number of digits that you specify.

Financial Functions

You can use financial functions to figure loan amounts, interest rates, savings results, and so on. Most financial functions use the same set of arguments, as listed in Table 12-2.

TABLE 12-2 Financial Functions

Argument	Description
rate	Interest rate. You have to match the rate to the term (nper). So if you are calculating a monthly rate and you have an annual interest rate of 10, you'll enter ".1/12."
nper	Number of periods. A five-year car loan has 60 monthly payments.
per	Period of interest. For instance, you'd enter "12" to get information on the 12th period.
pv	Present value. This is the amount of the loan or the amount of money you want to invest.
fv	Future value. This is the cash balance you want to attain. For some functions, this argument is optional. When you leave it out, Excel assumes 0, which is usually what you want.
type	When payments are made. This argument is optional. Use 1 for payments you make at the beginning of the period. Use 0 if you make payments at the end of the period. If you leave out this argument, Excel assumes 0 (payments at the end of the period), which is usually what you want.

Figure 12-11 shows some of the financial functions. The line below the function shows the function as it was inserted to get the results shown.

```
=PMT(rate,nper,pv,fv,type)
```

Figure the payment on a loan. The result is a negative number because it is cash you are paying out.

```
=PV(rate,nper,pmt,fv,type)
```

Start with the amount of money you can afford to pay monthly and then figure backward to tell you how much you can afford to borrow. Again, the result is a negative number because it is outgoing money. Be sure to divide the interest rate by 12.

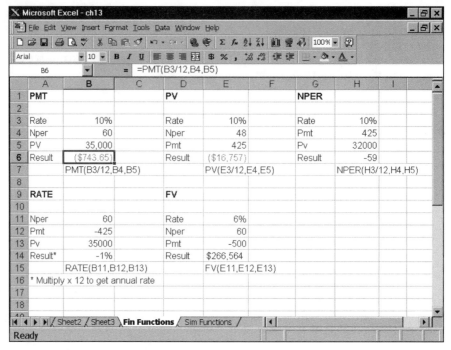

Figure 12-11 Use financial functions to calculate loan amounts.

```
=NPER(rate,pmt,pv,fv,type)
```

Tell how many payments you need to make on a loan.

```
=RATE(nper,pmt,pv,fv,type,guess)
```

Calculate the rate you are paying on a loan. Note that you must enter the payment as a negative number (cash going out). And the result is the monthly interest rate. Multiply by 12 to get the annual rate.

```
=FV(rate,nper,pmt,pv,type)
```

Calculate the future value of an investment. For example, if you save $500 a month for five years at an interest rate of 6 percent, how much will you have saved? Enter the money you are saving as a negative number.

Other Functions

```
=NOW()
```

Enter the current date and time in the worksheet cell. Note that this function requires no arguments; you just enter the two parentheses.

```
=IF(logical_text,value_if_true,value_if_false)
```

Do a logical test on two values and then display one value if the test is true, another if the test is false. If you want to display a message, enter the text within quotation marks. If you want to perform formulas for the true and false results, just type the formulas.

```
=NA()
```

Enters #NA in a cell so that it is clear which cells should contain values but do not at a given point.

The Quick Way to Enter Formulas

If you read the section on referencing, it should have clicked in your head that you don't have to create each formula in a worksheet. If you want to use the same formula, you can copy or fill it. For instance, take a look at the worksheet in Figure 12-1. Row 10 includes a sum function, but the same one would work for all the columns in that row. You can create the four formulas in this worksheet individually, or you can create it once and then copy it. Filling is the same as copying, so you can use either method.

To copy a formula, follow these steps:

1. Select the cell that contains the formula you want to copy.

2. Select **Edit** → **Copy** or click ⬚.

3. Select the cell or range where you want to copy the formula.

4. Select **Edit** → **Paste** , click ⬚, or simply press Enter. The formula is copied, and the references are adjusted accordingly.

X-REF **For more complete information on copying, see the next chapter.**

To fill a formula, follow these steps:

1. Select the cell that contains the formula you want to fill.

2. Drag the fill handle across the range you want to fill. The formulas are filled — that is, copied — to this range.

BONUS

Auditing the Worksheet

As mentioned, Excel won't make a mistake in its calculations, but you might. You might enter a wrong value or point to a wrong cell or type the formula incorrectly. To be sure your worksheet is accurate, you should audit it. Excel includes several tools for auditing or checking a worksheet. You can view the formulas or use the Auditing commands to trace formulas.

Displaying Formulas

To check your formulas, you can have Excel display the actual formulas rather than the results in the cells. Then you can go through and verify that you've created the formulas correctly. *Follow these steps:*

1. Select `Tools` → `Options`.

2. Click the View tab. You see the View tab of the Options dialog box.

3. Check the Formulas check box.

4. Click the OK button. Excel displays the formulas in the worksheet.

To return to the regular view, follow the same steps, but uncheck the Formulas check box.

Tracing Formulas

Excel also provides some commands for auditing a worksheet. To use these features, you should be familiar with the terms *precedents* and *dependents*. *Precedents* are cells that are referred to by a formula in another cell. To trace precedents, you start with a cell that contains a formula and then trace all cells referenced in that formula. *Dependents* are cells that contain formulas that refer to other cells. To trace dependents, select a cell that is referenced in a formula and then trace the formula that references it.

Follow these steps to trace formulas:

1. Select the cell you want to trace.

2. Select `Tools` → `Auditing`.

3. From the submenu, select what you want to trace: `Trace Precedents`, `Trace Dependents`, or `Trace Error`. You see the results.

To remove the errors, use the Remove All Arrows command under Tools → Auditing.

EDITING YOUR WORKSHEET

13

Things change. Prices go up or down. Interest rates rise and fall. Your income increases (hopefully). The entries in your Excel worksheet will also change. Maybe you entered a value incorrectly. You can change it. Maybe you forgot a budget category (ice cream!). You can add it. Maybe you included an expense category that isn't valid anymore. You can delete it. This chapter covers all the editing changes you can make to the entries in your worksheet.

Presto Change-O

Allowing you to change the values in your worksheet is what makes Excel such a valuable analysis tool. You can change a key value and see how it affects the bottom line. What if I take that vacation to Cancun? How will that affect my budget? What if I get that 10 percent raise? How does that affect my income? What if I win the lottery? What can I buy? You can edit your entries to correct them or just to see how a change affects the formulas in the worksheet.

Allowing you to change the values in your worksheet is what makes Excel such a valuable analysis tool.

To make a change, follow these steps:

1. Select the cell you want to edit.

2. Double-click the mouse button. The insertion point appears within the current cell. The buttons in the formula bar also become active (see Figure 13-1).

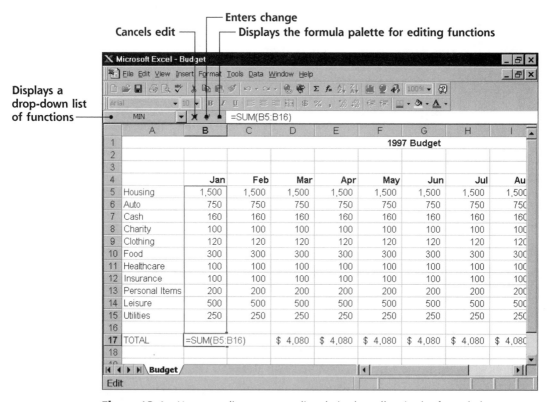

Figure 13-1   You can edit your entry directly in the cell or in the formula bar.

3. Make any changes to the entry. You can use the arrow keys to move around within the entry.

4. Press Enter or click the checkmark. Excel updates the entry.

If you are editing a function, you can click the equal sign (=) to display
the formula palette. You can use this palette to create or edit the
function. You can also click the down arrow next to the Cancel button
to display a drop-down list of functions. See Chapter 12 for more
information on creating functions.

Don't Want You No More

As you review your worksheet, you may need to delete some entries.
Maybe they are no longer valid. Or perhaps you entered several values
incorrectly and want to clear them and start again. You can delete the
contents of a cell. If the cell is referenced in a formula, that formula is updated.

TIP To delete the cells themselves, see the section "Take It Out!" later in this
chapter.

To delete data, follow these steps:

1. Select the cell or range you want to delete.

2. Press Delete.

If you delete a selected cell or range by accident, immediately select the
Edit → Undo command or click the Undo button.

Remodeling Your Worksheet

Even the best laid plans need adjustments. You may have spent a lot of
time thinking about how the data would be laid out in the worksheet. But
now something just isn't right. Those data would work better over here. Or
that column needs to come first. If you'd used the old paper method of tracking
numbers, you'd have to wear out an eraser to make any rearrangements. With
Excel, you can easily rearrange your data using the Cut and Paste commands.

And when you think of Cut and Paste, also think of Copy and Paste. You can
use Copy to copy data you want to use again in the worksheet. For instance, you
can copy formulas (as covered in Chapter 12). Or you may want to copy a list of
names or other entries. This section tells you how to move and copy using the
commands and then how to move and copy by dragging and dropping.

Moving Data

Moving data to a new spot in the worksheet is just as easy as pie. Excel also takes care of all the references when you move cells that are referenced in a formula. All relative references are adjusted to reflect the new location. All absolute references remain the same.

To move data using commands, follow these steps:

1. Select the cell or range you want to move.

2. Select **Edit** → **Cut** or click ✂. Excel displays a moving marquee around the selected cells (see Figure 13-2). You are prompted to select a destination.

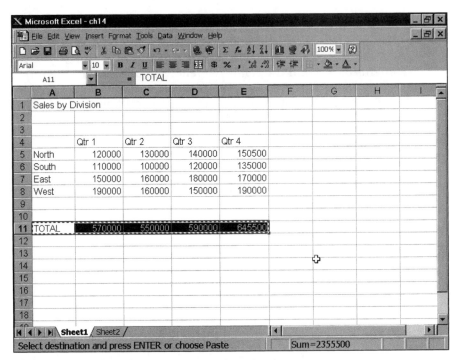

Figure 13-2   Select where you want to move the data.

3. Select the cell at the upper-left corner of where you want the pasted cells. Keep in mind that Excel will overwrite any cells in the destination area. (One way not to overwrite cells is to select a blank area or to insert the cells) Be sure to select a blank area or an area that you want to overwrite.

4. Press Enter, select **Edit** → **Paste**, or click 📋. The selected cell or range is moved to the new location (see Figure 13-3).

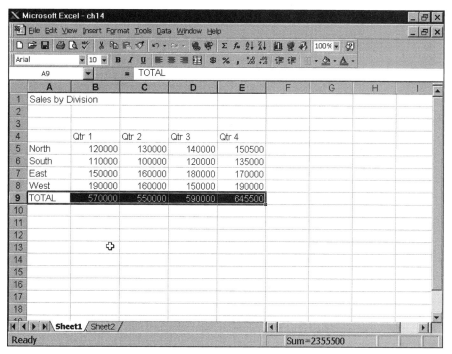

Figure 13-3   The data are moved to its new location.

TIP   You can also use these keyboard shortcuts: Ctrl+X for cut, Ctrl+C for copy, and Ctrl+V for paste.

Copying with Commands

Copying is a great shortcut when you are entering data. Rather than type anything twice, copy it if you can. Copying works much like moving data. If you copy formulas, all the relative references are adjusted. All absolute references stay the same. (See Chapter 12 if you don't know the difference between these references.)

When you copy, you can copy a cell to another cell or a cell to an entire range. You can also copy a range to another range. The original range and the copied range must be the same size.

Follow these steps to copy data:

1. Select the cell or range you want to copy.

2. Select ░Edit░ → ░Copy░ or click 🖻. Excel displays a marquee around the selected cell or range.

3. If you selected a range, select the cell at the upper-left corner of where you want the pasted cells. If you selected a single cell and want to paste it to a range, select the range. Figure 13-4 shows the original cell (B9) about to be copied to a range (C9:E9).

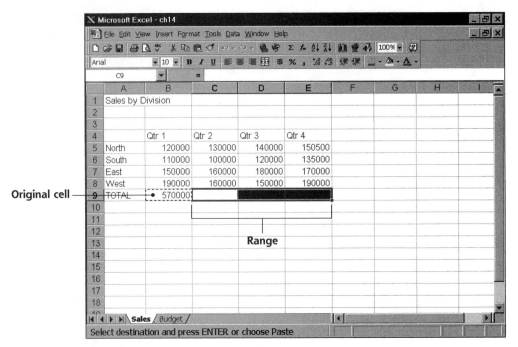

Original cell — 9 TOTAL • 570000

Range

Figure 13-4 You can copy a single cell to a range.

4. Press Enter, select **Edit** → **Paste**, or click ⬛. Excel pastes the copy or copies (see Figure 13-5).

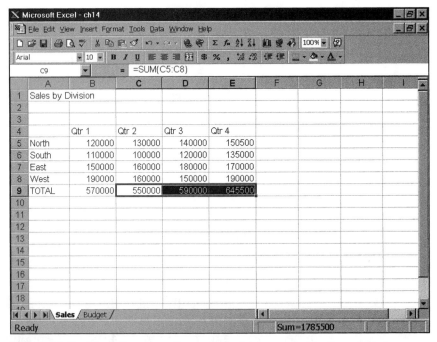

Figure 13-5 The cell contents (here a formula) are copied to the selected range.

CAUTION If you select a range to copy and then select a different size range for the paste, you get an error message that says the copy and paste areas are different shapes. Click the OK button. Either select a range the same size and shape or just select the upper-left corner for the pasted range.

Drag-and-Drop Moving or Copying

If you want to move or copy a selected range a short distance, you can use the drag-and-drop method. This method takes some practice — you have to get the mouse pointer in just the right spot. If you put it in the wrong spot, you may deselect the range or fill the range. Still once you get the hang of it, you can drag and drop rather than use the commands to copy or move.

Follow these steps to drag and drop a selected range:

1. Select the cell or range you want moved or copied.

2. Move the mouse pointer over the selection's border. The mouse pointer should change to an arrow.

3. To move, drag the border. To copy, hold down the Ctrl key and drag the border. As you drag, you see an outline of the selected data (see Figure 13-6).

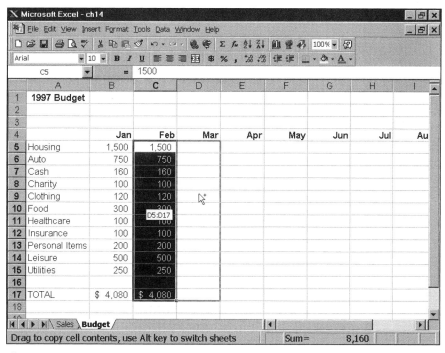

Figure 13-6 You can drag data to a new location.

4. When the selection is in the spot you want, release the mouse button.

New Sheets, New Names

When you start Excel, you don't have just one worksheet available, you have three sheets of worksheet paper. For simple worksheets, you may just use the first sheet. For more complex worksheets, you may want to use several sheets. For instance, you can enter sales for quarter 1 on one sheet, for quarter 2 on another sheet, and so on. Chapter 11 covered how to move to another worksheet. Here you learn how to add additional worksheets, use more descriptive names, and delete worksheets.

Inserting a Sheet

A new workbook starts off with three sheets. *If you need more sheets, you can add them by following these steps:*

1. Select the worksheet . The new worksheet will be inserted before this worksheet.

2. Select **Insert** → **Worksheet** . Excel inserts a new sheet.

 TIP You can also use the shortcut menu. Point to a sheet tab and click the right mouse button. Click the command you want.

Naming a Sheet

The default names, Sheet1, Sheet2, and so on, aren't very descriptive. If you use several sheets in a workbook, you should rename them so that you know what each sheet contains. *To rename a sheet, follow these steps:*

1. Double-click the sheet tab you want to rename. The sheet name is highlighted (see Figure 13-7).

Figure 13-7 Type a name for the worksheet.

2. Type a new name. You can include spaces in the name.

3. Press Enter. Excel renames the sheet.

 Don't confuse worksheet names with workbook names or filenames. They aren't the same. You still need to name and save the workbook, as described in Chapter 3.

Deleting a Sheet

If you don't want extra sheets in your workbook, you can delete them. Keep in mind that Excel will delete not only the sheet but all the data on that sheet. Be sure that you don't delete information you need. Also keep in mind that you can't undo a worksheet deletion.

Follow these steps to delete a sheet:

1. Select the sheet you want to delete.

2. Select Edit → Delete Sheet . You are prompted to confirm the deletion.

3. Click the OK button. The worksheet and all its data are deleted.

You can also rearrange the sheet tabs in a different order. To do so, click the tab you want to move and then drag it to the new location.

Move Over and Make Room

f you'd used pencil and paper to create a worksheet and forgotten something, you'd have to do a lot of erasing to make room. With Excel, though, you can easily insert cells, rows, and columns if you leave something out or need to add something later.

SIDE TRIP

SCROLLING THROUGH THE WORKSHEETS

When you have just three sheets, you can see all the tabs, so selecting the one you want is easy. When you have several sheets, you may be able to see only the first few sheet tabs. To display the other ones, use the sheet scroll tabs at the bottom-left corner of the worksheet.

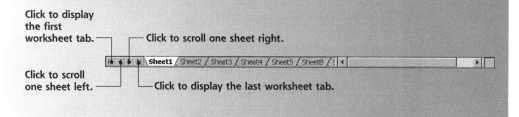

Click to display the first worksheet tab.

Click to scroll one sheet right.

Click to scroll one sheet left.

Click to display the last worksheet tab.

Inserting Cells

You can plunk down a new cell or cells right in the middle of the existing ones if needed. *Follow these steps:*

1. Select the cell where you want to insert a new cell. If you want to insert several cells, select the number of cells you want to add.

2. Select Insert → Cells . You see the Insert dialog box (see Figure 13-8).

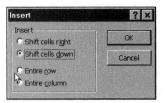

Figure 13-8   Select how to shift the existing data.

3. Select how you want to shift the existing data: Shift cells right or Shift cells down.

4. Click the OK button. Excel inserts the cell(s) and moves existing data to make room.

Inserting a New Row

When I create a worksheet, it seems that I always leave out one row of information. I need a new, empty row right in the middle. *If you too find yourself needing a new row, you can add one by following these steps:*

1. Click within the row that you want to follow the new row. The new row will be added above the current one. If you want to insert several rows, select the number of rows you want to insert.

2. Select Insert → Rows . Excel inserts the row(s) and moves existing rows down.

Inserting a New Column

Just as you can insert a row, you can easily insert a column and move existing columns over. *Follow these steps:*

1. Select the column that you want to follow the new column, which will be inserted to the left of this column. If you want to insert several columns, select the number of columns you want to insert.

2. Select Insert → Columns . Excel inserts the column(s) and moves existing columns over.

Take It Out!

J ust as you can add cells, rows, and columns, you can also delete them. This is similar to pulling out a plank of wood. All the surrounding rows and columns move up or over to fill in the gap left by the empty row or column. One difference is that when you delete cells, rows, or columns, all data in that row or column are deleted. Be sure to check the row or column before you delete it.

CAUTION If you delete a cell, row, or column that is referenced in a formula, you see the error message #REF in the formula cell. You need to edit the formula to take care of the missing reference.

Removing Cells

You've already learned how to delete cell contents, but what if you want to yank the cells out of the worksheet? For instance, say that you have entered data in the middle of a worksheet and then decide you don't want those data. You don't want to delete just the contents, because that will leave a hole in the middle of the worksheet. You want to delete both the contents and the cells so that existing data move up to fill in the blank cells. *To do so, follow these steps:*

1. Select the cell or range you want to delete.

2. Select █ Edit █ → █ Delete █. You see the Delete dialog box (see Figure 13-9).

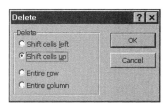

Figure 13-9 Select how to shift the remaining cells.

3. Click Shift cells up or Shift cells left to tell Excel how to shift existing data.

4. Click the OK button. Excel deletes the cells and the contents and moves existing data.

Taking Out a Column

If you include a column in your worksheet that you no longer need, you can delete it. When you delete the column, remember that you delete all the data in that column. Be sure there's nothing in the column you need to keep.

To delete a column, follow these steps:

1. Select the column or columns you want to delete. You can select a column by clicking the column letter.

2. Select <kbd>Edit</kbd> → <kbd>Delete</kbd>. Excel deletes the column.

Pulling Out a Row

Deleting a row is similar. *Follow these steps:*

1. Select the row (or rows) you want to delete by clicking the row number.

2. Select <kbd>Edit</kbd> → <kbd>Delete</kbd>. Excel deletes the row and all its data, and moves existing rows up.

Checking Your Spelling

The last chapter covered how to check your formulas. But what about the text entries? Nothing messes up an otherwise perfect worksheet more than a glaring typo or misspelling. To avoid these embarrassing mistakes, check your spelling.

The spell-check works by comparing the words in the worksheet (all values, hidden cells, text boxes, and buttons) to the words in its dictionary. It flags any words it cannot find. That a word is flagged doesn't necessarily mean it is misspelled. It just means Excel can't find the word in its dictionary. You can correct or ignore the flagged word.

 You still need to proofread your text. The spell-check only knows weather (whether) the word is spelled correctly, not weather (whether) you have used it correctly!

To check the spelling in your worksheet, follow these steps:

1. Select a single cell to check the entire worksheet.

2. Select <kbd>Tools</kbd> → <kbd>Spelling</kbd> or click . The speller stops on any words it cannot find in its dictionary (see Figure 13-10).

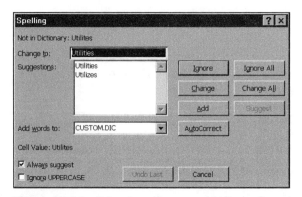

Figure 13-10   Select how to correct this flagged word.

3. For each of the flagged words, do one of the following:

If the word is misspelled and you see the correct spelling in the Suggestions list, click the word. Then click Change to change just this occurrence. Click Change All to change all occurrences.

If the word is misspelled but the correct spelling is not listed, type the correct spelling in the Change to text box. Then click Change to change just this occurrence. Click Change All to change all occurrences.

If the word is spelled correctly, click Ignore to ignore this word and continue. Click Ignore All to ignore this word throughout the document.

If the word is spelled correctly and you don't want it to be flagged again, add it to the dictionary by clicking Add.

If the word is one you often misspell and you want Excel to correct your misspelling with the correct spelling automatically, click AutoCorrect.

4. If you started in the middle of the worksheet, you are prompted to start checking at the beginning. Click Yes. When you see a message saying the spell-check is complete, click the OK button.

BONUS

13

Making Your Worksheet Easier for Others to Use

Many times you won't be the only person using a worksheet. Perhaps you create a worksheet that others use as well. Or maybe someone at your workplace gives you the worksheets you need to use. In either case, you can do some things to make a worksheet easier to use.

As one thing, you can use names to make formulas easier to understand. Compare this formula:

```
=SUM(A1:A5) - SUM(B1:B5))
```

To this one:

```
INCOME - EXPENSES
```

The second formula — which uses range names — is easier to figure out. This section tells you how to create and use names.

As another thing, you can add comments to cells. These comments might explain the assumptions for the formula, include a reminder of what values you need, or just describe the setup of the formula or worksheet. This section also explains how to add comments.

Naming Cells and Ranges

As you know, Excel uses *range names* to refer to ranges. Rather than use the references (A1:A10), you can use a range name. Range names are easier to include in formulas, and it's much easier to remember a name such as QTR1 than the cell address that refers to that range. Once you create a name, you can use it in formulas, as covered here.

CREATING A NAME

You can name a single cell or a selected range in the worksheet.

Follow these steps to create a name:

1. Select the cell or range you want to name.

2. Select **Insert** → **Name** → **Define**. You see the Define Name dialog box. Excel displays the range coordinates and suggests a name (see Figure 13-11).

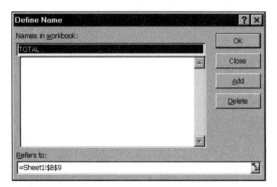

Figure 13-11 Type a name for the range.

4. Type the range name. Begin the range name with a letter or an underscore. You can include upper and lowercase, and you can include up to 255 characters. Don't use a range name that looks like a cell reference, and don't include spaces.

5. Click the OK button. Excel names the range. When the range is selected, it appears in the Name box in the formula bar.

TIP If you want to name a range and use the column or row headings as the names, use the Insert → Name → Create command. Use the Office Assistant to get help on using this command.

USING A NAME IN A FORMULA

After you name the range, you can easily insert the name in a formula. To do so, simply type the range name where you want to use it in the formula. If you can't remember the range name, you can paste it in the formula using the Insert → Name → Paste command. From the dialog box that appears, select the name to paste and then click the OK button.

GOING QUICKLY TO A NAMED RANGE

To go to a named range, follow these steps:

1. Click the down arrow next to the Name box in the formula bar. You see a list of names.

2. Click the one you want to go to.

Adding Comments

Another way to remind others or yourself how a worksheet is set up is to add comments. You can attach a comment to any cell in the worksheet, as covered in this section.

CREATING AND DISPLAYING COMMENTS

To add a comment to a cell, follow these steps:

1. Select the cell you want to contain the comment.

2. Select **Insert** → **Comment**. You see a comment box with your name.

3. Type the comment.

4. When you are finished, click back in the worksheet. Excel attaches the comment and displays a small red triangle in the upper-right corner of the cell.

You can tell which cells have notes because of the little red indicators. To display a comment, simply put the pointer on an indicator; the comment box pops up (see Figure 13-12).

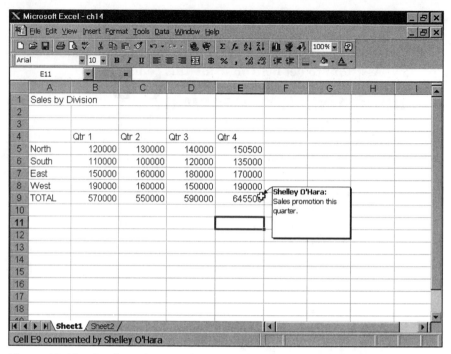

Figure 13-12 Put the pointer on the note indicator to display the note.

EDITING AND DELETING COMMENTS

When you see the comment, you may want to make changes or even get rid of the comment. You can't do so by simply displaying it.

You must follow these steps:

1. Select the cell that contains the comment.

2. Select ⟦ **Insert** ⟧ → ⟦ **Edit Comment** ⟧. The comment box is displayed with the insertion point inside it so that you can make changes.

3. To edit the comment, make the changes and click back in the worksheet.

   To delete the comment, click the border of the comment box and press Delete.

FORMATTING YOUR DATA

LEARN THESE KEY SKILLS:

I f you think all you need to do is enter the data for your message to be clear to your audience, think again. Compare the two worksheets shown in Figure 14-1. In the worksheet on the top, it's unclear what the data represent. In the worksheet on the bottom, the message or purpose of the worksheet is clear. The numbers as well as what they represent are easy to figure out.

To create a professional-looking worksheet, you need to spend some time working with the appearance of the data. You can change the number format, align titles, change the column width, add borders, and more. This chapter covers some of the formatting changes you can make to a worksheet's data.

X-REF   For information on formatting worksheet pages, see the next chapter.

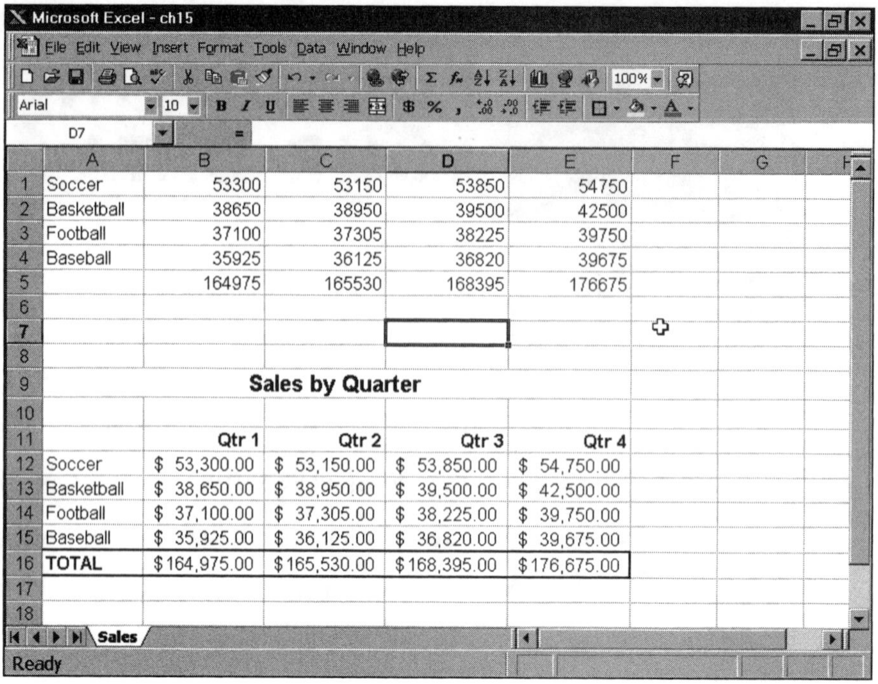

Figure 14-1 Spend some time formatting your worksheet to make the purpose of the worksheet easy to understand.

Looky Here!

Most of the time you want your reader to notice certain things about a worksheet. For instance, you may want to make the worksheet title stand out. Likewise, the row and column headings should be easy to spot. You may want to emphasis totals. You can call attention to certain entries in the worksheet in many ways. Here are some ideas:

* You can make entries bold, italic, or underline.
* You can use a different font or font size. (For more information on fonts, see Chapter 7 in the Word part.)
* You can change the color of entries.
* You can apply a fill or background color to entries.

The fastest way to make any of these changes is to use the toolbar buttons. Use this method when you want to make a change and you know the change you want to make — that is, you don't need to see a preview. You can also use the Font tab of the Format Cells dialog box. Use this method when you want to make several changes at once and when you want to preview the changes before applying them.

Fast Formatting Using the Toolbar

Excel conveniently provides buttons for the most common formatting changes. To make a change, select the range you want to format and then do any of the following:

* Click **B** to make entries bold.
* Click *I* to make entries italic.
* Click U̲ to underline entries.
* Click the down arrow next to Times New Roman ▾. From the list of available fonts, click the one you want.
* Click the down arrow next to 10 ▾ and then click the size you want.

TIP **To undo the change, click the Undo button.**

* To use a different color for entries, click the down arrow next to A ▾ and select the color you want.
* To use a color for the background of the cell, click the down arrow next to ◇ ▾ and then click the color you want.

Figure 14-2 shows some different types of changes you can make. Note that the gridlines have been turned off in this figure so that you can see underlines. To turn off gridlines, select Tools → Options and then click the View tab. Uncheck the Gridlines check box and then click OK.

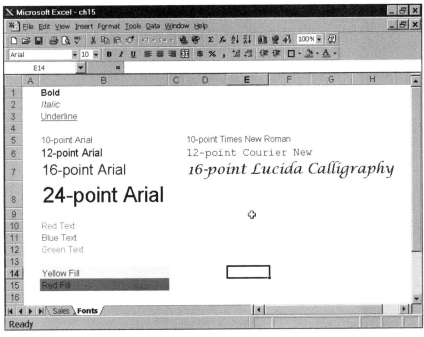

Figure 14-2   You can change the font, style, size, and color of entries.

More Options with the Font Tab

The toolbar is quick but not so quick if you have to select five or six fonts until you find one you want. If you aren't sure which font you want to use, you may want to use the Font tab in the Format Cells dialog box. This dialog box shows a sample, plus you can make several changes at once. Also, some options are available only from the dialog box.

To change the look of entries using the Font tab, follow these steps:

1. Select the text you want to change.

2. Select Format → Cells .

3. If necessary, click the Font tab to display the Font options.

4. In the Font list, click the font you want. Notice that you see a sample of the text in this font in the Preview area.

5. In the Font style list, click the style you want.

6. In the Size list, click the font size you want.

7. To change the font color, select the color you want from the Color drop-down list.

8. To underline text, display the Underline drop-down list and select the style of underline that you want.

9. To use any special effects, check the effect you want: Strikethrough, Superscript, or Subscript.

10. Click the OK button. Excel makes the change.

SIDE TRIP

CHANGING THE DEFAULT FONT

By default, Excel uses the Arial 10-point font for all worksheet entries. If you find yourself changing to a different font over and over again, you can change the default font used for new worksheets. This change won't affect any worksheets you've created previously. Only new worksheets will use this new font.

To change the default font, follow these steps:

1. Select Tools → Options .

2. Click the General tab.

3. Display the Standard font drop-down list and select the font you want.

4. Display the Size list and select the default font size you want.

5. Click the OK button.

Snapping to Attention

Because numbers are aligned to the right and text to the left, your worksheet may look a little off kilter. You can tidy things up by aligning the column heads, data entries, and worksheet titles. You can select left, right, or center. You can also use a handy Merge and Center button for worksheet titles. Read on to find out how to get your entries to snap to attention.

Left, Center, Right

The three most common alignments are available as toolbar buttons. *To make a change, follow these steps:*

1. Select the cell or range you want to change.

2. To center the range, click 🔲.

   To align the range with the right edge of the cell, click 🔲.

   To align the range with the left edge of the cell, click 🔲.

Figure 14-3 shows examples of each of the different alignments.

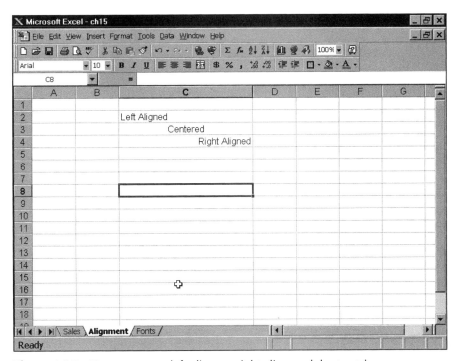

Figure 14-3   You can center, left-align, or right-align worksheet entries.

FEATURE FOCUS New with Excel 97 are the Indent buttons. You can use these to indent entries within a cell. To indent an entry, click ⊞. To unindent an entry, click ⊞.

Centering Across Columns

Most worksheets include a title, and the best place for that title is centered above the worksheet values. You can try to eyeball the title and place it somewhere in the center, but it won't align exactly. Instead, center the entry across the columns. When you do this, Excel creates one cell that spans several columns. *Follow these steps:*

1. Select the range that contains the heading and the range that you want to center across.

2. Click ⊞. The cells are merged, and the title is centered, as shown in Figure 14-4.

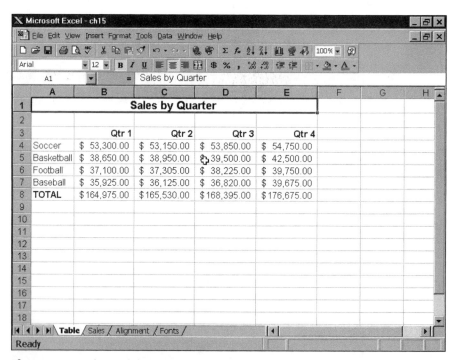

Figure 14-4 The worksheet title has been centered.

Wrapping Text and Other Cool Effects

Excel includes some other neat effects that you can only access from the Format Cells dialog box. *To try some of these other alignments, follow these steps:*

1. Select **Format** → **Cells**.

2. Click the Alignment tab. You see the Alignment tab of the Format Cells dialog box.

3. To change the horizontal alignment, display the <u>H</u>orizontal drop-down list and select the alignment you want. These options are the same as the alignment toolbar buttons.

4. To change how the cells align top to bottom, display the <u>V</u>ertical drop-down list and select an alignment: Top, Center, Bottom, or Justify.

5. To indent text, select the indent amount in the <u>I</u>ndent text box. (This option is available only when you select left alignment.)

6. To rotate text, drag the rotate bar in the Orientation area or enter the number of degrees you want to rotate.

7. Check any text control options you want to use. <u>M</u>erge cells combines the cells. <u>W</u>rap text wraps a long text entry within the cell. Shrin<u>k</u> to fit shrinks the text size so that it fits within the cell.

8. Click the OK button. Figure 14-5 shows examples of these effects.

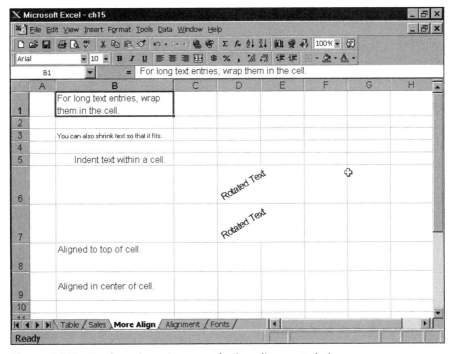

Figure 14-5 Get fancy by trying some further alignment choices.

Dollar ign and Other Formats

Numbers can mean different things depending on how they are formatted. For instance, compare 9000 to $9,000. It's clear what the second 9,000 represents. Compare .1 to 10%. Again, the meaning of the second number is clear. When you enter a number in Excel, it's displayed in the General format, which doesn't include commas, dollar signs, or any other formatting. It's just a plain old number. You can select a number format that is more appropriate. The fastest way is to use the toolbar buttons, but to see additional options, try the Number Format tab of the Format Cells dialog box. Both methods are covered here.

Click for Styles

If you want to use currency, comma, or percent formatting, you can use the buttons on the formatting toolbar. *Follow these steps:*

1. Select the cell or range you want to change.

2. For currency, click $\boxed{\$}$.

   For percents, click $\boxed{\%}$.

   For commas, click $\boxed{,}$.

3. Click $\boxed{}$ to show more decimal places. Click $\boxed{}$ to show fewer decimal places.

Excel applies the appropriate number format. Figure 14-6 shows examples of each of these number styles.

TIP   Try these keyboard shortcuts:

Ctrl+Shift+!	**Comma style**
Ctrl+Shift+$	**Currency style**
Ctrl+Shift+%	**Percent style**

More Control: The Number Tab

The three most common number styles are available on the toolbar, but Excel provides many additional number formats to select from. Not only does this command give you access to many other styles, it also enables you to preview the style before you make the change. *To use the Number tab to select a number format, follow these steps:*

1. Select the cell or range you want to change.

2. Select $\boxed{\textbf{Format}} \rightarrow \boxed{\textbf{Cells}}$.

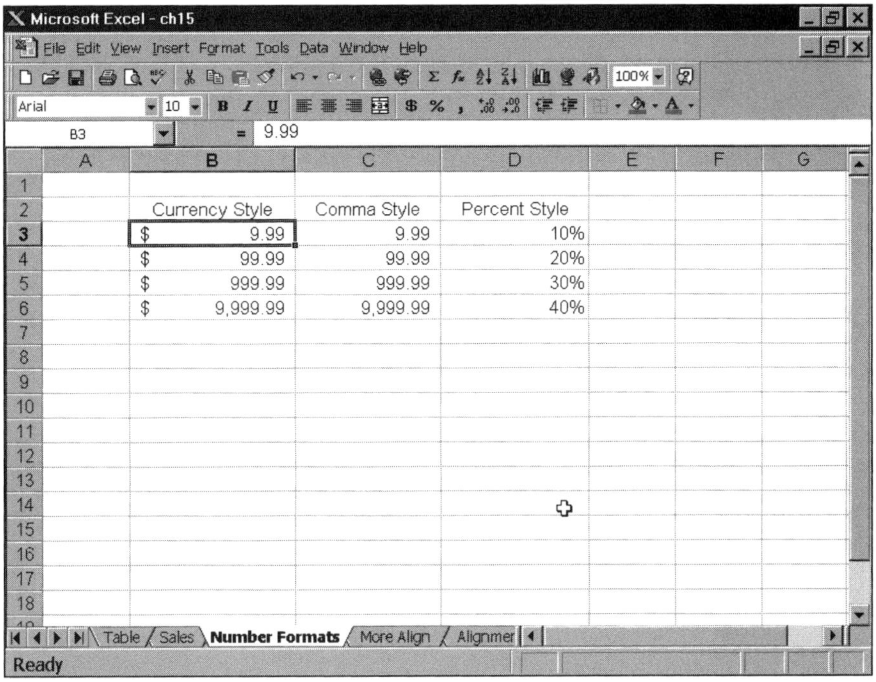

Figure 14-6 Use the toolbar buttons for currency, percent, or comma styles.

3. Click the Number tab. You see the Number tab of the Format Cells dialog box.

4. In the Category list, click the category you want. The right side of the dialog box displays the options for this category. For instance, for currency, you can select the number of decimal places, the symbol, and how negative numbers are displayed.

5. Make any changes to the options for this number style.

6. Click the OK button. Excel makes the change.

Fatter! No, Skinnier!

In a new worksheet, all the columns are the same size. But it's unlikely all your entries will be the same size. Some columns may contain just a few characters. Some may contain several. Some entries may spill over to the next cell or be chopped off. (If the next column contains an entry, Excel truncates the display of the long entry. The cell still contains the entire entry; you can see only the first part of it.) You may see something weird in a cell such as "1E+08" or "####." (When you enter a number that is too big to fit in a cell, Excel will apply the scientific number style — that's when you'll see "1E+08." When you make a column too small to display a number, you see the number signs.) In all these instances, you can make a change by changing the column width. Excel provides some quick methods to make this change.

The easiest way to change the column width is to drag the border. Using this method, you can visually see the changes. When the column is as wide as you want, you can quit dragging. *Follow these steps:*

1. Point to the right column heading border. The pointer will change to a thick line with arrows on either side of it. This indicates the pointer is in the right spot.

2. Clicking and holding down the mouse button, drag to a new width. As you drag, you see an outline of the column border. A measurement of the width also appears in the reference area of the formula bar.

3. When the column is the width you want, release the mouse button.

You can also have Excel adjust the column width to fit the largest entry in that column. To do so, double-click the right column border, next to the column letter. Or select the F_ormat → _Column → _AutoFit Selection command.

Finally, you can enter an exact value for the column width by selecting F_ormat → _Column → _Width command. Type the value you want (the number of characters that will fit) and click OK.

Notice Me! Notice Me!

If you want to highlight certain sections of your worksheet, you can add a border or a pattern. For example, you may want to add a border under your row headings to make them stand out. Or you may want to double-underline your totals. If you set up a database in Excel, you may want to shade every other row to help separate the rows. You can apply a border with the toolbar or with a command. You can apply a pattern with a command.

If you want to highlight certain sections of your worksheet, you can add a border or a pattern.

Adding a Border

Want to add a border to data? Outline key data? Underline totals? Add a line above and below the data? You can select all of these border placements and more using the toolbar or the Border tab of the Format Cells dialog box.

ADDING A BORDER USING THE TOOLBAR

If you want to use one of the most common border styles and placements, use the toolbar. *Follow these steps:*

1. Select the range to which you want to add a border.

2. Click the down arrow next to . You see a palette of different border placements (see Figure 14-7).

Figure 14-7 Select the border style and placement you want.

3. Click the button that represents the border style and placement you want. Excel applies the border.

To remove a border, select the range again. Click the Border button and then click the None option. (It's the first button.)

ADDING A BORDER USING THE BORDER TAB

If the Border button doesn't include the line style you want, you can use the Border tab of the Format Cells dialog box. This method gives you access to several different line styles and placements. You can use the dialog box to change the color of the line as well.

To add a border using the Border tab, follow these steps:

1. Select the cell or range you want to change.

2. Select **Format** → **Cells** .

3. Click the Border tab. You see the Border tab of the Format Cells dialog box (see Figure 14-8).

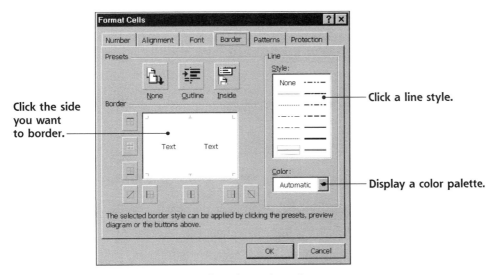

Figure 14-8 Use this tab to select where to place the border, the line style, and the color.

4. To use a different line style, click the one you want in the Style list.

5. To use a different color, click the down arrow next to the Color list. Then click the color you want.

6. In the Border area, click where you want to place this border.

7. Follow steps 4–6 for each border you want to add. You can use a different line style for each border.

8. Click the OK button. Excel applies the border.

Shading a Range

Shading a range with a color or pattern is another good way to add emphasis. *You can select the pattern and color you want by following these steps:*

1. Select the cell or range you want to change.

2. Select Format → Cells .

3. Click the Patterns tab. You see the Patterns tab of the Format Cells dialog box (see Figure 14-9).

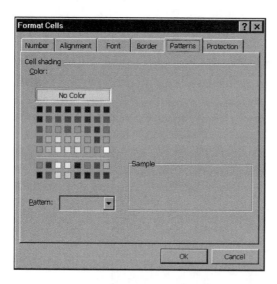

Figure 14-9 Select the color and pattern you want to use.

4. To add a color, click the color you want in the Color area.

5. To add a pattern, display the Pattern drop-down list and select the pattern you want. If you want to use a different color for the pattern, display this list again and then click the color to use for the pattern. You see a preview of your selected pattern.

6. Click the OK button. Excel applies the pattern.

Don't Touch These Data!

You may have noticed that so far this chapter has covered all of the tabs in the Format Cells dialog box except the Protection tab. Well, you can check off Protection because it's covered here.

You can use this tab to protect your data from change. For example, you might set up the skeleton of a worksheet and then have someone else do the data entry. You can lock the cells that shouldn't be changed — for instance, those that contain formulas — and unlock the cells that you want data entered into.

Protecting data is a two-step process: locking and unlocking the cells and then turning on protection. By default, all cells are locked, but the option has no effect unless worksheet protection is on. Once you turn on worksheet protection, all locked cells cannot be changed or deleted.

Because all cells are locked by default, you have to unlock the ones you want to be able to change. Then you turn on protection. *Follow these steps:*

1. Select the cells that you want to unlock. These are the cells you *do* want to be available for change or deletion.

2. Select   **Format** → **Cells** .

3. Click the Protection tab. You see the Protection tab of the Format Cells dialog box.

4. Uncheck the Locked check box and click OK.

5. Select   **Tools** → **Protection** → **Protect Sheet** . You see the Protect Sheet dialog box (see Figure 14-10).

Figure 14-10   This dialog box turns on worksheet protection.

6. If you want to assign a password to this sheet, type it and click the OK button. When prompted to confirm the password, retype it and click the OK button.

7. Select what you want protected: Contents (the data), Objects (any pictures, charts, drawings), Scenarios (a feature for forecasting different results from a worksheet model).

8. Click the OK button. Excel protects all the locked cells in the worksheet. If you try to change a locked cell, you see an error message.

To turn off worksheet protection, select Tools → Protection → Unprotect Sheet. If you assigned a password, type the password to turn off the protection. You can now modify any locked cells.

BONUS

Formatting Shortcuts

Excel provides many time-saving formatting features. For example, if you get a range formatted just right and then want to use the same formatting on another range, you can copy the formatting. You can also use a set of predefined formats called AutoFormats. These shortcuts are covered here.

Note that you can also set up styles, similar to Word styles. For more information on Excel styles, consult the Office Assistant help feature.

Copying Formatting

Copying formatting is a quick way to save time and effort. Suppose that you've selected a range, added a border, changed the alignment, and used a different number format. You've got the range just how you want it. In fact, you like it so well that you want to format another range using the same formats. To save time, copy the formatting. *Follow these steps:*

1. Select the cells that contain the formatting you want to copy.

2. Click . The mouse pointer displays a little paintbrush next to the cross.

3. Select the cells that you want to copy the formatting to. The formatting is applied to the selected range.

TIP   If you want to clear all formatting from a cell or range, select it and then use the Edit → Clear → Formats command.

Using AutoFormat

As another option, you can let Excel apply a set of formatting options — borders, font styles, colors, and such — for you. *To do so, follow these steps:*

1. Put the pointer within the data that you want to format. Excel will select and format all surrounding data.

2. Select **Format** → **AutoFormat**. You see the AutoFormat dialog box (see Figure 14-11).

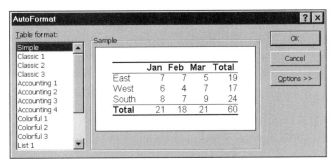

Figure 14-11   Select an AutoFormat from this dialog box.

3. In the Table format list, select the format you want. You can get an idea of the formats by checking out the sample table in the dialog box.

4. Click the OK button. Excel formats your data.

FORMATTING YOUR WORKSHEET PAGES

LEARN THESE KEY SKILLS:

I n the previous chapter you learned how to make the insides or content of your worksheet look good. But that's just part of creating a good-looking worksheet. You also have to think about how the worksheet looks on the page. Is it all crammed in the upper corner of the page? If so, you may need to adjust the margins. Is the worksheet wider than long? If so, you may want to print sideways on the page. Is the worksheet more than one page? If so, you may want to use headers and footers as well as continue the column or row headings on the following pages. This chapter covers how to make these changes and more so that when you print your worksheet it is picture perfect.

More White Space!

H ow does your worksheet flow on the page? A good way to get an idea is to preview the entire page using File → Print Preview. Using this view, you can check the overall page layout. For example, the worksheet in

Figure 15-1 looks crammed at the top of the page. To fix this problem, you can adjust the margins to better place it on the page.

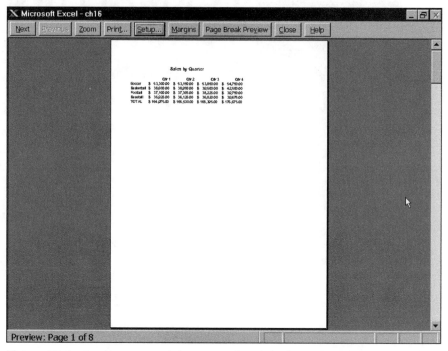

Figure 15-1   Preview your worksheet to see how it looks on the page.

By default, Excel creates 1-inch top and bottom margins and .75-inch left and right margins. Headers and footers have .5-inch margins. You can change these settings using an exact method (dialog box) or a visual method (print preview).

Using Print Preview to Change the Margins

If you are previewing the document, you can visually drag the margin guidelines and set them as you want. This method is easiest because you can see how the changes affect the overall page. *Follow these steps:*

1. If you are not already previewing the document, do so by selecting File → Print Preview or clicking ⊡. You see a preview of the worksheet (refer to Figure 15-1).

2. Click the Margins button. You see dotted margin guidelines for each margin (see Figure 15-2).

3. Click and drag the margin guideline you want to change. Do this for each margin (top, bottom, left, right, header, footer) that you want to change.

4. Click the Close button to return to the worksheet.

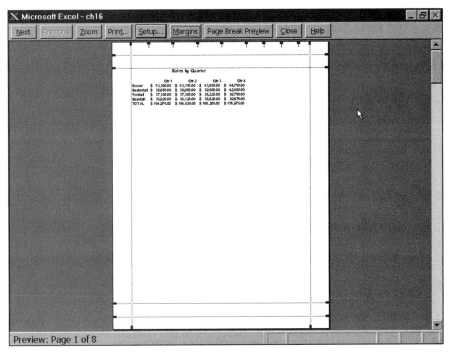

Figure 15-2   Use these guidelines to change the page margins.

TIP   You can also display the preview and margin guidelines by clicking the Print Previe_w_ button in the Margins tab of the Page Setup dialog box.

Using the Margins Tab to Change Margins

If you have a precise measurement in mind, you can use the Margins tab. You can see a sample preview, but it doesn't show your data. *Follow these steps to change the margins using this method:*

1. Select `File` → `Page Setup`.

TIP   You can display the Page Setup dialog box from Print Preview by clicking the _S_etup button.

2. Click the Margins tab. You see the Margins tab of the of the Page Setup dialog box (see Figure 15-3).

3. Click in the margin text box you want to change: _T_op, _B_ottom, _L_eft, _R_ight, He_a_der, or _F_ooter.

4. Type the new value or use the spin buttons to enter the value.

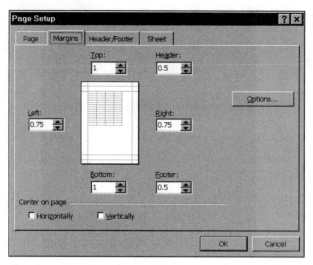

Figure 15-3 Enter the margins you want.

 TIP If you can't get your printout to look right on the page, try centering it. Check the Horizontally check box to center the page horizontally. Check the Vertically check box to center the page vertically.

5. Click the OK button. Excel makes the changes.

Pages Every Which Way

Getting a big worksheet to fit on the page can involve some work. You don't want to have one page full of data and then another sheet that shows just one lonely column. Or another ugly option is a few rows printed on about 15 sheets of paper. Both of these printouts scream for a makeover.

When you have more columns than rows, one way to make the printout look better is to change the orientation to landscape.

When you have more columns than rows, one way to make the printout look better is to change the orientation to landscape. This orientation prints sideways across the paper so that you can fit more columns on the page.

Another option is to have Excel scale a worksheet so that it all fits on one page. You can make the adjustment percentages yourself or just have Excel scrunch it on the page for you. You can find these and other page options on the Page tab.

Follow these steps to make a change:

1. Select File → Page Setup.

2. Click the Page tab to display these options (see Figure 15-4).

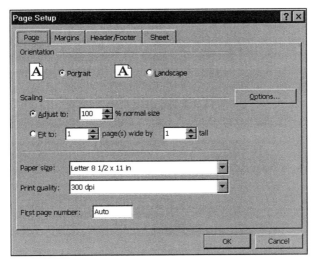

Figure 15-4 Use this tab to set page options such as the orientation.

3. Select an orientation: Por̲trait or L̲andscape.

4. If you want to scale the page, click the A̲djust to option and enter a percentage to scale. Or click the F̲it to page option and enter the dimensions of the pages (1 by 1, for instance).

5. If you want to change the paper size, display the Paper si̲ze drop-down list and then select the size you want.

6. If you want to change the print quality, display the Print q̲uality drop-down list and select the quality you want.

7. If you want to start numbering pages with a different number, enter the number you want to use in the Fi̲rst page number text box.

8. Click the OK button. Excel updates the page.

Three Sheets to the Wind

Sheet options control what prints — gridlines, notes, row headings, and so on. For your worksheet, you may want to make some changes. For example, you may want to turn on gridlines so that each cell border prints on the page. If you are printing and checking a worksheet, you may want to print the row and column headings (the row numbers and column letters) so that you can easily check formulas. When I teach a training class, for instance, I always print the gridlines and row and column headings for the handouts so that the students can easily find and follow the references to certain cells.

If you have a worksheet that is several pages long and the rows or columns continue onto the next page, you should consider printing the row and column headings (not the letters and numbers, but your row and column headings) on the other pages. For instance, suppose that your two-page sales worksheet lists the sales rep name in the first column, and the rest of the columns print the monthly sales amount, six months per page. The first page is fine, but you won't be able to figure out which sales rep goes with which month on the second page. To fix this problem, repeat rows (or columns) on the other pages, using the Sheet tab.

Follow these steps to set up the sheet:

1. Select File → Page Setup .

2. Click the Sheet tab. You see the Sheet tab of the Page Setup dialog box (see Figure 15-5).

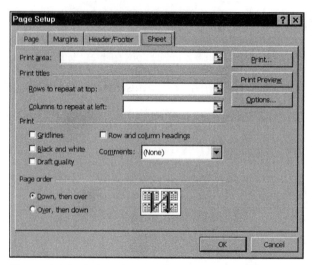

Figure 15-5 Select sheet options from this tab.

3. If you want to print just a range, enter the range in the Print area text box. (If the worksheet is not longer than one page, this option is not available.)

4. To print titles, click in the Rows to repeat at top and/or the Columns to repeat at left text boxes. Then click the worksheet row or column you want to repeat. Excel enters a row or column reference — for instance, $A:$A indicates column A will be repeated.

5. Check which elements to print: Gridlines, Black and white, Draft quality, Row and column headings, and Comments.

6. Click a page order: <u>D</u>own, then over or O<u>v</u>er, then down.

7. Click the OK button.

Perfect from Top to Bottom

You should include a title on your worksheet to identify the contents. In addition, you may want to print certain information — the worksheet name, date, author, page number, or what have you — on each page. This information helps your audience identify and keep worksheets in order. For instance, you can include your name and title Financial Wizard so that everyone knows that this is *your* worksheet.

You can print information at the top of each page (in the header) or at the bottom of each page (in the footer). You can select from some of Excel's prefab headers and footers or create your own. All of this and more is covered right here in this very section.

Letting Excel Pick the Header or Footer

Excel lists some predefined headers and footers that combine different information. Check these before you go to the trouble of creating your own custom header. You can select to print the page number, the worksheet title, your name, the filename, "Confidential," or any combination of these options.

To use one of Excel's suggested headers or footers, follow these steps:

1. Select `File` → `Page Setup`.

2. Click the Header/Footer tab. You see the Header/Footer tab of the Page Setup dialog box.

3. To use a suggested header, click the down arrow next to the He<u>a</u>der list box and then click the one you want to use (see Figure 15-6).

4. To use a suggested footer, click the down arrow next to the <u>F</u>ooter list box, under the Header/Footer tab of the Page Setup dialog box, and then click the one you want. These are similar to the ones shown in Figure 15-6. You see a preview of the header and footer in the text boxes in the dialog box.

5. Click the OK button. In the Normal view of the worksheet, the headers and footers aren't displayed. To see them, preview the worksheet.

TIP If you don't want to use a header or footer, display the Header/Footer tab, click the down arrow next to the He<u>a</u>der drop-down list or <u>F</u>ooter drop-down list, and then click None.

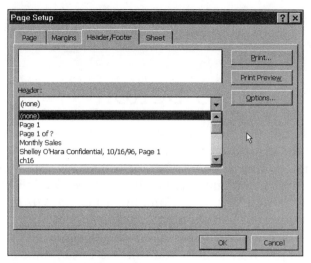

Figure 15-6   Select the header you want to use.

Typing Your Own Header or Footer

If none of Excel's suggested headers or footers are to your liking, you can create your own. You can type any text you want to include. You can also use handy buttons to insert the page number, date, time, worksheet name, or filename.

To create a custom header or footer, follow these steps:

1. Select File → Page Setup .

2. Click the Header/Footer tab. You see the Header/Footer tab of the Page Setup dialog box.

3. Click the Custom Header button to create a custom header or the Custom Footer button to create a custom footer. Figure 15-7 shows the Header dialog box. The Footer dialog box looks the same only the name is different, and the text you enter will be inserted at the bottom of the page.

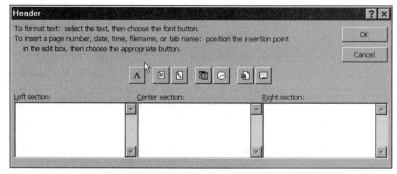

Figure 15-7   Enter the text for your header or footer in each of the three sections.

4. Notice that you can enter text in three different sections of the header or footer: the <u>L</u>eft section, <u>C</u>enter section, and <u>R</u>ight section. Click in the section you want.

5. Enter the text you want. You can also use the buttons to insert special information:

Button	Use To...
A	Change the font
#	Insert the page number
	Insert number of pages
	Insert the date
	Insert the time
	Insert the file name
	Insert the worksheet name

6. Click the OK button twice. Excel creates the header or footer. To see how the header or footer looks on the page, preview the worksheet.

What's Printed? Where?

In a single-page worksheet, you don't have to worry about setting the print area or checking the page breaks. Everything prints on one page. Simple. If the worksheet is more than one page, you may need to tinker with these options. You will want to check the page breaks to be sure they don't leave data hanging somewhere in limbo. You may also want to print just part of the worksheet. In that case, you can set the print area. This section tells you how to make both of these checks or changes.

Checking and Setting Page Breaks

Excel will enter page breaks automatically according to the page setup options you have selected (margins, scaling, and so on). It's a good idea to check where these page breaks will fall.

To check page breaks, follow these steps:

1. Select `View` → `Page Break Preview`. You see the worksheet broken into pages. You can check the page order as well as the breaks from this view. Each page break is indicated with a dotted line. You can adjust the page breaks by clicking and dragging these lines.

2. If the dialog box telling you about setting page breaks appears, close it by clicking the OK button.

3. If you want to make a change to any of the breaks, click and drag to set a new page break.

4. To return to Normal view, select `View` → `Normal`.

Dragging a page break is the easiest way to change it because you can see exactly how the pages are divided. *You can also insert a page break within the worksheet by following these steps:*

1. Select the cell where you want to insert the page break. The page break will be inserted above the selected cell.

2. Select `Insert` → `Page Break`. On screen you see a dotted line indicating the page break.

    To remove a page break, select the cell immediately below the page break. Then select the `Insert` → `Remove Page Break` command.

Setting the Print Area

In a large worksheet, you may want to print just part of the worksheet. If so, you can set the print area and include just the range you want to print. *Follow these steps:*

1. Select the range you want to use as the print area.

2. Select `File` → `Print Area` → `Set Print Area`.

    To clear a set print area, use the `File` → `Print Area` → `Clear Print Area` command.

BONUS

Using a Spreadsheet Template

Setting up a worksheet — all the data, formulas, and formatting — can be time-consuming. You may wish you had some worksheets already created that you could just fill in. Well, you do. Excel includes a couple of spreadsheet templates that you can use to create a specific kind of worksheet. For instance, Excel includes an expense statement, an invoice, and a purchase order. You can also get information about custom spreadsheet design from Village Software. You can get information on this company by selecting this template.

To try one of these spreadsheets, follow these steps:

1. Select **File** → **New** . You see the New dialog box.

2. Click the Spreadsheet Solutions tab. You see the available templates. You can preview the template by clicking the one you want. Figure 15-9 shows a preview of the Expense Statement.

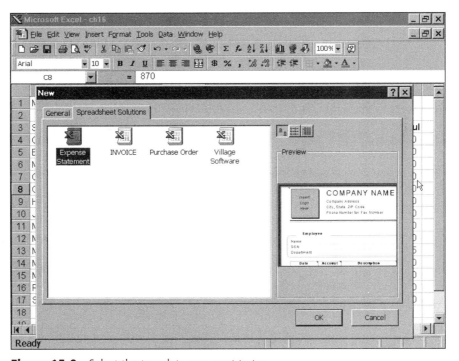

Figure 15-9 Select the template you want to try.

3. Select the template you want and click the OK button. Excel creates a new worksheet based on this template. You can then complete the template to create your own worksheet.

CREATING EXCEL CHARTS

LEARN THESE KEY SKILLS:

HOW TO PLAN A CHART   PAGE 262

HOW TO CREATE A CHART   PAGE 264

HOW TO EDIT A CHART   PAGE 267

HOW TO CHANGE CHART APPEARANCE PAGE 272

Y ou can look at a grid of numbers and figures and calculations until you go nutsy-cuckoo. You can flip it, turn it, calculate it, massage it, and so on and still miss the obvious. Sometimes you need to "see" the data, and the best way to see other meanings in data is to chart them. A chart can show you trends, relationships of one set of data compared to another (like one product versus another or one quarter versus another), individual volume compared to total sales, and so on.

Excel is more than just a calculation program; it also offers sophisticated charting tools. You can use these tools to create charts of all types, as covered in this chapter.

FEATURE FOCUS The process of creating a chart is somewhat similar to previous versions, but the steps have been simplified. You can also find some new chart types as well as handy features such as the ScreenTips that appear for each chart element.

Decisions, Decisions

Before you start wildly charting every little thing in your worksheet, you should understand a few concepts about charts. Most important, you should have a good idea of the different chart types. Doing so will help you select the one most suitable to your message. For example, if you want to show how sales increased from 1992 to this year, a pie chart isn't going to help. You'd end up with pie on your face, so to speak. If you want to show how your total sales break down by product, a line chart isn't the "right" chart. This section explains the different chart types as well as other decisions to think about before you start charting away. Think of this section as picking the "right" outfit for different occasions.

Selecting the "Right" Chart Type

When you create a chart, Excel selects a column chart by default. But you don't have to use this chart type. Excel has several chart types to choose from, and each chart has several subtypes or styles. You should try to match the message you want your data to convey to the best chart type. Which chart type is best? It depends. Table 16-1 explains each chart type so that you can have some ideas of what to try when you create your chart.

TABLE 16-1 Types of Charts

Example	Chart Type	Description
	COLUMN CHART	The default chart type. Use this chart when you want to compare items but emphasize change over time. The values are charted vertically. Subtypes include stacked, 3D, and 100% stacked charts.
	BAR CHART	Similar to the column chart, but the values are plotted horizontally rather than vertically. The horizontal plotting puts more emphasis on comparison, rather than time. Subtypes of this chart type include a stacked bar chart (values are stacked on each other), 3D, and 100% stacked (the percentage of each value is stacked).
	LINE CHART	Use this chart type when you want to show trends or emphasize change over time.
	PIE CHART	Use this chart type when you want to show the relationship of the individual values to the whole. You can chart only one data series in a pie chart.

Example	Chart Type	Description
	XY SCATTER CHART	Use this chart type to show the relationship of values in several chart data series. The chart shows clusters or uneven intervals in the data, a feature that is useful in charting scientific data.
	AREA CHART	Use this chart type when you want to show change in volume or magnitude over time. This chart type is similar to a line chart, but an area chart emphasizes the amount of change. The line chart emphasizes the rate of change.
	DOUGHNUT CHART	Similar to a pie chart, this chart shows the relationship of the parts to the whole, but in a doughnut chart, you can chart more than one data series.
	RADAR CHART	Use this chart when you want to show changes relative to a center point. This plotting shows which data series covers the most area.
	SURFACE CHART	Similar to a topographical map, this chart type is useful for finding relationships that may otherwise be difficult to see, such as the best combination between two sets of data.
	BUBBLE	A type of XY scatter chart. The difference is that the size of the data marker indicates the value.
	STOCK	Often called a high-low-close chart, it is used for charting stock prices or other scientific data.
	CYLINDER	Another style of a column or bar chart, but cylinders are used to plot the data series.
	CONE	Another style of a column or bar chart but cones are used for the data series.
	PYRAMID	Another style of a column or bar chart that uses a pyramid.

Deciding Where to Place the Chart

You may not know exactly what chart type you want until you start tinkering around, but the preceding table should give you a good idea of which chart types might be applicable. The next thing you should think about is where you want to place your chart. You can include a chart as a graphic object on the worksheet. Use this option when you want to show your data from the worksheet and the chart on the same page. You can also include a chart as a separate sheet in the workbook. Use this when you want to create a separate page for your chart.

Deciding What to Chart

You start a chart by selecting the data that you want to chart. This may seem simple enough, but keep a few points in mind:

* Excel will use the column and row headings as the axis titles and legend. (You can select which is which.)

* If your chart includes a total row, you most likely will not include this in the charted data. For example, if you are charting the sales of products over four quarters, you won't want to include the totals. Instead, just include the individual data series.

* In a pie chart, you can chart only one series — that means you can select only one set of data to chart.

Charting Your Course

I f you are starting to think that charting may be more trouble than it's worth, don't. Excel makes creating a chart simple with the Chart Wizard. This wizard leads you step by step through the process and shows you visually how your choices affect the chart. You can create a chart in four simple steps. (This is *much* easier than previous versions without the Chart Wizard, where you may have been tempted to simply color a chart rather than figure out how to set up a chart.)

Excel makes creating a chart simple with the Chart Wizard.

Follow these steps to create a chart:

1. Select the range that you want to chart. (See the preceding section on selecting data.)

2. Select `Insert` → `Chart` or click ▥. Excel displays the first step of the Chart Wizard. Here you select the chart type (see Figure 16-1). Notice that you can select the chart type and the style (or subtype).

3. In the Chart type column, select the type of chart you want to create. In the Chart sub-type list, Excel displays the available styles of this chart type.

TIP If you want to get help on the different chart types, click the Help button in the dialog box. You can also click the Press and hold to view sample button to see how your data will be charted using the selected chart type.

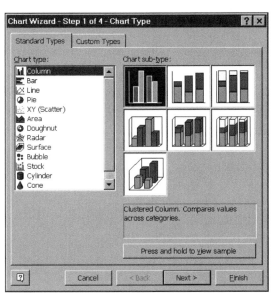

Figure 16-1 Select the chart type you want to use.

4. Select the chart subtype you want and click Next. You see Step 2 of the Chart Wizard. Here you can select how the data are charted and the series order (see Figure 16-2).

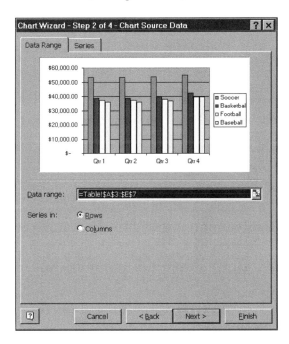

Figure 16-2 Select how the data are charted.

If you change your mind, click the Back button to go backward through the Chart Wizard steps and make changes.

5. On the Data Range tab, confirm the correct range is selected in the Data range text box. If not, drag across the correct range in the worksheet.

Also, select whether the rows or columns are the series. For example, in Figure 16-2, the rows are the series, which means each quarter is charted as a group. You could do the reverse — use the columns (here the products) as the series. Compare Figure 16-3 with Figure 16-2 to see the difference.

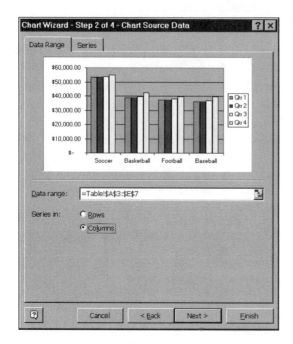

Figure 16-3 Compare this sample chart to the one in Figure 16-2. In this one, the columns are the data series.

6. If you selected the data correctly, you shouldn't have to make any changes to the series, so you can skip this step. Excel guesses pretty well what to use as the axis label, the series names, and the values. If you want to confirm or change any of these, click the Series tab and make any changes (see Figure 16-4). Click the Next button.

When you click the Next button, you see Step 3 of the Chart Wizard, shown in Figure 16-5. Again, the defaults will work for most charts. You can always start with the defaults and then make changes, as covered later in this chapter. Or you can click any of the tabs and make changes.

7. Make any changes to any of the chart options tabs and then click the Next button. You are prompted to select a location for the chart — on the worksheet or as a new sheet (see Figure 16-6).

8. Select where to place the chart and click the Finish button. If you selected the new sheet option, Excel creates the chart on a new, separate sheet in the workbook. If you selected to include the chart as an object in the worksheet, the chart is placed on the worksheet (see Figure 16-7). You may have to adjust the size and placement as covered later.

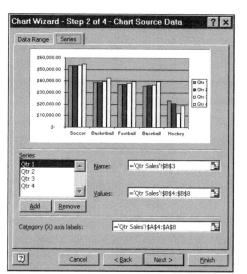

Figure 16-4 Change the axis labels, series names, values charted, or series order using this tab.

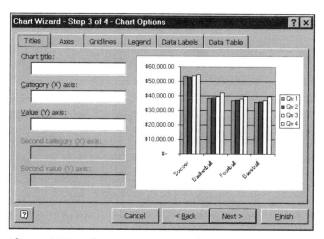

Figure 16-5 Change or enter any chart options for titles, axes, gridlines, legend, data labels, or the data table.

What If I...

Your first concern with the chart should be that the data are represented accurately and that the chart as a whole is OK. Then you can worry about the individual elements of the chart. First, if you placed the chart on the worksheet, is the chart the right size? In the right place? If not, you can move it around or resize it. Second, is the chart the right type? If not, you can select another chart type. Third, are the data right? You can make changes to the data — and poof! — the chart is updated. Finally, if you don't like what you got and want to start over, you can delete the chart.

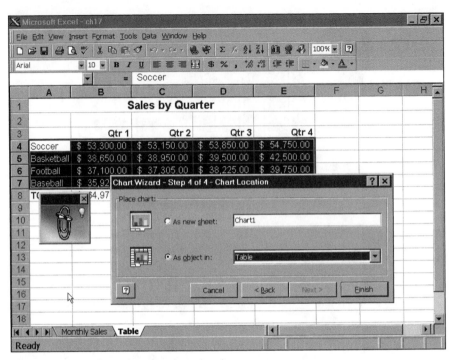

Figure 16-6 Select where to place the chart.

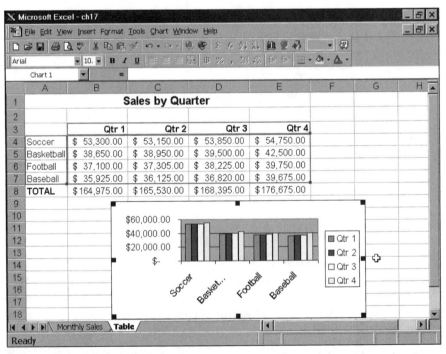

Figure 16-7 Excel creates the chart and places it on the worksheet (shown here) or as a new sheet.

Moving, Resizing, and Deleting the Chart

If you included the chart on the worksheet, Excel plunks down the chart right in the worksheet. Maybe right on top of your data. If that happens, you move it out of the way. Also, the chart may be too small. You can change the size. And if you messed up in a big way, you can just delete the chart and start over. (You can't resize or move a chart that is on a separate sheet. You can delete the chart by deleting the sheet.)

To make any changes to the chart, start by selecting it. To do so, click the chart object once. You should see black selection handles around the outside of the chart (see Figure 16-8). Now you can make any of the following changes:

✳ To move the chart, place the pointer on a chart border, but not on one of the selection handles. Drag the chart to the new location.

✳ To resize the chart, place the pointer on a selection handle and drag. Use the handles at the top and bottom to make the chart taller. Use the handles on the sides to make the chart wider. Use the handles in the corners to change both the height and width.

✳ To delete the chart, press the Delete key.

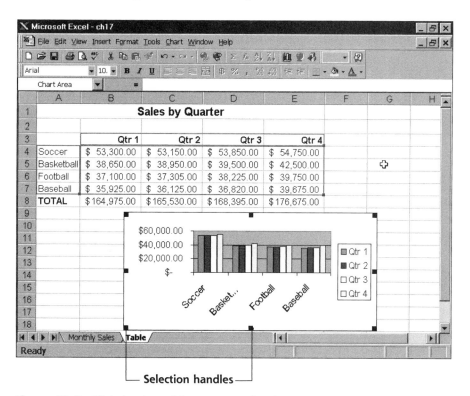

Selection handles

Figure 16-8 Click the chart object once to select it.

Be sure the selection handles are around the outside border of the chart — not within the chart area. You want to select the entire chart, not part of it.

Changing the Chart Type

Charting takes some trial and error. The more you work with charts, the easier it gets. When you see how your data turn out in a chart, you may think "that's not it." You may want to try another chart type. *Rather than recreate the chart, you can select a different chart type by following these steps:*

1. If the chart is on the worksheet, click the chart once to select the entire chart object. If the chart is on a separate sheet, click that sheet tab to display the chart.

2. Select `Chart` → `Chart Type`. You see the Chart Type dialog box, which is similar to Step 1 of the Chart Wizard.

3. Select the chart type and subtype and click OK.

Changing Charted Data

The connection between the chart and the data it represents is "live" — that is, if you make a change to the worksheet data, the chart is updated. If you delete data in the worksheet, the matching data series will be deleted in the chart. Pretty cool! You might want to make a change even if one isn't necessary to test this out. Hey, go ahead (see Figure 16-9).

Just as you can change the worksheet data to update the chart, you can also change the chart and update the worksheet data. *To make this type of change, follow these steps:*

1. If the chart is on the worksheet, click the chart once to select the entire chart object. If the chart is on a separate sheet, click that sheet tab to display the chart.

2. Click the data point you want to change. When a single data point is selected, black selection handles appear along the borders of the area. Also, the Name box displays the selected data point, and the formula bar displays the entire series references.

3. Drag the data point up or down. The corresponding worksheet data are updated to reflect the change.

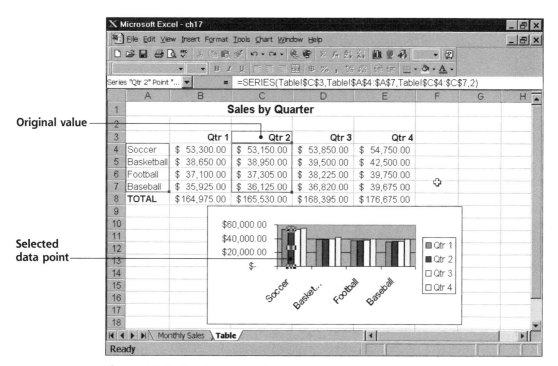

Original value

Selected
data point

Figure 16-9 Try changing a data point.

Adding Chart Data

If you insert a row or column into the worksheet, those data are not added to the chart automatically. *If you want to include the data on the chart, you can do so by following these steps:*

1. In the worksheet, select the data you want to add to the chart.

2. Drag the selection onto the chart. The series are updated to include the new data.

If the worksheet is on a separate page, you can use the <u>C</u>hart → <u>A</u>dd Data command to add the data to the worksheet. Select the command and then when prompted, select the range that contains the data you want to add.

Changing the Chart Location

Change your mind about where you want the worksheet? Then you can move it from the worksheet to a separate sheet or vice versa. *Just follow these steps:*

1. Select the chart.

2. Select <u>Chart</u> → <u>Location</u>. You see the Chart Location dialog box which is similar to Step 4 of the Chart Wizard (refer to Figure 16-6).

3. Select As new sheet to move the chart to a new sheet. Select As object in and then select which worksheet you want from the drop-down list to move the chart to a worksheet.

4. Click the OK button.

Chart Makeovers

Many different elements make up a chart — the data points, the collection of data points or series, the axes, the legend, and more. You can change each individual element of the chart. To start, you have to figure out what the element is called. Then you can make a change. This section describes generally how to make a change. As with a lot of Excel features, you can tinker with many, many different options to control how the chart looks. The best way is to experiment. You can also consult the Office Assistant for complete information on each command and option.

Knowing What's What on a Chart

One thing new with Excel 97 is that you can figure out the different parts of a chart by simply placing the pointer on the area you want. A pop-up name appears (see Figure 16-10). These names can help you get a handle on what's what in a chart. On most charts, you typically have the elements shown in Table 16-2. This table also explains the changes you can make to each element.

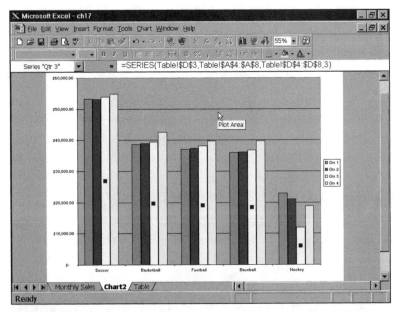

Figure 16-10 Use the pop-up names to figure out what each part of the chart is called.

TABLE 16-2 Chart Elements

Chart Element	Description
CHART AREA	The entire area the chart covers. You can change the pattern used for the chart area, add a border, or use a different font.
DATA SERIES	The individual series of data charted — for example, in Figure 16-9 all the Quarter 1 data. Each data series is represented with a certain color, identified in the legend. You can change the outline and color used for each series, which axis the data are plotted on, the labels used, the series order, and the overlap and gap width between each series or point.
PLOT AREA	The area where the data series are plotted or graphed. You can change the pattern and color used as well as the border of the plot area.
GRIDLINES	The lines displayed in the plot area. You can select a different line style, color, and weight. You can also select a different scale.
VALUE AXIS	The vertical or y-axis of the grid. You can change the pattern of the line, the format of the tick marks, the tick mark labels, the scale, the font, the number format, and the alignment of the axis labels.
CATEGORY AXIS	The horizontal or x-axis of the grid. As with the value axis, you can change the line, scale, font, number, and alignment.
LEGEND	The key to the chart, which shows by color plot what each series represents. You can change the outline and color of the legend as well as the font and placement. For example, you can move the legend to the top, bottom, corner, right, or left of the chart.

Making a Change to a Chart Element

To make a change or simply get an idea of what you can change, follow these steps:

1. Double-click the chart element you want to change. For example, double-click the data series you want to change. You see a dialog box with tabs for each set of options you can change. For example, Figure 16-11 shows the Format Data Series dialog box with the Patterns tab selected.

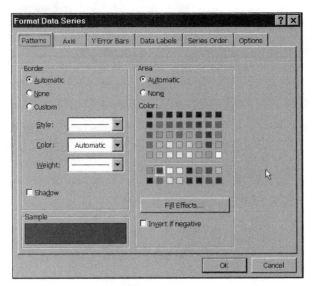

Figure 16-11 Make changes to any of the tabs in the chart dialog box.

2. Select the tab you want and make any changes. For example, if you did not like the color used for this particular series, you could select another color on the Patterns tab.

3. Click the OK button when you are finished making changes.

Changing Chart Options

You can also change the chart options that you selected when you created the chart (Step 3 of the Chart Wizard). Here you can add titles, select how the gridlines are displayed, and what appears as data labels. Some of these options overlap with options you can change by double-clicking the chart item.

To make a change, follow these steps:

1. Select the chart.

2. Select ⟨**Chart**⟩ → ⟨**Chart Options**⟩. You see the Chart Options dialog box, which is similar to Step 3 of the Chart Wizard (refer to Figure 16-5).

3. Select the tab you want. Use the Titles tab to add a chart, x-axis, or y-axis title. Use the Axes tab to select whether the x- and y-axes are displayed. You can also select a format for the x-axis. Select whether gridlines are displayed for the x- and y-axes on the Gridlines tab. Select whether a legend is included and if so its placement on the Legend tab. Use the Data Labels tab shown in Figure 16-12 to select how data labels are displayed. If you want to include the data table as part of the chart, use the Data Table tab.

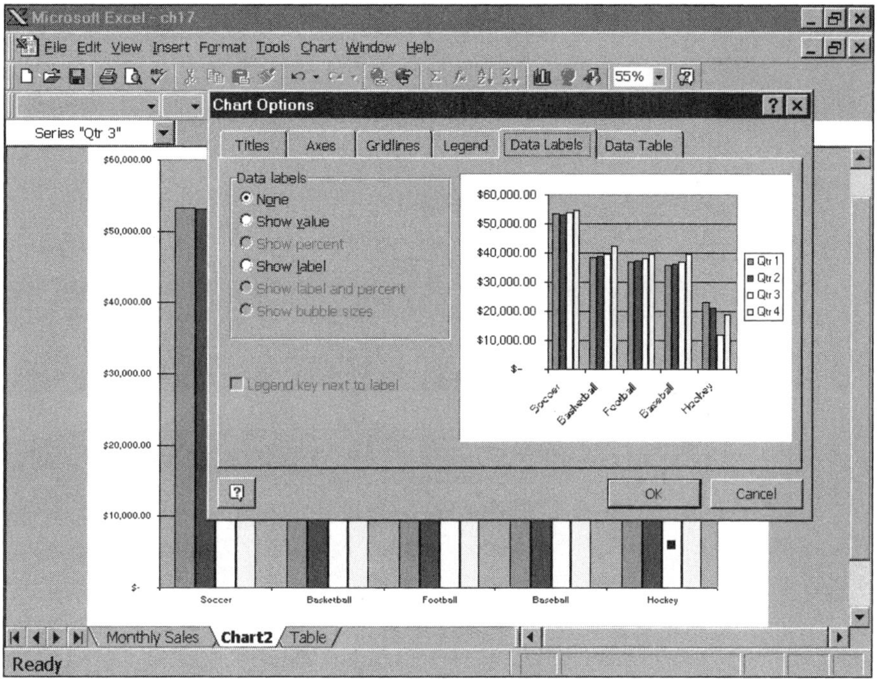

Figure 16-12 You can elect to show data labels as label, value, percent, or label and percent.

4. Make any changes and click the OK button.

BONUS

Adding Other Types of Graphics

Charts aren't the only visual elements you can include in a worksheet. You can also insert pictures — clip art images provided with Office or graphics files from other sources. And if you are quite the artist yourself, you can even use the Drawing tools to add your own scribbling to the worksheet. This bonus section tells you how to jazz up your worksheet with other fun stuff.

Inserting a Picture

If you aren't an artist, you can insert some "canned" art provided with Office. You can select from a variety of pictures — places, foods, business images, buildings, and so on. Don't go overboard, though. You don't really need a clip art image of the Statue of Liberty in your worksheet on travel expenses.

To insert a clip art image, follow these steps:

1. Select ▐ **Insert** ▌→ ▐ **Picture** ▌. From the submenu that appears, select <u>C</u>lip Art. You see the Microsoft Clip Gallery.

2. In the category list, click the category you want to view. Excel displays the images in that category in the middle of the dialog box (see Figure 16-13).

Figure 16-13 Select the image you want to insert.

3. Click the image you want to insert.

4. Click the <u>I</u>nsert button. Excel inserts the image in the worksheet. It is sized to its "ideal" size, but you can also change the size.

To move the object, click it once and then drag it to the new location. To resize an object, click it once and then drag one of the selection handles. To delete an object, click it once to select it and then press the Delete key.

Drawing on the Worksheet

Want to get someone to notice some key value on the worksheet? Then draw an arrow that says "Look here!" Want to add note, similar to a Post-it note, that explains something? Draw a text box. Can't draw even a square? Then try an AutoShape. You can add these and other shapes to your worksheet using the Drawing toolbar.

USING THE DRAWING TOOLBAR

When you want to be artistic, display the Drawing toolbar and then use any of the tools (described in Table 16-3) to express yourself.

TABLE 16-3 The Tools for Drawing Objects

Button	Name	Use to...
Draw ▾	DRAW	Display a menu with commands for working with the object
	SELECT OBJECTS	Select the object you want to work with
	FREE ROTATE	Rotate an object
AutoShapes ▾	AUTOSHAPES	Display the AutoShapes toolbar for drawing an AutoShape
	LINE	Draw a line
	ARROW	Draw an arrow
	RECTANGLE	Draw a rectangle or square
	OVAL	Draw an oval or circle
	TEXT BOX	Draw a text box
	FILL COLOR	Fill an object with a color or pattern. Click the color you want from the palette that appears.
	LINE COLOR	Select a line color. Click the color you want from the palette that appears.
	FONT COLOR	Select a font color (available for only objects, like text boxes, that have text). Click the color you want from the palette that appears.
	LINE STYLE	Select a line style. Click the style you want.
	DASH STYLE	Select a dash style. Click the style you want.
	ARROW STYLE	Select a style and placement for arrows. Click the style and arrow placement.
	SHADOW	Add a shadow. Click the shadow effect.
	3-D	Select a 3D effect. Click the 3D effect.

16

DRAWING A SHAPE

When you want to draw something, you follow the same basic steps:

1. Click the button for the shape you want to draw. The mouse pointer changes to small crosshairs.

2. Click within the document and drag to draw the object. Figure 16-13 shows a text box and arrow added to the worksheet.

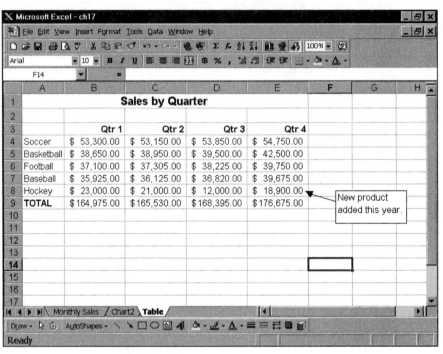

Figure 16-13   You can add text boxes, arrows, and other drawn objects to your worksheet.

TIP   To draw a straight line, square, or circle, select the appropriate tool (line, rectangle, or oval) and then hold down the Shift key as you drag.

CHAPTER SEVENTEEN

MANAGING DATA WITH EXCEL

17

As you saw in the last chapter, Excel is much more than a spreadsheet. You can also use it to create charts. And — as you learn in this chapter — you can use it to keep track of simple data lists. If you don't want to learn Access (the database program included with Office) and your database needs are simple, you can use Excel instead. Excel provides several tools for working with data lists. You can use a data-entry form, sort data, display a subset of information, and more. You learn all about the database features in this chapter.

It's Just a Worksheet, Really!

Have a simple database you want to track? Maybe you want to keep a list of product prices or inventory. Or you may keep track of a simple schedule or a list of clients or sales reps or other names. You don't have to learn anything special to set up a data list because all you do is create a worksheet, which you know how to do. You just have to understand the basics of a database, as covered here.

Database Stuff Defined

To understand a database, you just have to get straight two concepts: records and fields. Think about a simple product pricing database, shown in Figure 17-1. This database includes a list of product names and prices. Each individual piece of data is called a *field.* For example, in the product database, you have just two fields: one for the product name and one for the price. In Excel, each field is stored in a separate column and is identified with a column heading or field name.

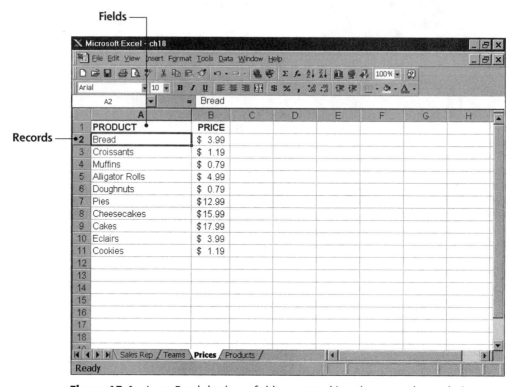

Figure 17-1   In an Excel database, fields are stored in columns, and records, in rows.

One set of information — that is, one set of completed fields — constitutes a *record.* For example, the information about one product, say cookies, is one record. In Excel, records are stored in rows.

Creating Your Excel Database

Once you understand the difference between rows and columns, you can easily set up a worksheet that you can use as a database. You simply enter a field name for each field you want to include, that is, one field name per column. As you enter the field names, keep these points in mind:

* Include one field for each bit of data you want to include. For instance, if you are keeping track of people include columns for the first name and the last name. Doing so gives you more flexibility in arranging or sorting the data list.

* Use unique names for each column.

* Remember that the database is an ordinary worksheet. You can edit the data using all of the commands and features covered in this part of the book. For example, if you forget a field, you can insert a new column. If need be, you can adjust the column width.

* Consider formatting the column headings (that is, the field names) so that they stand out from the data. You can increase their point size or make them bold or add borders or all three!

* If you want to keep track of the records in the order you entered them, include a field for the record number.

Filling in Those Fields

Once you enter the field names, you can start entering the data into the worksheet. After all, what good is a database without data? You can use the regular worksheet or a special data-entry form to enter the data, as covered here.

Using the Worksheet

If you like the regular worksheet style of entering data, you can just enter data directly in the rows. Select the cell and then type the entry. After you complete the entries for the first record (all the columns for that record), move to the next row to add the next record.

One handy tip for entering data in a worksheet is to freeze the column headings at the top of the worksheet so that you can always tell what field you are in.

One handy tip for entering data in the worksheet is to freeze the column headings at the top of the worksheet so that you can always tell what field you are in. Say that you are in row 33 and forget what column (what field) you are in. You can keep the row with the field names frozen at the top so that the field names always are displayed. *Follow these steps to freeze the field names:*

1. Put the pointer in the first column in the row below the column headings. Excel "freezes" all rows and columns above and to the left of the active cell.

2. Select Window → Freeze Panes . The top row with the field names will now always be displayed no matter which row you are in.

To unfreeze the column headings, use the Window → Unfreeze Panes command.

Using the Data Form

If you are distracted by all the rows of data, you may prefer to look and work on one record at a time. If so, you can use the data form and see each field in a neat fill-in-the-blank form. You complete that form and then move to the next. You don't have to do anything special to set up this form; Excel will create it for you. *To use the data form to enter records, follow these steps:*

1. Put the pointer within the data list you have set up.

2. Select Data → Form . You see a data form. Excel includes text boxes for each of the fields in the database. The name of the worksheet becomes the title of the dialog box (see Figure 17-2).

Figure 17-2 You can use a data form to enter data.

3. Type the entry for the first field. You can type more information than the size of the field in the data form. As you type, the information scrolls to the left.

4. Press Tab to move to the next field. (You can also press Shift+Tab to move backward through the fields.) Complete all the fields for the record.

5. To add the new record and display a blank form, click the New button.

6. Complete the next record. Follow steps 3–5 for each record you want to add.

7. When you are finished entering data, click the Close button. You are returned to the worksheet.

Keeping Those Records Current

Any database is only as good as the data that are entered. If something changes, you need to update your records. For example, you may need to update a price or delete a product you no longer carry. Or you may need to update the names and addresses of your client list. If you use Excel to track friends and enemies, you may have to update the status of friends versus enemies. When you want to make a change, you can use either the data form or the regular worksheet.

Regular Worksheet Editing

You can edit a field directly in the record row and field column. To edit a field, select the cell you want to change. Double-click the cell, make any changes, and press Enter.

 TIP **If you make a mistake and don't want to make the entry, press Esc rather than Enter.**

To delete a record in the worksheet, simply delete the row. Click the row number and then use the Edit → Delete command. The row along with the information it contains is deleted from the worksheet.

To delete a field in the worksheet, simply delete the column. Click the column letter and then use Edit → Delete. Keep in mind that the field and all the contents of that field are deleted.

 TIP **Delete something by mistake? If you make a mistake, you can undo it using the Edit → Undo command.**

Using the Data Form

If you don't like the clutter of all the data on screen, you can edit using the data form. You can use this form to display and work on a single record at a time. You can make changes and delete records as needed. *To edit or delete a record, follow these steps:*

1. Select Data → Form .

2. Click the scroll arrows to display the record you want to change or delete. You can also click the Find Prev or Find Next buttons until the record you want is displayed.

 TIP **In a really big database, scrolling to find the record takes too much time. Instead, search for the record as covered in the next section, "Where Is the Record For..."**

3. To update any entry, click in the text box and make any changes.

To delete a record, click the <u>D</u>elete button and then confirm the deletion by clicking the OK button.

4. When you finish making changes, click the Close button to close the data form.

Where Is the Record For...

I f your data list is pretty short, you can probably skim through the records to find the one you want. On the other hand, if your database is really big, skimming and scrolling is a waste of time. Move to the record you want by searching for it. You can search for a match based on any field. The easiest way to set up a search is to use the data form, as covered here. *To search for a record, follow these steps:*

1. Select ⬛ **Data** → ⬛ **Form** . You see the data form on screen.

2. Click the <u>C</u>riteria button. You see a blank record on screen (see Figure 17-3).

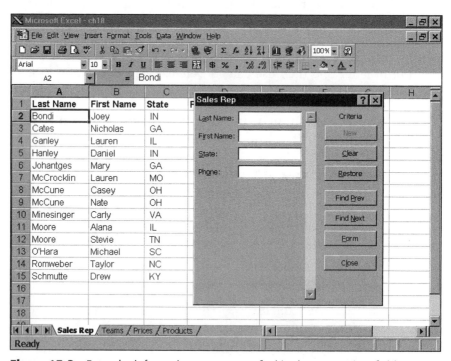

Figure 17-3 Enter the information you want to find in the appropriate field.

3. Move to the field on which you want to search. For instance, if you want to find a sales rep based on last name, go to the last name field. If you want to list all sales reps in a certain state, move to the State field.

4. Type what you want to find. You can type all or part of the entry. For instance, if you wanted to find the rep Moore, you can type **M**, **Moo**, or **Moore**.

5. Click the Find <u>N</u>ext button. Excel displays the first matching record. Continue clicking the Find <u>N</u>ext button until the record you want is displayed.

If Excel can't find a match, you won't see an error message, but you will hear a beep, and Excel will return to the data form. Try a different search — try a partial entry or use a comparison formula. Or try searching on a different field.

Order! Order!

When you enter the records in your database, don't become obsessed with putting them in a particular order. You can easily rearrange the database. You can sort by any of the fields in the database. For instance, in an address database, you can sort by last name or zip code or state. *To sort the database, follow these steps:*

1. Select any cell within the database.

2. Select ⬛**Data** → ⬛**Sort** . Excel displays the Sort dialog box (see Figure 17-4).

Figure 17-4 Use this dialog box to select a sort order.

3. Display the Sort by drop-down list and click the column that you want to sort by first. For instance, if you were sorting by last names, you'd select last name from this list.

If the Header row option button is selected, Excel uses the column headings as choices in the drop-down list, and Excel will not include this header row in the sort. If you don't have column headings, Excel will display the first value in the column in the drop-down list. To make it do this, click the No header row option button so that Excel will include the first row.

4. Click Ascending or Descending order.

TIP **To sort on more than one field, display the Then By drop-down lists and select the other field(s) you want to sort on.**

5. Click the OK button. Excel sorts the database in the order you selected.

As a shortcut, you can also click within the column you want to sort on. Then click ![icon] to sort the entries in ascending order or click ![icon] to sort the entries in descending order.

I Just Want to See...

In a big database, you may want to see or just work on a subset or partial list of data. For example, you may want to take a look at a particular type of product or sales reps in one state or clients in one area or teams at one level. Excel provides a pretty nifty feature, called AutoFilter, for viewing just one set of data. *To filter your database using AutoFilter, follow these steps:*

1. Select `Data` → `Filter` → `AutoFilter`. Drop-down arrows appear next to each column in your database (see Figure 17-5).
2. Move to the column heading for the column on which you want to filter. For example, Figure 17-5 shows a database that tracks different teams. If you wanted to view just a certain team level, you could filter on the team column.

3. To display the filter list, click the arrow or press Alt+`↓`. You see a list of entries in that column as well as some general choices.

4. Select what records you want to match:

Select `All` to display all records in that column.

Select `Top 10` to display the ten highest values in that field. You can use this option only on numeric or calculated fields.

Select `Custom` to display the Custom dialog box and enter a custom filter.

	A	B	C	D	E	F	G

CIWTL 96-97 Season

3	Coach ▼	Team ▼	Practice Day ▼	Time ▼			
4	Ludo	Open	Monday	11:30 to 1:00			
5	Mark	Open	Monday	1:00 to 2:30			
6	Miguel	A	Monday	2:00 to 3:30			
7	Ludo	A	Tuesday	9:00 to 10:30			
8	Mark	A	Tuesday	10:30 to 12:00			
9	Jim	B	Monday	11:30 to 1:00			
10	Miguel	B	Monday	1:00 to 2:30			
11	Ludo	B	Tuesday	10:30 to 12:00			
12	Mark	B	Wednesday	11:30 to 1:00			
13	Jim	C	Wednesday	10:30 to 12:00			
14	Miguel	C	Wednesday	11:30 to 1:00			
15	Mark	C	Wednesday	1:00 to 2:30			
16	Slater	C	Thursday	9:00 to 10:30			
17	Jim	Q	Thursday	10:30 to 12:00			
18	Miguel	Q	Thursday	11:30 to 1:00			

Figure 17-5 Use the AutoFilter arrows to display the filters you can apply to particular column of data.

Select the specific value you want to match. For example, in Figure 17-5, you could filter the Team column to show just A teams or just B teams or just C teams. Likewise, you could filter the database on the Practice Day field and show just teams that practiced on Monday (or on Tuesday or Wednesday or Thursday or Friday). As another example, you could filter the database on the Coach field to show just the teams for a particular coach.

Select **Blanks** to display only rows that are blank in this column. This option is available only when there are blank fields within some of the records.

Select **NonBlanks** to display only rows that contain values in this column. This option is available only when there are blank fields within some of the records.

When you select the option, Excel displays only those records that meet the selected criteria. All other rows are still in the database; they are just hidden. You can tell the database has been filtered because the filter arrow is a different color. For example, Figure 17-6 shows the team database filtered to show Ludo's teams.

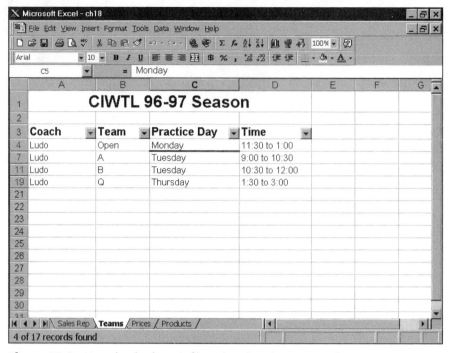

Figure 17-6   Here the database is filtered to show just one coach's teams.

To display all records again, display the filtered column's drop-down list and select (All). To display all records and turn off the filter, select the Data → Filter → AutoFilter command. The drop-down arrows disappear, and all records are displayed.

BONUS

Calculating Subtotals

Some of your databases are likely to contain numeric entries, even calculations. You may want to do some analysis on these data. For example, Excel includes a cool Subtotals command that you can use not only to sum, but to count, average, or perform other functions on the data. You just select what you want, and Excel inserts the necessary rows and formulas.

To start, you have to arrange the database in the order you want. For example, if you wanted to figure total sales for each product, you'd need to sort by product type first. Use the Data → Sort command and select the field to sort on.

Once the records are sorted, you can create the subtotals. *To calculate subtotals, follow these steps:*

1. Click within any row in the database.

2. Select **Data** → **Subtotals**. You see the Subtotal dialog box, shown in Figure 17-7.

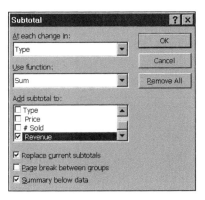

Figure 17-7 Use this dialog box to set up how the subtotals (or other functions) are calculated.

3. Select which column you want calculated from the <u>A</u>t each change in drop-down list. For instance, if you wanted a new calculation each time the Company changed, you'd select Company. If you wanted to calculate the total for each product type, you'd select Type.

4. By default, Excel sums the entries, but you can also display the <u>U</u>se function drop-down list and select another function. You can select Count or Average, for instance. (For more help on functions, see Chapter 12.)

5. In the A<u>d</u>d subtotal to list, check the boxes that you want subtotaled. This isn't the same entry as in step 3. For instance, you can't total company names or product types. Instead, you want to calculate the revenue here, so be sure that's the check box that's checked. (Excel makes pretty good guesses at what to do.)

6. Make any changes to the other settings. To replace any existing subtotals, uncheck the Replace <u>c</u>urrent subtotals check box. To insert a page break before each group, check the <u>P</u>age break between groups check box. By default the subtotals and grand totals appear at the end of the data group. If you prefer to show these totals before the data group, check the <u>S</u>ummary below data check box.

7. Click the OK button.

Excel inserts a subtotal row for each time the selected field changes and performs the selected function on the column you selected for step 5. In the product example, Excel created a subtotal for each product type and a grand total of all sales (see Figure 17-8). You have to scroll to see the grand total.

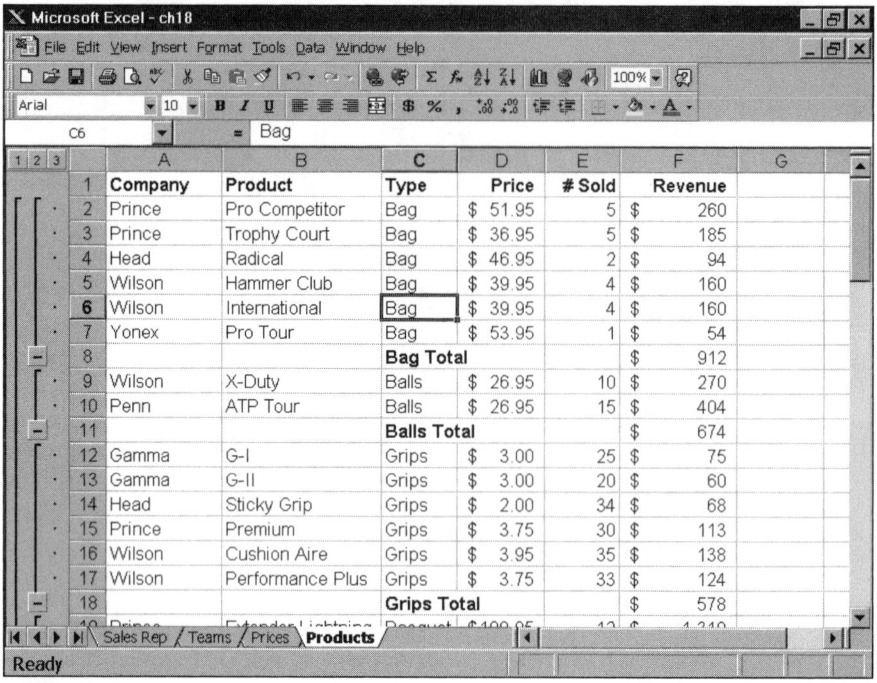

Figure 17-8 This database has been sorted and subtotaled by product type.

To remove the subtotals, select the <u>D</u>ata → Su<u>b</u>totals command. Click the <u>R</u>emove All button.

CREATING PRESENTATIONS WITH POWERPOINT

THIS PART CONTAINS THE FOLLOWING CHAPTERS:

Whether you give presentations all the time or just on rare occasions, you'll find PowerPoint can help you create a simple presentation or a sophisticated one in no time at all. In this part you learn the different ways to create a presentation, the different types of slides you can include, and the many special effects you can try. For help on creating, editing, and formatting a presentation, review this part.

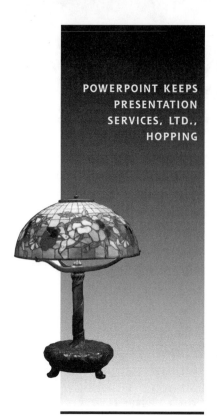

"We have a customer base of about 270 clients, and 80–85 percent of them use PowerPoint in their work," says John Kuhlman, president and owner of Presentation Services, Ltd., (PSL) based in Greenwood Village, Colorado.

Presentation Services is a full-service graphic design service bureau, consulting firm, and custom design company. The service bureau arm takes a variety of graphic and other files and outputs them to slides, color overheads, or prints, including large formats. Everything is done in house, which allows PSL to provide fast turnaround to its customers. The company also has mailboxes at certain companies where clients can upload files to be transferred to film. Kuhlman then logs on and dumps them to his own system.

In addition, PSL is a fully integrated graphic design company, creating everything from corporate logos to complete slide presentations. "Since most of our customers have standardized on Microsoft Office, it makes sense to create their presentations in PowerPoint so they can use them back at the office." Kuhlman has been working with PowerPoint since it first arrived on the scene, and he feels that "Version 3.0 really turned the page for improvement and ease of use."

In spite of its ease of use, Kuhlman has seen an increase in the need for training as PowerPoint continues to improve and include more advanced and complex features. "Now that PowerPoint is a little more complex, we are providing training to help clients get the most out of the software."

For those companies who prefer to have PSL do the work, Kuhlman and his staff also provide custom templates. After consulting with clients about their needs, PSL develops PowerPoint templates specifically for the client, including a logo and other trademarks and insignia. This enables the company to have a completely unique design for presentations, a service that is especially helpful when the company uses the presentation on the road. "They avoid duplicating the look of another company who may have used one of the templates that ships with PowerPoint," explains Kuhlman. "We work closely with them to produce a template that not only looks good but will be easy to use. Often the client can select the template, turn on Outline view, and type in the text for the presentation. Just about everything else is there for them in the template."

In addition to running PSL, Kuhlman is co-owner with Mike Ellis of Trailhead Interactive, which provides fully interactive digital presentations. Trailhead develops Computer Based Training (CBT), CD-ROM based applications, 3D animation, multimedia Web sites, and other media-based products.

CREATING A POWERPOINT PRESENTATION

18

LEARN THESE KEY SKILLS:

D o you have to make a sales presentation? Present a new product idea? Motivate your staff? Give your bosses an overview of your business plan? Whenever you need to present any kind of idea to an audience, use PowerPoint to help you create an effective presentation.

PowerPoint is the presentation program included with Microsoft Office. You can use it to create presentations of any kind. This chapter starts by telling you how to get started and how to create a presentation.

What's in Your Toolbox This Time?

PowerPoint is a little different from some of the other Office programs in that you don't start with a blank document. Instead, PowerPoint starts by displaying a dialog box, similar to a wizard, asking what you want to do. You select whether to create a new presentation (and how) or to edit an existing presentation. Depending on what you choose, you will be prompted to make other selections. The section "Ready, Set, Go" covers how to get started with the program and also provides an overview of the different tools available in PowerPoint.

TIP A wizard is an automated method for creating a particular type of document. The program prompts you to make selections and then helps you create the document.

Figure 18-1 shows a blank slide added to a new presentation. You'll learn about working with slides later. For now, take a look at some of the tools in the PowerPoint program window. As in other program windows, you see the title bar and menu bar at the top of the window. (For more information on these elements, see Chapter 2.) PowerPoint also includes several toolbars. Tables 18-1 and 18-2 describe the buttons in the top two toolbars — the Standard and Formatting toolbars. Chapter 19 explains the View buttons, and Chapter 20 covers the Drawing toolbar. In addition the PowerPoint window includes a Common Tasks toolbar. The commands in this toolbar are pretty self-explanatory. You'll learn how to use them in this and the next two chapters.

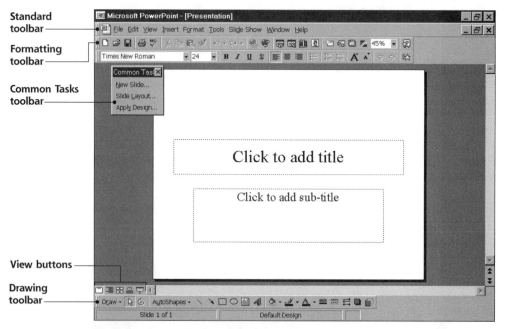

Figure 18-1 PowerPoint includes several tools for creating a presentation.

TABLE 18-1   The Standard Toolbar

Button	Name	Description
	NEW	Create a new presentation
	OPEN	Open a previously saved presentation
	SAVE	Save the presentation
	PRINT	Print the current presentation
	SPELLING	Check your spelling
	CUT	Cut selected text or object
	COPY	Copy selected text or object
	PASTE	Paste cut or copied text or object
	FORMAT PAINTER	Copy formatting
	UNDO	Undo the last command
	REDO	Redo the last command
	INSERT HYPERLINK	Insert a link to a file or a Web address
	WEB TOOLBAR	Display a toolbar with buttons for creating Web documents
	INSERT MICROSOFT WORD TABLE	Insert a Word table. See Chapter 29 for more information on sharing data among programs.
	INSERT MICROSOFT EXCEL WORKSHEET	Insert an Excel worksheet. See Chapter 29 for more information.
	INSERT CHART	Insert a chart on the slide
	INSERT CLIP ART	Insert a clip art image
	NEW SLIDE	Insert a new slide
	SLIDE LAYOUT	Select a different slide layout for the current slide
	APPLY DESIGN	Select a presentation design to apply to the presentation
	BLACK AND WHITE VIEW	Display the presentation in black and white
45%	ZOOM	Zoom in or out on the current slide
	OFFICE ASSISTANT	Display (or turn off) the Office Assistant

TABLE 18-2 The Formatting Toolbar

Button	Name	Description
Times New Roman	FONT	Select a different font
10	FONT SIZE	Select a different font size
B	BOLD	Make selected text bold
I	ITALIC	Make selected text italic
U	UNDERLINE	Underline selected text
	SHADOW	Add a shadow to selected text
	ALIGN LEFT	Align selected data to the left edge of a text box
	CENTER	Center selected text within a text box
	ALIGN RIGHT	Align selected text to the right of a text box
	BULLETS	Create a bulleted list
	INCREASE PARAGRAPH SPACING	Add more space between paragraphs
	DECREASE PARAGRAPH SPACING	Use less space between paragraphs
A	INCREASE FONT SIZE	Make selected text bigger
A	DECREASE FONT SIZE	Make selected text smaller
	PROMOTE	Indent selected paragraphs
	DEMOTE	Unindent selected paragraphs
	ANIMATION EFFECTS	Add animation effects to the slide

First Things First

Now that you are familiar with what's available, you should think about your presentation. PowerPoint includes a few ways to create a new presentation and several different slide types. If you just sit down and get started, you may feel overwhelmed with all the choices. You may get halfway through and realize that there's a better way. Avoid all these missteps by taking a look at this section, which gives you an overview of the different elements to consider before you create a new presentation.

What's the Message?

If you have a good idea of what you want to do, you can then pick the tools most suited for accomplishing that goal. So think about your overall presentation and content. Ask yourself these questions:

* What is the goal or message of the presentation? To inform? Persuade? Teach? Sell? Recommend? You should have one clearly defined goal in mind.

* Who's the audience for your message? Peers? Students? Bosses? Coworkers? Potential investors? Anyone that will listen? What will *they* be thinking? What is their background? You should have a good idea of the audience and of audience members' various perspectives.

* How can you convey your particular message to your particular audience? Do you need to explain a lot of stuff? Do you need financial information? Do you need tables of information? Do you need to show charts? What exactly will convince your audience to "buy" what you are "selling"?

Once you answer these questions, you can think about how to put together the actual presentation. On to planning step 2. What's the best way to create the presentation?

Ways to Create a Presentation

When you start PowerPoint, you are given three choices as to how to create a new presentation (besides the choice of opening an existing presentation):

* Use the AutoContent Wizard. With this option, PowerPoint leads you step-by-step through the process of creating a presentation. You select the presentation type, output options, presentation style, and presentation options. You can select from many different types, including project overview, status, financial overview, marketing plan, and so on.

PowerPoint adds some typical slides with sample data. Replace the sample data with your own to create a presentation. This option is helpful for users who are new to creating presentations and may need some help in deciding the content of a presentation.

✳ If you don't like the idea of replacing sample data with your own but do want some initial help in selecting the look of the presentation, you can use a template. A template defines the colors, font, text placement, and other formatting features of a presentation. You can then add the slides you want.

✳ If you don't choose to mess with someone else's design, you can start with a blank presentation. You can then add the slides you want and select formatting options such as color scheme and special effects to your slides.

The section "Ready, Set, Go" covers how to start a presentation using each of these three methods.

Types of Slides You Can Include

A presentation is a collection of slides, and those slides convey the information to your audience. When you planned your presentation, you should have thought about how best to convey your message. Now you can see the different ways to put your thoughts before your audience. You can select from several basic slide layouts. Take a look at Table 18-3 for a general idea of each slide layout as well as a description.

The rest of this chapter covers how to create these slides and add them to a new presentation.

TABLE 18-3 Slide Layouts

Slide Layout	Type	Description
	TITLE	This slide includes text placeholders for a title and a subtitle. Most presentations start with a title slide that defines the name or purpose of the presentation.
	BULLETED LIST	This slide includes a title and an area for a bulleted list. Use this slide to present a series of points, such as an agenda, a summary of accomplishments, or a list of goals.
	2 COLUMN TEXT	This slide includes a title and two columns of text. Use this to present text in two columns.

TABLE 18-3

Slide Layout	Type	Description
![table icon]	TABLE	This slide includes a title and a table. You can present numerical data or other tabular data on this slide.
![text & chart icon]	TEXT & CHART	This slide includes a table, an area for text, and an area for a chart.
![chart & text icon]	CHART & TEXT	This slide, similar to the preceding one, includes an area for a title, text, and a chart.
![org chart icon]	ORGANIZATION CHART	This slide includes a title as well as an area for an organization chart.
![chart icon]	CHART	This slide includes a title as well as a place for a chart.
![text & clip art icon]	TEXT & CLIP ART	This slide includes a title, a text area, and an area for a picture.
![clip art & text icon]	CLIP ART & TEXT	This is similar to the preceding slide layout.
![title only icon]	TITLE ONLY	This is a title chart with just one title.
![blank icon]	BLANK	This is a blank slide. You can add text, charts, pictures, or other elements anywhere you want.

Ready, Set, Go

Now that all that background information is stored solidly in your mind, you can get to the fun stuff — actually creating a new presentation. *Follow these steps to start PowerPoint and start a new presentation:*

1. Click the Start button, select **Programs**, and then select **Microsoft PowerPoint**. The program is started, and you see the PowerPoint dialog box, which prompts you to select how to create a new presentation (see Figure 18-2).

TIP To open a new presentation, select <u>O</u>pen an existing presentation and then select the one you want to work on. See Chapter 3 for more information on opening Office documents.

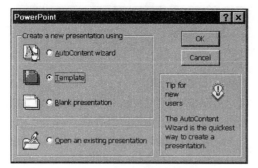

Figure 18-2 Select which method you want to use to create your new presentation.

2. Select a method to create a new presentation — using the AutoContent wizard, a template, or a blank presentation — and then click the OK button. The rest of this section describes each method, so go to the selection you made and follow the remaining steps.

Using the AutoContent Wizard

If you selected the AutoContent Wizard to create a new presentation, you see the first dialog box for this wizard. This dialog box gives you an overview of the process (see Figure 18-3).

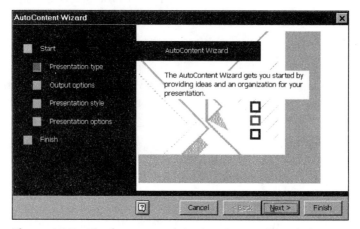

Figure 18-3 The first screen of the AutoContent Wizard gives you an overview of the process.

Follow these steps to complete the setup:

1. Review the initial screen and then click the Next button. You are prompted to select the type of presentation (see Figure 18-4). By default, PowerPoint lists all of the presentation types, you can narrow the list by selecting a category in the dialog box.

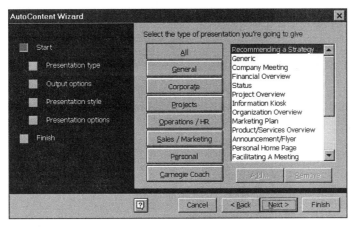

Figure 18-4 Select the type of presentation you want to create.

2. Select the type of presentation and click the <u>N</u>ext button. You are prompted to select the output options (see Figure 18-5).

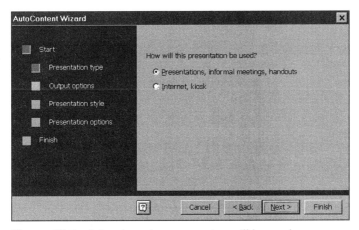

Figure 18-5 Select how the presentation will be used.

3. Select <u>P</u>resentations, informal meetings, handouts for a regular presentation. Or select <u>I</u>nternet, kiosk for those types of output media. Click the <u>N</u>ext button. You are prompted to select the type of output (see Figure 18-6).

X-REF For information on Internet publishing, see Chapter 31.

4. Select the type of output. You can choose to present the presentation on a computer screen, as black-and-white overheads, as color overheads, or as a slide show. You can also choose whether you want handouts. After you make your choices, click the <u>N</u>ext button (see Figure 18-7). You are prompted for information for the title slide.

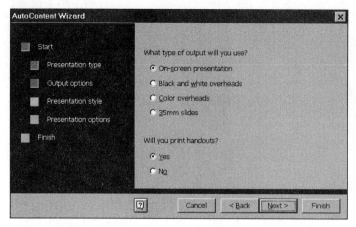

Figure 18-6 Select presentation style options from this dialog box.

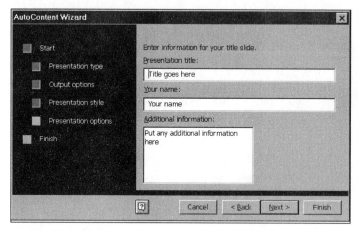

Figure 18-7 Enter the information for the first slide.

TIP **If you make a mistake or change your mind about your selections, click the Back button to go back to a previous dialog box and make different choices.**

5. Type your presentation title, your name, and any additional information you want to include on the title slide. Click the Finish button.

PowerPoint creates the presentation and some sample slides for that specific type of presentation. For example, Figure 18-8 shows a Company Meeting presentation. You can then edit each slide in the presentation. The next chapter covers how to edit a presentation. You may want to turn to that chapter next. You can also use the information in the rest of this chapter to learn how to add other new slides to this presentation.

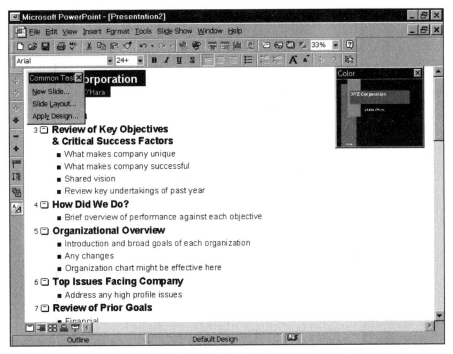

Figure 18-8 Here's a presentation applicable to a company meeting.

Using a Template

If you chose to create a new presentation based on a template, you see the New Presentation dialog box shown in Figure 18-9. You also see this same dialog box if you use the File → New command to create a new presentation once you've started PowerPoint. *Follow these steps to select the template:*

1. In the New Presentation dialog box shown in Figure 18-9, select the presentation template you want to use. If you aren't sure what they look like, select the template and then view a preview in the dialog box.

2. Click the OK button. PowerPoint sets up a new presentation using the design styles from the template and displays the New Slide dialog box so that you can select the first slide in the presentation.

Turn to the section "Show Me Slides" to learn how to add slides to this presentation.

Creating a Blank Presentation

If you chose to create a blank presentation, you see the New Slide dialog box. Here you can select the first slide to add to your presentation. This topic is covered in the very next section. Keep reading!

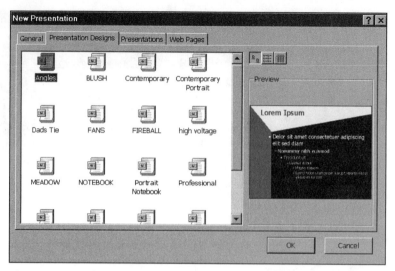

Figure 18-9 From this dialog box, select the presentation template you want to use.

Sliding for Home

When you create a presentation based on a template or a blank presentation, you see the New Slide dialog box. The first step in adding a new slide — whether it's the first or last — is to select the type of slide you want.

The first step in adding a new slide is to select the type of slide you want.

From this dialog box, select the type of slide you want to add and then click the OK button. PowerPoint adds the slide and includes placeholders for each element included on that slide type. For example, if you've added a title slide, you see placeholders for the title and the subtitle. If you added a bulleted list, you see placeholders for the title and the bulleted list. The next sections describe how to create each type of element on the slide.

To add another slide to the presentation, click the New Slide command in the Common Tasks toolbar, click ⌧, or select the Insert → New Slide command. Again, you see the New Slide dialog box where you can select the type of slide you want to add. The new slide is added after the current one.

Continue adding new slides and creating the slides until you complete the presentation.

Get Your Text Here!

S everal slide layouts contain mostly text. For example, if you add a title slide, you have placeholders for the title and the subtitle (see Figure 18-10). You can simply replace the placeholder text with the actual text.

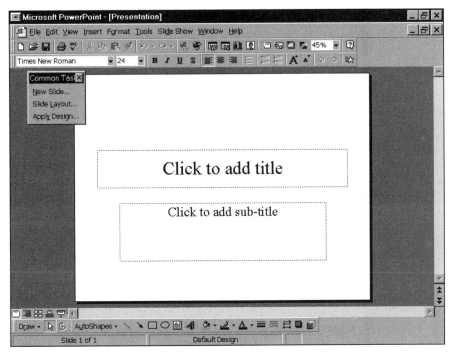

Figure 18-10   You can add text to a title slide.

To add text to any type of slide, follow these steps:

1. Click the placeholder.

2. Type the new text.

3. Click outside the placeholder.

TIP   **For information on formatting the text, see Chapter 20.**

When you are working with text, you can make any changes you need. The same editing techniques you use when working with text in Word or Excel apply to PowerPoint. For example, you can do the following:

✳ As you type, you can press Enter to insert a paragraph break. Pressing Enter on title placeholders does not move you to the next placeholder. You must click in the next chart area to move there.

* If you are creating a bullet slide, pressing Enter ends the paragraph and inserts a new bullet.

* To edit text, start by moving the insertion point. You can use the mouse to point and click or you can use the arrow keys.

* To select text, drag across it much like you do in Word.

* To delete text to the left of the insertion point, press Backspace. To delete text to the right of the insertion point, press Del. If you have a lot of text to delete, drag across the text to select it and then press Del.

* To copy or cut text, select the text first. Then use the Copy, Cut, and Paste buttons or commands.

* If you make a mistake when editing text, use the Undo button or command to undo the change.

* If you add a table chart, you see an area for the table. Double-click that area and then select the number of columns and rows you want. The table is added to the slide. Type each entry in the table cells and use Tab to move to the next one. For more information on working with tables, see Chapter 9, which covers working with Word tables.

* Be sure to save your presentation as you add new slides. Saving documents is covered in Chapter 3.

* When you're done adding slides, check the spelling of the text using the Spelling button. The command works much like the spell-check feature in Word or Excel (see Chapter 6).

Show Me Slides

In addition to text slides, you can include slides with charts. For instance, in a sales meeting, you may want to chart sales performance for each quarter. For a company meeting, you might show annual profit by year. For a new product launch, you might show projected income.

Creating a chart in PowerPoint is a lot like creating a chart in Excel. You can select from similar chart types, and you enter data in a mini worksheet. This section covers how to set up a chart.

TIP You can use charts or data from Excel in your PowerPoint presentation. For information on this topic, see Chapter 29.

Displaying the Chart Tools

When you select a slide layout that includes a chart, you see an icon for the chart area (see Figure 18-11). To get started, double-click the Chart icon. PowerPoint displays the datasheet with sample data and the chart (see Figure 18-12).

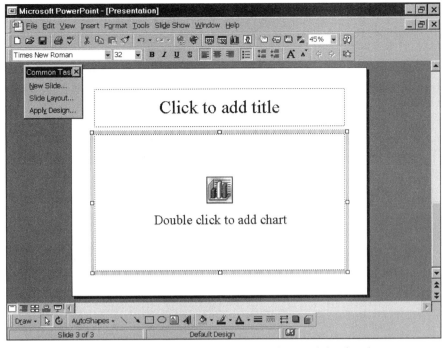

Figure 18-11 Double-click the icon to display the chart and the datasheet.

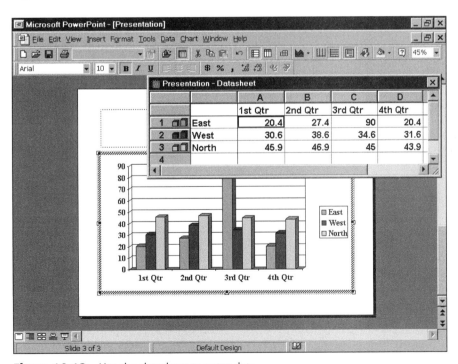

Figure 18-12 Use the datasheet to enter data.

TIP You can also use the Insert → Chart command or Insert Chart button to add a chart to an existing slide.

Entering Data

The datasheet is just like a mini worksheet — that is, a grid of rows and columns (refer to Figure 18-13). The sample data give you an idea of how the data should be entered. You replace the sample column and row headings with the data you want to chart. You also replace the numerical data with the data appropriate to your chart.

To select a cell for editing, click it or use the arrow keys (just as you move around in Excel). Type the new entry and press Enter to replace the current entry. If the chart you want to create includes more columns or headings than the sample data, simply enter the data in the appropriate row and column. If the chart contains less data, be sure to delete the inappropriate sample data. To delete data, select the range (drag across the cells to highlight them) and then press Del.

When data entry is complete, click back on the slide. PowerPoint closes the datasheet and adds the chart object to the slide using the data you entered (see Figure 18-13).

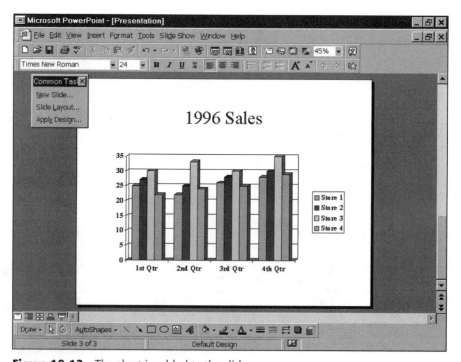

Figure 18-13 The chart is added to the slide.

X-REF For information on editing a chart — such as changing the chart type — see the next chapter.

Who's Who

In addition to regular charts, you can also include organization charts on a slide. These come in handy when you want to present the staff of a company or department. With an organization chart, you can show any type of hierarchy of people or ideas.

To add this type of slide, simply select the layout that includes the organization chart. You see a slide with an area for a title and an area for the chart (see Figure 18-14). You can also add an organization chart to an existing slide by selecting the Insert → Picture → Organization Chart command.

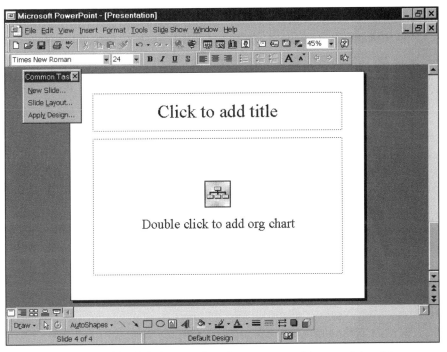

Figure 18-14 Double-click the Org Chart icon to create this part of the slide.

Double-click the Org Chart icon to start Microsoft Organization Chart, a separate mini application you use to create a chart. You see boxes for a top-level manager and three next-level managers (see Figure 18-15).

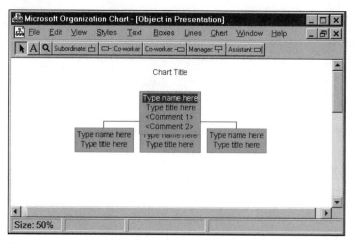

Figure 18-15 Use this application to create your organization chart.

To complete the organization chart, follow these steps:

1. Type the name for the top-level position and press Enter. You move to the title line.

2. Type a title for this position and press Enter. You move to the first comment line.

3. If you want, type an optional comment and press Enter. Type a second comment.

4. Click the next organization box and follow the same steps to add the name, title, and optional comments for each box.

You aren't stuck with just three boxes on your org chart. You can add other boxes or get rid of boxes you don't need. You can do any of the following:

* To add another box on the same level, use the Coworker button in the toolbar. Click the button and then click the box to which you want to attach the new one. Type the information for the new box.

* To add a subordinate to one of the boxes, click the Subordinate button and then click the box to which you want to attach this new one. Type the information for the new box.

* To add an assistant, click the Assistant button and then click the box to which you want to attach the assistant. Type the information for the box.

* To add a manager (box above), click the Manager button and then click the box to which you want to attach the manager. The selected box is demoted one level, and a new box is added above it.

* To delete a box, click it and press the Delete key.

When you are finished creating the boxes, click back on the slide to add the org chart to the slide. Figure 18-16 shows an organization chart added to a slide.

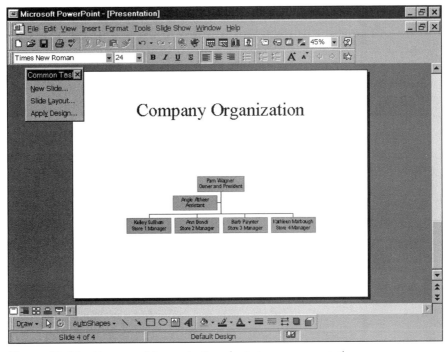

Figure 18-16   You can add organization charts to your presentation.

 X-REF   **For information on editing an organization chart, see Chapter 19.**

Pictures

A final type of element you may want to include on a slide is a picture. You can use clip art included with Office, and you can select a slide layout that includes clip art. If so, you see a placeholder for the clip art image. You can also use the Insert → Picture → Clip Art command or the Insert Clip Art button to insert clip art to a slide.

To insert the clip art image, follow these steps:

1. Double-click the Clip Art icon if you are adding the image to a slide that includes clip art as part of the layout. Or select Insert → Picture → Clip Art or click 🔳. You see the Microsoft Clip Art gallery (see Figure 18-17).

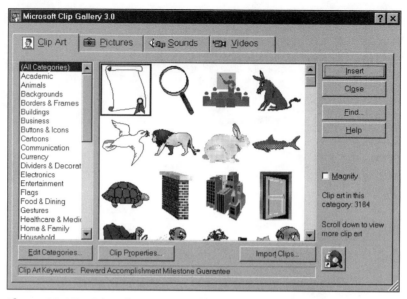

Figure 18-17   Select the category and then the image you want to insert.

2. In the category list, click the category you want to view.

3. Click the image you want to insert.

4. Click the Insert button. The image is added to the slide (see Figure 18-18).

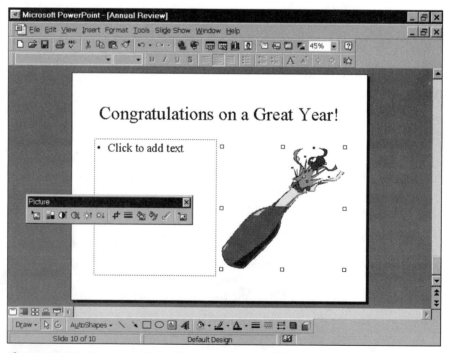

Figure 18-18   You can include clip art as part of a slide.

BONUS

Using an Outline to Create a Presentation

If you like to think about the whole shebang first and then concentrate on the individual pieces, you may prefer a different method for creating the presentation. You may want to work from an outline. You can type in the slide titles and set up the entire presentation. Then you go back and create each individual slide.

To create a presentation from an outline, follow these steps:

1. Create a new presentation, as covered earlier in this chapter. You can create a presentation based on a template or a blank presentation. If you create one based on an AutoContent wizard, the content is added, and you can simply edit it.

2. Select **View** → **Outline** or click the Outline view button.

3. Type a title for the first slide and press Enter. PowerPoint adds a new slide.

4. If you want to add other text to this slide, click the Demote button and type the text. Press Enter. Continue typing text for this slide and pressing Enter until you complete all the text. Then press Ctrl+Enter.

5. Continue typing slide titles and any other text until you complete the outline.

6. To edit the slide, double-click it. You see the slide in Slide View, where you can make any editing and formatting changes you want.

EDITING A POWERPOINT PRESENTATION

LEARN THESE KEY SKILLS:

19

Y ou practiced your presentation in front of your spouse and he got a con- fused look on his face. Or worse yet, he laughed. "You're really funny!" That's great except when you didn't *mean* to be funny. When you review your presentation either in front of a practice audience or just by yourself, you may find that you need to make some changes. You may want to use a different order for the slides. You may have to add slides or get rid of slides that don't make sense. You may need to rework the text on a slide.

The topic of this chapter is editing a presentation, and here you learn how to make these changes and more. To get ready for prime time, check out this chapter.

View Master

W hen you create a slide, you see a single slide on screen. This view (called Slide view) helps you concentrate on that particular slide. You can work on the text or the look (covered in the next chapter). After you've added a few slides, you may need to go back or forward. How do you move to the next slide? How do you see all the slides? This section covers how to move from slide to slide in Slide view as well as how to try some of the other views for working with a presentation.

Moving Around

You can move from one slide to the next using the vertical scroll arrows. If you click the arrow once, you move one slide in that direction (see Figure 19-1). You can also drag the scroll box. As you drag, you see a pop-up box next to the scroll bar indicating the current slide. Drag until you see the slide number you want; then release the mouse button. PowerPoint displays that slide.

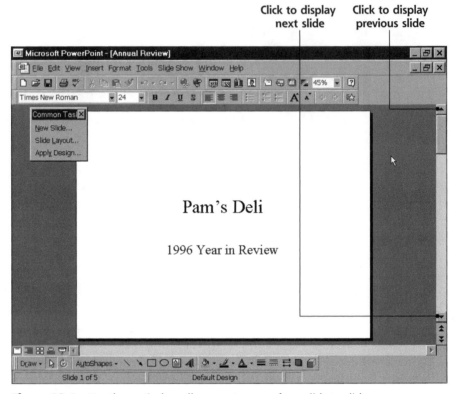

Figure 19-1 Use the vertical scroll arrows to move from slide to slide.

TIP Press the Page Down key to move to the next slide. Press Page Up to move to the previous slide.

Trying Other Views

As mentioned, the default view, called Slide view, is great for working on a single slide at a time, but it's not the only view you can use. When you want to check and make changes to the order of the slides in a presentation, you can use Slide Sorter view. When you want to see an outline of your presentation, use Outline view. You can also view the notes page or see your presentation as a slide show. (These topics are covered in the next chapter.)

The fastest way to change to another view is to use the slide view buttons in the lower-left corner of the screen. Click the button to change to that view, as seen in Table 19-1.

TABLE 19-1 Views

View	Name	When to Use
🗔	SLIDE VIEW	Use this view when working on individual slides.
⊞	OUTLINE VIEW	Use this view to see the presentation as an outline. Figure 19-2 shows this view of a presentation. You can check the overall flow of a presentation as well as edit the text. Chapter 18 explained how to create a presentation in this view.
⊞	SLIDE SORTER VIEW	Use this view to see a thumbnail view of each slide. This view is good for checking the flow of the presentation and making any adjustments (as covered later in this chapter). Figure 19-3 shows a presentation in Slide Sorter view.
🖳	NOTES PAGE VIEW	Use this view to set up speaker notes. This topic is covered in the next chapter.
🖵	SLIDE SHOW	Use this view to view an on-screen slide show of your presentation. This topic is covered in the next chapter.

Ch-Ch-Changes

As you take a look at the overall presentation, you may find that some slides stick out and scream "Fix me! Fix me!" Perhaps the text isn't succinct. Perhaps the chart you're using isn't quite the right one for the data. You can make any changes — adding text, changing the text, reworking the charts and organization charts, as covered here.

X-REF This chapter covers how to make editing changes. You can also tinker with the look of each slide and the entire presentation. This is the topic of the next chapter.

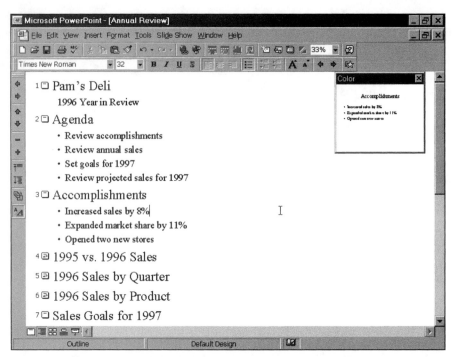

Figure 19-2   In Outline view, you see the overall structure of the presentation.

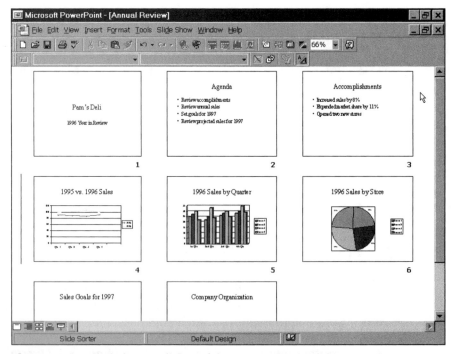

Figure 19-3   Check the overall flow of the presentation in Slide Sorter view.

Editing Text

When you include text on a slide, you should strive to make that text clear and easy to understand. You don't have a lot of room, so you want your text short and to the point. As you look at each slide, you should ask yourself "Is my point clear? Is there a better way to word this?"

If you need to make a change, you can easily do so. The best view for working on individual slides is Slide view, so start in that view. Then display the slide you want to change. *To edit the text, follow these steps:*

1. Click within the text area. The entire text area should be selected, and the insertion point should appear where you clicked (see Figure 19-4).

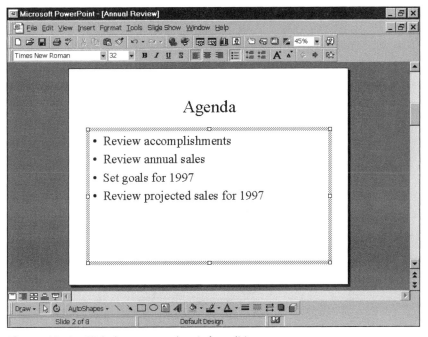

Figure 19-4 Click the text to select it for editing.

2. Do any of the following:

   To add text, click where you want the new text and start typing. You can press Enter to insert additional lines. If you press Enter within a bulleted list, you create another bulleted item. To type normal text, click outside the bulleted text box. Or click the Bullets button to turn off bullets.

   To delete text, position the insertion point and use Backspace or Delete. Or select the text and press Delete.

   You can copy and cut text using the Copy, Cut, and Paste buttons in the toolbar.

3. Click outside of the text area when done.

Editing a Chart

If your slide includes a chart, you may need to make some adjustments to the data in the chart. Perhaps you forgot a value. Or maybe you want to change the chart type. *To edit a chart and access the many features and commands for working with a chart, follow these steps:*

1. Display the slide that contains the chart.

2. Double-click the chart. PowerPoint selects the chart and displays the datasheet. You also see a different set of menus and commands — ones for working with the chart.

3. Make any of the following changes:

   To change one of the values, click in the cell you want to change and make the change.

   To delete any values, select them and press Delete.

   To add values, enter them in the next blank row or column. The new data are included in the chart.

   To change the chart type, select   Chart → Chart Type . You see the Chart Type dialog box (just like the one from Excel), which is shown in Figure 19-5. Select the chart type and subtype you want and click the OK button.

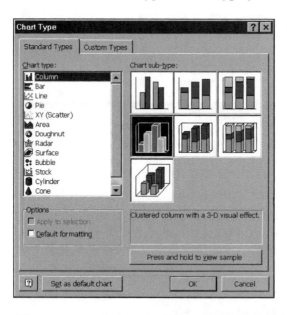

Figure 19-5 Select the chart type and subtype from this dialog box.

4. When you are finished editing the chart, click back on the slide to close the datasheet and update the slide.

X-REF For complete information on the different chart types, review Chapter 16 in the Excel part of this book.

Editing an Organization Chart

If your slide includes an organization chart, you may need to update it. Perhaps someone won a promotion. Or maybe the boss's nephew was finally fired. Or perhaps you were given that assistant you requested. *You can easily make any changes by following these steps:*

1. Display the slide that contains the organization chart.

2. Double-click the organization chart. PowerPoint selects the chart and starts the program Microsoft Organization Chart so that you can make changes (see Figure 19-6). Microsoft Organization Chart can also be used with other Office programs.

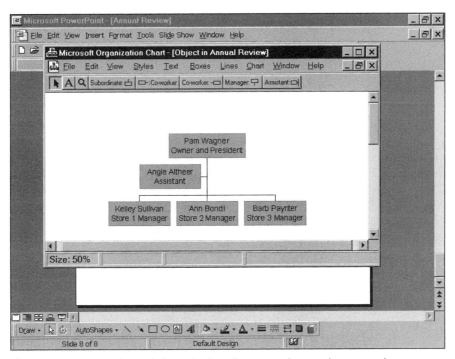

Figure 19-6 Use Microsoft Organization Chart to make any changes to the organization chart.

3. Make any of the following changes:

To change the text in one of the boxes, click within the box you want to change. Then edit the text.

To delete a box, click the box to select it and then press Delete.

To add a box, click the appropriate box type from the toolbar. Then click the box to which you want to attach the new one. Type the information for the new box.

4. When you are done working on the organization chart, click back on the slide to close the Microsoft Organization Chart program and update the slide.

Slip Slidin' Away

A slide is actually made up of different objects. You can have a text object, a chart object, an organization chart object, a clip art object, a table object, a bulleted list object, and so on. By default, these objects appear in the locations set by the slide layout you chose. That doesn't mean you can't make a change! You can move these objects around on the slide — for example, you can move the title to the bottom. You can also change the size of the objects — make an organization chart bigger. And if you decide you don't want to include that particular object, you can — zap! — delete it.

To start, select the object you want to change. To select it, simply click the object once. You should see white selection handles around the selected object. Figure 19-7, for example, shows an organization chart object selected.

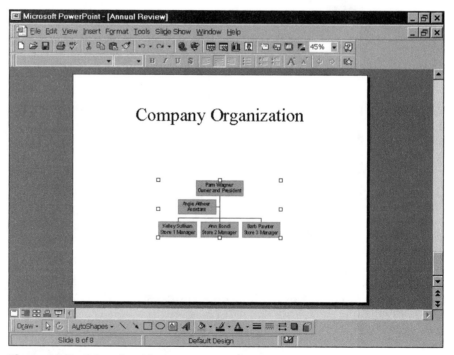

Figure 19-7 Select the object you want to change.

Then do any of the following:

* To delete an object, press Delete.
* To move an object, put the pointer within the selected object. The pointer should look like a four-headed arrow. Drag to the new location.
* To resize an object, put the pointer on one of the selection handles and drag to resize.

 TIP **If you change your mind, undo the change by clicking the Undo button or selecting Edit → Undo.**

Does It Make Sense?

After you carefully eyeball and fine-tune each slide, you still have a few content checkpoints. You should check the overall flow of your presentation and make any adjustments. For example, you may want to change the order of the slides. Or delete a slide that isn't necessary. Or add a new slide. This section describes how to make these adjustments.

Rearranging Slides

The best view for checking the overall flow of a presentation is Slide Sorter view. Using this view, you can easily make changes to the order of the slides. *Follow these steps:*

1. Click the Slide Sorter View icon to change to this view.

2. Click the slide you want to move. You should see a black box around the selected slide (see Figure 19-8).

 If you double-click a slide in Slide Sorter view, you change to Slide View and display the selected slide. To change back, click the Slide Sorter View icon again and be sure to click just once on the slide you want to select.

3. Hold down the mouse button and drag the slide to the new location. As you drag, you see a line and small slide icon indicating where the current slide will be placed. Release the mouse button. PowerPoint reorders the slides in the presentation.

Deleting Slides

If your presentation contains slides that aren't needed, you can delete them. The best view for working with the overall presentation is Slide Sorter view.

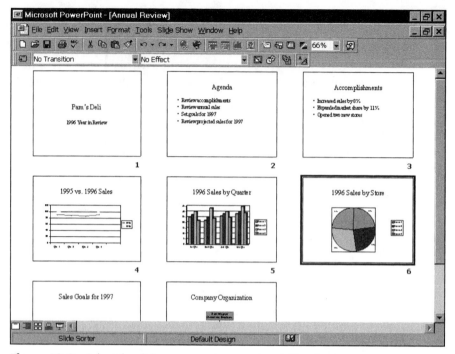

Figure 19-8   Select the slide you want to move by clicking it once.

Follow these steps:

1. In Slide Sorter view, click the slide you want to delete. You should see a black box around the selected slide.

2. Press Delete. The slide is deleted.

To delete a slide in Slide view, display the slide and then select Edit → Delete Slide.

Adding Slides

You can add a new slide to the presentation also, and you can do so in any view you choose. *To add a new slide, follow these steps:*

1. Start where you want the new slide placed. The new slide will be inserted after the current slide.

2. Do any of the following:

    Click [icon].

    Select **Insert** → **New Slide**.

    Press Ctrl+M.

    Click New Slide in the Common Tasks toolbar.

    You see the New Slide dialog box (see Figure 19-9).

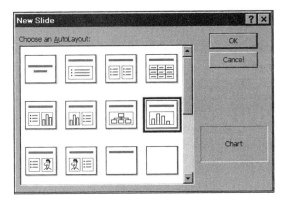

Figure 19-9 Select the layout for the new slide.

3. Select an autolayout for the slide and click the OK button.

4. Create the new slide as described in Chapter 18.

BONUS

Checking the Presentation

It's a good idea to check your presentation before you present it before an audience. You may want to print and proofread each slide carefully. You may want to practice in front of an audience. These are all good ideas. You can also have PowerPoint check the presentation for you. PowerPoint will not only check the spelling, but will also make some style recommendations.

To check a presentation, follow these steps:

1. Select Tools → Style Checker . You see the Style Checker dialog box, shown in Figure 19-10. Notice that this command checks style as well as spelling.

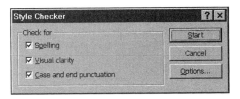

Figure 19-10 You can check the spelling, visual clarity, and punctuation of a presentation.

2. Click the Start button. PowerPoint starts checking the presentation. For spelling errors, you see the Spelling dialog box shown in Figure 19-11.

TIP If you don't want spelling checked, uncheck the Spelling check box. You can also check spelling alone using the Spelling button or the <u>T</u>ools → <u>S</u>pelling command.

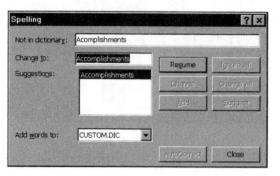

Figure 19-11 The checker will flag any spelling problems.

3. For spelling errors, make any corrections. You can do any of the following:

   If the word is spelled incorrectly and the correct spelling is listed as a suggestion, click the suggestion you want to use and then click <u>C</u>hange or Change A<u>l</u>l.

   If the word is misspelled but none of the suggestions are right, type the correct spelling in the Change <u>t</u>o text box and then click <u>C</u>hange or Change A<u>l</u>l.

   If the word is misspelled and you frequently make this mistake, select the correct spelling and then click the AutoCo<u>r</u>rect button. PowerPoint will make this correction automatically whenever you mistype it.

   If the word is not misspelled, click <u>I</u>gnore or Ignore All. To add this word to the dictionary so that it will not be flagged again, click <u>A</u>dd.

4. If the checker finds any style problems, you see a dialog box similar to the one shown in Figure 19-12. To make a change, click <u>C</u>hange or Change A<u>l</u>l. To ignore the problem, click <u>I</u>gnore or Ignore All.

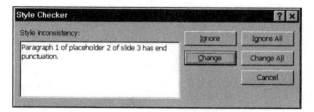

Figure 19-12 Correct any style inconsistencies.

5. When the checker is complete, you see a message saying so. Click the OK button to close the dialog box.

FORMATTING AND DISPLAYING A POWERPOINT PRESENTATION

LEARN THESE KEY SKILLS:

20

The first part of creating a presentation is to work on the content. Without content, there's nothing to build on. No matter if you have laser sound effects and dancing text, the presentation will be a bust without good content. The previous two chapters covered how to work on the content to make it award-winning.

Now you need to add the snap, crackle, pop to the presentation. That is, you need to work on the look of the presentation. Does the presentation look appealing? Is the font easy to read? Are the colors good? You need to review the entire presentation and make any changes. This chapter covers ways to enhance the appearance of your presentation.

Dazzling Text

The style, size, and alignment of text on a slide are determined by the slide layout and template you are using. PowerPoint selects readable, well-placed text so that you don't have to spend so much time making changes. But if you need to, you can change any element of the text — the font, font style, alignment, and so on. Read this section to see how to make your text shine!

Changing the Font for Selected Text

If you don't like the font that is selected, you can always make changes. You can change the typeface, the size, and the style (bold, italic, underline, or shadow). The fastest way to make a change is to use the toolbar. *Follow these steps:*

1. Move to the slide that contains the text you want to change. Select the text you want to change.

   To change the look of just some text, click the text box and then drag across the text you want to change. To change all the text within a text box, click the box once. Then click the box border. Figure 20-1 shows an entire text box — the title — selected for change.

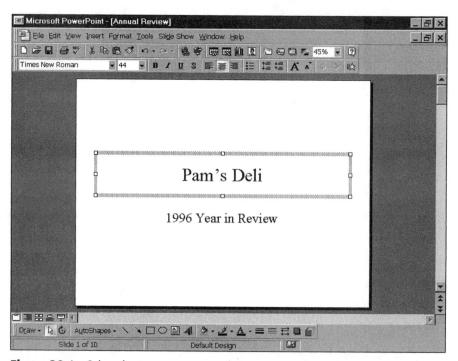

Figure 20-1 Select the text you want to change.

2. Do any of the following:

   To change the font, click the down arrow next to Times New Roman and then select the font you want.

To change the size of the text, click the down arrow next to $\boxed{10 \; \blacktriangledown}$ and click the size you want.

To change the style of the text, click $\boxed{\text{B}}$ for bold text, $\boxed{I}$ for italic text, $\boxed{\underline{u}}$ for underlined text, or $\boxed{\blacksquare}$ for shadowed text.

TIP **To make selected text larger or smaller, use the Increase Font Size and Decrease Font Size buttons in the toolbar.**

3. Click outside the text box to deselect it. Figure 20-2 shows a slide title using different font, font size, and shadow types.

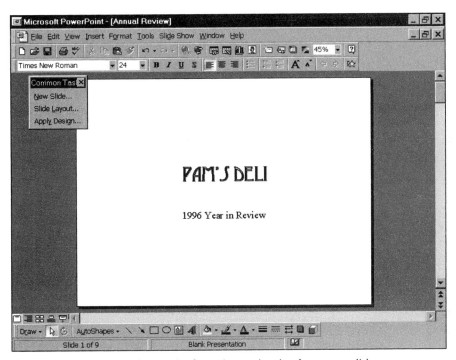

Figure 20-2 You can change the font, size, and style of text on a slide.

Changing the Font on All Slides

The font used throughout the presentation is determined by the template you selected. If you don't like that font, you don't have to change each piece of text on the slides. Instead, you can replace the font with another font of your choosing. *Follow these steps:*

1. Select $\boxed{\text{Format}} \rightarrow \boxed{\text{Replace Fonts}}$. You see the Replace Font dialog box.

2. Display the Replace with drop-down list and select the font you want to replace.

3. Display the <u>W</u>ith drop-down list and select the new font you want to use.

4. Click the <u>R</u>eplace button. PowerPoint makes all the replacements.

5. Click the Close button to close the dialog box.

Changing the Alignment of Text

Where the text appears within the text box — that is, how it is aligned — depends on the layout you selected. Just as with most other options, if you don't like the placement of the text, you can make a change. You can choose left, center, right, or justified.

TIP **You can also move the text object around on the slide. For example, you may want to put a subtitle after the title. For help on moving objects, see Chapter 19.**

Follow these steps to change the alignment of text:

1. Click within the paragraph or line you want to change.

2. To center the text, click ▤ or select Fo<u>r</u>mat → <u>A</u>lignment → <u>C</u>enter .

To align the text with the left edge of the text box, click ▤ or select Fo<u>r</u>mat → <u>A</u>lignment → <u>L</u>eft .

To align text with the right edge of the text box, click ▤ or select Fo<u>r</u>mat → <u>A</u>lignment → <u>R</u>ight .

To justify text (this works only for more than one line of text), select Fo<u>r</u>mat → <u>A</u>lignment → <u>J</u>ustify .

TIP **You can also use these keyboard shortcuts: Ctrl+L for left, Ctrl+E for Center, or Ctrl+R for right.**

PowerPoint makes the change. Figure 20-3 shows a subtitle that is right-aligned.

SIDE TRIP

FORMATTING LINES OF TEXT

If you have several lines of text (paragraphs), you can change how these appear. Follow these steps:

1. Select the text you want to change.

2. To add a bullet to these lines, click ▤.

3. To use more or less space, click ▤ or ▤.

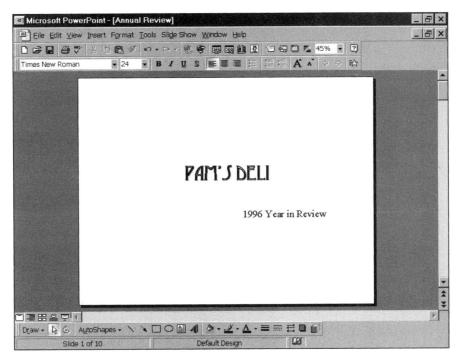

Figure 20-3 You can change the alignment of the text boxes.

Minor Look Changes

Text is only one part of the slide. You can also change the overall look of the slide, adding other objects, such as a simple logo. You can use a different slide layout or change the colors used in a chart. For organization charts, you can change how the boxes look. When you want to tinker with some part of the slide that's not text, try this section. The next section in this chapter covers how to update the look of the entire presentation.

Changing the Slide Layout

What if you don't like the slide layout you selected? You can make changes manually by dragging and resizing the objects the slide does include and then adding any other objects you do want to include. You'll also need to get rid of objects that you don't want and possibly change the formatting of the text. Whew! That's a lot of work.

Instead of going to all that trouble, you can update the layout by simply selecting another layout. *Follow these steps:*

1. Select **Format** → **Slide Layout** or click ⬚ or select Slide Layout from the Common Tasks toolbar. You see the Slide Layout dialog box, shown in Figure 20-4.

2. Click the layout you want and then click the OK button. PowerPoint updates the layout of the slide.

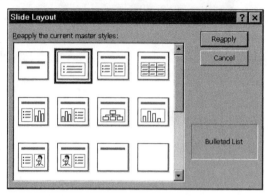

Figure 20-4 Select the layout you want from this dialog box.

Adding Objects to a Slide

What if you like the layout that you have, but you just want to add some other object to the slide — such as text, or a chart, or a picture. You can easily add any object to a slide:

✳ To add text, click 📧 or select Insert → Text Box . Click the slide and drag to draw the text box. Then type the text for the text.

✳ To add a chart, click 📊 or select Insert → Chart . Create the chart as covered in Chapter 18.

✳ To add an organization chart, select Insert → Picture → Organization Chart . Create the organization chart as covered in Chapter 18.

✳ To add a clip art image, click 🖼 or select Insert → Picture → Clip Art . Select the image as covered in Chapter 18.

✳ To draw on the slide using the Drawing tools, see the next section.

You select a placement for text boxes, but for other objects PowerPoint places the object right in the middle of the chart. You will have to move and possibly resize the object to integrate it with existing content. Figure 20-5 shows a clip art image added to a slide. This image was resized and moved to the lower-right corner.

Drawing on a Slide

You may want to call attention to an important point on a slide. Or you may want to add a simple logo. Even if you don't have any artistic talent, you can use the simple shapes on the Drawing toolbar displayed at the bottom of the PowerPoint screen to draw on the slide. These are the same tools you find in

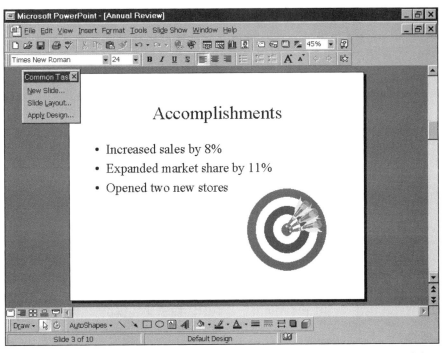

Figure 20-5 You can add any type of object, including clip art, to an existing slide.

Word and Excel, so you should be pretty familiar with them. You can do any of the following:

* To add a predrawn shape, click $\boxed{\text{AutoShapes } \cdot }$. You see the AutoShapes menu. Select the type of shape you want to add and then click and drag on the slide to draw the shape.

* To draw a line, click $\boxed{\diagdown}$ and click and drag to draw the line. Hold down Shift key as you drag to draw a straight line.

* To draw an arrow, click $\boxed{\diagdown}$ and click and drag to draw an arrow. Click $\boxed{\rightleftarrows}$ to select a different style for the arrow. Figure 20-6 shows an arrow drawn on a slide.

* To draw a rectangle or square, click $\boxed{\square}$ and click and drag to draw the shape. To draw a square, hold down the Shift key as you drag.

* To draw a oval or circle, click $\boxed{\bigcirc}$ and click and drag to draw the shape. To draw a circle, hold down the Shift key as you drag.

* For rectangles and squares, you can fill the object with color by clicking $\boxed{\diamondsuit}$ and then selecting the color you want from the palette that appears.

* To use change how the lines are drawn, click $\boxed{\diagup}$ and select a line color, or click $\boxed{\equiv}$ and select a different line style, or click $\boxed{\equiv}$ and click the style you want.

* For special effects, try $\boxed{\blacksquare}$ to add a shadow or $\boxed{\square}$ to add a 3D effect.

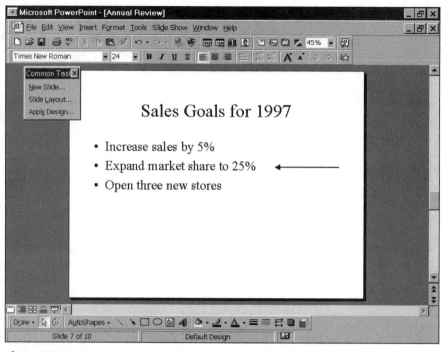

Figure 20-6 You can draw on a slide — for example, draw an arrow as shown here.

Changing the Look of a Chart

When you create a chart, PowerPoint does a good job of creating a chart with a good design. If you aren't exactly happy with what you get, you can modify the chart options and make changes to the chart's appearance. *Follow these steps:*

1. Double-click the chart object. You see the datasheet. Also, the `Chart` menu now appears in the menu bar.

2. Select `Chart` → `Chart Options`. You see the Chart Options dialog box. The tabs and options that appear vary depending on the chart type. Figure 20-7 shows the options for a pie chart.

3. Click the tab you want and make any changes. If you aren't sure what each one does, try experimenting. The dialog box shows how your chart will appear with the options you have selected. You can also get help by right-clicking the option and selecting the What's This? command.

4. When you are finished making changes, click the OK button. PowerPoint updates the chart.

5. Click back on the slide. Figure 20-8 shows a pie chart with percent labels added and the legend moved to the left side.

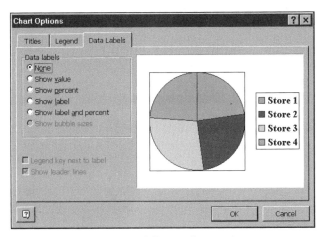

Figure 20-7 Select the different chart options you want to use.

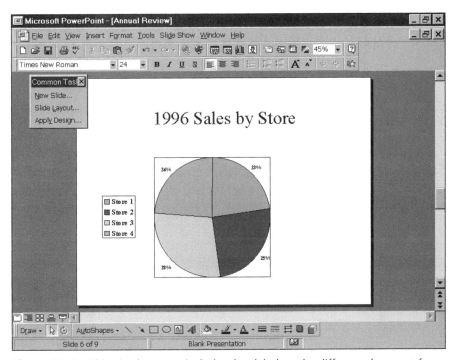

Figure 20-8 This pie chart now includes data labels and a different placement for the legend.

Changing the Look of an Organization Chart

Just as you can change how a chart looks, you can also change the appearance of an organization chart — using different styles for the boxes, using different colors, changing the font, and more. *To make a change, follow these steps:*

1. Double-click the organization chart to start Microsoft Organization Chart, the program used to create and modify this type of chart.

2. Select the box you want to modify.

TIP **To select multiple boxes, hold down the Shift key and click each box you want to select.**

3. Use the Styles menu to select how the boxes are arranged. The menu gives you a good idea of how each choice affects the boxes (see Figure 20-9).

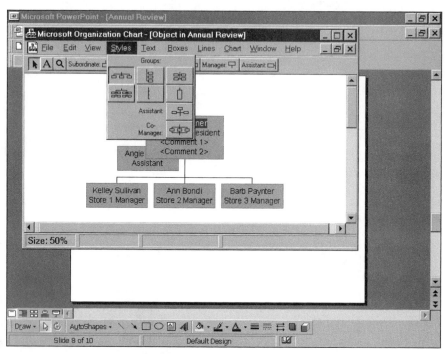

Figure 20-9 You can change the arrangement of the boxes in an organization chart.

4. Use the Text menu to select the font, color, and alignment of the text.

5. Use the Boxes menu to select a color, shadow, border style, border color, or border line style for the boxes.

6. Use the Lines menu to change the thickness, style, and color of the lines that connect the boxes.

7. When you are finished making changes, click the Close button for the application. When prompted to update the slide, click Yes.

Figure 20-10 shows an organization chart with some changes — different text styles, border style, shadow, and color.

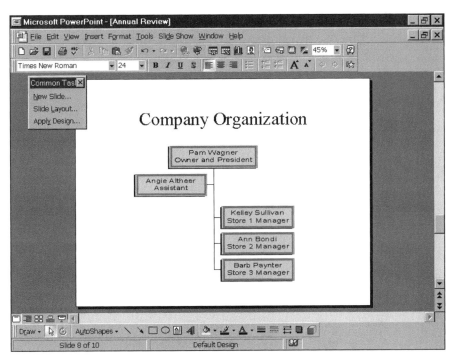

Figure 20-10 You can change the look of the boxes, text, and lines in an organization chart.

Major Look Change

The preceding sections covered how to change individual slides, which can help you fine-tune the look of the presentation. When you make individual changes, you need to be careful not to end up with colors and styles that are a mish-mash rather than a unified design. Be sure these individual changes improve the overall appearance of the presentation.

In your presentation, be careful not to end up with colors and styles that are a mish-mash rather than a unified design.

Working with individual slides is one way to improve the presentation. As another way, you can make changes to the presentation as a whole. For example, you can use a new design that includes colors, slide layouts, fonts, and other selections. Or you can change the background color or color scheme used on the slides. This section discusses these changes.

Note that you really shouldn't mess with the color scheme, background, and design all together. Instead, update the entire presentation using a new design or tinker with the color scheme and possibly background colors, but not all three. Also, while you can change the background color and color scheme for individual slides, I wouldn't recommend it. The colors are one thing that unifies a presentation. If you go hog wild on the colors, you may end up just distracting your audience. But hey, it's your presentation.

Applying a Design

When you create a new presentation, you select the template you want to use. The template affects the fonts used, the color scheme, the location/alignment of the slide objects, and other formatting options such as the style and color for bullets. If you don't like the template that you selected, you can make a change. Using a different template (or design) is also a good way to change the overall appearance of the presentation. When you apply a new template, PowerPoint updates all design elements for the entire presentation.

To apply a new design, follow these steps:

1. Select **Format** → **Apply Design**, click 🖼, or select Apply Design in the Common Tasks toolbar. You see the Apply Design dialog box.

2. To get a preview of the selected design, select the one you want in the Name list. Figure 20-11 shows a preview of the Dads Tie design.

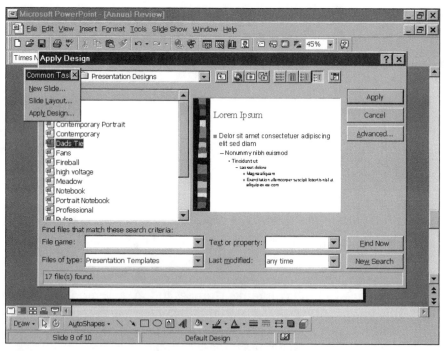

Figure 20-11 Preview the design before you apply it to your presentation.

3. Click the Apply button to apply these changes to the presentation.

Changing the Color Scheme for the Presentation

If you look at a presentation, you'll notice more than just a few color choices. PowerPoint uses one color for the background, one for the text, a set of colors for any charts, and so on. The collection of colors used in a presentation is called the *color scheme*. If you don't like the colors, you can select a different color scheme.

To use a different color scheme, follow these steps:

1. Select **Format** → **Slide Color Scheme**. You see the Color Scheme dialog box, shown in Figure 20-12. In each scheme, you can see the colors that are currently used for each of the presentation elements (title, bullet, background, and charts).

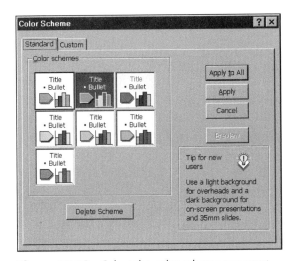

Figure 20-12 Select the color scheme you want.

2. Select the color scheme you want to use.

3. To apply this scheme to all slides in the presentation, click the Apply to All button. The presentation is updated.

Using a Different Background

If you don't like the background color used for the slides, you can select a different one. The available colors depend on the color scheme you have selected. *Follow these steps to change the background color:*

1. Select **Format** → **Background**. You see the Background dialog box, shown in Figure 20-13. The dialog box shows the colors of other elements so that you can be sure these elements will look OK on the new background.

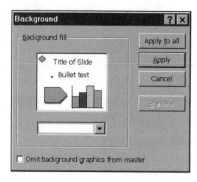

Figure 20-13 Select the background color or fill you want.

2. Display the drop-down list and select the color you want to use.

3. To apply this scheme to all slides in the presentation, click the Apply to All button. The presentation is updated.

Lights, Camera, Action

Once the look is perfect-o, you can think about presenting your presentation. You can give your presentation in a couple of ways. You can print transparencies and use an overhead to give the presentation. Or you can have slides created and use a slide projector. Or you may simply hand out a printed copy of the presentation and go over the slides without a visual display. Another method for giving the presentation is to use your computer. You can display your presentation on your monitor, or you can use special equipment and the PC to display your presentation as a slide show on a larger screen.

TIP For information on printing, see Chapter 3 of this book. For information on creating slides, check with a local printing service bureau in your area. They should be able to tell you what they need from you to print the slides for the presentation (usually just the file).

Setting Up a Slide Show

Any PowerPoint presentation is in effect a slide show. You don't need to do anything special to create a PowerPoint slide show. How about that for a short section?

Viewing a Slide Show

The show's already set up, so all you have to do is check it out and add any special effects. *To start a slide show, follow these steps:*

1. Select   Slide Show → View Show . You see the first slide in the presentation (see Figure 20-14).

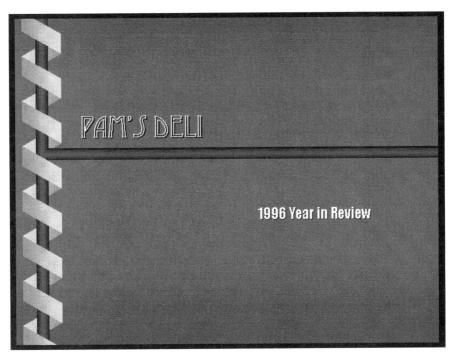

Figure 20-14 Slides are displayed one at a time on your monitor during a slide show.

2. To display the next slide, click the mouse button or press the Spacebar.

3. Continue moving through each slide. When you get to the end, PowerPoint returns you to the last view you were in.

 TIP To stop the presentation, right-click the slide and select End **S**how.

SIDE TRIP

ANIMATE TEXT

If you are planning on giving your presentation as a slide show, you may want to try out some of the animation effects for text. For example, you can have text appear typed one character at a time. You won't notice these effects on the slide; they appear only during the slide show. Follow these steps to animate text:

1. Select the text you want to animate.

2. Click 🌠. You see the Animation Effects toolbar, which contains buttons for common animation effects.

3. Click the effect you want.

4. Close the toolbar by clicking its Close button.

5. View the effect by viewing the slide show.

Adding Transition Effects

PowerPoint provides some special effects for drawing a new slide on the screen. For example, you can have the new slide drawn as blinds, as a checkerboard, as stripes, and so on. Transition effects can jazz up the delivery of a presentation. *To select a transition effect, follow these steps:*

1. Select Slide Show → Slide Transition . You see the Transition dialog box (see Figure 20-15).

Figure 20-15 Use this dialog box to set the transitions for the slides in your slide show.

2. Display the Effect drop-down list and select the effect you want. The dialog box shows you an example of this effect.

3. To add a sound, display the Sound drop-down list and select the sound you want.

4. Select whether you want to advance to the next slide only when the mouse is clicked or automatically after the amount of seconds you specify.

5. Click the Apply to All button to apply these effects to the presentation. To see them in action, view the slide show.

You can set individual effects for each slide, but you don't want to make your audience dizzy. Instead, stick to one transition type per presentation.

BONUS

Creating Speaker Notes

When you are creating a presentation, you most likely have some additional things to talk about for each slide. You don't want to stand up in front of audience like "Duh?" And you probably don't want to rattle off whatever pops in your head. Or worse yet, you don't want to simply read each slide to your audience. Instead, you probably will prepare some notes.

You can type up your notes separately and hope you know what idea goes with what slide. Or you can create speaker notes for yourself. These notes show the slide at the top and include a big area for you to type your script. *To set up notes, follow these steps:*

1. Select `View` → `Notes Page`. You see the Notes page, shown in Figure 20-16. The view is too small, so zoom to a larger zoom percentage. Click `45% ▾` and select a larger number to zoom the notes.

2. When the notes are big enough for you to see and work with, click the text placeholder and type the text for this slide.

3. Display the next slide and add notes for this page. Do this for each slide you want notes for.

4. When you are finished adding notes, click the Slide View button to return to Slide view.

5. To print the notes, select `File` → `Print`.

6. In the Print dialog box, display the Print what drop-down list and select Notes Pages.

7. Click the OK button. Now you are ready to give the presentation. Good Luck!

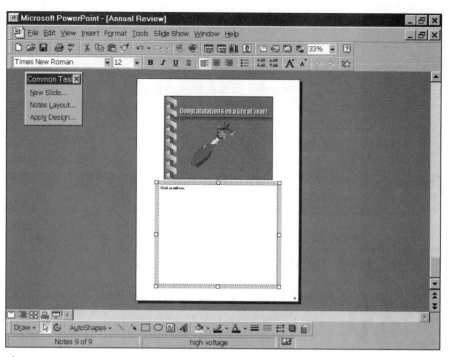

Figure 20-16   Type your notes on this page.

Microsoft refers to Access as a "Relational Database Management System." That's a fancy way of saying "I keep your data stuff organized." A relational database lets you set up all your data in such a way that you can connect items easily, find what you need, and add and remove things when necessary. In this section, you learn what it takes to get a database up and running, starting with an introduction to databases and continuing through printing your data in readable reports.

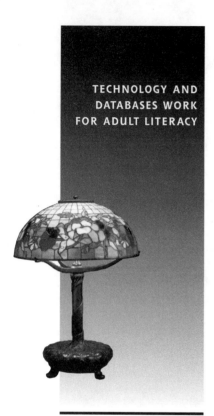

The National Center on Adult Literacy (NCAL), along with other literacy organizations, has made a strong commitment to using technology to improve the quality of adult literacy programs nationwide. Established in 1990, NCAL "seeks to improve the quality of adult literacy programs," and one way they've expressed their commitment is by founding the Literacy Technology Laboratory (LTL), which works "to meet the challenge of adapting new technologies to adult literacy learning and instruction." This includes not only promoting the use of effective instructional software, hardware, and networking solutions, but also keeping in touch with the instructional needs of those working in the field of adult literacy.

Among many projects at the LTL, the staff maintains an electronic database of adult literacy software. "We update the database every 18 months or so, depending on when new software and updates become available," explains Chris Hopey, Project Director. Interested parties can search the database, which the LTL maintains on the NCAL Web site. The database, which has received much positive feedback, is also available on disk and as hard copy. Through phone, mail, and a variety of giveaways at conferences and workshops, Hopey estimates that over 4,000 people have received the database in some form.

The LTL sees the Internet as the next great forum for disseminating adult literacy information, resources, and products. They have developed materials to help practitioners and program instructors gain access to the Internet and use it more effectively.

Chris Hopey sees the use of technology in adult literacy expanding in two directions: "First, self-directed instruction, especially over the Internet for the GED and pre-GED learner." According to Hopey, the second direction is geared to teachers. Several companies are developing products and resources — such as classroom-based materials and lesson plans — that will be available on the Internet.

For more information on NCAL, visit their Web site at `http://ncal.literacy.upenn.edu`. For more on the literacy software database, visit `http://ncal.literacy.upenn.edu/Products/prdat.htm`.

CREATING AN ACCESS DATABASE AND TABLES

YOU LEARN THESE KEY SKILLS:

Though many people use the familiar address book as an example of a simple database, a database is more than a list of names and addresses. With Microsoft Access, you can not only maintain a list but quickly change it, review only certain names based on criteria you determine, and more. In this chapter, you begin your journey into the world of databases by creating your own database and your first *table*, the building block of every database.

Entering the Database Zone

If you are asking yourself "What's a database?" read on for some basic database concepts. If you are saying "Get on with it!" skip down to "Shoving Off" to learn how to create your first database.

A *database* is a collection of information that shares a common theme or subject. No doubt you use some or all of the following databases on a regular basis — a phone or address book, a photo album, or an organized grocery list. Each of these is a database, with the information ordered in a particular way, such as alphabetically in the case of an address or phone book, chronologically in the case of the photo album, or by item type (produce, canned goods, or what have you) in the case of the grocery list. (I know what you're thinking: who has time to organize a grocery list? Answer: me. My in-laws gave us a preprinted list that has little boxes for each category. Scary, but true.)

An *electronic* database allows you to maintain your collections of information on your computer. You can manipulate the information in a variety of ways, including sorting it (show me all of Aunt Martha's calls in chronological order, starting with the most recent), extracting information according to specific criteria (show me all the people who owe me money so that I can send in my heavies), and printing reports to present the information in a meaningful way.

Microsoft Access takes the database concept even further by providing a *relational* database management system. This means that you can have several collections of information and tie them together in different ways. Let's say you have a home office and provide financial services to a variety of clients. You want to maintain several lists of information — clients, services you offer and rates, and an inventory of materials you send or leave with clients. Access refers to these "lists" as *tables,* and you can store each of these lists in a separate table.

What's the advantage of separate tables? Two of the biggest advantages are manageability and efficiency. If your information is divided into logical tables, you can find what you need more quickly. Also, such an arrangement prevents you from having to repeat identical information in several locations. For example, if several clients receive your Budget Planning service, you can tie each client to the Budget Planning service in your list of services, rather than repeating this service in the list of clients. And anytime you want to see what services you've provided to Jane Brown and when you provided them, you can ask Access to tell you (see Figure 21-1). You will learn more about asking Access for information in upcoming chapters.

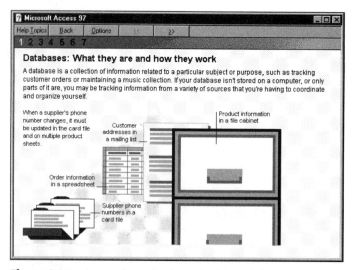

Figure 21-1 Learn about databases in Access help.

Access refers to the elements that make up a single database as *objects*. Objects include tables, reports, forms, queries, macros, and modules. Huh? Take a peek in your closet. Each piece of clothing — pair of pants, shirt, or shoe — is like a database object. In the case of these clothing objects, each has a different function in helping you look presentable each day. In the case of database objects, each has a different function in helping you manage your data. You will learn more about most of the database objects in upcoming sections and chapters.

Shoving Off

Access ships with several predefined database types, such as Contact Management, Inventory Control, and Order Entry. You may find that you can use many of these predefined databases for your own work. However, before you can use these effectively, you need to understand how Access puts a database together. The best way to do that is to create your own database from scratch.

Starting Access

Follow these steps to create a new database:

1. At the Windows desktop, start Microsoft Access. For more information on starting an Office application, refer to Chapter 2.

2. Access starts and displays the Microsoft Access dialog box (see Figure 21-2). Here you decide whether you want to create a new database or open an existing one.

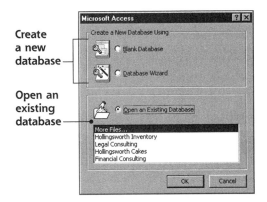

Create a new database

Open an existing database

Figure 21-2 Create a new database or work on an existing one.

Every time you start Access, you will see this dialog box. You'll create a new database using the Database Wizard.

As you have seen in the Word, Excel, and PowerPoint sections, one of the hallmarks of Microsoft applications is the Wizard, a handy helping tool that leads you through a task by asking a series of questions and creating a database, table, or other object based on your answers. It's like your own personal tutor, taking you by the hand and walking you through the steps you need to complete a task.

Creating a Database

As I mentioned previously, you will create a database from scratch to get an understanding of what makes a database and how it's put together.

Follow these steps to create a database using the Database Wizard:

1. Click Database Wizard under Create a New Database Using, and then click OK. Access displays the New dialog box (see Figure 21-3), where you can select the type of database you would like to create.

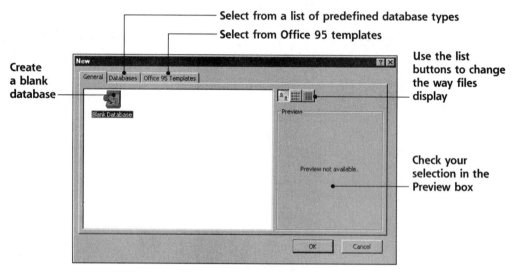

Select from a list of predefined database types

Select from Office 95 templates

Create a blank database

Use the list buttons to change the way files display

Check your selection in the Preview box

Figure 21-3   Select the type of database that best suits your needs.

2. Make sure Blank Database is selected on the General tab, and then click OK. Access displays the File New Database dialog box. Access is one of the few applications that requires you to name your file before you do anything with it. It is also the only Office program that automatically saves your databases when you exit so that you aren't put in danger of losing data.

3. Type a name for your database in the File name text box and then click Create. Access displays the Microsoft Access window and the message "Verifying system objects" on the status bar. You then see the Database window for your database, with six tabs (see Figure 21-4).

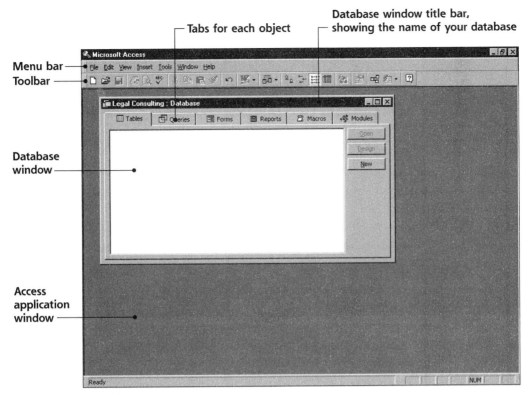

Menu bar

Toolbar

Tabs for each object

Database window title bar, showing the name of your database

Database window

Access application window

Figure 21-4 Create or select objects in the Database window.

Next you'll create the all-important foundation of your database — tables.

The Wizard of Table Street

The building blocks of every database are its tables. Earlier I mentioned that you can store collections of related information in individual tables. Think of a table as one individual file in a hanging file folder and the database itself as the hanging folder. Each file folder (table) may contain a client list, a list of products you sell, or — to continue with the financial planner example — your list of services. Access uses the tables as the basis for creating reports, building queries, and working with forms.

A table consists of columns and rows. Each column contains a *field,* which is like a label describing the type of information contained in the column. Each row contains a *record*, which is a collection of fields related to a single person, event, or item. For example, in your client list, the fields would consist of such labels as first name, last name, company, address, city, state, zip, phone, fax, e-mail, and so on (see Figure 21-5). Each record would consist of the information associated with each person.

TIP Try to lay out the different tables you think you'll need and the data contained in each table before you begin. Though you can easily modify your tables later, it helps to have a "map" to start out.

Columns (fields)

Field heading
or label

Rows
(records)

Mailing List ID	First Name	Last Name	Title	Organization N	Industry	Address
1	John	Walden	Partner	Walden & Jones	Law Firm	1234 E. Main S	De
2	Barbara	Smith	Partner	Otis, Mann, & L	Law Firm	5678 E. 51st Av	En
3	Lynn	Becker	Partner	Becker, Becker	Law Firm	23 N. Centennia	An
4	Matthew	Raymond	Partner	Perkins & Johns	Law Firm	4575 E. Cherry	Gle
5	Walter	Stanford	Partner	Fair & Middlon	Law Firm	23 E. 38th St.,	De
6	Stephanie	Chaucer	Partner	Chaucer & Chau	Law Firm	1455 N. Master	Au
7	Christopher	Bryce	IS Manager	Sigmund Insura	Insurance	3457 S. Brighto	Co
8	Vincent	Music	IS Manager	Needless Insura	Insurance	9878 W. 54th S	De
9	Michelle	Davis	IS Manager	U-Safe Insuranc	Insurance	3234 E. Piney F	De

Record: 1 of 20

Figure 21-5 A table consists of columns and rows.

Creating a Table Using the Table Wizard

Access provides several methods for creating tables, with the easiest one being the Table Wizard.

To create a table with the Table Wizard, follow these steps:

1. With the Database window displayed, select the Tables tab, if it is not already displayed.

2. Click New.

3. Select Table Wizard from the list in the New Table dialog box and click OK. Access displays the Table Wizard dialog box (see Figure 21-6).

Fields you wish to use

Sample table type

Business

Personal

Fields selected for your table

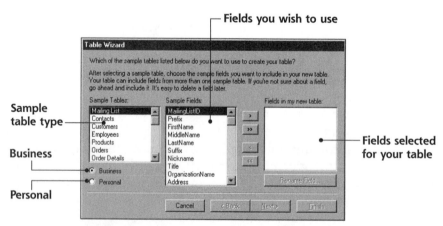

Figure 21-6 Select the type of table that best suits your needs.

4. Select Business or Personal at the bottom of the dialog box to display a list of appropriate sample tables.

5. Select the table that best suits your needs from the Sample Tables list.

6. Select the field you wish to include from the Sample Fields list and then click ⟩. If you want to use all the fields in the Sample Fields list, click ⟩⟩.

Fields appear in the table in the order you select and insert them into your list. Though you can change them later, it's easier to select them in the order you wish them to appear now, before copying them to the Fields in my new table list.

7. When you're finished adding all your fields, click <u>N</u>ext.

8. Type a name for your table and then read the information in this dialog box about *primary keys*, which are fields or sets of fields that create a unique identifier for each record in a table to avoid duplication.

TIP When you're just starting out, it's best to let the Access Wizard set the primary key for you. Later, when you feel more comfortable with how your tables interrelate, you may want to set your own key.

9. Click <u>N</u>ext to let Access set the primary key for you. Access displays the next Table Wizard dialog box, asking if you wish to modify the table design or enter data.

SIDE TRIP

INSERTING AND REMOVING FIELDS

It's easy to insert and remove fields in this dialog box if you make a mistake.

✴ To insert a field quickly, double-click it.

✴ To remove a field from your list, select the field and then click ⟨ or just double-click the field.

✴ To remove all fields, click ⟨⟨.

✴ To insert a field between two existing fields, select the field in the Fields in my table list that you wish to *precede* the new field and then double-click the new field in the Sample Fields list.

✴ To rename a particular field, select it in your list and then click Rename Field. Type the new name in the <u>R</u>ename field text box and then click OK.

X-REF For information on modifying the table design, see "Rearranging the Furniture" in Chapter 22. You'll learn more about entering data using a form in Chapter 24, "Working with Forms."

10. Click Finish to accept the default.

Access displays your new table in table Datasheet view (see Figure 21-7). This view shows your data in columns and rows, allowing you to see more of your records at once. You will learn more about views in the next chapter. Notice the field names at the tops of all the columns. If you let Access set your primary key for you, you'll see an "ID" column as the first column in your table. Access will add a unique number to each record to help identify it.

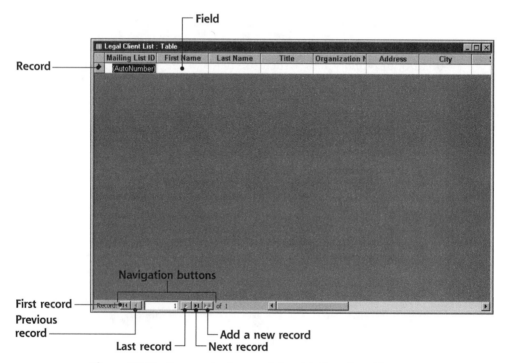

Figure 21-7 Enter and edit records in table Datasheet view.

Exploring the Datasheet Toolbar

Just like all Microsoft applications, Access has a variety of toolbars to help you complete the current task. As you begin to create different objects and use different views, you will see the toolbar change to reflect its new surroundings. Table 21-1 provides a description of the buttons on the Table Datasheet toolbar.

To use a toolbar button, merely click the desired button. If a button has a down arrow next to it, click the arrow to display a list of options, and then select the desired option.

TABLE 6-1 The Table Datasheet Toolbar

Button	Name	Description
	VIEW	Displays the table in Datasheet or Design view.
	SAVE	Saves the document.
	PRINT	Prints the current table.
	PRINT PREVIEW	Displays a preview of the table.
	SPELLING	Checks the spelling in the table.
	CUT	Cuts selected text.
	COPY	Copies selected text.
	PASTE	Pastes cut or copied text from the clipboard.
	FORMAT PAINTER	Copies formatting such as colors and line styles. Not available in table Datasheet view.
	UNDO	Undoes the last command or commands.
	INSERT HYPERLINK	Inserts a link to a file or a Web page. Available only when you've defined a hyperlink address field in the table.
	WEB TOOLBAR	Displays a toolbar with buttons for creating Web documents.
	SORT ASCENDING	Sorts the table in ascending order (A to Z) based on the current field.
	SORT DESCENDING	Sorts the table in descending order (Z to A) based on the current field.
	FILTER BY SELECTION	Filters records by selected fields.
	FILTER BY FORM	Displays the Filter By Form window so that you can specify filter criteria.
	APPLY FILTER	Applies the current filter to the data. Available only when you've set filtering criteria.
	FIND	Searches for a string of information in the table.
	NEW RECORD	Adds a new record as the last record.
	DELETE RECORD	Deletes the current record.

(continued)

TABLE 6-1 (continued)

Button	Name	Description
⊡	DATABASE WINDOW	Displays the Database window.
⊡	NEW OBJECT	Creates a new object.
⊡	OFFICE ASSISTANT	Displays the Office Assistant.

Entering Records into a Table

Once you've created the table structure — that is, once you've defined the fields for your table — you can begin entering information. *Follow these steps*:

1. Press Tab to move to the first empty field.

2. Type the information for the field.

3. Repeat steps 1 and 2 for each new field. When you press Tab from the last field in a row, Access moves to the next row (record).

4. Press Tab to move to the next empty field and type the information for the field.

When you finish entering records into your table, you can close it. Access will automatically save the data. You can also save the data periodically using the Save feature you learned in Chapter 2.

Getting Hitched

At the beginning of this chapter, I talked about a relational database and the advantages of using related tables instead of having all your information in a single location (one table). These advantages include not having to repeat information in several places, and having information in manageable chunks that you can work on individually.

When you create another table using the Table Wizard, Access automatically asks you to define the relationship between the new table and any existing tables. When you define relationships between tables, it's important to determine the *primary table* you will use in the relationship. The primary table is the one that begins each relationship and maintains the relational integrity between the tables. For example, if you have your client list in one table and your services list in another, you can relate one client in the first table to several services in the second table. This is called a *one-to-many relationship* because your one client may use several services, and thus the client table is the primary table. Figure 21-8 in the next section provides a visual representation of this kind of relationship.

Creating a New Table and Defining Its Relationship

Before beginning, determine the contents of your new table and how it will relate to the existing table. You can have three types of relationships — one-to-one, one-to-many, or many-to-many — but you will focus on the most common relationship — one-to-many. In a one-to-many relationship, a record in Table 1 can have one or more matching records in Table 2, but a record in Table 2 has only one or no matching records in Table 1. For an example of this relationship, see Figure 21-8.

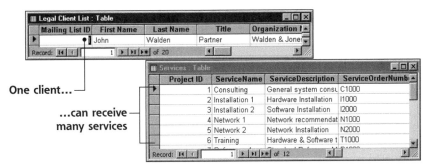

Figure 21-8   One client can receive many services in a one-to-many relationship.

You will add a new table and define its relationships using the Table Wizard. *To define relationships between tables, follow these steps:*

1. From the Database window, select the Table tab and click New. Otherwise, if you have a table open, click 🖼 on the Table Datasheet toolbar.

2. Select Table Wizard from the list in the New Table dialog box, and then click OK to display the Table Wizard dialog box.

3. Select your options as you did for the previous table, choosing Business or Personal, Sample Table, and sample fields. Then click Next.

4. Type a name for your table and then click Next to have Access set the primary key for you. Access displays a dialog box asking about the relationships between your tables.

5. Click Relationships to display the Relationships dialog box, and then select the one-to-many option that reflects the relationship you want.

6. Click OK and then click Next.

7. Click Finish to complete the table and display it in table Datasheet view.

8. Enter the data and then save the table.

If you are finished working with Access, you can exit the application, using the steps you learned in Chapter 2.

BONUS

Working with Databases

Now that you understand how databases work, you can explore some of the database models available through the Database Wizard, and learn how to open an existing database and change the name of a database.

Using a Predefined Database

As mentioned at the beginning of the chapter, Access ships with a number of pre-defined database models, many of which may suit your data management needs. *To create a new database based on one of these models, follow these steps*:

1. In Access, click **File** → **New Database**. Then click Database Wizard under the Create New Database Using box.

2. Select the Database tab, select the predefined database that represents the type of information you wish to store, and click OK.

3. Type a name for the database in the File name text box and then click Create. Access creates and displays the Database window for the new database and then immediately displays the opening Database Wizard dialog box (see a sample in Figure 21-9). This first dialog box describes the type of data you can store in the selected database.

4. Click Next to display the next dialog box for the Database Wizard. This dialog box lists suggested tables for your database and recommended fields for each table (see Figure 21-10).

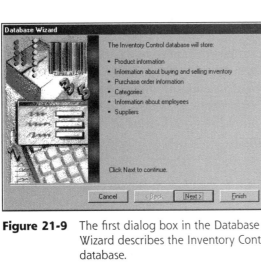

Figure 21-9 The first dialog box in the Database Wizard describes the Inventory Control database.

Remove a field from the selected table

Recommended tables

Recommended fields for each table

Include sample data

Figure 21-10 Select the tables and fields for your database.

5. Select each table and remove any fields you don't want.

6. Click the check box at the bottom of the dialog box if you wish to include sample data in the table. Then click Next. Access displays a dialog box asking what background style you would like to use, if any.

7. Select the desired background, noting the sample that appears in the box at left. If you don't wish to use a background, select Standard and click Next. Access asks how you wish the labels to appear for printed reports.

8. Select the desired style, noting the sample that appears in the box at left. If you wish to use the default, select Casual and click Next. Access asks for the title of your database.

9. Type a title and then click the check box if you wish to include a picture on each page of forms and reports. Click Next.

10. Click Finish to set up the database.

11. If this is the first time you've used one of the database templates, Access displays a message box telling you that you need to enter your company name and address. Click OK and fill in the form that displays. Close the form to save the information. Access builds all the tables, forms, and reports for your database and then displays the Main switchboard, where you can select which task you'd like to perform first.

When you use the Database Wizard to create a database, Access creates a *switchboard* that helps you to work with your database. This switchboard appears when you open the database as a sort of a "What would you like to do?" page. It contains a list of tasks with buttons that you can click to add records, open forms, and perform other common tasks with your database.

12. Select the task and proceed.

 X-REF For information on using forms and reports, see Chapter 23, "Working with Forms," and Chapter 24, "Working with Reports."

Renaming a Database

You can't change the name of a database from within Access. You must use Windows Explorer or My Computer. *To change the name, follow the steps below*:

1. Make sure you close the database you wish to rename.

2. Using My Computer or Windows Explorer, display the folder containing the database file.

 TIP If you are unsure where the file is located, open the database and then click File → Properties. Select the General tab, note the folder next to Location, and then click OK.

3. Click the filename (not the file icon) once to select it, and then click it again to activate edit mode.

4. Type the new name for the database, including the .MDB extension if you aren't hiding DOS extensions, and then press Enter.

5. Close My Computer or Windows Explorer.

 When you start Access, you see the Microsoft Access window, which lists existing databases under Open an Existing Database. If you have renamed a database, the new name will not be reflected here. You must choose More Files under Open an Existing Database and then click OK to display the Open dialog box, where you can select the database with the new name.

WORKING WITH YOUR DATA

LEARN THESE KEY SKILLS:

C hange is inevitable in life and in databases. Now that you've had a chance to create your own database and entered records into a table, you can explore the methods for editing your data and modifying the actual table structure to reflect additions or deletions in the way you want to maintain your data.

Doing the Data Dance

D o you use whiteout, white tape, or the old scratch-out method when changing someone's information in your address book? Or maybe you really think ahead and have entries in pencil so that you can erase the old information and enter the new. Whatever method you use, you know that change is inevitable. People move, change jobs, or change Internet service providers, and you've got to keep your information up to date.

Access provides a variety of ways to make changes to your data, including editing existing records, adding new records, deleting records, and freezing columns so that you can view different parts of the table at the same time.

Before you can make changes, you need to open your database. If Access is open and running, you can open your database as you would any document. Refer to Chapters 2 and 3 for information on starting an application and opening a file.

However, if Access is not running, go ahead and start it using the methods described in Chapter 2. Then select a database name from the Open an Existing Database list and click OK (see Figure 22-1). If you don't see your database listed, select More Files in the list, and then display the folder containing your database. Select the database name and click Open.

Recently used database files appear here

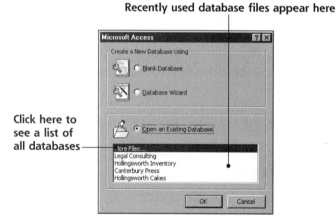

Click here to see a list of all databases

Figure 22-1 Select the database that you wish to work on.

 X-REF When you open a database that contains a *switchboard*, Access opens the database file and then displays the switchboard so that you can select the task you wish to perform. For more on switchboards, see the Bonus section in Chapter 21.

Adding a New Record

When you add a new record, Access places it after the last existing record. You can add a new record using the keyboard, the toolbar, or a menu.

 X-REF To organize records in a specific order, see "Order in the Court!" in this chapter.

To add a new record, follow these steps:

1. Select the Tables tab in the Database window.

2. Select the table containing the data you wish to change, and then click Open. Access displays the table in Datasheet view.

3. Select one of the following methods to add the new record, and then type the information for the new record:

* From the last field in the last record, press Tab.
* Click on the Table Datasheet toolbar or next to the record number box at the bottom of the table window.
* Click Insert → New Record.

Modifying a Record

Once you've opened your database, you can modify individual records to reflect new information.

To modify an existing record in a table, follow these steps:

1. Select the Tables tab in the Database window.

2. Select the table containing the data you wish to change, and then click Open. Access displays the table in Datasheet view.

3. To locate the record you wish to modify, use the vertical scroll bar or use one of the keyboard navigation methods listed in Table 22-1.

4. Click in the field you wish to change and edit the information. You can use the standard editing keys — Delete, Backspace, and Insert/Overtype — to make changes. In Access, press the Insert key once to turn Overtype on, and then press it again to turn Overtype off and Insert on. When you use Overtype, Access selects the next character so that you can replace it with a new one.

TIP If you prefer to keep your fingers on the keyboard as you work with your data, you can work in *navigation mode*, which allows you to move around your table using a variety of keyboard combinations. To activate navigation mode, press Tab, Shift+Tab, ⬆, or ⬇ to select the entire contents of the field without the insertion point being visible. You must use one of these methods. Merely selecting the contents of a field by double-clicking doesn't place you in navigation mode, because you can still see the insertion point.

CAUTION If you use keyboard navigation methods to move to a field, as indicated in Table 22-1, Access selects the entire contents of the field. If you don't want to replace the entire contents, make sure you click in the field before making changes. This gets you out of navigation mode and allows you to move between characters within the field.

TABLE 22-1   Moving Around in a Table

This Key	Will
TAB	Move to the next field.
SHIFT+TAB	Move to the previous field.
→	Move to the next field in a row, in navigation mode. Otherwise, it moves to the next character in the current field.
←	Move to the previous field in a row, in navigation mode. Otherwise, it moves to the previous character in the current field.
↓	Move to the next row.
↑	Move to the previous row.
HOME	Move to the first field in a row, in navigation mode. Otherwise, it moves to the beginning of the current field.
END	Move to the last field in a row, in navigation mode. Otherwise, it moves to the end of the current field.
CTRL+END	Move to the last record in a table, in navigation mode. Otherwise, it moves to the end of current field.
CTRL+HOME	Move to the first record in a table, in navigation mode. Otherwise, it moves to the beginning of the current field.
F5	Activate the record number box. Type the record number you wish to go to, and then press Enter.

If you have made several changes to your table, consider saving it before continuing.

Deleting a Record

If a contact or client has declined to remain on your list, or if you no longer need a record for some other reason, you can easily remove it. *Follow these steps*:

1. If your table is not displayed, select the Tables tab in the Database window, and then select the table containing the data you wish to change and click Open.

2. Display the record you wish to delete and then select it by clicking in any field, or click the record selector (the gray box) to the left of the first field in the record. See Table 22-2 for an explanation of symbols that appear on the record selector.

3. Click or choose Edit → Delete Record .

TIP If you've selected the entire record, you can press the Delete key to delete the record. Otherwise if you press the Delete key, you will delete only parts of a record depending on where the insertion point is located or what you have selected.

4. Click Yes or No to confirm deletion of the record.

 Note that the confirmation message box informs you that you won't be able to undo this action once you say yes. Make sure you definitely want to remove the record permanently before responding.

TABLE 22-2 Record Selector Symbols

This Symbol	Indicates That
▶ CURRENT	The record is currently active.
✳ NEW	You are in a new record and can begin entering information.
✎ EDIT	You are currently editing this record and haven't saved the changes.
⊘ LOCKED	Someone has locked this record and you cannot make changes to it.

Rearranging the Furniture

You can change how your table presents information by making modifications in table Datasheet view or table Design view. Changes you make in table Datasheet view don't affect the underlying structure of the table.

Freezing and Unfreezing Columns

Okay, you've got tons of fields in your table and you want to change Hector Snodgrass's social security number. You find Hector's record and move to the social security field, which happens to be beyond the north 40, perhaps even in the next county — in other words, one of the last fields in the record. But now you can't see Hector's name and you're not positive you're really in the right record after all. What's a person to do?

Enter the Freeze. If you've worked in Excel, you may know this feature already. You can freeze a column so that it remains stationary while you display other columns. For example, you could freeze the Last Name column so that you could always see the last name as you traveled around the various fields in your table (see Figure 22-2).

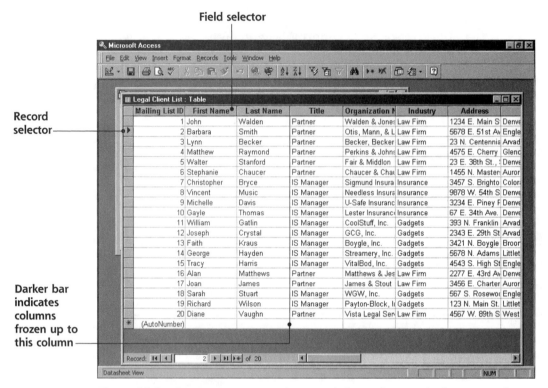

Figure 22-2 Freeze one or more columns to help you keep track of your records.

To freeze a column, follow these steps:

1. Select the column(s) you want to freeze. If you want to freeze the first column, click the field selector once. If you want to freeze any other column, select all columns up to that column.

2. Click **Format** → **Freeze Columns** . Access places a black line to the right of the last column selected. When you use the horizontal scroll bar or tab to display or move to the remaining fields, the frozen columns stay put.

3. To unfreeze the columns, Click **Format** → **Unfreeze All Columns** .

TIP To select multiple columns, click the first column field selector and continue pressing the mouse button. Then drag over the remaining column field selectors to extend the selection.

If the column you wish to freeze is not the first column in the table, make sure you select all columns up to the column you wish to freeze. If you don't, and instead select the column by itself (say Column 3), Access will not only freeze this column, it will move it so that it's the first column in the table.

For inquiring minds, you can't and don't need to freeze rows in Access since the field headings remain visible at all times.

Adjusting Column Widths

If you can't see the complete field name in a particular column while you're in Datasheet view, or a name doesn't need the full width allotted to it, you can adjust the widths using the mouse. Adjusting the width of columns in Datasheet view doesn't affect the underlying structure in Design view. *Follow these steps to adjust columns:*

1. If you aren't currently using Datasheet view, click ▦▾ on the toolbar or choose View → Datasheet View if you're not already using this view.

2. Point to the right or left edge of the column you wish to adjust until you see the pointer change to a sizing pointer (see Figure 22-3).

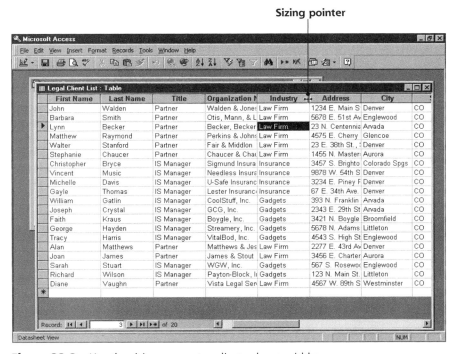

Figure 22-3 Use the sizing arrows to adjust column widths.

3. Click and drag right or left to increase or decrease the column width.

Moving a Column

If you want your columns to appear in a different order, you can move them in Datasheet view. Moving columns in Datasheet view does not affect their underlying structure in Design view. *Follow these steps to move a column:*

1. If you aren't currently using Datasheet view, click 〔▦ ▾〕 on the toolbar or choose 〔**View**〕 → 〔**Datasheet View**〕.

2. Click the field selector for the column you wish to move, to select the entire column. You can also click and then drag to extend the selection to several columns.

3. Point to the selected column(s), and then click and hold down the mouse button. You'll see a white vertical line appear to the left of the selection, and the move box will attach to the pointer.

4. Drag to the new location. When you release the mouse button, the columns remain in the new location.

Renovating This Old House

You've had that trusty address book for years. You've erased and changed information, added new people, and scratched out those that you no longer need to contact. But hold on, now all these people have e-mail addresses and you don't have a place for them. Maybe not in that old address book, but in Access you can make changes to the table *structure* as well as the *data*, adding "space" for new information and things changed. Changing the structure includes adding, modifying, moving, or deleting fields.

Switching Views

Whenever you open an existing table, Access displays it in Datasheet view. However, if you want to perform any structural changes to the table, you must use table Design view. The View button on the table Datasheet toolbar works like a light switch, switching between Design and Datasheet views as you click it. The icon on the button is always the opposite from the current view. So if you're using Datasheet view, the icon on the button will be the Design icon, 〔▨ ▾〕. If you're in Design view, the button will display the Datasheet icon, 〔▦ ▾〕.

To switch to Design view, click 〔▨ ▾〕. You can also click the arrow next to the button and then select the desired view or choose View → Design View. Access displays the current table in Design view (see Figure 22-4).

Select the field you wish to edit

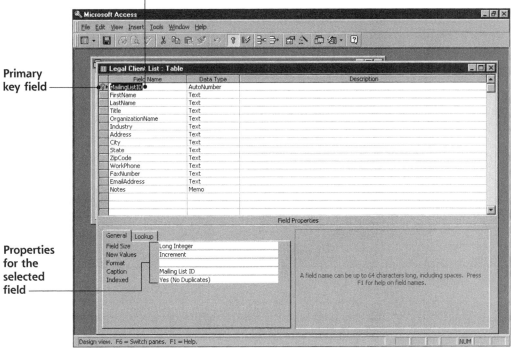

Figure 22-4   Change the table structure in table Design view.

Notice that the toolbar changes to reflect the new view. Table 22-3 describes the buttons that are unique to the table Design toolbar.

Table 22-3   The Table Design Toolbar

Button	Name	Description
	PRIMARY KEY	Sets or removes the current field as the primary key.
	INDEXES	Displays the Index window so that you can view, create, or edit indexes.
	INSERT ROWS	Inserts a row above the currently selected row.
	DELETE ROWS	Deletes the current row or selected rows.
	PROPERTIES	Displays the property sheet for a selected item.
	BUILD	Displays a builder for the selected item or property.

TIP You move around in table Design view much as you do in table Datasheet view, using Tab, Shift+Tab, and the arrow keys or clicking in the desired locations.

Adding a New Field

You can add a new field before or after any existing field in the table. Use Figure 22-5 as a guide when adding a new field. Note that Access refers to fields as *rows* for editing purposes.

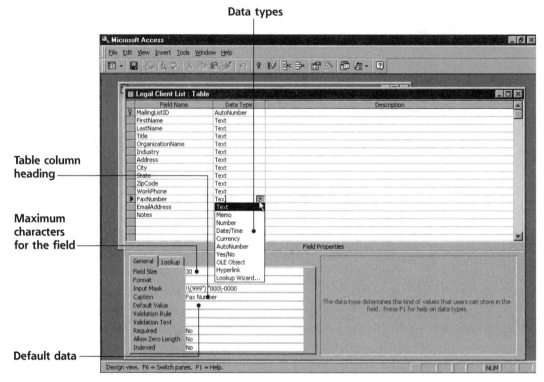

Figure 22-5 Customize the field using data types and properties.

To add a field, follow these steps:

1. Once you've displayed table Design view, select the location for the new field. Fields are inserted above the selected field.

2. Click ⧉ on the Table Design toolbar or right-click the field, and then select Insert Rows. Access inserts the new row.

3. In the Field Name box, type a name for the new field, and then press Tab. Notice Access adds an arrow button to the Data Type box and displays the field properties on the General tab at the bottom of the

window. You can select from several types of data, such as text (the default), date/time, and currency. Indicating a data type forces a specific kind of data entry when you enter records. For example, if you select date/time, you can type any of these: **1-2-97**, **January 2, 1997**, or **Jan 2 1997**, and Access will automatically convert the value to 1/2/97 in that field.

4. Click the Data Type arrow button, and then select the desired type.

5. Make any changes to the properties for the field.

6. Repeat steps 1–5 for all new fields you wish to add.

7. Save the table design.

Moving a Field

If you find you would prefer a field to be in a different location, you can move it. For example, if you have a list of clients, you may decide you want their last names before their first names.

Follow these steps to change the order of the fields in table Design view.

1. Use the record selector to select the fields (rows) you wish to move.

2. Click and hold down the mouse button in the row selector again. Access displays a thin, white horizontal line just above the last selected row and attaches the move box to the pointer.

3. Drag the selected field(s) to the new location. Note that the fields will come in above the target field when you release the mouse button.

Moving fields in table Design view changes the order in which Access stores the fields in the table. It also changes the column order in table Datasheet view.

Deleting a Field

If it no longer matters when your client began receiving your newsletter, or you don't want to include middle initials anymore, you can permanently remove a field. Once you do so, all data associated with the field are deleted as well.

You delete a field in Design view much as you delete a record in Datasheet view:

1. Select the row(s) you wish to delete.

2. Press Delete or choose Edit → Delete .

 TIP If you want to delete only a single row, position the insertion point anywhere in the row, and then click Edit → Delete Rows.

3. Click <u>Y</u>es or <u>N</u>o to confirm deletion of the record. As with records, you cannot undo a field deletion, so make sure you want to delete it before responding.

CAUTION

Remember, any data associated with the deleted field are also removed!

If you don't save the table structure before leaving table Design view, Access will prompt you to save the table before either closing the table or returning to Datasheet view.

Looking for Data in All the Right Places

Earlier in this chapter you explored ways to move to a particular record by using scroll bars, keystrokes, and the record number box. But let's face it. It isn't often you're going to say "I've got to change Jennifer Pompadour's address. She's record 246." Yeah, right. You're not going to know her record number and you probably won't remember where she falls in the table. That's where the Find feature, which you may be familiar with, comes in.

Follow these steps to use Find to locate data:

1. Click the Tables tab in the Database window, and then select the table you wish to use and click <u>O</u>pen. If you're already using a table, make sure you're in Datasheet view, clicking **View** → **Datasheet View** if necessary.

2. Select the field (column) in which you wish to search. Or position the insertion point in any field to search the entire table.

TIP

If you limit your search to a specific field, Access can find your data much faster.

3. Click 🔍 on the toolbar or click **Edit** → **Find** . Access displays the Find dialog box (see Figure 22-6).

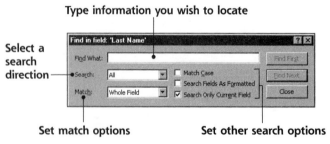

Type information you wish to locate

Select a search direction

Set match options   Set other search options

Figure 22-6 Set Find options to locate your data.

4. Type the information you wish to locate in the Find What text box. If you want to search for partial words or phrases, you can use wildcards. Refer to Table 22-4 for some of the most common wildcard characters.

5. Set any other options in the Find dialog box. If you only want to search the current field, make sure the Search Only Current Field check box is checked.

6. Click Find First to locate the first occurrence of the information or click Find Next to locate a subsequent occurrence.

7. Click Close when you have finished.

8. Make any desired changes to the record you've located.

You can locate a record based on the contents of any field. You can even use *wildcard characters* to stand in for other characters. Use wildcard characters when you:

✳ Don't know the complete word or value you're looking for.

✳ Want to locate data that start with a specific letter or match a particular pattern.

TABLE 22-4   Using Wildcards in Find

This Character	Finds This
*	Any number of characters. Use as the first or last character. **Example:** *sw** finds Swanson," "swim," and "switch."
?	Any single alphabetic character. **Example:** *d?n* finds "Dan," "den," and "din."
[ ]	Any single character within the brackets. **Example:** *d[ae]n* finds "Dan" and "den" but not "din."
-	Any one of a range of characters. The range of characters must be specified in ascending order. **Example:** *d[a-i]* finds "Dan," "den," and "din" but not "Don."
#	Any single *numeric* character. **Example:** *1#3* finds 103, 113, 123.
!	Use for exclusion to match any character not contained in the brackets. **Example:** *D[!ae]n* finds "din" but not "Dan" or "den."

CAUTION If the data item you want to locate contains an asterisk (*), a question mark (?), a number sign (#), an opening bracket ([), or a hyphen (-), you must place brackets around this character so that Access will treat it as a data character and not a wildcard character. For example, to locate an asterisk, type [*]. If you want to locate an exclamation point (!) or a closing bracket (]), you don't need to place either in brackets. You only use this ! wildcard character within brackets. You can't search opening and closing brackets ([ ]) together.

TIP You can also replace existing data with new data by choosing Edit → Replace. The steps and options are similar to those for Find except that you include replacement text in the Replace With text box.

You can use wildcard characters when you don't know the complete value you're looking for or want to locate data that match a particular pattern.

Order in the Court!

f you don't need to find a specific record but merely want to order your data either chronologically or by last name, you can use the sort feature. Sorting provides a way to display your information in a more readable, logical fashion. *To sort the data in your table, follow these steps*:

1. Click the Tables tab in the Database window, and then select the table you wish to use and click Open. If you're already using a table, make sure you're in Datasheet view, clicking View → Datasheet View if necessary.

2. Select the field (column) by which you wish to sort. For example, to sort by last name, select the Last Name field. To sort by date, select the Date field.

TIP You can also just position the insertion point in the desired field.

3. Click A↓ to sort the data in ascending order or click Z↓ to sort the data in descending order.

When you sort data in a table, they only remain sorted until you close the table. To sort a table permanently, you must create a query on the table. For more on queries, see the following Bonus section.

BONUS

Querying Your Data

Your Access database is fabulous and contains all the information you will possibly need to complete your work. And you know how to sort and find the data you need. Great. So what more could you possibly want? Well, what if, for example, you need to refer only to those clients who work in the banking industry? Or those who received a brochure from you within the last sixth months? How do you find records meeting specific criteria? You use a feature called *querying*.

A *query* is the result of selecting and manipulating data within your database. You can ask Access to display records meeting a certain criterion (for instance, only clients in the banking industry). You can also ask that you see only certain fields for these banking records (for instance, only the Contact Name, Bank Name, and Phone Number). It's like opening a box of candy and selecting only those that are chocolate and putting them on a plate. The underlying table is the box of candy, your criterion is "chocolate," and the resulting *dynaset* is the plate of chocolates.

Once you create a query, Access stores the resulting data in a *dynaset*. A dyna-*what*? No, Microsoft hasn't done some Jurassic Park thing. This animal, the dynaset, is a separate object in your database that looks identical to a table. It's what Access refers to as a "dynamic view" of the table, organized based on the criteria in that query. You can move, edit, and change information within the dynaset just as you do that in a table. When you do so, these changes affect the underlying table.

You can query more than one table if you want to display information from several tables at once.

You can create a query from scratch or use the trusty Query Wizard to assist you. However, the Query Wizard doesn't provide you the flexibility you have when you actually design a query.

Creating a Query

So you want to show only those records that meet your criteria. *Follow these steps to create your first query*:

1. Make sure you have your database open.

2. At the Database window, select the Queries tab and click <u>N</u>ew. Access displays the New Query dialog box.

3. Make sure Design View is selected in the list, and then click OK.

4. Select the table(s) you wish to base the query on in the Show Table dialog box, and then click <u>A</u>dd.

5. Click <u>C</u>lose. Access displays a blank query in Design view (see Figure 22-7).

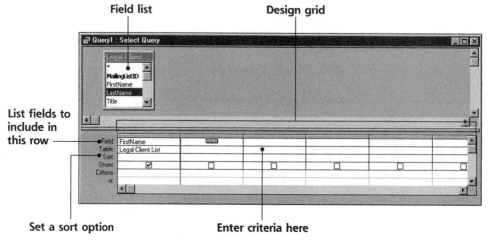

Field list   **Design grid**

List fields to include in this row

Set a sort option   **Enter criteria here**

Figure 22-7   Set query criteria in query Design view.

6. Determine which fields you wish to use in your query, and then click and drag each field from the Field list to the desired column in the Design grid.

TIP   **Use the horizontal scroll bar to display more empty field columns in the Design grid. If you want to use a field in your query but not have the field itself show up in the resulting dynaset, click the check box in the Show row for that field.**

Entering Criteria

When you enter criteria in a query, you are restricting Access to identifying only specific records with which you want to work. In my earlier example, I mentioned that you could see only those clients in banking, instead of all clients. To do this, you specify criteria that limit the results to records whose Industry field is "Banking." Access refers to the information you type in the Criteria cell as an *expression. Follow these steps*:

1. Position the insertion point in the Criteria cell for the field for which you want to set criteria.

2. Type the criteria expression. Use Table 22-5 for available operators and examples. Note that if you don't include an operator, Access assumes the equal operator (=), which means the criteria must match exactly.

TIP To sort by a particular field, click the Sort arrow button for the field, and then select Ascending or Descending.

3. Repeat steps 1 and 2 for all fields that should contain criteria. Make sure you remember to place the criteria in the proper row for And or Or operation.

4. When you're finished defining your query, click 💾 on the toolbar or click File → Save .

5. Type a name for the query, and then click OK.

6. Close the Query design window.

TABLE 22-5 Expression Operators

Operator	Description
>	The data must be greater than the criterion. **Example:** *Brochure Sent >5/15/97* displays all records for clients who received a brochure *after* May 15, 1997.
<	The data must be less than the criterion. **Example:** *Last Name <Jones* displays all records whose last name comes before Jones alphabetically (Johnson, Christianson, Adams, and so on).
>=	The data must be greater than or equal to the criterion. **Example:** *Brochure Sent >=5/15/97* displays all records for clients who received a brochure *on* or *after* May 15, 1997.
<=	The data must be less than or equal to the criterion. **Example:** *Last Name <=Jones* displays all records for clients whose last name *is* Jones or comes before Jones alphabetically (Johnson, Christianson, Adams, and so on).
Or	The data can match either of the two criteria. **Example:** *Last Name =Jones or Smith* displays all records whose last name is *either* Jones or Smith.
Between/And	The data occur between two criteria. **Example:** *Brochure Sent Between #5/1/97# And #8/31/97#* displays records for all clients who received a brochure between May 1 and August 31, 1997, inclusive.

22

Using a Query

You can see the results of a query by opening the query from the Database window or, if you are currently in query Design view, running the query. Use one of these methods to open or run a query:

* If you are currently in query Design view and wish to run the query, click Query → Run.

* If you don't have query Design view open, display the Database window and then select the Query tab. Select the query you wish to use, and then click Open.

Access displays the dynaset with the results of the query.

Deleting a Query

If you find you no longer need a particular dynaset, you can delete the query that creates it.

Follow these steps:

1. Display the Database window.

2. In the Database window, select the Queries tab.

3. Select the Query you wish to delete, and then press Delete or click Edit → Delete .

4. Click Yes to confirm the deletion.

CHAPTER TWENTY-THREE

CREATING FORMS

LEARN THESE KEY SKILLS:

U p to this point, you've used tables to enter your data, moving from field to field to work with your records. Now it's time to make Access imitate real-world work. By using forms rather than tables to enter and modify data, you can use a familiar tool for home and business — the fill-in-the-blank form.

Start Making Sense (of Forms)

A ccess forms are electronic fill-in-the-blank forms, similar to such forms as job applications, insurance forms, claim forms, or renewal forms. They have a heading or label and then a blank box for the user to type in the necessary information. You use forms to add or modify records in your database, just as you used the table Datasheet view. The advantage to using a form is that the information is displayed in a more logical fashion and you view only one record at a time. You can include calculations in forms to add, subtract, multiply, divide, and perform more advanced calculations on numeric data you may include.

23

An Access form contains *controls*, which are text boxes, buttons, rectangles, graphics, lines, and other elements that make it easier to enter your data. You can include drop-down menus on your form so that the person filling in the form can select from a predefined list. You can also add a series of buttons to the form to perform particular actions more quickly (See Figure 23-1).

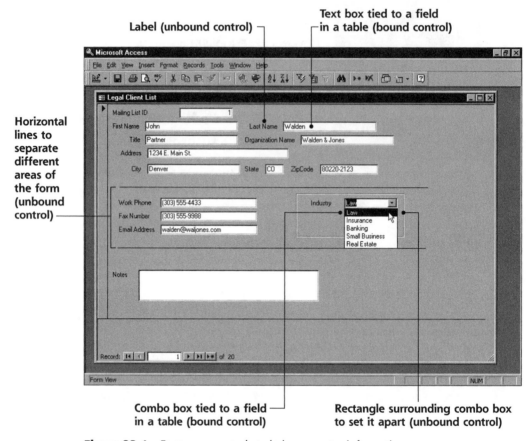

Figure 23-1 Forms use controls to help you enter information.

Controls can be bound or unbound. A bound control is one that is connected to a specific field within the table or query. For example, you would create a bound control for a text box to contain the last name of a client. This control would tie to the last name field in your table. Unbound controls are not connected to a specific field within a table or query but include design elements or buttons that help organize the form, such as lines, labels, rectangles, and other objects. A horizontal line separating personal information from business information is an example of an unbound control.

Snap! Instant Forms!

As mentioned previously, one of the advantages of a form is that, depending on how many fields you have, you can often see all fields for one record at once. The form also allows you to enter your data in a manner that is familiar — the fill-in-the-blank form. To create a form, you should already have a table created, whether or not it contains data. Access will need to tie the form controls to the fields in the table to create the form.

One advantage of a form is that you can often see all the fields for one record at once, and you can enter your data in the familiar fill-in-the-blank format.

The easiest way to create a form for an existing table is by using the AutoForm feature. *Follow these steps to create an AutoForm:*

1. If you don't have a database open, open the one you wish to use (Chapter 21 explains how) and then select the Tables tab in the Database window.

2. Select the table on which you wish to base the form.

3. Click 🔲 or click Insert → Auto Form. Access displays a standard form. Notice the table headings have become the form labels, data appearing in boxes after each label (see Figure 23-2). Access automatically displays the first record from your table in the form. If you already have data in the table, you will see the form filled in with information for Record 1.

Use It or Lose It

Once you have an AutoForm displayed, you can use it to view, edit, or add records. You use many of the same navigation buttons and keys here that you do to move around a table in Datasheet view. Table 23-1 recaps these methods for you.

TABLE 23-1 Navigation Keys and Buttons for Autoforms

Use	To
Tab	Move to the next field.
Shift+Tab	Move to the previous field.
▶	Move to the next record.

(continued)

TABLE 23-1   *(continued)*

Use	To
◀	Move to the previous record.
◀◀	Move to the first record.
▶▶	Move to the last record.
▶✳	Create a new record.

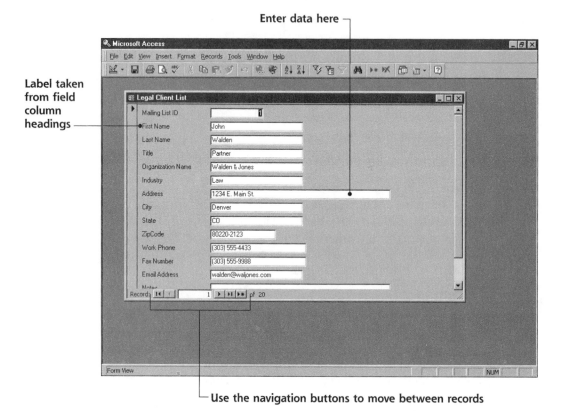

Enter data here

Label taken from field column headings

Use the navigation buttons to move between records

Figure 23-2   An AutoForm has been created from an existing table.

Finding and Modifying a Record

Just as in table Datasheet view, you can use Find to locate a record you need to modify. Otherwise, you can use the navigation buttons to view the desired record. *Follow these steps*:

1. Position the insertion point in the field you wish to search. For example, if you want to search for "Friendly Felines, Inc.," position the insertion point in the Company Name field.

2. Click on the toolbar or click **Edit** → **Find** . Access displays the Find dialog box (see Figure 23-3).

Current field

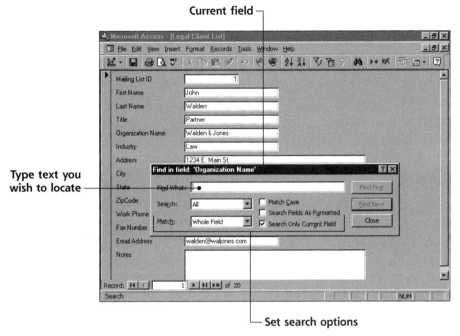

Type text you
wish to locate

Set search options

Figure 23-3 Use Find to locate a record.

3. Type the information you wish to locate in the Find What text box.

X-REF **If you want to search for partial words or phrases, you can use wildcards. Refer to Table 22-4 in Chapter 22 for more information.**

4. Set any other options in the Find dialog box. If you want to search only the current field, make sure the Search current field only box is checked.

5. Click Find First to locate the first occurrence of the information or click Find Next to locate a subsequent occurrence.

6. Click Close when you've reached the correct record.

7. Make any desired changes to the record you've located.

Adding a New Record

If you have additional clients to add to your mailing list, or if you've decided to add a new service to the list of services you already offer, you can easily do the job using a form. *To add a new record, follow these steps*:

1. Click ▸⁕ on the Table Datasheet toolbar or click Insert → New Record .

2. Type the information for the first field, and then press Tab.

3. Repeat step 2 for all fields to contain information.

Deleting a Record

You can delete a record in Form view just as you did in table Datasheet view. *Follow these steps*:

1. Display the record you wish to delete.

2. Click ⋈ or click Edit → Delete Record .

3. Click Yes to confirm deletion of the record.

Remember that once you say yes, you can't bring the data back.

Switching to Datasheet View

If you want to work in table Datasheet view while using Form view, use one of these methods:

✴ Click the arrow next to the View button on the toolbar to display the drop-down list, and then click Datasheet View.

✴ Click View → Datasheet View .

TIP Once you create a form and use it, Access automatically saves changes and additions to your underlying table. However, if you want to save the form itself, you need to let Access know. If you close the form and you haven't saved it, Access will prompt you to do so. Otherwise, you can use the Save command. Once you save a form, you can use it over and over to view, modify, and add records.

Form Over Substance

The AutoForm is nice, but it isn't very fancy. And wouldn't it be great to have the last name field on the same line as the first name field, instead of beneath it? In other words, can you rearrange those fields so that they appear a little more organized? Absolutely. Just as you can change the design of your tables, you can also change the design of your forms. However, designing forms is much different from designing tables. This section looks at some basic form design techniques to improve the look and usability of your form.

Switching to Form Design View

In Chapter 22, you looked at table Design view, learning how to modify the structure of a table by adding, removing, or changing fields. Here, you'll explore form Design view, which may seem a bit strange until you understand its elements and how you work with them. To change the look of your form, you must be in form Design view.

Note that this section assumes you have an existing form (such as the AutoForm you may have saved in the previous section) to work with. If you don't, go ahead and create an AutoForm following the steps in the previous section and saved it with a name. *Then follow these steps*:

1. Click the Forms tab in the Database window.

2. Select the form you wish to work with, and then click Design. Access displays your form in Design view (see Figure 23-4). Here you can move things around, change text and box appearance, and generally wreak havoc.

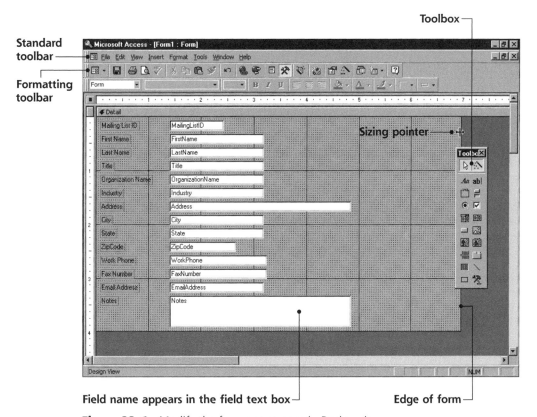

Figure 23-4 Modify the form appearance in Design view.

A FORM WITH A VIEW

If you are currently using your form, you can use one of the following methods to display it in another view.

* Click If you don't see the Design icon on the View button, click the arrow next to the View button to display the drop-down list, and then click Design View.

* Click View → Design View.

Increasing the Width of the Form

In Figure 23-4, you see that the edge of the form doesn't fill the window when you maximize the window. You can increase the form width to gain more room to rearrange your controls.

Maximize the window, if you haven't already done so, and then point to the edge of the form until the pointer changes to a sizing pointer Finally, click and drag to the right to extend the form area.

> **CAUTION** When you increase the width of the form in Design view, you will usually need to maximize your form before you will be able to see all your fields.

Selecting and Resizing Controls

If the information you will add to a field may require more room than the current text box allows, or if the text box is much too wide for the information, you can increase or decrease its size. Sizing affects only the text box, not the label.

If you want to resize a control, you must select it first. Keep a careful eye on the shapes and sizes of handles so that you can distinguish between Move handles and Sizing handles (see Figure 23-5). *To resize the control, make sure you're in form Design view and follow these steps:*

1. To select a control, click the attached label for the control.

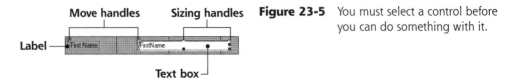

Figure 23-5 You must select a control before you can do something with it.

TIP To select multiple controls at once, point next to (not directly on) one of the controls you want to select, and then click and drag diagonally to include all the controls. As you drag, you'll see a rectangle surround the controls to indicate your selection. When you release the mouse button, Access selects all the controls within or touching the rectangle. If you aren't a click and drag expert, you can press and hold Shift, and then click each control you wish to select.

2. Resize the control using one of the methods in Table 23-2.

TABLE 23-2 Resizing Controls

To Change	Do This
Box height	Drag the top or bottom sizing handles.
Box width	Drag the left or right sizing handles.
Box height and width	Drag a corner sizing handle.

Moving a Field and Its Label

As mentioned before, you may dislike the location of a particular field and want to move it to a more logical spot. *If you want to move a field and its label to another part of the form, follow these steps*:

1. Make sure the control you wish to move is *not* selected. If it is, click anywhere outside it to deselect it. If you try to move the control while it is selected, you may end up moving the text box and label separately from one another. See the next section for information on this.

2. Point anywhere within the control (either the label or the text box), and then click and hold the mouse button. You should see the pointer turn into a black hand (see Figure 23-6).

Hand pointer ⌐

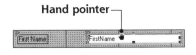

Figure 23-6 The hand pointer indicates you are ready to move.

3. Drag the control to its new location, and then release the mouse button.

Moving a Text Box or Label Separately

If you want to get really fancy, you can move a text box without moving its label, or vice versa. Why would you do this? Well, you may want to place the label above or below the text box, rather than to the left of it. When this is the case, you must move them separately.

To move a field or label separately, follow these steps:

1. Select the control containing the field or label you wish to move.

2. Point to the move handle for the label or the field, until the pointer changes to the Move pointer (see Figure 23-7). Notice that this move pointer has only one finger extended. This is different than the Move pointer that moves both the label and field.

Single finger on hand pointer

Figure 23-7 The Move pointer to move a label or a field text box separately has a distinctive look.

3. Click and drag the label or field to its new location, and then release the mouse button.

Make sure you save your form once you've made changes to your satisfaction!

TIP If you want your form to start automatically when you open your database, click Tools → Startup to display the Startup dialog box. Click the Display Form down arrow and select the form you wish to display, and then click OK.

BONUS

Customizing Forms Using the Toolbox

In addition to moving and resizing controls on your form, you can add color, depth, and other elements to make your form more interactive and useful. You will use the Toolbox to perform many of these design techniques. Use Figure 23-8 to become familiar with the tools on the Toolbox.

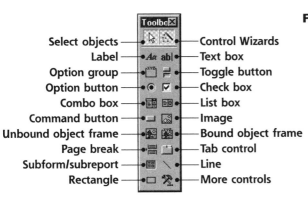

Select objects ——— Control Wizards
Label ——— Text box
Option group ——— Toggle button
Option button ——— Check box
Combo box ——— List box
Command button ——— Image
Unbound object frame ——— Bound object frame
Page break ——— Tab control
Subform/subreport ——— Line
Rectangle ——— More controls

Figure 23-8 Select a tool from the Toolbox to customize your form.

Adding a Title

As you saw earlier, a label is a control that provides information. In earlier examples, it labeled the field text box on the form. You can also have labels that aren't associated with a text box but merely provide instructions or other information you would like to appear on your form. For example, you might want to include a title at the top of your form or provide a note to let users know that they don't need to fill in certain fields. These are perfect uses for a freestanding label. To add a freestanding label for a title to your form, you will place it in the form header, which appears at the top of each form page. Make sure you're in form Design view first. *Then follow these steps*:

1. Click `View` → `Form Header/Footer`. Access displays the Form Header area above the detail area and the Footer area below the detail area.

2. If the Toolbox is not displayed, click 🛠 or choose `View` → `Toolbox`.

3. Click `Aa` on the Toolbox. The pointer changes to a label pointer — a crosshair with the letter A attached.

4. Click in the location for the label and type the text for the label.

5. Press Enter when finished.

6. Resize the label to suit your needs using any of the methods listed in Table 23-2.

Use the instructions in the next section to change the title appearance.

TIP **You can also click and drag the label tool to create a box first. The text you type will automatically wrap within it.**

Changing the Look of Text

You can change the appearance of text in your labels by changing their font, size, and color, along with the appearance of the control itself.

To change the look of text, select all labels you wish to change and then choose from these options:

* Select the font 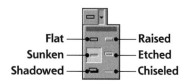 and size `10` ▼ on the Formatting toolbar.

* Select bold, italic, or underlining if desired.

* Use the Font/Fore Color button $\boxed{A}$ ▼ to change the text color.

TIP **To add a combo box to your form, click the Combo Box button on the Toolbar and click in the loaction for the combo box. Follow the instructions in the Combo Box Wizard.**

Formatting Control Appearance

You can change the control appearance to make your text boxes and labels look really cool and different. Do this by selecting the label(s) you wish to change and using the the Special Effect feature (see Figure 23-9).

Flat —— Raised
Sunken —— Etched
Shadowed —— Chiseled

Figure 23-9 The Special Effect feature gives you several useful options.

Also, experiment with the Line ◥ and Rectangle ▢ tools to set different areas of your form apart from other areas.

Adding a Combo Box to Your Form

If you'd like those who will use your form to be able to pick from a list of options for some of the data they must fill in, you can easily add a combo box. A combo box provides a text box with a default response in it. If the user clicks the arrow next to the text box, a list of all responses drops down and the user can select one of these (see Figure 23-10). Access provides a Wizard that leads you through the steps of creating the combo box. The best use of a combo box is when you have a particular field that has a limited number of responses. For example, let's say your clients work in five different industries and you include this information in your Industry field. You could place these five industries in your combo box list and tie the combo box to your Industry field. Then whenever you add a new client, you can select his or her industry type from the combo box list.

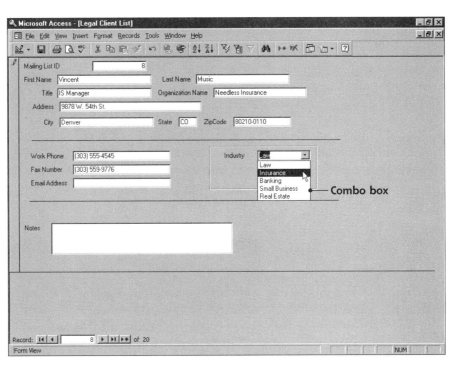

Figure 23-10   An example of a combo box is shown.

To add a combo box with your own list and tie it to a field, follow these steps:

1. Open your form in Design view by selecting the form on the Forms tab and clicking Design.

2. Locate the field you wish to tie the combo box to, and then select and delete it. For example, if you want a list of industries, locate the Industry field on your form. The combo box will replace the field.

3. Click 🖩 on the Toolbox.

4. Click the location on the form where you want to place the combo box. Access immediately starts the Combo Box Wizard. You must first decide how you will add the list of options (values) to your combo box.

5. Select the second option — I will type in the values that I want — and click Next. Access displays the next dialog box in the Wizard, allowing you to enter the values you wish to display in the combo box list (see Figure 23-11).

Type each value in a new cell

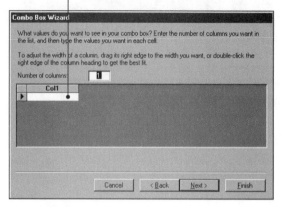

Figure 23-11 Enter your list values in the column.

6. Position the insertion point in the first column cell and then type the first value. Press Tab and then type the next value, repeating for all values.

 Your list will appear exactly in the order you've entered, and with the appearance you've given it here. Check for misspellings or other errors before continuing.

7. Click next to display the next Wizard dialog box and select the second option — Store that value in this field.

8. Click the arrow button next to the option and select the field that will tie to the combo box (for example, Industry), and then click Next.

9. Type a label for the combo box (the name of the field you selected in step 8 is a good choice), and then click Finish.

10. Make any adjustments to the combo box and label that you wish.

11. Save the form design and return to form view.

To use the combo box, click its down arrow and select the option. Access will save your selection with the record.

 FEATURE FOCUS You can create a form that has tabs — just as the Database window contains tabs — using the Tab control. See online help for more information.

CHAPTER TWENTY-FOUR

WORKING WITH REPORTS

LEARN THESE KEY SKILLS:

HOW TO USE AND UNDERSTAND REPORTS PAGE 393

HOW TO CREATE AN AUTOREPORT PAGE 394

HOW TO VIEW AND PRINT AN AUTOREPORT PAGE 396

HOW TO SAVE A REPORT PAGE 398

HOW TO CUSTOMIZE A REPORT PAGE 405

Now that you've explored how to set up your data and even how to enter them using a nice fill-in-the-blank form, you're ready for the final frontier — showing your data to other people. What does this mean? It means putting all your stuff down on paper so that others can take a look. And to make it look good and make *you* look good, you'll use a report.

Reporting for Duty, Sir!

A report is the final printed presentation of your data, something you provide to others so that they can read and understand the information you wish to present. Your report could show a complete list of all your clients, or it could be a summary of your services, who received them, and when. A report could also be a set of mailing labels based on your client list that you could use to send out a brochure or announcement.

You can be as creative with reports as your information allows, adding pictures, graphs, and other objects to enhance its presentation, as well as including calculations to provide totals and subtotals where appropriate. Once you create a report, you can save it to use again and again. Each time you use the report,

Access will use the latest updated data when it displays and prints the report. The report itself will always look the same, but the data within the report will reflect the most current information (see Figure 24-1).

Like an Access form, a report contains *controls*, which are text areas and other elements the form uses to present your data in a readable manner.

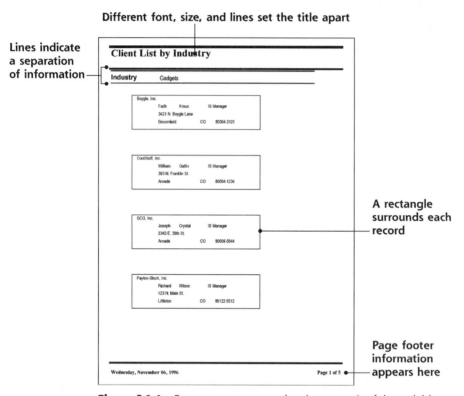

Different font, size, and lines set the title apart

Lines indicate a separation of information

Client List by Industry

Industry   Gadgets

Boygle, Inc.
        Faith   Kraus   IS Manager
        3421 N. Boygle Lane
        Broomfield   CO   80304-2121

CoolStuff, Inc.
        William   Gatlin   IS Manager
        393 N. Franklin St.
        Arvada   CO   80004-1234

GCG, Inc.
        Joseph   Crystal   IS Manager
        2343 E. 29th St.
        Arvada   CO   80006-5544

A rectangle surrounds each record

Payton-Block, Inc.
        Richard   Wilson   IS Manager
        123 N. Main St.
        Littleton   CO   80122-5512

Page footer information appears here

Wednesday, November 06, 1996   Page 1 of 5

Figure 24-1   Reports present your data in a meaningful, readable way.

Just as they are in a form, report controls can be bound or unbound. A *bound* control is connected to a specific field within the table/query, such as the name and address of a client. *Unbound* controls are not connected to a specific field within a table or query but include design elements or buttons that help organize the report. The rectangle surrounding each record as in Figure 24-1 is an example of an unbound control.

Report It Now!

The fastest way to get a report containing all the data in your table or query is to use the AutoReport feature. Like AutoForm, AutoReport will ask you which table or query you wish to base the report on and then create a report with a basic design.

The fastest way to get a report containing all the data in your table or query is to use the AutoReport feature.

Follow these steps to create an Auto Report:

1. In the Database window, select the Tables tab.

2. Select the table on which you wish to base the form.

3. Click the New Object arrow on the toolbar to display the list of objects and then click AutoReport or choose Insert → AutoReport . Access displays a standard report. Notice that the table headings have become the report labels, with the data appearing to the right of each label (see Figure 24-2). The records appear in the order in which they are listed in the table or query. The AutoReport creates an extremely basic report. Notice that page numbers do not even appear for each page of the report.

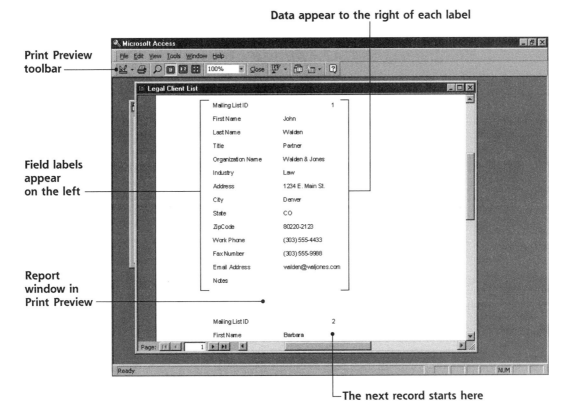

Figure 24-2 An AutoReport has been created from an existing table.

Taking a Peek

When you first create an AutoReport, Access displays it in Print Preview at 100 percent, providing you with a look at how the report will appear when you actually print it out. Let's review the Print Preview toolbar and look at some ways you can view your report in Print Preview.

The Print Preview Toolbar

The Print Preview toolbar provides several buttons for viewing the report in different ways. Table 24-1 describes these buttons and how to use them.

TABLE 24-1   The Print Preview Toolbar

Button	Name	Description
	VIEW	Selects Design Preview, Print Preview, Layout Preview.
	PRINT	Prints the current report.
	ZOOM	Zooms in 100% or out to full page.
	ONE PAGE	Displays one page at a time.
	TWO PAGES	Displays two pages at a time.
	MULTIPLE PAGES	Displays multiple pages at a time.
	ZOOM BOX	Lists zoom percentages.
	CLOSE	Closes the Print Preview window.
	OFFICELINKS	Converts the report to an RTF document for use in Microsoft Word.
	DATABASE WINDOW	Displays the Database window.
	NEW OBJECT	Lists new objects you can create.
	OFFICE ASSISTANT	Starts the Office Assistant.

FEATURE FOCUS   The Multiple Pages and Office Assistant buttons are new features in Office 97.

Viewing Your Report

Notice that when you move your pointer anywhere in the report, it changes to a magnifying glass. This allows you to switch between having a full page view and zooming in at 100 percent on a particular part of the report. To use the zoom pointer, merely point to the area you'd like to take a look at and click. The first click will take you to full page, where you get a bird's eye view of an entire page of your report. The second click will take you back to 100 percent, showing you the area in which you clicked.

 TIP You can also click 🔍 on the Print Preview toolbar to zoom in and out.

* To view the report in a percentage other than 100 percent or full page view, click the Zoom box arrow to display other percentages and then select the desired percentage.
* To view two pages of your report at a time, click 🗐 .
* To view multiple pages of your report at a time, click 🗐 and then select the matrix of pages you wish to display. For example, selecting 2×2 pages will display four pages — two pages in each of two columns.

 FEATURE FOCUS If you have the Microsoft Intellimouse, you can use the wheel button to move around the current page in a report.

Printing Your Report

If you like what you see when you preview your report, you can send it to the printer. You can either print the entire report with one click or select specific pages to print using the Print dialog box. To print all the pages of your report, click 🖨 .

To select print options before printing your report, follow these steps:

1. Click **File** → **Print** . Access displays the Print dialog box (see Figure 24-3).

2. Select a range of pages or records to print under Print Range.

3. Indicate the number of reports you wish to print under Copies.

4. Click OK.

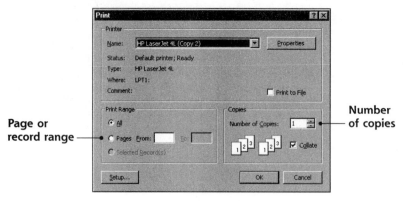

Page or record range ⟶

Number of copies ⟵

Figure 24-3 Set print options in the Print dialog box.

Repeat Reports

As with table structures and forms, Access doesn't keep a permanent copy of your report until you save it. If you close a report that you haven't saved, Access will prompt you to do so. Otherwise, you can use the Save command. Once you save a report, you can use it over and over to present your data, always using the most up-to-date information from the underlying table or query.

Report Construction Ahead

As you saw, the AutoReport is very bare bones. If you want to add some visual impact to your report with lines, fonts, and page numbers, you should use the Report Wizard. The Report Wizard even allows you to group your data by a specific field. For example, if you want all of your clients to appear by industry, you can group by the Industry field. If you want them to appear by city or state, you can indicate this field. In this section, you use the Report Wizard to create your report and then explore some basic design techniques in report Design view.

Using the Report Wizard

The fastest and easiest way to create a slick-looking report without a lot of fuss is to use the Report Wizard. You will need to determine which fields you wish to appear on your report and if you want to group records by a particular field (such as city, state, or industry). *To use the Report Wizard to create a report, follow these steps:*

1. In the Database window, click the Tables tab.

2. Select the table you wish to base your report on, click the New Object arrow on the toolbar to display the list of objects, and choose Report or click **Insert** → **Report**. Access displays the New Report dialog box.

3. Select Report Wizard in the list.

4. Make sure the correct table is listed in the box at the bottom of the dialog box and then click OK. Access displays the first Report Wizard dialog box, where you indicate which fields you wish to appear on your report (see Figure 24-4).

Select fields here →

Insert a field

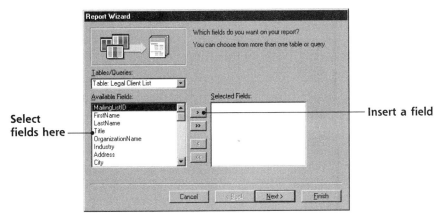

Figure 24-4   Indicate the fields you wish to appear on your report.

5. Double-click each field you wish to appear in the report or click **»** to insert all fields. Then click Next. Access displays the next Report Wizard dialog box, which asks if you want any grouping levels.

6. If you wish to group your records, double-click the field by which you wish to group them. If you select more than one, indicate which field Access should use first by using the Priority arrow buttons. Your selection will appear in blue in a separate box above the other fields (see Figure 24-5). Notice that the field you selected is no longer part of the lower list.

7. When you finish selecting a group field, or if you don't want to group them, click Next. Access displays the next Report Wizard dialog box, asking if you want to sort your records.

8. Use the arrow button next to each numbered box to indicate which field or fields you wish to sort by (such as by last name or company name).

9. Use the Ascending/Descending button to indicate the order in which Access should sort and then click Next. Access displays the next Report Wizard dialog box, which asks how you wish your report to look (see Figure 24-6).

Grouping field

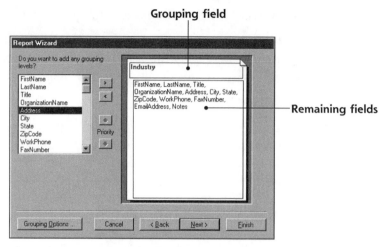

Remaining fields

Figure 24-5 You can group your data by a particular field.

An example of your selection

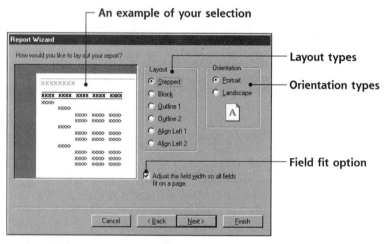

Layout types

Orientation types

Field fit option

Figure 24-6 Indicate a layout for your report.

10. Make your layout selections.

If you accept the default option that adjusts field width so that all fields fit on the page, you may find that your fields are too small to display your data. Keep this in mind as you preview the report, because you will probably have to move and resize your fields.

11. Click <u>N</u>ext. Access displays the next Report Wizard dialog box, asking what text style you would like to use.

12. Select the desired style and then click <u>N</u>ext. Access displays the last dialog box in the Report Wizard.

13. Type a name for the report and then click Finish. Access sets up the report and then displays it in Print Preview.

TIP **Use a name that accurately describes what information the report provides and how it provides it (such as "Client List by City").**

Moving and Deleting Fields and Labels

Once you've created a report using the Report Wizard, you have a good basis with which to work. One of the first things you may want to do is rearrange the fields and remove any unnecessary labels. For example, you may want the client address beneath the client name, rather than beside it. And you may not need to have the labels "address," "city," and "state" because this information is clear on your report. Let's look at ways to rearrange fields and remove any unnecessary labels.

The first thing you need to do is get into report Design view. If you've worked through previous chapters on table and form design, you'll be familiar with this. While you're still in Print Preview, click the View arrow button to display the list of options and then click Design View or choose View → Design View. Access displays the report in all its designing glory (see Figure 24-7). See Table 24-2 for a description of each area.

Report header

Page header

Group header

Detail area

Page footer

Report footer

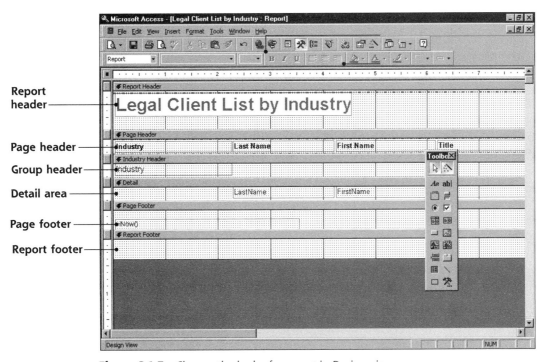

Figure 24-7 Change the look of a report in Design view.

TIP If the Design icon is displayed on the View button on the toolbar, you need only click the button to switch to report Design view.

TABLE 24-2   Report Design Areas

Area	Note
REPORT HEADER	Appears once at the top of the first page of a report.
PAGE HEADER	Appears at the top of each page of the report.
GROUP HEADER	Appears only if you've chosen to group records by a particular field.
DETAIL AREA	Contains the fields that will appear on the report.
PAGE FOOTER	Appears at the bottom of each page of the report.
REPORT FOOTER	Appears once at the bottom of the last page of the report.

Note that the group header uses the field name. For example, in Figure 24-7, the group header is called "Industry Header."

MOVING A FIELD

Probably the most frequent task you will perform when working with a report is moving your fields around. Depending on what style of form you've selected, your fields and labels may be together or separate, in the same area or different areas on the report. If you don't like where they've ended up, you can rearrange them or remove them altogether.

If you want to move a field to another part of the form, follow these steps:

1. Point anywhere within the control and then click and hold. You should see the pointer turn into a black hand, as you saw in the previous chapter in form Design view. This moves both the label and the field. You can also use the Move handle, as indicated in Figure 24-8, to move the label or the field separately.

2. Drag the control to its new location and then release the mouse button.

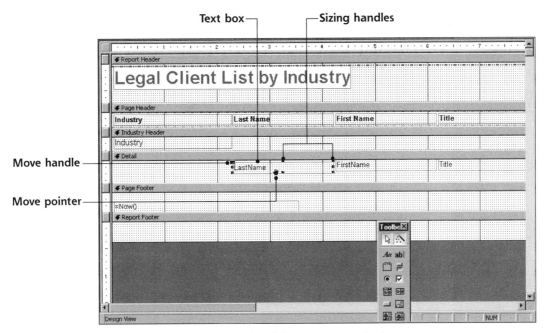

Figure 24-8 Select a control and then move or resize it.

RESIZING CONTROLS

If, while using the Report Wizard, you allowed the default option that fits all fields on a page, you may find your fields are not wide enough to display all of your data. Or you may find that some fields (like the State field) are too wide. You can easily increase or decrease the width of a control by clicking and dragging.

If you want to resize a control, you must select it first. Keep a careful eye on the shape and size of handles so that you can distinguish between Move handles and Sizing handles (refer back to Figure 24-8). To resize the control in report Design view, follow these steps:

1. Click the control to select it.

TIP   **To select several controls at once, press and hold Shift and then click each control you wish to select.**

2. Resize the control using one of the click and drag methods you learned in Chapter 23, Table 23-2.

SECRETS TO RESIZING

If you need more room, you can increase the height of the detail area by clicking and dragging the bottom of the detail area. This is also true for other areas, such as the report header or footer.

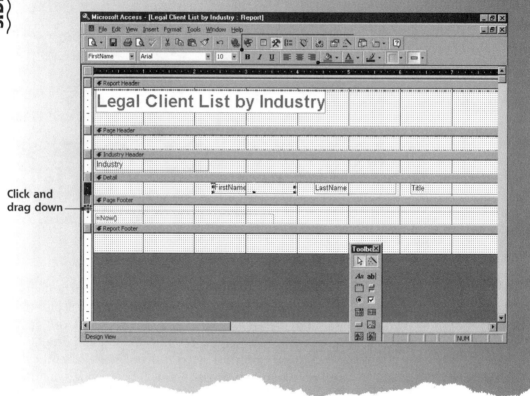

Click and drag down —

DELETING A LABEL

Once you begin moving your field controls around, you may find that you don't need the labels the Report Wizard associated with each one. It's easy to delete the labels you don't want. Just select the control(s) and press the Delete key. You can also delete fields this way if you decide you don't want the data associated with a field to show up on your report.

Keep in mind that, depending on which report layout you've selected, the label controls may be in the Page Header section. If this is the case, they will appear only *once* per page. If you place a label control in the Detail section, it will show up for *each record*. For example, if you move the Last Name control from the Page Header section to the Detail section, you will see "Last Name Jones," "Last Name Smith," "Last

Name Robinson" on your report. If, because you've rearranged your field controls, you don't want your labels to run across the top of the page, delete the labels.

Make sure you save your modified report so that you will have the changes for future reports.

Hey, Good Lookin'!

Though rearranging and resizing controls is one of the most common tasks you'll perform in report Design view, you may also want to do a few other things to add flair to your report. You can change text font, size, and color, add borders to field controls, and add vertical lines. You can make many of these changes using the Standard and Formatting toolbars. However, some of them require the Toolbox, as you will see.

 X-REF To refresh your memory on the Toolbox tools, refer to Figure 23-8 in Chapter 23 for a description of each tool.

Changing the Look of Text

You can change the appearance of text in your labels and field controls by changing their font, size, and color, as well as the appearance of the control itself.

To change the look of text, select all labels you wish to change and then choose from these options:

✳ Select the font `Times New Roman` and size `10` on the Formatting toolbar.

✳ Select bold `B`, italic `I`, or underline `U` if desired.

✳ Use the Font/Fore Color button `A ▾` to change the text color.

Changing the Look of Controls

Not only can you change the appearance of text within labels and fields, you can change the actual control box surrounding the text.

To change the control appearance:

1. Select the label(s) you wish to change.

2. Click the Special Effect arrow button to display a list of effects (see Figure 24-9).

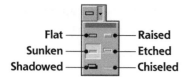

Flat — Raised
Sunken — Etched
Shadowed — Chiseled

Figure 24-9 Select a special effect from the list.

3. Select the desired effect.

Select and use the following to add color and/or change border thickness for controls:

✳ Use the Line/Border Color button ![button] to change the line or border surrounding a control.

✳ Use the Line/Border Width button ![button] to change the text color.

Adding Lines and Rectangles

You can add horizontal or vertical lines to separate different areas of a report, or you can set a particular area off by placing a rectangle around it. For examples of lines and rectangles, see Figure 24-1 at the beginning of this chapter.

To add a line to your report:

1. Click ![abl] or click [**View**] → [**Toolbox**] to display the Toolbox.

2. Click ![line] to select the Line tool.

3. Click in the location for the beginning of the line and then drag to the location for the end of the line.

To surround an area with a rectangle:

1. Make sure the Toolbox is displayed. If it isn't, click ![abl] or select [**View**] → [**Toolbox**] to display it.

2. Click ![rectangle] to select the Rectangle tool.

3. Click in the location for one corner of the rectangle and then drag to the opposite corner of the rectangle (see Figure 24-10).

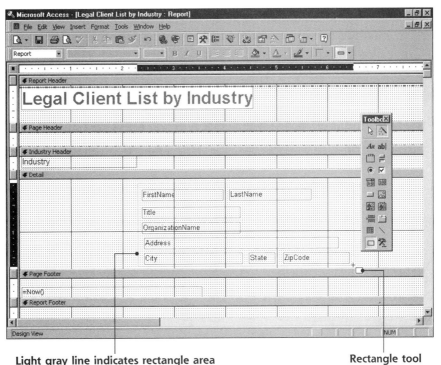

Light gray line indicates rectangle area

Rectangle tool

Figure 24-10   Click and drag around an area to enclose it in a rectangle.

BONUS

Using Calculations in Your Report

Throughout this chapter, you've learned how to present your data in a readable and meaningful manner on paper. But wait, there's more. (Isn't there always?) If you really want to impress your colleagues or boss, you can add subtotals and totals, as well as other calculations to your report. A few well placed functions and voilà! Instant numeric data. Here you learn how to insert a number that shows the total records within a group, as well as the total number of records in the entire report.

Counting Records in Your Report

Does your report need totals and subtotals? Would it help to know how many records appear in each group? Do you have a list of sales for the quarter that you would like to total at the end of the report? For any of these instances, you can add a calculated control to do the math for you. If the data change, the calculation will update to reflect the change. In this section, you learn how to total the number of records in a group. In Figure 24-11, the number indicated actually comes from a special function inserted in the Report Design. The function has added the number of records in the Insurance group and inserted the result at the appropriate spot. If your report doesn't break records into groups, skip to "Totaling Records at the End of a Report." If you wish to add other calculations to your report, see "Adding Calculations with the Expression Builder" at the end of the Bonus section.

This number uses a calculated control ——

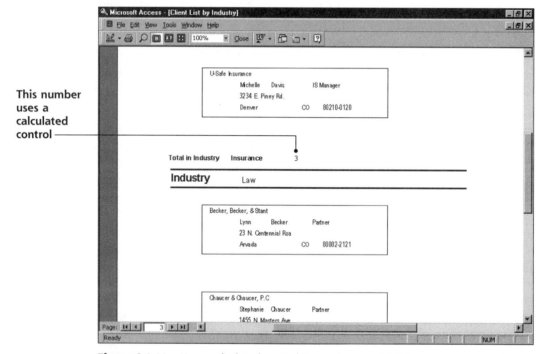

Figure 24-11 Use a calculated control to produce a subtotal.

Displaying a total for each group is a two-step process. First, you must tell Access to count each record in a group. Second, you must display the Group Footer and tell Access to display the count for each group in the Group footer area.

ADDING A CALCULATION CONTROL FOR EACH GROUP

As just indicated, the first step to displaying a record count is to tell Access to count the records for each group. To do that, you must add a control and then edit the control's properties so that it will count. *Follow these steps:*

1. In the Database window, select the report you wish to use and click Design.

2. Make sure the Toolbox is displayed. If it isn't, click or choose **View** → **Toolbox** to display it.

3. If you need more room in the Detail section, click and drag the lower bar down to increase the area.

4. Click **abl** on the Toolbox.

5. In the Detail area, click to place the text box in the desired location. Move and adjust the label and text box as necessary.

6. Select the text box and then click 🖼 on the toolbar or choose **View** → **Properties**. Access displays the Properties dialog box for this control (see Figure 24-12).

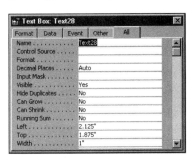

Figure 24-12 Set control properties in the Properties dialog box.

7. Type a label name, such as **RecordCount**, in the Name text box. You will refer to this name later.

8. Select the Data tab, position the insertion point in the Control Source text box, and type **=1** to tell Access to count records.

TIP You can also type **=1** directly into the field box in report Design view.

9. On the Data tab, click in the Running Sum box and then click the arrow button and select Over Group.

10. Select the Format tab and then set the Visible option to No. You want Access to count, but you don't want the count to show up here. You will have the count show up in the Group Footer.

11. Close the Properties dialog box.

DISPLAYING THE RECORD COUNT IN THE GROUP FOOTER

The second step to counting your records is to display them in the group footer. This means Access will show you the total number of records at the end of each group of records. *To display the record count in a group footer, follow these steps:*

1. Click or choose **View** → **Sorting and Grouping**. Access displays the Sorting and Grouping dialog box (see Figure 24-13).

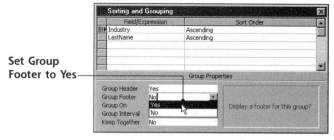

Set Group Footer to Yes

Figure 24-13 Display the group footer using this dialog box.

2. In the Group Properties section, set the Group Footer option to Yes so that it will display in your report.

3. Close the Sorting and Grouping dialog box. Access adds a group footer, using the field name for the footer name. For example, if you used the Industry field to group your records, the footer area will be called "Industry Footer."

4. Make sure the Toolbox is displayed. If it isn't, click abl or choose View → Toolbox to display it.

5. Click abl on the Toolbox.

6. In the Group Footer area, click once to place the text box in the desired location. Move and adjust the label and field boxes as necessary.

7. Select the text in the label box (indicated by **Textxx**, where *xx* is a number) and then type a new label (such as **Total in This Industry**).

8. Select the field control box (indicated by "Unbound") and then click on the toolbar or select View → Properties. Access displays the Properties dialog box for this control.

9. Select the Data tab and then position the insertion point in the Control Source text box and type =[*Name*] — where *Name* is the name you gave the control in the Detail area. In my example, I would use **RecordCount**, so my Control Source would read =[**RecordCount**]. This tells Access to use the total number it gets in the RecordCount calculated control created in the Detail area.

TIP You can also type =[*Name*] directly into the text box in report Design view.

10. On the Data tab, make sure the Running Sum is set to No.

11. Select the Format tab and then make sure the Visible option is set to Yes. You want Access to display the total number of records here.

12. Close the Properties dialog box.

Make sure the name you use in the Control Source for the Group Footer matches the name you used in the Detail section *exactly*. Otherwise, Access expects you to fill in a parameter when you preview the report.

When you preview your report, you should see the total number of records for each group displayed at the end of each group (the group footer).

TOTALING RECORDS AT THE END OF A REPORT

If you don't have your records grouped by a particular field, you can still indicate the total number of records at the end of your report. *Follow these steps*:

1. In report Design view, scroll down until you see the Report Footer area and then increase the area if necessary.

TIP   **If you don't see the Report Footer area, choose View → Report Header/Footer.**

2. Make sure the Toolbox is displayed. If it isn't, click abl or choose View → Toolbox to display it.

3. Click abl on the Toolbox.

4. In the Report Footer area, click once to place the text box in the desired location. Move and adjust the label and field text boxes as necessary.

5. Select the text in the label box (indicated by **Text*xx***, where *xx* is a number) and then type a new label (such as **Total Clients**).

6. Click in the field control box (indicated by "Unbound") to position the insertion point and then type =**Count(*)** to complete the process.

When you preview the report, Access will display the total number of records on the last page of the report.

Adding Calculations with the Expression Builder

If, at times, you want Access to perform actual calculations to indicate the total number of sales, or to display a percentage increase in revenue, Access requires that you create an *expression*. An expression consists of *identifiers* and *operators*. Identifiers refer to a field in a table or form, such as Price or Hourly Rate, and operators are those symbols that affect the calculation, such as addition (+), subtraction (–), multiplication (*), and division (/). You can also use symbols to include or exclude data, such as greater than (>) or less than (<). You can also use *functions* such as Sum, Avg, and Max or Min to display particular results.

An expression always begins with an equal sign. One of the easiest ways to create an expression is to use the Expression Builder. *To create an expression using the Expression Builder, follow these steps*:

1. In the Database window, select the report you wish to use and click Design.

2. Create a calculated control, such as a text box, in the desired area (Detail, Group Footer, Report Footer).

3. Modify the text label for the control so that it reflects the result of the expression (for instance, **Total Sales**), or delete it altogether.

4. Select the control and then click 🖼 or choose **View** → **Properties**.

5. Select the Data tab and then click **···** next to the Control Source text box. Access displays the Expression Builder dialog box (see Figure 24-14).

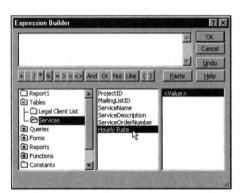

Figure 24-14 Create an expression using the Expression Builder.

6. Select the element you wish to use from the first column. For example, let's say you want to use the Hourly Rate field from the Services table. Select Tables and then select Services in the first column.

7. Select the element you wish to use from the second column. For example, select Hourly Rate. To the expression, click Paste.

8. If necessary, select the element you wish to use from the third column and then click Paste to add it to the expression.

9. Insert any operators you need (+, –, *, /) in the appropriate places. For example, if you wanted to multiply the Hourly Rate for a service by the number of hours spent on a project, your expression would look like this: [Hourly Rate]*[Project Hours]. Click OK when you're finished.

Here are some other examples to help you create your expressions:

=[Price]*.50 multiplies the value in the Price field by 50 percent.

=Sum([Sales]) totals all values in the Sales field.

=[Price]–([Price]*.15) indicates the price after it is reduced by 15 percent.

USING OUTLOOK

This part covers how to use Outlook, Office's new desktop information management program. You can use Outlook to handle e-mail, keep track of names and addresses, and maintain your schedule.

Outlook contains several applets that can help you when you're organizing a job search. For example, you can maintain a list of contacts, create notes for reminders, and schedule your appointments within Outlook. You can even use e-mail to make your initial contact with a potential employer.

E-mail has really come into its own with the rapid growth of the Internet. Not long ago e-mail was primarily used by companies to communicate within the confines of their own private networks. Now these same companies can also electronically correspond with customers, prospective employees, other interested parties, and even their competitors.

Many individuals and companies are adopting e-mail addresses in addition to their regular mailing address. With more and more companies coming online e-mail is becoming a viable way to contact certain prospective employers. Girl Tech, a private organization located in California, works with young women, helping them become technically savvy by stressing the importance of computer literacy. Using e-mail is one of the subject areas at Girl Tech. Janese Swanson with Girl Tech says, "E-mail is effective in some cases as an initial approach to companies. Busy people can find time to glance over an introductory e-mail, whereas a phone call may be more easily brushed aside. E-mail allows you to apply quickly to multiple organizations."

Using e-mail gives you many other advantages. E-mail offers 24-hour-a-day access and is faster than "snail mail" (letters sent via the U.S. Postal Service). It is relatively efficient. Storing and retrieving e-mail messages is easier, more cost-effective, and less bulky than using paper mail. And here's another benefit of using e-mail: If you limit your correspondence with chatty people to e-mail, you can save a lot of time. In fact, another bonus of e-mail is that it generally forces the message writer to be concise and to the point. Of course, e-mail is not always the best form of communication for all situations. Paper mail, telephone conversations, and faxes all have their place depending on the situation. For example, as Swanson notes, well-designed résumés also have their place in the job application process. A résumé can serve as the initial contact with the prospective employer, or it can be sent at a later point, after initial e-mail contact. One can even wax creative by putting the résumé on disk using animation and sound, if appropriate. Says Janese, "I think that more companies will provide a way for people to apply through the Internet, whether through listings or job applications that can be filled out online."

GETTING FAMILIAR WITH OUTLOOK

LEARN THESE KEY SKILLS:

O utlook is a *desktop information manager*, and it attempts to be your personal secretary. You can keep information about all of your contacts, friends, colleagues, and associates in the Contacts applet; you can keep a list of tasks that lie ahead (and their due dates) in the Tasks applet; and you can record what you've done in days past in the Journal applet. You can record appointments in the Calendar applet and get reminders in time to keep those appointments. Last, but not least, you can make impromptu little notes of incidental information very quickly with the Notes applet.

Outlook is a bit like the new shopping mall in town: It seems very busy at first and you don't know where to start or where your favorite shops are, but once you take a cruise through it and discover the places you are likely to use the most, it becomes a lot more comfortable and less confusing.

Setting Up

If you are using Outlook on a company network, you don't need to read this section — your system administrator will take care of setting up the mail service for you. Just do what they tell you.

If, however, you are using Outlook on your own computer, you will need to set up a mail service to run through Outlook. What it boils down to is this: Microsoft wants you to use The Microsoft Network (MSN). They make it ridiculously easy to set up an MSN account in Outlook, and ridiculously difficult to set up an account with any other service provider.

My advice is: If you are within an MSN local telephone access area, and you want to do things the easy way, just go with the flow and set up an MSN account. You can call MSN support at 1-800-386-5550 to find out if there is a local-access telephone number in your area.

But if MSN is a long-distance phone call for you, as it is for me, then you must either bite the bullet and pay the long-distance charges to use e-mail, or you must go through the more complex process of setting up an account with a local Internet access provider.

Unfortunately the procedures for setting up an Internet service provider account vary a little from service provider to service provider (and the names of things you need to type in the dialog boxes are different at every service provider, which only makes the process more annoying), but if your service provider is any good they will be able to provide you with detailed instructions on how to set up their service to run in Outlook.

Your Local Internet Service Provider

Ask your online friends and at computer stores in your area - get the names of several service providers, and then call them and ask them if they have detailed instructions for setting up their service in Outlook. If they say "Huh?", call the next service on your list.

Once you find a service provider who can tell you exactly how to set up in Outlook (because they've done it themselves and they have written out instructions for their clients), then set up an account with them and follow their instructions.

Setting up Your E-Mail Service

The first time you start Outlook, you'll see the Inbox Setup Wizard. It wants to know what means you'll be using to correspond with the world at large. Table 25-1 lists the options that you can choose from.

TABLE 25-1 Which Mail Service?

Choose this option	If you are sending mail on
MICROSOFT EXCHANGE SERVER	A company network that uses the Microsoft Exchange Server — a wizard guides you through setup and ask for information, like your mailbox name and path, that you'll have to get from your system administrator.
MICROSOFT MAIL	A company network that uses the Microsoft Mail Server — again, your system administrator will give you the information you need to set up.
INTERNET MAIL	An Internet Service Provider — your service provider will give you the information you need to fill in the blanks in this wizard.
MICROSOFT NETWORK	The Microsoft Network Online Service — this wizard guides you through setting up an account (have your credit card number on hand) and sets up Outlook for you.

The rest of the wizards' steps offer you default options and folder locations — my advice is that you accept each default and click Next, until you get to the last step where you click Finish.

Be sure you close Outlook and then restart it before you try to use your new mail service setup.

Telling Outlook Where to Check for Mail

You can have Outlook automatically check your mail service (or services, if you have several), or you can tell Outlook each time you go online which service you want to check. Frankly, I would have them all checked automatically each time I go online, except that some of the services involve a long-distance phone call, and I only want to check those once a day.

To tell Outlook which services to check automatically, follow these steps:

1. Select Tools → Options.

2. Click the E-mail tab.

3. Under Check For New Mail On, click the check box for your mail service.

   If you have installed more than one mail service, all of them will be listed here. Just check the ones you want Outlook to go online with automatically when you check for new mail.

If one of your services involves a long-distance phone call, for example, you might not want to check it ten times a day — but you can go online with a service separately by selecting a different command, which I'll tell you about in the next exercise.

4. Click OK.

Sending and Picking up Mail

You send Outlook on a mail run, and go get fresh coffee. To pick up and deliver your e-mail from services you check automatically, do this:

✳ On the `Tools` menu, click `Check For New Mail`.

Outlook dials up all the mail services you have set for automatic pickup (see the previous exercise), collects your waiting messages, and sends any messages that are in your Outbox.

When the transfer of mail is complete, Outlook signs off from the service and hangs up. You'll find your new e-mail in your Inbox, and messages that were in your Outbox are now in your Sent Items mail pile.

To pick up and deliver e-mail from a service that you don't want checked automatically (such as that long-distance service that you only want to check once a week), follow these steps:

1. On the `Tools` menu, click `Check For New Mail On`.

2. Click the check boxes for each service you want to check.

3. Click OK.

Outlook dials up the mail services you checked, collects your waiting messages, and sends any messages in your Outbox. When the transfer of mail is complete, Outlook signs off from the service and hangs up.

Start Your Engines

Before you begin to cruise around in Outlook, you need to start it. To do so, double-click the Outlook icon on the Windows 95 desktop (see Figure 25-1).

Figure 25-1   Double-click the Outlook icon to start Outlook.

By default, Outlook opens with the Inbox displayed (see Figure 25-2).

Folder banner

Menu bar

Toolbar

Outlook bar

Figure 25-2   The Inbox is your welcome screen when Outlook opens.

At the top are the familiar Microsoft menu bar and a toolbar. On the left side is the Outlook bar — clicking the Outlook, Mail, or Other button displays the Outlook, Mail, or Other group of icons. You'll learn how to navigate Outlook using the Outlook bar later in this chapter.

Below the toolbar is a bar called the Folder banner (the bar that says Inbox on the left side). The Folder banner tells you which folder or *applet* (small Outlook program) is open.

Below the Folder banner is a row of column headings, which work as sort buttons. You'll learn more about sorting later in this chapter.

Below the column headings is a list of e-mail messages you have received, because the Inbox is displayed. In a different applet or folder, a different list of items is displayed.

Next, you'll learn how to get into those different applets and folders.

Where Can You Go from Here?

E ven though e-mail may turn out be the most often-used Outlook feature, Outlook offers a lot more than e-mail. Outlook provides Contacts for keeping track of names, addresses, and incidental information; Calendar to schedule appointments and events; Tasks, which is a to-do list with deadlines so you can keep track of your projects; Journal, for tracking time spent on different activities; and Notes, which are electronic sticky notes. Outlook can also open other files on your computer or network for you.

You get into all these other features most easily by clicking the appropriate buttons and icons in the Outlook bar (see Figure 25-3).

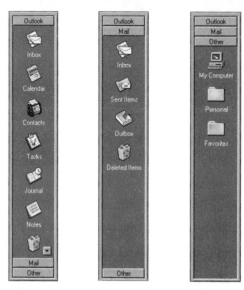

Figure 25-3 The three Outlook bar groups are Outlook, Mail, and Other.

What's in the Outlook Group?

To open the Outlook group, if it's not already showing, click the Outlook button in the Outlook bar.

The Outlook group is where the fun stuff is. The features (called *applets*) that Outlook offers include the following:

* **Inbox**, for a quick leap into your incoming mail pile.

* **Calendar**, where you can schedule anything — events, such as vacation or your dog's birthday; appointments, such as a lunch date; and recurring appointments, perhaps therapy sessions or haircuts.

* **Contacts**, which stores names, addresses, phone numbers, and miscellaneous information about your associates and friends. Contacts coordinates with Microsoft Word for mail merges, and with Journal for time-tracking.

* **Tasks**, which helps you prioritize your work and keep tabs on the progress of specific jobs.

* **Journal**, where you can record time spent in activities with associates in your Contacts list, create timelines to see where you were all week, and keep records of unusual situations and when they occurred.

* **Notes**, which are sticky notes you can paste all over your desktop as in-your-face reminders.

And the Mail Group?

To open the Mail group, click the Mail button in the Outlook bar.

The Mail group is an electronic version of the mail piles that accumulate on most desks. The mail piles are:

* **Inbox**, where e-mail messages to you are delivered when they arrive.

* **Sent Items**, where you can check whether you remembered to send a message that you wrote.

* **Outbox**, where the message you wrote but forgot to send can be found until you send it, whereupon it moves to the Sent Items pile.

   If you are on a company network instead of a standalone system, your mail is sent directly to the network server, where it waits in the server outbox until the server goes online to send and receive mail (or it goes directly to the server and then to your coworker's Inbox).

* **Deleted Items**, a sort of mini-recycle bin just for e-mail messages you delete and might want to retrieve.

To see what's in any particular mail pile, click its icon in the Outlook bar.

And the Other Group?

To open the Other group, click the Other button in the Outlook bar.

The Other bar is a portal to your files. The My Computer icon does exactly what the My Computer icon on your desktop does: It opens a window into your folders and files so you can play (or work) with them.

The Personal and Favorites folder icons are provided for your convenience and easy access, just in case you use them a lot. They open windows directly into your Personal and Favorites folders so you don't have to start My Computer and click, click, click your way into them.

You Can Get There from Here

Outlook has a lot of stuff all in one place, and the Outlook bar (that you saw previously in Figure 25-3) is the easiest, best, and main way to get from place to place.

To see what's in a certain mail pile, follow these steps:

1. Click the Mail button in the Outlook bar.

   The Mail group of icons appears.

2. Click the icon for the mail pile you want.

To get into another applet, follow these steps:

1. Click the Outlook button.

   The Outlook group of icons appears.

2. Click the icon for the applet you want to open.

Sorting Out Your Stuff

Every list, whether you are looking at an applet like Tasks, a mail pile, or a folder of business files, has column headings that serve as sort buttons (see Figure 25-4). Each sort button sorts the list of items according to the entries in that *field* (also called a *column*).

Figure 25-4 Column headings also serve as sort buttons. Click a column heading to sort the list by that field.

Suppose you want to find an e-mail message in your Inbox that you received last May. The easiest way to find it is to sort the Inbox list by Received date.

To sort the Inbox list by Received date, follow these steps:

1. Click the Received column heading.

   The list is sorted in ascending order based on the items in that column (for example, the Received field is sorted into date order).

2. Click the same column heading again.

   The list is sorted again but in the opposite order.

To find a message you received last May, scan the May entries for the message you want.

Getting Another View

The items in your lists can be viewed in many different ways. For example, Contacts can be viewed as a database-type list, with rows and columns, or as address cards that are laid out like rotary-index cards; Notes can be viewed as a database or (my favorite) as icons (see Figure 25-5). The variety of views makes it easy to tailor your views to your personal work style.

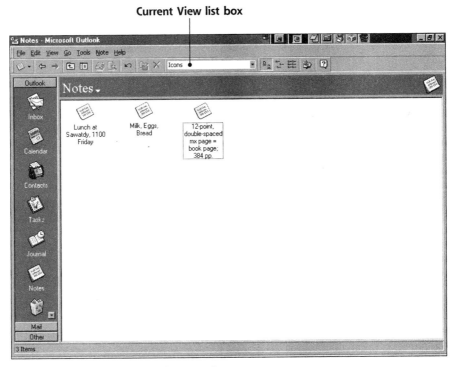

Figure 25-5 Notes appears in Icons view.

To change your view of any list, follow these steps:

1. On the toolbar, select a view from the Current View list box (see Figure 25-5).

   Try running through all the views just to see what's available!

2. If you get a Save View Settings dialog box, click OK.

   You won't lose anything, in spite of the ominous dialog box wording.

Updating Your Little Black Book

In Chapter 26 you'll learn about sending e-mail messages, but before you send messages you'll want to have addresses for them in your Personal Address Book. Your Personal Address Book is the heart of most e-mail operations, so you need to know how to enter names and e-mail addresses into it.

To add a name to the Personal Address Book, follow these steps:

1. Be sure you are in the Inbox or one of the other mail piles.

If you do not have a mail list displayed, the toolbar with the Address Book button will not be displayed, either.

2. On the toolbar, click ▣.

The Address Book dialog box appears (see Figure 25-6).

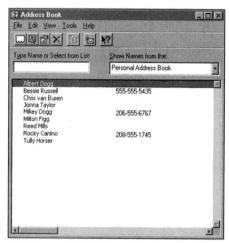

Figure 25-6 Add names to your Personal Address Book.

3. In the Show names from the list box, click Personal Address Book (if it is not already displayed).

4. In the dialog box toolbar, click ▣.

The New Entry dialog box appears.

5. Double-click the type of e-mail address you are adding.

Which types of e-mail addresses are displayed in your dialog box depends on the mail services installed on your computer or network. If you do not see an e-mail address type that matches the address you want to enter, use Other.

6. Enter the name and e-mail address on the Address tab in the dialog box that appears, and then click OK.

The new name appears in the list of names in the Address Book dialog box.

7. Click [×] to close the Address Book dialog box.

You're done playing with Outlook for the day? You'll want to exit Outlook before you shut down your computer — see Chapter 2 to learn how to exit Outlook (or any other Office 97 program).

BONUS

Starting Outlook Automatically

If you like to start up your computer in the morning and pick up your e-mail first thing while your coffee is brewing, there is an even easier way to start Outlook than by double-clicking the shortcut icon on your desktop: don't start it at all. Instead, put a shortcut to Outlook in the Windows Startup folder, and let Windows start Outlook for you when you boot up your machine.

To put a shortcut to Outlook in the Startup folder, follow these steps:

1. On the desktop, double-click the My Computer icon, which opens a window to the contents of your computer.

2. In the My Computer window, double-click your hard drive icon.

3. Double-click the Windows folder.

4. Double-click the Start Menu folder.

5. Double-click the Programs folder.

6. Finally, double-click the Startup folder.

The StartUp folder contains shortcuts to items such as the Microsoft Office shortcut bar that start automatically when you start your computer.

7. With the right mouse button, drag the Outlook icon from the desktop and drop it into the Startup folder window, as shown in Figure 25-7.

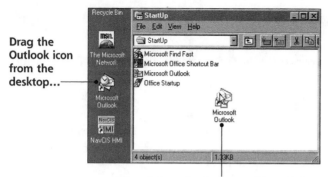

Drag the Outlook icon from the desktop...

...and drop it into the Startup Folder window

Figure 25-7 Drag the Outlook icon into the Startup folder.

The Outlook icon on your desktop is actually a shortcut icon (you can tell a shortcut by the little curvy arrow in the lower-left corner of the icon), not a real file — so you can copy it, cut it, even delete it at will without harming your computer.

8. On the shortcut menu, click Create Shortcut(s) Here.

9. Click ⊠ to close the Startup folder window. (If you have lots of windows open, click the X of the close box in each of them.)

That's all. Every morning, Outlook will start automatically and be at your bidding. If you want to prevent the automatic startup, just remove the Outlook icon from the Startup folder — either by dragging it from the Startup folder window to the Recycle Bin or by right-clicking the icon and clicking Delete (which also puts the shortcut icon in the Recycle Bin).

SENDING AND RECEIVING MESSAGES AND DOCUMENTS

LEARN THESE KEY SKILLS:

Okay, you are burning to send someone an e-mail message to tell them all about your new desktop information manager (I'm referring to Outlook). You can create a message from within any of Outlook's applets, but for simplicity's sake all of the figures in this chapter will show the Inbox.

E-mail is simply a medium for electronic messages. You type your message, give it an electronic mailbox address, and send it out on a telephone line. It travels to its destination via telephone lines, and your correspondent's e-mail program will unscramble the electrons so that he or she can read what you typed.

Creating a Simple Message

O n the far left end of the toolbar you'll find the New Mail Message button. It has a down arrow next to it that displays a list of new items to create, so you can create new tasks, calendar entries, and more from within Inbox, but while you are in Inbox the button face will always be New Mail Message.

To create a new message, follow these steps:

1. In the Outlook bar, click ![inbox icon].

2. On the toolbar, click ![new mail icon].

   The Untitled Message window appears (see Figure 26-1).

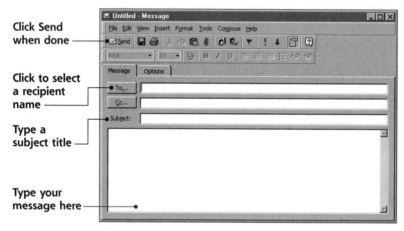

Click Send when done

Click to select a recipient name

Type a subject title

Type your message here

Figure 26-1 A new message is ready to be created.

3. Click the To button, and scroll through the names in your address book (see Figure 26-2).

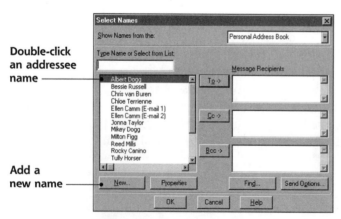

Double-click an addressee name

Add a new name

Figure 26-2 The Select Names dialog box appears.

4. Double-click the name of the person you want to send the message to.

The name you double-clicked appears in the <u>M</u>essage Recipients box. It is underlined, which indicates that Outlook recognizes the name as a valid address book entry and has an e-mail address for it.

5. Click OK.

The Untitled Message window reappears, containing a recipient name in the To... box.

6. Type an identifying phrase in the Subject box.

It's polite to tell your recipient what the message concerns so that he or she won't ignore it — your recipient might be downloading your message remotely, in which case he or she won't perform a wholesale download of all waiting messages but will download headers (subject lines) and then choose which messages to download on the basis of the subject headers.

7. After you type a Subject line, the window (and your message) are titled with your subject (see Figure 26-3).

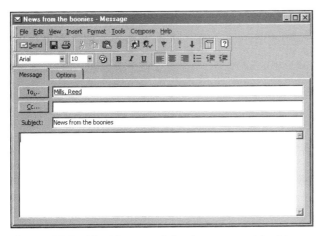

Figure 26-3 The Message dialog box gets an identity.

8. Type your message in the large box.

In the next section, you'll learn how to send the message.

Sending Your Words Forth

You have created a message, and now you are ready to send it. Sending a message is pretty straightforward, consisting of one or two steps, depending on your mail system.

Sending a Message from a Network Server

Sending mail takes only a single step:

✳ In the Message dialog box, click 🖂Send (see Figure 26-4).

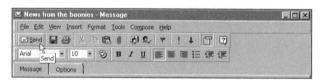

Figure 26-4   Click the Send button to send your message.

If you are on a company intranet, the message is sent to the company server and then into recipients' mailboxes.

Sending a Message over a Mail Service

If you are not on a network server but are instead using a mail service (such as Microsoft Network), the message is sent to your Outbox and you must send the mail from your Outbox to your mail service. To send out your message:

✳ On the   Tools   menu, click   Check For New Mail .

Outlook rings up the mail service, leaves your messages, and picks up any mail waiting for you.

Incoming!

As with snail mail (paper mail), getting mail is much more fun than sending it, and it's easier. Receiving mail is pretty much automatic, and after a message arrives in your Inbox, you can open it, read it, and reply to it if you want to.

Opening a Message

Very simple — to open a message you receive, follow these steps:

1. In the Outlook bar, click 📁 .

2. Double-click the message you want to open.

Previewing Messages with AutoPreview

AutoPreview is a nifty feature that shows you the first three lines of any new message. When mail arrives in your Inbox, the new messages appear with their first three lines displayed so that you can immediately tell which ones are important and which can wait until after lunch.

To preview new messages with AutoPreview, follow these steps:

1. In the Outlook bar, click [Inbox icon].

2. In the toolbar, in the Current View list box, select Messages With AutoPreview.

   All new messages will be displayed in AutoPreview when you get new mail (see Figure 26-5).

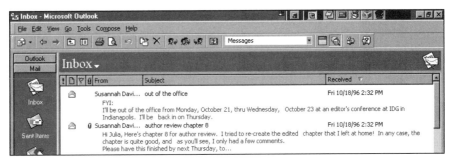

Figure 26-5 Messages are displayed in AutoPreview mode.

Sending It Back

Replying to a message is a lot faster than creating a new message to send as a reply. Not only are the address and subject line already filled in for you, but the text of the message you received is retained. You can reply directly to the sender's comments (which is a lot faster than copying text out of the old message and pasting it into your reply) so that your correspondent knows what you are talking about.

Replying to a Message

Suppose you have received a message from your coworker asking how to set up a special spreadsheet in Microsoft Excel — in the message to you, he asked several convoluted questions about Excel functions, and he wants you to answer each question as thoroughly as you can.

To reply to a message, follow these steps:

1. Open the message (see Figure 26-6).

   If the message is not already open, you can right-click the message and click Reply on the shortcut menu.

Reply to
the sender —

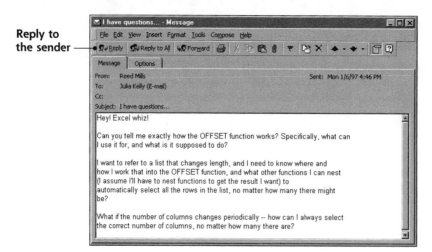

Figure 26-6 Open the message you want to reply to.

2. Click the Reply button.

   The text of the message you received is retained in your reply. You can delete all the excess trivia in that message (to shorten it) and then answer each of the sender's questions directly by typing your responses right into the paragraphs next to the questions.

3. Type your response, either at the top of the reply or within the text of the message.

4. Click ⌨ Send when you finish.

Transferring a Sender's Address to the Personal Address Book

Often you will get someone's e-mail address by receiving a message from them. When a message arrives in your Inbox and you want to keep the sender's e-mail address, it's easy to transfer the information directly into your Personal Address Book.

To transfer a sender's e-mail address into your Personal Address Book:

1. Open the message that contains the address.

2. Right-click the sender's name in the From line (see Figure 26-7).

3. In the shortcut menu, click Add To Personal Address Book .

4. Close the message.

   The sender's e-mail address has been added to your Personal Address Book.

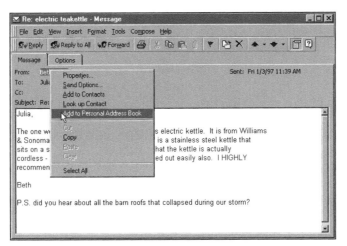

Figure 26-7 Transfer a sender's e-mail address to your Personal Address Book.

Sending and Receiving Attachments

The easiest and most direct way to send a file is to send it as an *attachment* to your message. An attached file is sent separately alongside your message, and the recipient can open it by clicking an icon in the message.

The easiest and most direct way to send a file is to send it as an attachment to your message.

A huge advantage of sending files in e-mail is their cross-platform capability: you can e-mail a binary file from a PC to a Mac computer, and neither computer knows the difference. This is a lot easier than messing with floppy disks and Mac versus PC disk formatting. (If you've ever tried to give a file on a floppy disk to a user on a different platform, you know what I mean, and if you haven't, be warned.)

Sending Attachments

If you send a file as an attachment, Outlook encodes the file so that it travels to its destination rapidly, and if your recipient has Outlook, the file is automatically decoded when it arrives. Other mail programs may not automatically decode, in which case the recipient must have a decoding program (such as Wincode) and decode the file manually, but that scenario is becoming more and more rare.

To send a file as an attachment to an e-mail message, follow these steps:

1. Create the message.

2. Be sure the insertion point (the I-beam that shows you where you are typing) is at the end of your message text.

3. On the toolbar, click ▣.

   The Insert File dialog box appears. By default, the Atta̲chment option button (on the right side of the dialog box) is selected — this is what you want, so *don't* change it.

4. Navigate to the folder that contains the file you want to send.

5. Double-click the file you want to insert.

   An icon representing the file is inserted into your message, as in Figure 26-8.

6. Click Send.

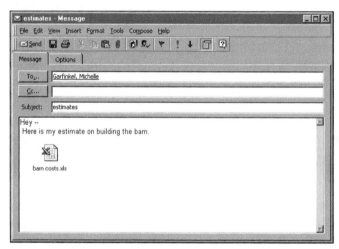

Figure 26-8   An icon for the attached file is inserted in your message.

Receiving Attachments

If you receive a message with an attached file, the file will be represented by an icon in the body of the message. Here's how to open an attachment you receive:

✳ To open the file, double-click the icon.

You can open the file from within the message, or you can drag the file from the message onto your desktop or into another folder (a copy will be placed where you drop the file icon).

Internet-Savvy E-Mail

Suppose you have heard of a Web site that might be interesting (perhaps through a television commercial or a magazine ad) and you have the address — those hard-to-remember addresses that begin with "http://www" — but you want one of your worker bees at the office to check it out for you because you are so busy being the boss. If you type the address in an e-mail message, your recipient can go online directly to the Web site by double-clicking the *hyperlink* you have created in your message.

A hyperlink (also called a hot spot or a jump) is colored, underlined text that you can click to jump to another file. You've probably seen them in help files — you click the underlined word and a definition of the word appears — and they work the same way in your e-mail message. Outlook recognizes the "http:/" part that you typed, starts your browser, and attempts to navigate to the Web page.

Creating a Hyperlink

Suppose you are hosting a gala shindig on your large getaway ranch in the Cascade mountains. It's a bit hard to find (and some guests are coming in from way out of town), so you decide to send e-mail invitations that include a map — better yet, a hyperlink to a map, so that anyone unfamiliar with the Cascades can study the lay of the land before they leave home. A great online map is the Virtual Tourist World Map (no kidding, this is real — try it!) at `http://www.vtourist.com/webmap`.

To create a hyperlink in your message:

1. Create the message.

2. Somewhere in the body of the message, type **http://www.vtourist.com/webmap**, as shown in Figure 26-9.

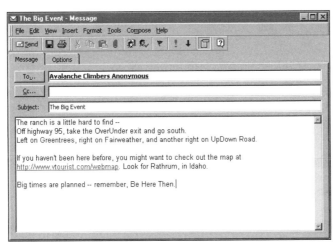

Figure 26-9 Type the Internet address — it will become a hyperlink automatically.

3. Finish the message.

4. Click ⌨️ Send .

Any guest who receives your message and has an Internet browser can click the hyperlink to start a browser and go directly to the site. Those without Internet browsers may get lost.

Editing a Hyperlink

Once you have typed the address and it has changed itself into a hyperlink, you cannot click it to correct a misspelling. Uh-oh.

To edit a hyperlink, follow these steps:

1. Press and hold down the Ctrl key.

2. While you are pressing the Ctrl key, use the left mouse button to select the part of the address that needs correction.

3. Type your changes.

BONUS

Adding an AutoSignature

A colleague sends me messages that always end with a Shakespeare-quote-of-the-week, and it changes every week. I thought he went to a lot of effort to do that until I learned it was automatic! Each week he typed up a new quote and created an AutoSignature out of it, and the AutoSignature was appended to the end of every message he sent (or replied to, or forwarded).

Outlook has an AutoSignature feature that automatically adds your text to the end of each message that you send (and reply to and forward, if you choose). You can AutoSign an advertisement for your business, or a Zen greeting, or even a cookie recipe. Whatever you want.

Creating an AutoSignature

To create an AutoSignature, follow these steps:

1. Be sure you are in Inbox.

2. On the Tools menu, click Auto Signature .

The AutoSignature dialog box appears (see Figure 26-10).

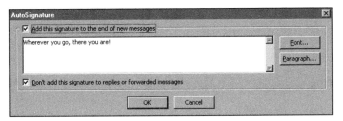

Figure 26-10   Create an AutoSignature for your messages.

3. Click the <u>A</u>dd this signature to the end of new messages check box.

   This adds the AutoSignature to all your messages. You can leave this check box cleared and add the AutoSignature to selected messages instead, if you like.

4. In the box, type the text you want.

   If the text is already typed out in another electronic document (such as a Microsoft Word file or an online encyclopedia), you can copy and paste it into the AutoSignature box.

5. To add the AutoSignature to replies and forwarded messages, clear the <u>D</u>on't add this signature to replies or forwarded messages check box.

6. Click OK.

Inserting an AutoSignature in a Message

If you create an AutoSignature but elect not to have it inserted automatically, you can include it only in those messages where you want it.

To insert an AutoSignature into a message (or any Outlook file except a Note), follow these steps:

1. Open the message.

2. Click where you want to insert the AutoSignature.

3. Select Insert → Auto Signature .

CHAPTER TWENTY-SEVEN

KEEPING TRACK OF CONTACTS AND YOUR CALENDAR

LEARN THESE KEY SKILLS:

HOW TO CREATE A LIST OF CONTACTS   PAGE 439

HOW TO UNDERSTAND THE CALENDAR   PAGE 445

HOW TO SCHEDULE APPOINTMENTS   PAGE 447

HOW TO SCHEDULE EVENTS   PAGE 450

his chapter covers two of Outlook's applets: Contacts and Calendar. Contacts is the Outlook applet in which you keep your directory of correspondents — people, companies, organizations, friends, Romans, and countrymen. You can store any kind of information you have about any individual or organization in the list and then find the information quickly when you need it.

Calendar is a combination daily, weekly, and monthly desktop calendar where you can record appointments and events, both one-time and recurring, and you can set reminders for your appointments and events so that they don't slip your notice.

You're on My List

long list of contacts is a useful thing to have, and the more information you have about each contact, the more useful your list is. The only way to get that enviable long list, however, is to create it, contact by contact.

To create a new contact, follow these steps:

1. In the Outlook bar, click .
2. On the toolbar, click .

   The Contact dialog box, shown in Figure 27-1, appears on the desktop.

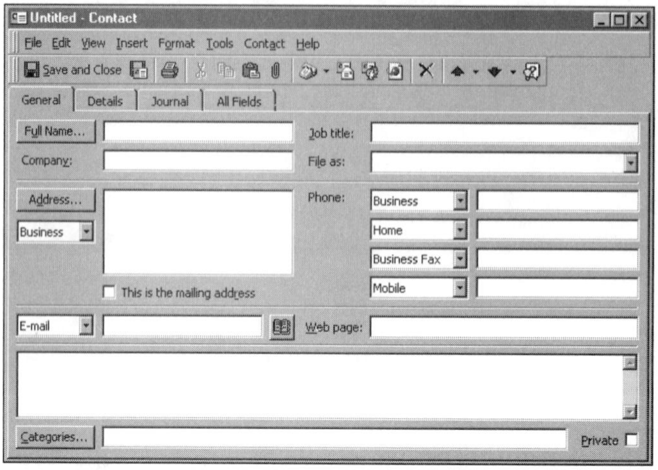

Figure 27-1 The Contact dialog box appears.

3. Be sure the General tab is displayed.

Entering the Contact Name

To enter the contact's name:

* Enter your contact's name in the Full Name box.

Type the full name of your contact. If you are concerned that Outlook may not recognize the various parts of your contact's name (for example, Outlook may think that "Van Buren" is a middle and last name, rather than a last name), click the Full Name button and type the parts of your contact's name into the appropriate boxes (see Figure 27-2).

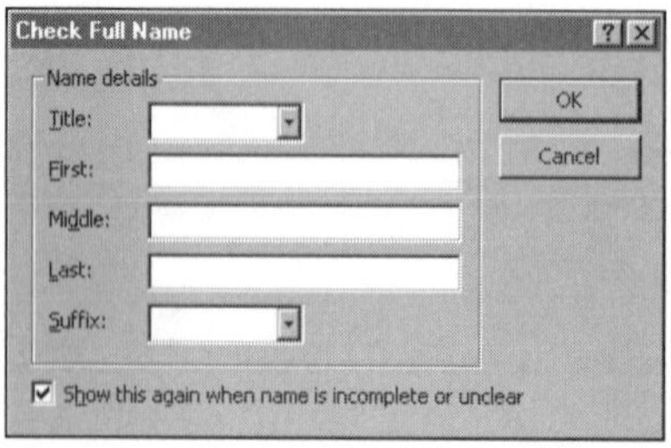

Figure 27-2 You can be sure parsing is done correctly by entering parts of the name into separate fields yourself.

If you want to enter two names in the First Name field (for example, Bob and Sue), you can type either **and** or an ampersand (**&**) between the names, and they will remain together in the First Name field.

If you want to file the contact by first name instead of last name (or vice versa), select a filing/sorting scheme from the File As list box.

Entering the Contact's Addresses

To enter the contact's various addresses, follow these steps:

1. In the Address section, select Business, Home, or Other from the list box.

2. Type the address in the large address box, shown in Figure 27-3.

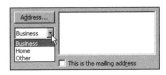

Figure 27-3 You can enter three addresses for a contact.

If you want to make sure the address is parsed into the appropriate fields, you can click the Address button and fill in the address fields (Street, City, State, Country, and so on) yourself (as shown in Figure 27-4). This can be important if you use your contacts list as a source of mail-merge addresses for a form letter in another program (such as Microsoft Word).

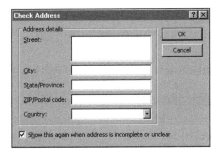

Figure 27-4 If you want to use Contacts as a mail-merge source, make sure the address is parsed into fields correctly.

If you have both a home address and a business address for a contact, select Business in the list box and enter the business address, and then select Home in the list box and enter the home address.

3. Display the specific address (Business, Home, or Other) that you want to use as a mailing address, and click the This is the mailing address check box.

If there is only one address entered, Outlook assumes that it is the mailing address.

Entering Phone Numbers

In the Phone section, you get to enter up to four phone numbers. *To enter the contact's various phone numbers, follow these steps:*

1. Click in one of the Phone boxes (see Figure 27-5).

Figure 27-5 Select a specific phone number type from each list box.

Each of the four list boxes can accept a slew of possible phone number types — select an appropriate phone number type from the list box for each number.

2. Type the number, including the area code.

    You can type the number in the format 555-123-4567, and when you move the insertion point away from the box, the phone number will be converted to the format (555) 123-4567. (And if you don't enter an area code, your computer's area code will be entered for you — how's that for insistent?)

Entering E-Mail Addresses

To enter the contact's various e-mail addresses, do this:

   ✳ In the box next to the E-mail 1 list box (see Figure 27-6), type your contact's e-mail address.

Figure 27-6 These boxes accept e-mail and Web addresses, as well as miscellaneous notes.

If there is more than one e-mail address (and often there is), click the down arrow on the E-mail 1 list box and select E-mail 2; the same goes if there is a third e-mail address. If there is a fourth, too bad.

Miscellaneous Notes about the Contact

Do you have miscellaneous information about a contact that you want to record somewhere, but it's just, well, miscellaneous? Like, perhaps, where you met this person and something about the person that you can use to break the ice when you speak with him or her again?

To enter miscellaneous notes about a contact, type the notes into the large, unnamed box near the bottom of the Contact dialog box.

Finished?

When you finish entering information, click the Save and Close button.

Working with Contacts

Once you have your Contacts set up, you'll probably want to do a few things with them as your contacts change and you need to update information. This section covers how to delete a contact, update contact information, and use your Contacts list as an address book for e-mail.

Deleting a Contact

I hate to delete contacts unless there's no chance in the world that I will need their information again (and you never know what you'll need five years from now), but sometimes it's necessary.

To delete a contact from your list, follow these steps:

1. Right-click the contact you want to delete.

2. Click Delete.

Updating Contact Information

When a contact's address or phone number changes, you will need to change the information in your Contacts list.

To update a contact's information, follow these steps:

1. Double-click the contact you want to edit.

   The Contact dialog box opens.

2. Add or change information.

3. Click the <u>S</u>ave and Close button.

Using the Contacts List as an Address Book

If you want to use both your Personal Address Book and your Contacts applet as sources of addresses for e-mail (which I highly recommend), you can include your Contacts applet in the list of address books that are available in the Select Names dialog box.

To make your Contacts applet available as a source of e-mail addresses, follow these steps:

1. In the Outlook bar, right-click 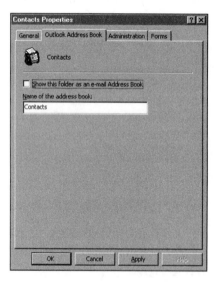.

2. On the shortcut menu, click **Properties** .

The Contacts Properties dialog box appears.

3. Click the Outlook Address Book tab.

4. Click the <u>S</u>how this folder as an e-mail address book check box (see Figure 27-7).

Figure 27-7 Click the check box on the Outlook Address Book tab.

5. Click OK.

The next time you create an e-mail message, you can select Contacts as an address book in the Select Names dialog box.

Where Did I Put My Weekly Schedule?

Now that you can enter your dentist's (or supervisor's or jogging partner's) name and phone number in your Contacts list, putting your appointments with that person on your calendar is efficient and logical. Outlook's Calendar provides several views of your upcoming schedule: you can choose a daily, weekly, or monthly view, depending on your needs.

Day/Week/Month view is where you'll find your daily calendar (see Figure 27-8). Here's how to display this view:

* Select Day/Week/Month in the Current View list box on the toolbar.

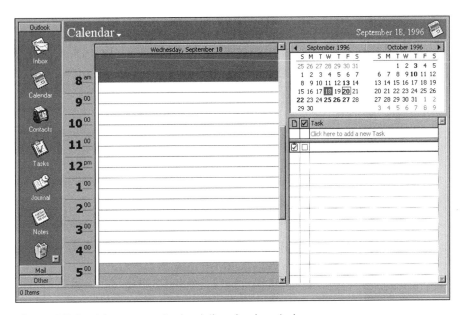

Figure 27-8 A lot goes on in the daily calendar window.

Stuff that Applies to Everything in Calendar

You open and delete all Calendar items (appointments and events) in the same way regardless of the item being opened or deleted. Here's how to open any Calendar item:

* Double-click the item you want to open.

To delete any Calendar item:

1. Right-click the item you want to delete.

2. Click Delete.

Changing Calendar Views

Calendar has several useful views, and you'll probably use several, depending on your intended task. Here's how to change your view:

✷ Select a different view from the Current View list box on the toolbar.

To see your calendar in a daily, weekly, or monthly view, follow these steps:

1. On the toolbar, select Day/Week/Month in the Current View list box.

2. Click the Day, Week, or Month button on the toolbar (the buttons are shown in Figure 27-9).

Figure 27-9   Change your views easily.

Tips for Calendar Views

Here are some tips for tweaking your Calendar views:

✷ To select a specific daily view, click that day in the thumbnail month.

✷ To select a different thumbnail month, click the thumbnail title bar and then click a different month in the list that appears.

✷ To scroll through the year in monthly view, drag the vertical scroll bar. (ScrollTips appear when you drag the scroll button, which tell you what date is displayed in the upper-left corner of the monthly view.)

SIDE TRIP

MAKING A DATE WITH AUTODATE

Microsoft's new electronic dating service for microserfs who work 100 hours a week and don't get to meet anyone really nice... (no, not really).

Suppose you want to set an appointment for two weeks from tomorrow. Instead of looking up what date that is (and perhaps entering the wrong date, which can be a real problem if someone is expecting you two weeks from tomorrow and you show up three weeks from tomorrow), you can type in **two weeks from tomorrow** and AutoDate will figure out the correct date for you — AutoDate turns your words into dates and times.

(continued)

SIDE TRIP

MAKING A DATE WITH AUTODATE (continued)

Here are a few examples of things you can type in date and time fields — almost anything will work, so be creative and see what happens!

one month from now	Halloween	now	noon
two days after Boxing Day	Valentine's Day	tomorrow	five fifteen am
three hours from now	next mon	last sat	three wks ago

Making Appointments for Fun and Profit

As a solitary writer with no company network, I use Calendar to keep track of my life. Important things like my quarterly IRS tax payment don't slip by unnoticed; I record them as appointments in my calendar and get a reminder two days in advance so that I have adequate time to write a check and mail it.

If you are on a company network, Calendar does more. You can designate an appointment's time slot as "busy," "free," "tentative," or "out of office," so coworkers (who have access to your calendar on the network) can see when you are busy, possibly available, and so on and plan meetings to accommodate your schedule.

Appointments can be solitary, or they can be set to recur on a regular basis (daily, weekly, the third Thursday of every month, and so forth).

Scheduling an Appointment

Suppose you are considering joining the local Chamber of Commerce, and you want to attend a meeting to see if it's an activity that really interests you. The Chamber meets only once a month, and you don't want to miss their next meeting, so you want to schedule an appointment (with a reminder) in your Calendar.

To schedule an appointment, follow these steps:

1. On the Outlook bar, click ▣ .

2. On the toolbar, click ▣▾ .

   The Appointment dialog box appears (see Figure 27-10).

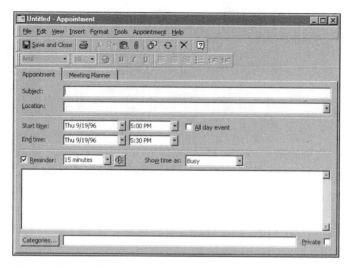

Figure 27-10 The Appointment dialog box allows scheduling of appointments.

3. In the Subject box, type a description, and in the Location box, enter the location.

4. Enter Start and End dates and times.

5. Click the down arrows and select dates and times, or (and this is more fun) type in something like **next Thursday** and **noon** and let AutoDate fill in the date and time for you.

6. In the Show time as box, select a classification for your time.

What you select here is what others will see when they look at your Calendar. By default, appointments display as busy and are blocked out, so others will know you are unavailable during that time slot.

Appointments will be visually differentiated as "busy," "free," "tentative," and "out of office" — the colored tab on the left of each appointment denotes the type of time you selected for each appointment. Figure 27-11 shows you how the appointments are visually differentiated in your daily calendar.

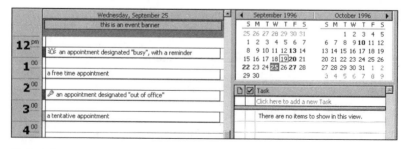

Figure 27-11 Appointments will look like this in your daily schedule.

7. Clear the <u>R</u>eminder check box if you don't want to be reminded.

If you do want to be reminded, but you want more than 15 minutes to get ready for your appointment, set a suitable remind-me-in-advance time allowance in the Reminder list box.

8. Type any miscellaneous notes to yourself in the large, unnamed box at the bottom of the dialog box.

These notes will show up only in the dialog box; to read them later, double-click the appointment in the calendar to open the dialog box.

9. Click the <u>P</u>rivate check box if you want to show the time as busy (and yourself unavailable) but don't want everyone on your network to know the nature of your business.

The subject will show up on your calendar but won't show up for anyone else on the network.

10. Click the <u>S</u>ave and Close button.

Scheduling a Recurring Appointment

A recurring appointment is an appointment that happens repeatedly on a regular basis (for example, the Chamber of Commerce meeting that happens the third Tuesday of every month at noon, and they are a really fun bunch, so you don't want to miss any meetings).

Setting a recurring appointment is the same as setting a single appointment, except that you also set a pattern for the recurrences.

To set a recurring appointment:

1. On the [<u>C</u>alendar] menu, click [**New Recurring Appointment**].

The Appointment Recurrence dialog box appears (see Figure 27-12).

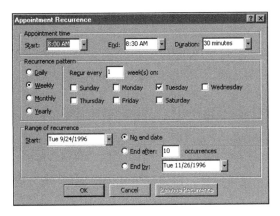

Figure 27-12 Set the appointment pattern in the Appointment Recurrence dialog box.

2. In the Appointment Recurrence dialog box, enter S̲tart and E̲nd times.

If you select a S̲tart time (say, noon) and a D̲uration (perhaps three hours), Outlook will set the E̲nd time for you (which saves your thinking energy for other, more important matters).

3. Click a Recurrence pattern option button.

Each option button will display a set of pattern options for the Recurrence pattern you selected.

4. Set the options that define the Recurrence pattern you've selected.

They have pretty much covered all the bases here, and you can set almost any kind of recurrence pattern you can dream up. For example, if you click the W̲eekly option button, you can set up a regular appointment to appear in your calendar every two weeks on Friday. You'll never again have to think of a lame excuse for missing the company Health & Safety Committee meeting.

5. Under Range of recurrences, you can set the appointments to cease after a specific number of appointments or on a specific date.

For example, if your tenure on the company Health & Safety Committee is over next July, you can type **July** next to the End b̲y option button, and Outlook will end the appointments next July.

6. Click OK to finish setting a pattern.

7. Fill in the Appointment dialog box with Subj̲ect, L̲ocation, and other pertinent info, following the steps in the previous section, "Scheduling an Appointment."

8. Click the S̲ave and Close button.

Remembering the Events in Your Life

Calendar defines events as lasting from midnight to midnight on the day(s) you schedule. Because events are things like birthdays, anniversaries, trade shows, vacations, and week-long motorcycle club reunions, they do not present a conflict with appointments in your calendar (Outlook assumes that you can keep a dentist's appointment during your week-long motorcycle club reunion). An event appears as a *banner*, a gray band that stretches across the day(s) involved in your calendar.

An "annual event" is an event that occurs yearly, like a birthday. Unlike ordinary events, which are scheduled as one-time happenings, annual events are scheduled to happen every year into eternity.

Scheduling an Event

Suppose you are planning on attending COMDEX, the extensive computer trade show in Las Vegas, but you are only going to attend this once. You can schedule it as a single event in Calendar.

To schedule an event:

1. Be sure Calendar is open.

2. Select **Calendar** → **New Event** .

    The Event dialog box appears (see Figure 27-13). It looks just like the Appointment dialog box, except that the All day event check box is checked (that's actually the only difference between an appointment and an event).

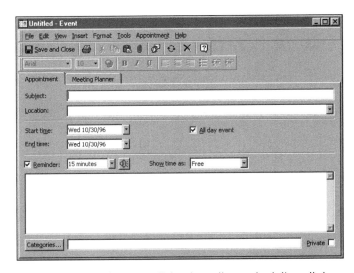

Figure 27-13   The Event dialog box allows scheduling all-day occasions.

3. Fill in the Subject and Location and other details, just as you would for an appointment.

4. Select Start and End dates for the event — no times are shown because events are all-day affairs.

    My advice is to clear the Reminder check box (or set it for a day or two), because you probably won't be around to be reminded.

5. Click the Save and Close button.

Scheduling an Annual Event

So you went to COMDEX and decided that it was the most fascinating, fun, really great time you've ever had (and you won $100 in a casino), and you want to attend *every year*.

To schedule an annual event:

1. Be sure you are in Calendar.

2. Select ⌈ **Calendar** ⌉ → ⌈ **New Recurring Event** ⌉.

   The Event dialog box appears, and the Appointment Recurrence dialog box appears on top of it.

3. Under Recurrence pattern, click the Yearly option button (see Figure 27-14).

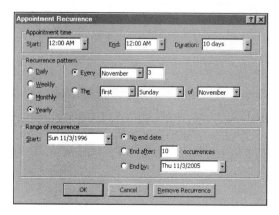

Figure 27-14 The Yearly recurrence options appear here.

4. Under Range of recurrence, set the annual Start date.

5. In the Appointment time area, set the Duration of the event.

   If the duration is longer than 2 days (for example, 10 days), the list box won't have a setting — instead, type **10 days** in the list box.

6. Click OK.

7. Fill in the Event dialog box just as you would for a single event.

8. Click the Save and Close button.

BONUS

Celebrating the Holidays

One of the very few disappointments about being self-employed (as most writers and computer consultants are) is that I tend to forget when the holidays are — and it's not nearly as delightful to take the day off when, really, I can take off any day I want to... (shhh, don't tell my editor). Calendar, however, helps me remember when the various holidays are by putting them into my calendar for me.

Holidays can be either all-day events or busy-time appointments, and if you open the holiday, the Location box on the dialog box tells you the country of origin for the holiday (clever, huh?).

To enter holidays into your calendar:

1. Select Tools → Options .

2. Click the Calendar tab.

3. Click the Add Holidays button.

   The Add Holidays to Calendar dialog box appears (see Figure 27-15).

Figure 27-15 Add holidays to your calendar.

4. In the Add Holidays to Calendar dialog box, click check boxes for the countries and religions whose holidays you want to add.

5. Click OK.

6. Click OK again to close the Options dialog box.

A great many holidays will be added to your calendar, probably including some you never heard of. You can, of course, delete those you don't want.

KEEPING TRACK WITH TASKS, JOURNAL, AND NOTES

LEARN THESE KEY SKILLS:

I n this chapter, you'll explore the Tasks, Journal, and Notes applets. Tasks are to-do lists where you can record projects that need to be done, along with due dates and billing information for each project.

Journal is an electronic diary. Everything that you normally write in your calendar (so that you can remember what you did, when you did it, and all the details about it), you can record in Journal. But Journal goes the paper diary one better — Journal can record activities, such as e-mail messages you send to your boss or spreadsheets you develop in Microsoft Excel, automatically.

Notes are a great way to keep temporary information close at hand, because they are simple to create and quick to access.

A Tisket, a Tasket

The Tasks applet is a convenient to-do list, a log of jobs that have yet to be done. To create a task, all that is minimally required is a subject, or title, for the task. You type a subject, press Enter, and you're done — the task is on your list for eternity, or until you delete it.

Outlook's Tasks has a lot more to offer, however, and all it needs is a bit more input from you.

Creating a Task

Your task can be singular, recurring, or regenerating, and all tasks are created in the same way (but you click a few extra check boxes for recurring and regenerating tasks).

To create a new task, follow these steps:

1. On the Outlook bar, click ![] to open the Tasks applet.

2. On the toolbar, click ![].

   The Task dialog box appears (see Figure 28-1).

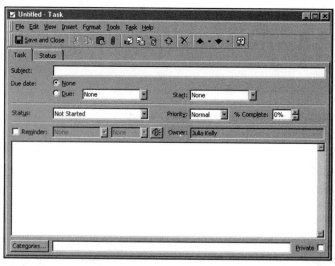

Figure 28-1 The Task dialog box provides for creation of all tasks.

3. Type a subject in the Subject box.

4. Decide whether there is a due date for the task.

   If your task is something like "Buy a more ergonomic computer chair" and there is no time limit on it, leave the None option button selected.

If your task has a due date for completion and/or a start date, set those dates in the Due and Start list boxes.

Remember AutoDate from Chapter 27? You can type a due date and a start date in words, such as **week from tomorrow**; or you can click the down arrow on each list box and then click a date on the thumbnail month that appears.

5. If you want the task to appear on your task list on a recurring basis (for example, every third Friday), on the toolbar, click .

You've seen the dialog box in Figure 28-2 before — it's the same one used by Calendar to set recurring appointments. As an example, to make your task appear on the Task List every third Friday, click the Weekly option button and then set Recur every 3 weeks, and finally click the Friday check box.

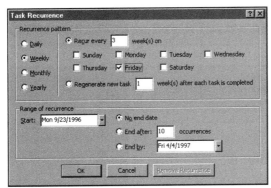

Figure 28-2   Set a recurring pattern in the Task Recurrence dialog box.

Recurring tasks appear on the Task List one at a time — when you mark one as complete, the next one pops up on your list.

6. If, instead, you want the task to reappear a specific amount of time after you complete the previous task (but *not* regularly every third week, or whatever), then you want to create a *regenerating* task.

An example of a regenerating task might be turning the compost pile in your garden — you want it to appear on your list one week after the last time you did it (and whether you turn the compost heap after four days or don't get around to it for ten days, the task will show up on your list again exactly one week after you mark it as complete). In Figure 28-3, scrubbing out the north pasture water troughs is a regenerating task.

**When this task
was marked
as complete...**
**...the next
occurrence
appeared
on the list**

			Subject	Status	Due Date	% Complete	Categories	
			Click here to add a new Task					
☑			~~scrub out north pasture water troughs~~	~~Completed~~	~~Mon 9/23/96~~	~~100%~~		
☑	!		get barn cat spayed!!	Not Started	Fri 10/4/96	0%		
☑			order winter feed supplies	Not Started	Mon 9/30/96	0%		
			muck out stalls in big barn	In Progress	Thu 9/26/96	50%		
☑	!		~~repair south pasture fence where bear broke thr...~~	~~Completed~~	~~Wed 9/25/96~~	~~100%~~		
			scrub out north pasture water troughs	Not Started	Mon 9/30/96	0%		

Figure 28-3 When you mark a regenerating task complete, the next
occurrence appears on your list.

To make a task regenerate rather than recur: in the Task Recurrence
dialog box, in the Recurrence Pattern area, click the Regenerate New
Task option button and type a number in the Week(s) after box.

7. If you set a schedule for recurrence or regeneration, click OK to close the
   Task Recurrence dialog box, and then continue filling in the Task dialog
   box.

   After you close the Task Recurrence dialog box, the Task dialog box is
   still open.

8. If you want to be reminded about the task before it's due, set a date and
   time next to the Reminder check box (in the Task dialog box).

9. If you want to keep the task subject shrouded from prying corporate
   eyes, click the Private check box (in the Task dialog box).

10. If the task is of especially high or low priority, set the priority level in the
    Priority list box (in the Task dialog box).

    Setting a priority allows you to sort your tasks by priority and thereby
    not overlook a high-priority task that languishes at the bottom of a long
    list.

11. Click [💾 Save and Close].

    The task you create appears in your Task List. If you set a due date, a
    reminder message will pop up on your computer screen the morning of
    the due date.

Deleting a Task

To delete a task, follow these steps:

1. Right-click the task you want to delete.

2. Click Delete.

Completing and Deleting Tasks

When you finish a task, you can delete it, or you can leave it in your list but mark it as completed (which gives you something to point to when asked "What have you been doing all day?").

To mark a task as complete, follow these steps:

1. Right-click the task.

2. Click **Mark Complete** .

The task will remain in your task list, but it will change color and be lined through.

Letting Outlook Keep Track of Things

Journal is a good way to keep track of your activities (such as the tasks you have already accomplished). Items you can enter in Journal automatically include e-mail messages you send from Outlook, meeting requests and responses that you send, task requests and responses that you send, and files you create or open in Microsoft Access, Excel, or Word.

Some activities (such as a conversation in the parking lot or a shopping expedition) can't be recorded automatically, but you can record anything you like manually. For example, you can record a phone call (no, not the actual voices, just the activity) and time the duration of the call with Journal's timer — the elapsed time will be recorded in the Journal entry.

Automatically Recording Items for Contacts

You probably don't want to record all of the e-mail messages you send to everyone, but you will want to keep a record of your contacts with certain people. You can automatically enter your messages to specific people. (And you can manually enter particular messages you send to people who are not on your "automatic" list.)

To automatically record all messages you send to specific contacts, follow these steps:

1. On the **Tools** menu, click **Options** .

2. Click the Journal tab (see Figure 28-4).

3. In the Automatically record these items box, click the check boxes for the items you want to enter automatically.

   Journal enters each item when it is sent (not when you create it).

Figure 28-4 Set automatic options on the Journal tab.

4. In the For these contacts box, click the check boxes for the contacts you want to enter activities for automatically.

All the activities you check are entered automatically for all the contacts you check.

5. Click OK.

TIP **To set up automatic recording when you enter a new Contact: in the Contact dialog box, on the Journal tab, click the Automatically record journal entries for this contact check box.**

Automatically Recording Documents

Suppose you create custom spreadsheet applications in Microsoft Excel for several clients — remembering to write down whose file you worked on, and when and for how long, can become somewhat haphazard on a busy day. There is a better way. You can have Journal keep track of your work on any file automatically, recording when you worked on it and for how long.

To automatically record the files you work in, follow these steps:

1. On the **Tools** menu, click **Options**.

2. Click the Journal tab.

3. In the Also record files from box, click the check boxes next to the programs whose files you want to automatically record in Journal.

4. All the files in each program you check will be recorded. (If you don't want a record of a particular file, you can delete it from Journal later.)

5. Journal records work automatically only in Microsoft Office files, but you can enter work in files from other programs manually.

Opening a Journal Entry

To open a journal entry, double-click the entry.

Deleting a Journal Entry

Even though Journal is a running log of your activities, occasionally you might want to delete an entry (for example, you'll want to delete the fake entries that you make while you read this book and experiment with making Journal entries).

To delete a Journal entry, follow these steps:

1. Right-click the entry.

2. Click Delete .

I'll Do It Myself

Automatic recording can save you from a sticky situation when it's the end of the month and you need to remember how many hours you worked on the Garden Gnome Collectors Club newsletter so that you can invoice the club properly, but you'll want to enter many items into your journal that cannot be recorded automatically.

Entering an Outlook Item Manually

If you have a specific e-mail message or task you want to enter in Journal (so that you can later recall when you worked on it and for how long), you can enter it manually. For example, although tasks cannot be entered automatically, you might want to record the time you spend on a task for future reference.

To enter an Outlook item manually, follow these steps:

1. Open the item you want to record.

   You can enter (and record the time spent on) any Outlook item — e-mail, a task, a contact, a lunch date on your Calendar, whatever (for example, the task in Figure 28-5).

2. In the dialog box, select Tools → Record in Journal .

   The Journal Entry dialog box appears (see Figure 28-6), filled in for the item you are recording.

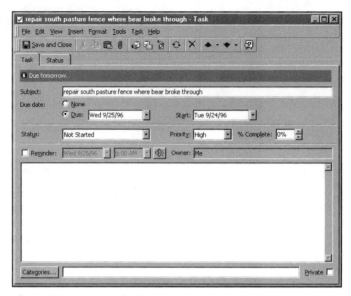

Figure 28-5 Open the item you want to record in Journal.

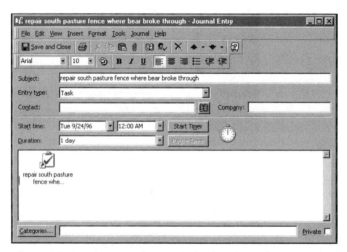

Figure 28-6 The Journal Entry dialog box is ready to complete.

3. Be sure the Start Time is correct.

To enter the current time as the Start Time, type **now** in the Start time boxes (for both the date and the time).

4. To record the time you spend on the item, click the Start Timer button and then deal with the item (have lunch with Harry, or fix the south pasture fence).

Although the dialog box must remain open for the timer to work, you can minimize the dialog box to get it out of your way. (Don't forget to stop the timer when you're done with the item!)

5. When you finish with the item (and you're ready to stop the timer) click 💾 Save and Close .

The item (along with the time the timer recorded) is entered into Journal.

Entering a Document Manually

It's understandable if you don't want Journal to automatically record every document you create in Microsoft Word, but there may be a single document that's important enough to keep a record of. You can manually record working on that one document. *To record a document manually:*

1. Locate the document you want to enter.

You can navigate to the document by any means (Outlook, My Computer, Windows Explorer, or your desktop).

2. Drag the document to the Journal icon in the Outlook bar, as shown in Figure 28-7.

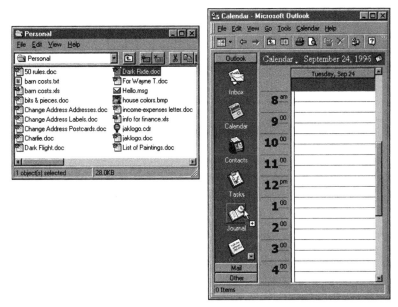

Figure 28-7 Reduce the size of each window to see them both.

It's a lot easier to drag a file to the Outlook window if you resize all the windows involved in the transaction, so that you can see all of them and drag from one to another.

A new Journal Entry dialog box appears, filled in with the current time and date, and with a shortcut to your file in the large box (see Figure 28-8).

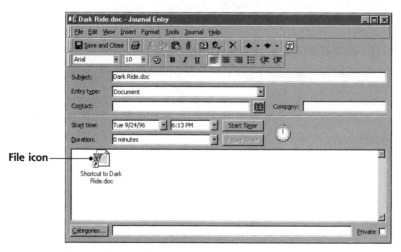

File icon

Figure 28-8 The new Journal Entry dialog box contains a shortcut to the file.

3. Click the Start Timer button to begin recording time you spend on this file, and then double-click the file to open it and begin work.

4. Remember to stop the timer by clicking [Save and Close] in the Journal Entry dialog box when you finish working in the file.

Manually Recording Any Activity

Any activity you want to record can be entered in Journal. For example, time you spend online (and let's face it, that can be considerable) can be recorded, along with the World Wide Web address(es) you've dialed up and any odd notes you feel like jotting down.

For example, suppose you are in charge of finding a suitable quote from one of Shakespeare's works for the marketing department to use in an ad campaign for a new walking shoe. If you record your activity in Journal, you can record not only how much time you spend online but also the Web address (as a hyperlink), so that you can open this journal entry at a later time and go directly online to the Shakespeare home page.

To record any activity in Journal, follow these steps:

1. Double-click in a blank space in the Journal window.

A new Journal Entry dialog box appears.

2. In the Subject box, type a description.

3. In the Entry type box, click the type of journal entry you are recording (such as phone call, conversation, or task).

You cannot create your own entry type, but there is a pretty long list from which to choose, so you can probably find an entry type that will suffice.

4. Type notes about the activity in the large empty box.

The large empty box is where you want to type your World Wide Web address for the Shakespeare home page — when you finish typing the **http:/** part of the address, the address becomes a hyperlink, like the one in Figure 28-9.

Type hyperlinks in the large box

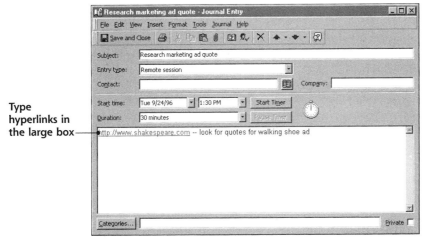

Figure 28-9 Type notes, including hyperlinks, in the large box.

5. If you are about to begin the activity (for example, if you are going online to search for that great quote), click the Start Timer button and then jump into your activity.

If you have already completed the activity and are belatedly recording it, type the time you spent engaged in the activity into the Duration box.

When you are finished with your activity, click [Save and Close] in the Journal Entry dialog box.

Better than a String around Your Finger

Outlook's Notes are the electronic equivalent of paper sticky notes that are stuck on the outside of computer monitors everywhere. They are terrific for jotting down bits of information like phone numbers and grocery lists.

Creating a Note

You can create a new note from within any applet or mail pile, because the New Note button on the toolbar is always available.

To create a note, follow these steps:

1. In the Outlook bar, click .

2. On the toolbar, click .

   A new note, like the one shown in Figure 28-10, appears on the desktop.

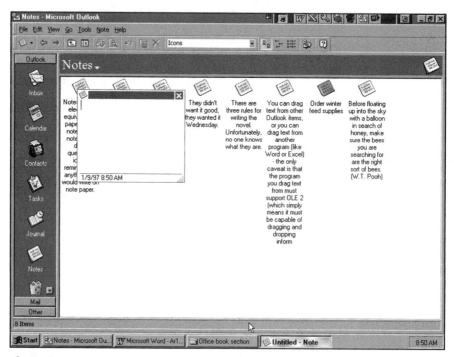

Figure 28-10   A new note appears.

3. Type the text you want in the note (as shown in Figure 28-11).

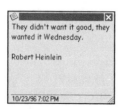

Figure 28-11   Type your note.

That's it! Your text is saved automatically.

4. Click in the Outlook window.

5. The note will be open but hidden behind the other applications on your desktop. To see the note, click the Note button on the taskbar at the bottom of your screen (see Figure 28-12).

Figure 28-12 An open note has a button on your taskbar.

Out of Sight, Out of Mind

Sometimes it's nice to have notes open on the screen and immediately available, but if you don't need to see the note until tomorrow, close it. Unlike a paper sticky, it won't get lost in the bottom of a drawer, never to be seen again — it will be stored in the Notes applet, easy to open when you need it. To close a note:

✳ Click X in the upper-right corner of the note.

What Did That Note Say?

It's tomorrow, and you need to open that important note you created yesterday.

To open a note, follow these steps:

1. In the Outlook bar, click 📝.

   The Notes applet appears in the Outlook window, as shown in Figure 28-13. By default, notes are displayed as icons, and the first few words in the note are in a caption below the note (so you can identify the note you want).

2. Double-click the note you want to open.

Tossing Old Notes

Notes are by nature impermanent, and deleting them is both important and simple.

DELETING AN OPEN NOTE

To delete an open note, follow these steps:

1. Right-click the note.

2. On the shortcut menu, click **Delete**.

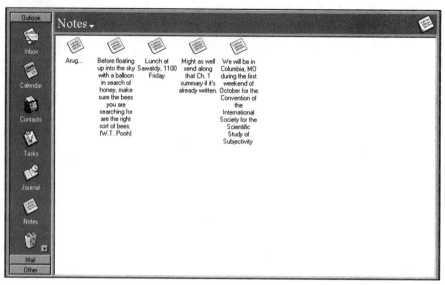

Figure 28-13   Double-click a note icon.

DELETING A CLOSED NOTE

To delete a closed note, follow these steps:

1. In the Outlook bar, click .

2. Right-click the note you want to delete.

3. Click **Delete** .

TIP   This book gives you only a brief introduction to Outlook, but an
introduction is just that. You can learn more about using Outlook in
Discover Outlook 97, by Julia Kelly (also published by IDG Books).

BONUS

How Long Did I Spend on That Job?

D o you keep records of billing information, mileage, contact names, and other assorted (but important) job details on scraps of paper in a little notebook? Or better yet, in the glove compartment of your car? The problem with paper-scrap records is that they tend to get disorganized and lost. You can record billing information in Tasks, however, and it will all be in one place when the time comes to invoice your client.

Recording Billing Information for a Task

To record important billing information for a specific task, follow these steps:

1. In the Tasks applet, double-click the task to open it.

2. Click the Status tab (shown in Figure 28-14).

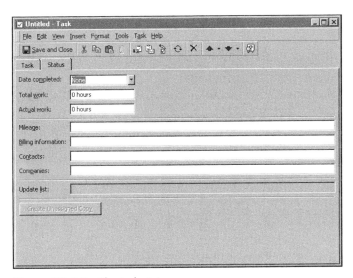

Figure 28-14   The task status.

3. Type billing information, such as hourly fee or account name/number, in the Billing Information box.

4. Type the mileage you traveled on a task in the Mileage box.

5. Type contact names in the Contacts box.

6. Type any company names you want to keep information on in the Companies box.

7. Record the number of hours you estimate the task will require in the Total work box.

   When you enter a number of hours, Outlook converts your entry to a number of days (based on a conversion factor of 8 hours per day and 40 hours per week).

8. In the Actual work box, type the number of hours you actually spend on a task as you complete it.

   Again, the number of hours you enter is converted into days.

9. Click .

TIP   To change the hours-per-day conversion factor: Select Tools → Options, click the Tasks/Notes tab, type a new number in the Hours per day box or the Hours per week box, and then click OK.

PART SEVEN

SHARING DATA AND WEB PUBLISHING

THIS PART CONTAINS THE FOLLOWING CHAPTERS:

As you get more and more proficient with Office, you'll find that you can create more sophisticated documents. For instance, you may want to combine data from several sources. Or you may want to create documents to be published on the World Wide Web. These topics are covered in this part.

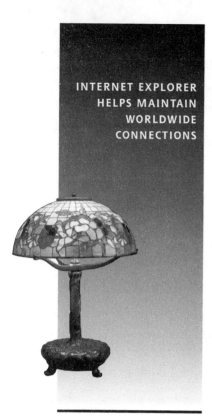

In its third annual Most Innovative New Products in Colorado contest, the *Denver Business Journal* reviewed more than 80 nominees, products ranging from the MountainBoard — a "snowboard" for summer fun — to a foam coating that helps prevent fire damage. The standout in the computer hardware and software category was OneWorld, an Internet-enabled business software package created by the phenomenally successful J.D. Edwards, based in Denver. Unlike many applications, OneWorld is designed to operate on a variety of platforms, enabling companies with national and worldwide operations to connect and work together without regard to the peculiarities of systems at each site.

Founded in 1977, J.D. Edwards has had explosive growth over the last few years. With more than 2,800 employees worldwide, this privately held independent software company is leading the way in cutting-edge business computing solutions. J.D. Edwards provides its "enterprise-wide software" to a broad range of clients, including those in the manufacturing, electronics, and pharmaceutical industries. All of J.D. Edwards software is designed to provide a solid foundation and the flexibility to adapt to ever-changing technology.

Within its own ranks, J.D. Edwards was quick to implement Internet access and develop its own extensive intranet, called the Knowledge Garden. The company has begun rolling out Internet Explorer, which will be the company standard within the next several months, internally. Every J.D. Edwards employee in the company has access to the Knowledge Garden and the World Wide Web. "An employee can browse through the Human Resources information in the Knowledge Garden and check out the benefits J.D. Edwards offers, as well as current job listings," says Wayne Applehans, Internet/Intranet Communications Manager for the Media Creators group at J.D. Edwards. "Or the employee could read recent press releases or find out when a particular product is planned for release."

No doubt J.D. Edwards will remain on the cutting edge, continuing to expand its products and its valuable intranet site, the Knowledge Garden.

To learn more about OneWorld and the J.D. Edwards vision, visit their Web site at http://www.jdedwards.com.

CHAPTER TWENTY-NINE

SHARING DATA AMONG APPLICATIONS

LEARN THESE KEY SKILLS:

HOW TO SHARE DATA BETWEEN APPLICATIONS
PAGE 474

**HOW TO INCORPORATE DATA FROM OTHER APPLICATIONS
INTO WORD DOCUMENTS** PAGE 480

**HOW TO INCORPORATE DATA FROM OTHER APPLICATIONS
INTO EXCEL SPREADSHEETS** PAGE 488

**HOW TO INCORPORATE DATA FROM OTHER APPLICATIONS
INTO POWERPOINT PRESENTATIONS** PAGE 492

W hen you run or work in a business, you don't rely on one type of information to keep that business successful. You may create reports about new trends or new products. You may review and present financial information to your staff. You may use charts to show your sales staff where you stand in terms of market share. You may keep track of inventory, sales, or orders. You use and work with a variety of data. That's what makes Office 97 so handy.

Office 97 is a suite of products, and you have available the tools to work with many types of data — documents, worksheets, presentations, databases, schedules, and so on. But while you can do a lot with each program individually, you aren't limited to one program for one task. You can also use data from different programs together to create a complex document. For example, you can insert a worksheet from Excel into your annual report created in Word. You can use charts you created in Excel in PowerPoint. If you use Access to keep track of your clients, you can use this list and Word to do a mail merge.

Being able to share data helps you pick the best tool for the task and spares you from having to recreate data. Why reenter all the names and addresses for a mail merge when this information is already available as an Access database? Why redo charts in PowerPoint when you've already used Excel to create charts for a worksheet?

This chapter starts by explaining the different ways you can share data and then shows you some specific examples for each type of application.

Share and Share Alike

You can use any of several methods to incorporate data from another program into your present document. Which one works best for you depends on the type of document you are creating and the results you want. Here are the three basic ways:

* **Copy data.** You can simply copy data from one application to another. For instance, you can copy an Excel worksheet and paste it as a table into Word. With this type of data sharing, the two files remain separate. If you change the worksheet in Excel, the data in Word are not updated. Also, you cannot use any of Excel's commands and features to modify the worksheet once it is placed in the Word document.

* **Link data.** You can insert a linked object. With this type of data sharing, the two files remain separate, but if you change the source file, the destination file is also updated. For instance, if you insert a linked Excel worksheet into Word and then change the worksheet, the Word document is updated as well. The Word document includes only the location of the source file and pulls the data from this file.

* **Embed data.** You can insert an embedded object. With this type of data sharing, the embedded object becomes part of the destination file. For instance, if you embed an Excel worksheet into Word, that worksheet becomes part of the Word file. You can use the Excel commands and features to modify the worksheet, but if you modify the original Excel worksheet, the embedded worksheet is not updated.

So the key questions are these:

* Do you need to keep the data updated?
* Do you want to be able to modify the data using commands and features from the other program?

If the answer to both questions is no, just copy the data. If the answer to both question is yes, link the data. And if the answer to the first one is no and the second is yes, embed the data. This section explains briefly how to copy, link, and embed data. The rest of the chapter gives you some specific examples of sharing data using Microsoft Office programs.

Note that you can also save a file as another file type. For example, you can save an Excel worksheet as an Access database and vice versa. This method for sharing data is covered later in this chapter.

Copying Data

You can think of copying and pasting as using a photocopier to make a copy. With a photocopy, the original remains intact in the original location, and you have the copy. You can manipulate the copy in any way that you want. You can edit it, delete part of it, highlight it, and so on, all without affecting the original. This method of sharing information works best when you simply want to use the same information in another program.

When you copy and paste without using a special command, the data are not linked. If you make a change to the original document, that change is not reflected in the pasted copy. If you want to keep the two documents in sync, link them (covered in the next section).

The application will try to paste the data into a suitable format in the receiving document. For example, when you paste an Excel worksheet into Word, the information is formatted as a table. In some cases (when you cannot edit the information in the receiving application), the information is pasted as an object.

The benefits of this method are that you don't have to maintain links and your file size will be smaller than if you used linking or embedding.

To copy and paste data, follow these steps:

1. Move to the document that contains the data you want to copy. To switch among applications, click the application you want in the taskbar.

2. Select the data you want to copy. Figure 29-1 shows Excel data selected.

3. Select **Edit** → **Copy** or click 🗈. The selection is copied to the Windows Clipboard.

4. Move to the document where you want to paste the data. Again, you can use the taskbar to switch applications.

5. Move the insertion point to where you want to paste the data.

6. Select **Edit** → **Paste** or click 🗈. The data are pasted into the document. In Figure 29-2 you see the results of pasting Excel data into Word. Notice that this data item is pasted as a table. Depending on what you copy, you'll get different results. Data such as Excel worksheets and Access data are pasted as a table. Pictures such as an Excel chart or a PowerPoint object are pasted as an object by default.

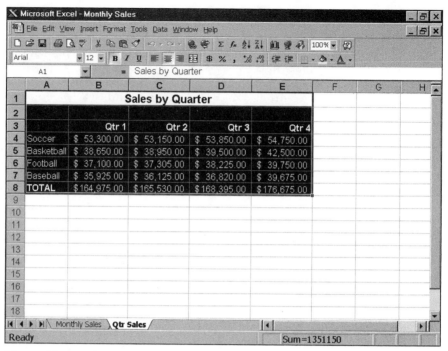

Figure 29-1   Select the data you want to copy.

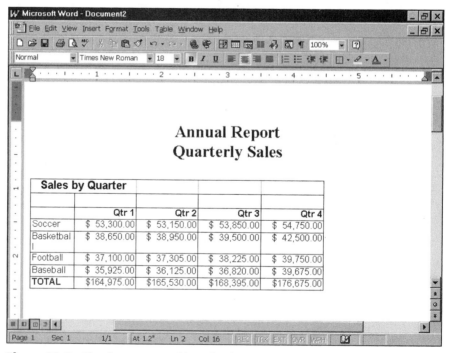

Figure 29-2   The data are pasted into the document.

Linking Data

In many cases, you may be creating a document with data from several sources. You could wait until each document is absolutely, completely finished and then copy the appropriate data, but things can — and usually do — seem to change up to the last minute. To avoid including outdated information in your final document, you can create a link between the two documents. Then when data in the original document (called the source document) are changed, the data in the new document (called the destination document) are updated too. Here are the key points to remember about linking data:

* You use the Copy command to copy the data you want to link, but you follow a different procedure for pasting the information.

* You can link data between Excel, Word, PowerPoint, Access, and any other document that supports linking.

* When you link data, you have two separate documents, stored in two separate files. Compare this to embedding (covered next).

* Use this method when you need to keep the data updated. Also, this method works best when you use the same data in several documents. You can maintain one source document and update that document as needed. All destination documents are then updated.

Follow these steps to insert a linked object:

1. Move to the document that contains the data you want to link. To switch among applications, click the application you want in the taskbar.

2. Select the data you want to link.

3. Select **Edit** → **Copy** or click 📋. The data are copied to the Windows Clipboard.

4. Move to the document where you want to paste the data. Again, you can use the taskbar to switch applications.

5. Move the insertion point to where you want to paste the data.

6. Select **Edit** → **Paste Special**. You see the Paste Special dialog box (see Figure 29-3). Here you can paste the data as just regular data or as a link.

7. Select the Paste link option. You can then select how the object is pasted: as an object, formatted text, unformatted text, a picture, a bitmap, or a hyperlink.

8. Select what you want the object pasted as and click the OK button. The data are pasted into the document and linked to the source. Figure 29-4 shows a worksheet object pasted into Word. If you make a change to this worksheet in Excel, the Word document is updated.

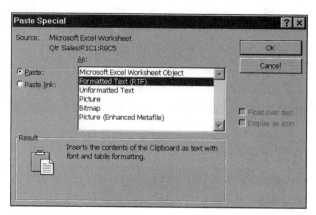

Figure 29-3   Use this dialog box to select how the data are pasted.

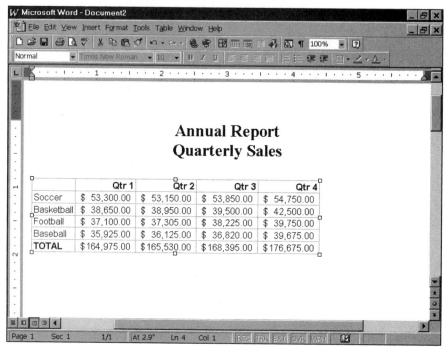

Figure 29-4   You can paste linked data into a document.

If you paste the data item as an object, it is like a picture. You can move it around within the document, but you cannot adjust the columns or edit the data from within the receiving program. If you want to make a change, you can double-click the object. Double-clicking in this case opens that application and displays that file. You can then make a change and go back to the receiving document. Contrast this with double-clicking an embedded object, covered next.

Embedding Data

In some cases you will want to be able to manipulate the data using the program you used to create the data. But you won't need to keep two separate files. In that case, you can embed the data as an object into the document. Keep these points in mind about embedding data:

✳ When you embed an object, that object is saved with the main document. For example, if you start in a Word document and embed an Excel worksheet, the worksheet is saved as part of the Word document. (If you are having trouble keeping all of the documents straight, think of embedding as a file folder. You stick all the information you need into that folder.)

✳ You can edit an embedded object using the original application. When you double-click an embedded object, you switch back to the program you used to create the object. (You can see both documents on the screen, but the toolbar and menu commands change for the appropriate application.) You can then use any commands to edit or format the object. Keep in mind that you must have the original application.

✳ The drawback to this method is that you can end up with a pretty big file. The benefit is that you don't have to maintain the links to other documents and you don't have to switch to another application to edit the embedded object.

Follow these steps to embed data:

1. Move to the document that contains the data you want to embed. To switch among applications, click the application you want in the taskbar.

2. Select the data you want to embed.

3. Select **Edit** → **Copy** or click 🗐. The data are copied to the Windows Clipboard.

4. Move to the document where you want to paste the data. Again, you can use the taskbar to switch applications.

5. Move the insertion point to where you want to paste the data.

6. Select **Edit** → **Paste Special**. You see the Paste Special dialog box (refer to Figure 29-3). Here you can paste the data as an embedded object. (Notice that this process is similar to pasting a link, only you do not select the Paste link option.)

7. Select the type of object. For example, for worksheets, select Microsoft Excel Worksheet Object.

8. Click the OK button. The data are pasted into the document.

Although the results look the same as pasting a link, they are not. For instance, if you make a change to this worksheet in Excel, the Word document is *not* updated. Also, you can double-click the worksheet to edit it. Rather than go to that source file, you see the Excel commands and toolbars and a miniworksheet within the Word document (see Figure 29-5). There are not two separate files when you embed data. The worksheet is saved with the Word document.

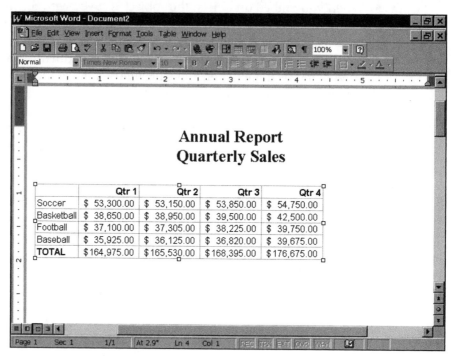

Figure 29-5   The embedded object becomes part of the document.

Everything into a Word Document

You get the most flexibility when working with text and objects with Word, so often that's the main document you start with. Then you just plunk everything else you need into Word. Word's like a big ol' handbag where you just throw everything in. This section explains how to start with Word and then insert data from other applications.

Inserting an Excel Worksheet

Now that you know your choices, you can use these skills to try some specific cases. This section covers how to insert Excel data into a document. If you are creating a report, you may want to include some of the worksheets you have created in Excel — sales, budgets, expenses, income, and so on. You can insert the data in the three ways covered in the last section:

* **As a table.** To do so, just use a straight copy and paste. The data will not be updated if you change the original worksheet.

* **As a linked object.** To do so, use the Paste Special command to paste the data and select the Paste link option. Here you have two separate files. If you change the source file (the Excel worksheet), the destination file (the worksheet object in the Word document) is updated.

* **As an embedded object.** To do so, use the Paste Special command and paste the data as an Excel Worksheet Object. Here you have just one file — the Word document. If you change the worksheet in Excel, the worksheet in Word is *not* updated.

For specific steps, refer to the preceding section. That section uses pasting Excel data as its example.

Including an Excel Chart

In addition to Excel worksheets you can also insert an Excel chart into your Word document. You might include a pie chart showing sales, a line chart of expenses, a bar chart showing income. You can keep the chart linked or simply embed it as an object.

To insert an Excel chart into a Word document, follow these steps:

1. Move to the Excel document that contains the chart. To switch among applications, click the application you want in the taskbar.

2. Select the chart you want to insert by clicking it. You should see selection handles around the chart (see Figure 29-6).

3. Select **Edit** → **Copy** or click 🖹. The chart is copied to the Windows Clipboard.

4. Move to the Word document where you want to paste the chart. Again, you can use the taskbar to switch applications.

5. Move the insertion point to where you want to paste the chart.

6. To paste the chart as an embedded object, select **Edit** → **Paste** or click 🖻.

   To paste the chart as a linked object, select **Edit** → **Paste Special**. In the Paste Special dialog box, select Paste link and click the OK button.

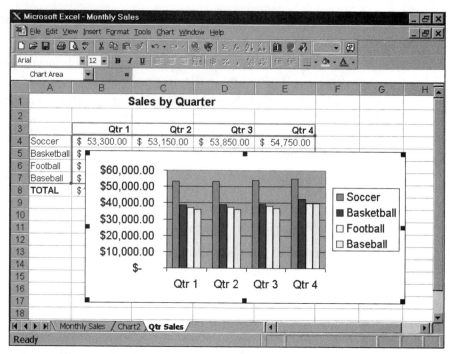

Figure 29-6   Select the chart you want to insert into Word.

Both charts look the same when inserted into Word (see Figure 29-7). But the linked object will be updated if you change the original. The embedded object will not. If you double-click the linked object, you open the application and that separate document file. If you double-click the embedded object, you have access to all the Excel commands, but you are not working in a separate Excel file. The worksheet is saved as part of the Word document.

You can move the object around and also change how text flows around the object. This object is just like a picture you've inserted. Refer to Chapter 9 for more information on formatting and working with objects.

Inserting a Slide from PowerPoint

If you do a lot of presentations, you may use PowerPoint, the presentation program included with Microsoft Office. You may want to include some of the slides from a presentation in your Word document. You can paste the slide as a picture (which you cannot edit with PowerPoint) or as a Microsoft PowerPoint Slide Object (which you can edit with PowerPoint). You can also choose whether to paste it as an embedded object or as a linked object.

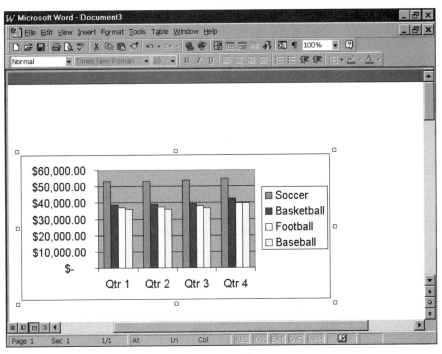

Figure 29-7 You can embed a chart into Word.

Follow these steps to copy a slide from PowerPoint to Word:

1. Move to the PowerPoint presentation that contains the slide. To switch among applications, click the application you want in the taskbar.

2. If necessary, switch to Slide Sorter view so that you can select the entire slide.

3. Click the slide you want to copy to Word. You should see a black border around the selected slide (see Figure 29-8).

4. Select **Edit** → **Copy** or click 📋. The slide is copied to the Windows Clipboard.

5. Move to the Word document where you want to paste the slide. Move the insertion point to where you want to paste the slide.

6. To paste the slide as an embedded object, select **Edit** → **Paste** or click 📋.

   To paste the slide as a linked object, select **Edit** → **Paste Special**. In the Paste Special dialog box, select Paste link and click the OK button.

   To paste the slide as a simple picture, select **Edit** → **Paste Special**. In the Paste Special dialog box, select Picture and click the OK button.

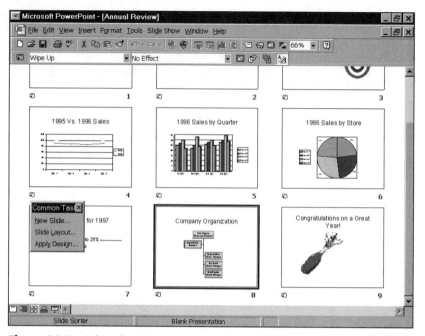

Figure 29-8 Select the slide you want to copy to Word.

Figure 29-9 shows a slide pasted as a picture. You can use any of the picture formatting options included with Word, but you cannot edit the slide using PowerPoint.

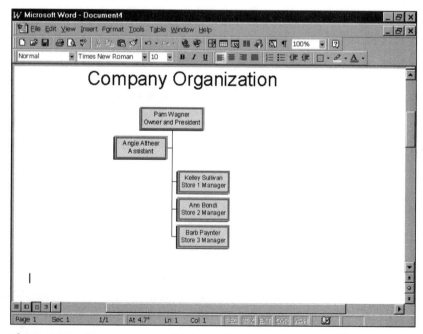

Figure 29-9 You can paste a slide into a Word document.

TIP You can move the object around and also change how text flows around the object.

Using an Access Database for a Mail Merge

If you have to keep track of a lot of data, you may use Access, a more sophisticated database program. If you use Access to track names and addresses, you may want to use these data to create form letters with Word. *You can do so by following these steps:*

1. Start in Word with a blank document on-screen.

2. Select   Tools   →   Mail Merge . You see the Mail Merge Helper dialog box.

 X-REF For complete information on doing mail merges, refer to Chapter 10.

3. Under Main document, click the Create button and select Form Letters. You can also use the database and set up labels or envelopes.

4. When prompted to use the current window or a new window for the main document, click the Active Window button.

5. Click the Get Data button and select Open Data Source. You see Open Data Source dialog box.

6. Display the Files of type drop-down list and select MS Access Databases as the file type. Then use the Look in drop-down list to change to the drive that contains the file you want to use. Also, change to the folder that contains the Access database. You should see your database file listed (see Figure 29-10).

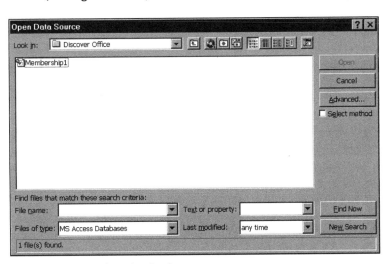

Figure 29-10 Select the database you want to use.

7. When you see the file listed, double-click it. If the database contains more than one table, you see the Microsoft Access dialog box, shown in Figure 29-11.

Figure 29-11   Select the table you want to use.

8. Select the table you want to use for the mail merge. Word lists this filename in the Mail Merge Helper dialog box. Word also establishes a DDE (Dynamic Data Exchange) link so that the data are linked. (This may take a while.)

When the links are established and the data records are read, you are prompted to set up the main document.

9. Click the Edit Main Document button. You see the main document on-screen.

10. Type the text of the letter.

11. When you get to a spot where you want to insert variable information from the Access database, click the Insert Merge Field button. You see a list of fields from the Access database (see Figure 29-12).

Figure 29-12   The fields from your Access database are available as merge fields in your Word merge document.

12. Click the field you want to insert.

13. Continue typing and inserting fields until you complete the document.

14. To save the main document, select **File** → **Save**. Enter a name and location for the main document. You can now merge the two.

15. Select **Tools** → **Mail Merge**. You see the Mail Merge Helper dialog box, which lists all the file information. Notice that the data source is an Access table.

16. Click the <u>M</u>erge button. You see the Merge dialog box. (For information on selecting options in this dialog box, see Chapter 10.)

17. Make any changes to how you want the merge performed and then click the <u>M</u>erge button. Word merges the letters and displays each one on a separate page (if you merged to a new document). Word uses the data from the Access database for the letters. Figure 29-13 shows one of the letters from a merge.

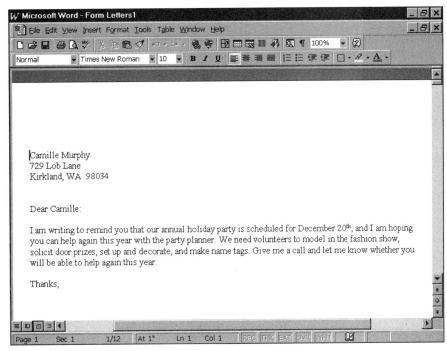

Figure 29-13 The merged letter pulls data from your Access database.

18. Print the letters using the **Edit** → **Print** command.

Sweet Figures

Are numbers your thing? Do you feel most comfortable with a calculator within fingertip reach? If so, you might want to move data from other programs into Excel. For example, you might set up a table in Word and then want to copy it to set up a worksheet. I do that a lot with book outlines. I have the outline in Word, but I want to set up a tracking sheet in Excel. Instead of retyping, I just copy the chapter names from Word to Excel. This section explains how to copy a Word table as well as other data from another program to Excel.

Copying Word Text into an Excel Worksheet

Data can go both ways. In the last section you learned how to copy Excel data to Word, and here you learn how to do the reverse — take text from Word and copy it to Excel.

What you select controls how the data are pasted into the worksheet. If you select paragraphs, each paragraph is pasted into a separate cell. If you select a table, each table cell is pasted into a worksheet cell. *Follow these steps to copy Word data to Excel:*

1. In Word, select the text you want to paste into Excel (see Figure 29-14).

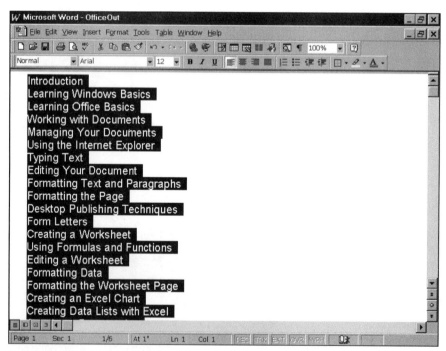

Figure 29-14 In this example, text is selected to paste into Excel.

2. Select **Edit** → **Copy** or click 📋.

3. Switch to Excel and select the cell where you want to paste the text.

 Be sure to select a blank range. Otherwise, you'll overwrite the existing data.

4. Select [**Edit**]→[**Paste**]. The data are pasted into the appropriate cell(s). You can make any necessary adjustments to the formatting and column widths (see Figure 29-15).

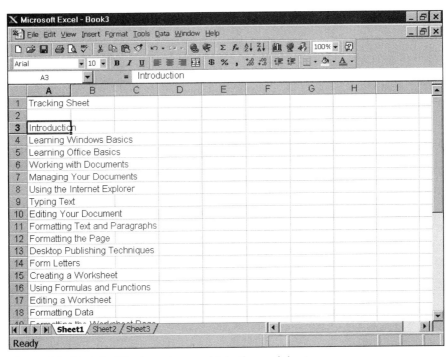

Figure 29-15 The Word text is pasted into the worksheet.

SIDE TRIP

ACCESS TABLE INTO WORD

You can also include Access data as a simple table in Word. To do so, follow these steps:

1. In Access, display the database in Datasheet view.

2. Select the records you want to copy.

3. Select [Edit]→[Copy] or click 📋.

4. Move to the Word document where you want to paste the data.

5. Select [Edit]→[Paste] or click 📋. The Access data are pasted as a table.

Saving an Access Database as a Worksheet

Access is great for manipulating information — sorting records, querying for matches, finding data, and so on. And you can perform some calculations on fields by creating reports, but report creation can be complex, and you don't have the same flexibility as you do in Excel.

If you want to do some number crunching with your Access data, you can turn them into an Excel worksheet. This identity change is called *exporting*. That is, you save the Access data in another format. The resulting Excel worksheet will include the same field names and all the records from the table. You can then insert new fields, edit the records, perform calculations, and so on, in Excel.

Follow these steps to export a database:

1. In Access, open the table you want to export.

2. Select File → Save As/Export. You are prompted whether to save the table as an external file or within the current database.

3. Select to export the database as an external file. You see the Save Form dialog box.

4. Display the Save as type drop-down list and select Microsoft Excel 97.

5. Select the drive and folder where you want to place the exported file. Also, if you want to use a different name, type a filename in the File name text box.

6. Click the Export button. Access exports the table. If you want to check the new file, you can switch to Excel and open the file. Figure 29-16 shows an exported Access table.

Exporting and Calculating Your Billing Information

If you enter billing information, such as mileage and hours worked, for each task, how can you make your computer do the work of totaling and organizing that information?

If you have Microsoft Excel, you can easily total the mileage and billing information you have typed into each task by exporting Tasks to an Excel file. (You can export to a number of file types, but I'll use Excel to demonstrate because it's one of my favorite programs.)

To export Tasks to an Excel file, follow these steps:

1. On the Outlook bar, click 📋.

2. Select File → Save Import And Export.

   The Import And Export Wizard starts.

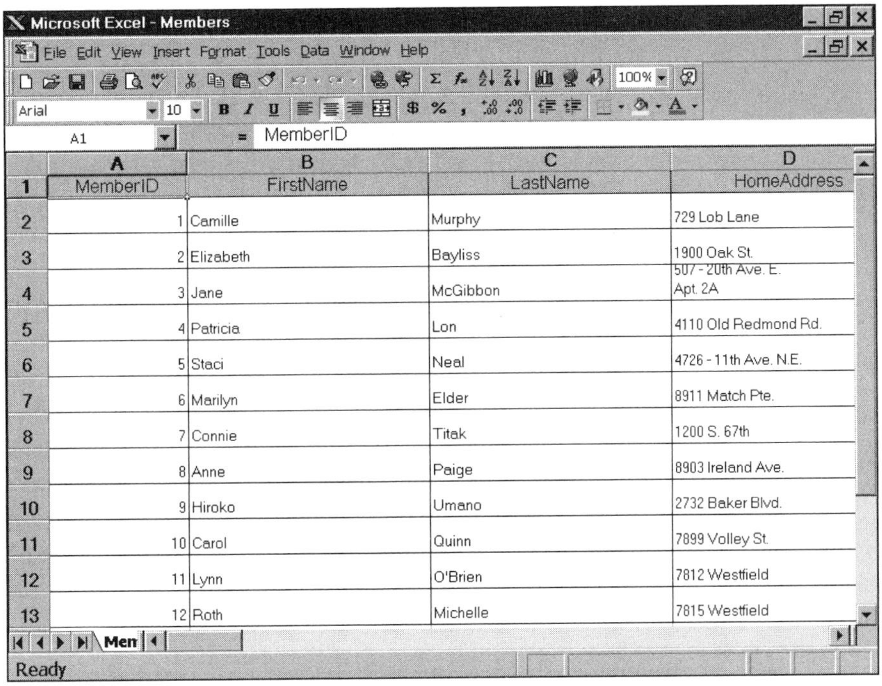

	A	B	C	D
1	MemberID	FirstName	LastName	HomeAddress
2	1	Camille	Murphy	729 Lob Lane
3	2	Elizabeth	Bayliss	1900 Oak St.
4	3	Jane	McGibbon	507 - 20th Ave. E. Apt. 2A
5	4	Patricia	Lon	4110 Old Redmond Rd.
6	5	Staci	Neal	4726 - 11th Ave. N.E.
7	6	Marilyn	Elder	8911 Match Pte.
8	7	Connie	Titak	1200 S. 67th
9	8	Anne	Paige	8903 Ireland Ave.
10	9	Hiroko	Umano	2732 Baker Blvd.
11	10	Carol	Quinn	7899 Volley St.
12	11	Lynn	O'Brien	7812 Westfield
13	12	Roth	Michelle	7815 Westfield

Figure 29-16 This worksheet was originally an Access database.

3. Click Export To A File, then click Next.

   The second wizard dialog box appears, and Tasks is selected in the dialog box folder list.

4. Click Next.

   The third wizard window appears.

5. Click Microsoft Excel to export the tasks to an Excel file, and then click Next.

   The fourth wizard window appears.

6. In the Save exported file as box, type a filename for the exported file (it will be saved in your Personal folder).

7. Click Next.

   The Fifth (and last) wizard window appears.

8. Click Finish.

   Your tasks are copied to the new Excel file.

To calculate the Tasks billing information, open the new file in Microsoft Excel. A workbook will open with a column for each of the fields in the Task dialog box — you can delete all the columns you don't need (such as Status, Priority, and Reminder).

Now all your tasks billing information is gathered into one table, and you can use Excel's features to organize and sum it all. Use AutoFilter to display the data for a specific client, and then use AutoSum to total the mileage and hours.

Power Up!

PowerPoint is perfect for creating presentations, but it might not be your tool of choice for creating, manipulating, and charting the data you want to present. For instance, if most of your financial data are stored as Excel worksheets, don't waste your time retyping the information in PowerPoint. Instead, copy and paste the worksheets or charts you want to use. If you like to outline your presentation, but prefer Word's outlining tools, use that program to create the outline. This section describes ways to use data from other programs in a PowerPoint presentation.

Using a Word Outline to Create a Presentation

If you use Word a lot for writing, you may prefer to use it to do all of your compositions, including planning a presentation. You can create an outline in Word and then set up a presentation based on the outline. When you do this, PowerPoint creates a slide for each topic that is formatted as Heading 1 (the top-level heading in an outline). The Heading 1 is used as the slide title. Any additional text you include in the outline is formatted as bulleted text.

Follow these steps to create a PowerPoint presentation from a Word outline:

1. Create the outline using Word. To do so, type the text and then assign the heading styles for each paragraph — Heading 1 for the top-level topics, Heading 2 for the next level, and so on. These heading styles are already set up and available in the default template.

   Or change to Outline view and type the outline. You can use the Outline toolbar or the Tab and Shift+Tab key combinations to arrange the headings. To decrease a heading's level, press Tab. To increase a heading level, press Shift+Tab.

   Figure 29-17 shows a Word outline about to be made into a PowerPoint presentation.

2. Select File → Send To → Microsoft PowerPoint. The outline is copied to PowerPoint, and a new presentation is created based on this outline. The PowerPoint program is started, and you see your new presentation (see Figure 29-18). You can make any changes as needed.

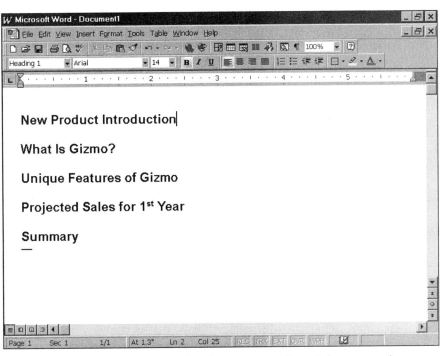

Figure 29-17 You can use a Word outline to create a PowerPoint presentation.

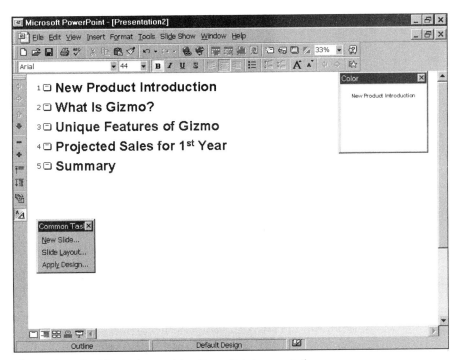

Figure 29-18 This is the resulting PowerPoint presentation.

Inserting an Excel Worksheet

As mentioned, you may prefer to do most of your financial information-keeping and charting in Excel. You can use any of the data and charts you've created with Excel in a PowerPoint presentation. *Follow these steps:*

1. In Excel, select the data you want to paste onto a PowerPoint slide.

2. Select **Edit** → **Copy** or click 🔲. The data are copied to the Windows Clipboard.

3. Use the taskbar to switch to PowerPoint, and display the slide where you want to place the worksheet data.

4. To paste the worksheet as an embedded object, select **Edit** → **Paste** or click 🔲.

   To paste and link the worksheet data, select **Edit** → **Paste Special**. In the Paste Special dialog box (refer to Figure 29-3), select Paste link and click the OK button. The worksheet is pasted onto the slide (see Figure 29-19).

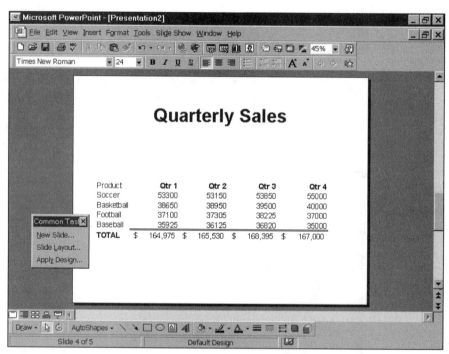

Figure 29-19 You can include Excel worksheets on a PowerPoint slide.

You may need to move and resize the worksheet object.

 TIP You can also insert a new worksheet onto a slide. Display the slide where you want to insert the worksheet or chart. Click 🔲 and then drag across the number of rows and columns you want to insert in the worksheet. Create the worksheet using any of the commands and features of Excel.

Inserting an Excel Chart

Just as you can copy worksheet data, you can also copy a chart you've created in Excel. *Follow these steps:*

1. In Excel, select the chart you want to copy. You can select the chart by clicking it.

2. Select **Edit** → **Copy** or click 📋. The chart is copied to the Windows Clipboard.

3. Switch back to PowerPoint and display the slide where you want to copy the chart.

4. To paste the chart as an embedded object, select **Edit** → **Paste** or click 📋.

   To paste the chart as a linked object, select **Edit** → **Paste Special**. In the Paste Special dialog box, select Paste link and click the OK button. The chart is pasted onto the slide as shown in Figure 29-20.

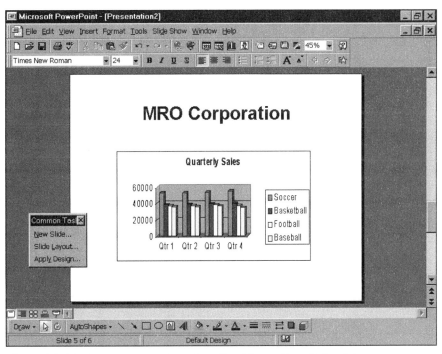

Figure 29-20 You can paste charts from Excel into a PowerPoint slide.

BONUS

Importing Data into Access

Access is a difficult program to copy data to — probably the most difficult — because it has such a particular format for its data. Still, one thing you can do is import an Excel worksheet and create an Access database from it.

You may start by using Excel as a simple database program. But if your needs become more complex, you may want to jump up to a more powerful database program, such as Access. Access offers you much more control in manipulating and working with the data. Rather than reenter the Excel worksheet in Access, you can import the Excel worksheet and create a new database table.

When you import a worksheet, you not only set up a new table with the same fields, but you also import all the records you have entered. Once you've imported the worksheet, you can then make changes to the structure of the database — add new fields, change field types, set new field widths, and so on — using any of Access's commands and features. You can also edit, delete, or add new records.

Follow these steps to import data:

1. In Access, open the database where you want to place the new table. Display the Tables tab and click the New button to create a new table.

2. Select Import Table as the method for creating the new table and click the OK button. You see the Import dialog box (see Figure 29-21).

3. Change to the drive and folder that contain the Excel worksheet.

4. Display the Files of type drop-down list and select Microsoft Excel.

5. Select the file you want to import and click the Import button. You see the first step of the Import Spreadsheet Wizard, shown in Figure 29-22. If your workbook contains more than one worksheet or named range, you start by selecting the range or worksheet you want.

6. Select the worksheet that contains the database you want to import and click the Next button. You are next prompted to tell Access whether the first row contains the column headings.

7. If your first row contains field names, check the First Row Contains Field Names check box and then click the Next button. You are prompted to select whether to store the data as a new table or an existing table.

8. Select where to place the new data and click the Next button. You are prompted to specify other information for each field (see Figure 29-23).

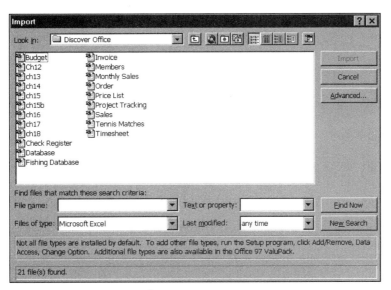

Figure 29-21   Select the file you want to import.

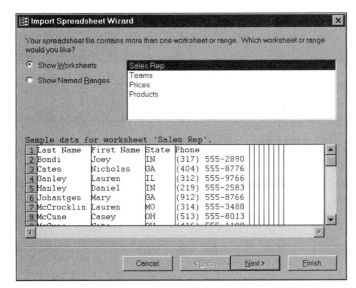

Figure 29-22   For the first step of the wizard, select which
worksheet you want to import data from.

9. Make any changes to the field name, index, and data type and click the
    Next button. You are prompted to select the primary key for the table.

10. Select whether to let Access add the primary key, choose your own, or set
    no primary key. Click the Next button.

11. Type a name for the table and then click the Finish button. Access
    processes all the records and displays the results of the import.

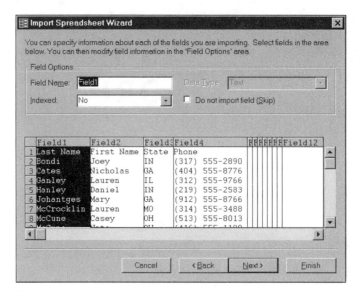

Figure 29-23   Set up the field names.

12. Click the OK button. You can then open the new database table (see Figure 29-24).

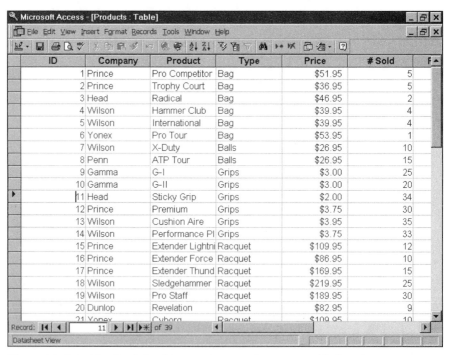

Figure 29-24   The Excel database was imported as a new table into Access.

USING INTERNET EXPLORER

I f you have never heard of the Internet, you must live in a cave. The Internet is virtually everywhere — on TV, in the news, in advertisements, in movies, in schools, everywhere. But just because you have heard of this oh-so-cool thing, you may not *really* know what it is and why it is so cool. Don't worry. You aren't alone. The Internet is hard to describe, and even though many have heard of it, they may not know a lot about this new phenomenon.

This chapter starts by defining what the Internet is. You then learn how to get connected and how to navigate around using the Internet Explorer.

TIP   The Internet is a topic unto itself. You can find entire books, volumes of books, devoted to this topic. If you want a more complete reference, try *The Internet for Dummies*, published by IDG Books Worldwide.

Is It a Bird? Is It a Plane?

L et's start by first defining what the Internet is, what you can do with it (if you haven't already heard!), and why you might want to jump in the swim and join other Internet "surfers."

The Internet is a group of hundreds of thousands — no one has an exact figure — of different networks, all loosely connected. Your company network is hooked to your main office network, which is hooked to a local university network that's hooked to a government network that's hooked to another company network and so on and so on. It's kind of like a highway system. All kinds of connecting roads exist, letting you visit all kinds of cities, that is, Internet sites. Once you have access to the Internet, you have access to the information on each of these networks, as if you were connected directly.

What You Can Do on the Internet

What makes the Internet so cool is that there are so many different networks and so many different users (estimates range upward from 40 million users!). That means you can get access to information from a wide, wide, wide variety of resources. And you can contact and communicate with people from around the world. With your Internet connection, you can do the following basic things:

* **Send and receive e-mail.** You can send mail to any one of the other millions of users that are connected. If your college best friend in South Carolina has an e-mail address, you can send her mail. For more information on sending mail, check out Part VI of this book, which covers how to use Outlook to send and receive mail.

* **Read and post messages** on bulletin boards, called *newsgroups*. A newsgroup is a group devoted to a particular topic. You can find newsgroups on practically any topic imaginable — Elvis sightings, quilting, fantasy sports, and more. Anyone can join (subscribe) to a newsgroup and then post and review messages posted on the bulletin board. (This book does not cover newsgroups.)

* **Download files** — for example, bug fixes, shareware, documents, and so on — from another network to your PC. You can also upload files — for example, I can upload my chapters to my editor.

* **Browse the World Wide Web** (often called the Web for short). The Web presents information in a graphical format. A Web page, for instance, may contain text, graphics, animations, sounds, video clips, and links to other pages. You can use the links to jump from page to page, which is often called "surfing the Net." To browse the World Wide Web, you need a Web browser, such as the Internet Explorer, Microsoft's Web browser. The rest of this chapter explains how to use Internet Explorer to browse the Web.

What You Need to Get Connected

To get connected to the Internet, you need the following stuff:

* A modem
* A phone line
* An Internet service provider

This section describes these three necessities.

YOU NEED A MODEM

Modem stands for MODulator-DEModulator; a modem is a device that enables you to send information via the phone lines. The modem takes PC-language data (digital) and translates them into a signal that can be carried on the phone lines (analog). The information is sent to another PC with another modem, which then demodulates or translates the information from "phone speak" to "PC speak."

Many new PCs come with a modem, so you may already have one installed. If you don't have a modem, you can purchase one and add it to your PC system. (Adding a modem isn't a very difficult upgrade, and they are not very expensive. You can get a modem for $150 or so.)

YOU NEED A PHONE LINE

Your connection — your on-ramp — to the Internet is through the phone line. You hook up a phone line to your modem, and the modem can then communicate via the phone line to other networks. You can use an existing phone line for your modem and connection, but you'll have to coordinate when the line is a "modem" and when the line is a "phone." Doing so may be more hassle than you really want. Instead, you can have the phone company install a separate phone line for your modem.

YOU NEED AN INTERNET SERVICE PROVIDER

You have the modem, and it's hooked up to the phone line, but who ya gonna call? To get connected, you have to have an Internet Service Provider — a service that provides access to the Internet. You can use an independent Internet Service Provider, or you can get access through other commercial online companies. For instance, you can use Microsoft Network to get connected to the Internet. (This chapter covers this method.)

TIP If you use the Internet a lot, you may want to investigate an independent service provider. Microsoft Network is a good way to get started and see whether you want to use the Internet and how much you'll use it, but it can be more expensive than other Internet Service Providers.

WHO OWNS THE INTERNET?

No one person or company controls the Internet. Instead, each person or company owns their particular network. The people in charge of the network determines what information is made available via the Internet. They also determine any charges for visiting that site. (Most don't charge. See the section "What Does It Cost?")

That means that no one company or entity is dominating the Internet market. Lots of companies benefit, which is one thing that makes the Internet so great. It is truly an open forum.

If you work in an office, you may have connections using other networking and connecting protocols. You don't need to worry so much about how to get connected. Just check with your system administrator.

What Does It Cost?

For the most part, the information on the Internet is free. Most companies do not charge to visit their Internet site or get information, but you will find some that do. For instance, you can subscribe to an Internet version of the *Wall Street Journal,* but you have to pay a subscription fee.

You do have to pay your Internet Service Provider, though, and this fee varies depending on your provider and which plan you select. Most companies offer unlimited access for a set fee. For instance, you may be able to get a plan with unlimited access time for $20 a month from a local Internet provider. Because of stiff competition, major providers such as Microsoft Network, America Online, Prodigy, and CompuServe are now offering unlimited access for around $20.00 per month, with small local companies charging less. You can also review the different plans available for MSN.

Hello, World

As mentioned, you can get connected to the Internet using an independent service provider or through a commercial service such as Microsoft Network (MSN). Microsoft, of course, wants you to use MSN, so they make it easy to get connected and try out the service. Some versions of Office may include a free trial subscription. This section briefly covers how to get connected.

Basically, you get connected to the Internet by setting up an account with an Internet Service Provider. This company will need information about you (name, address, credit card number, and so on). They also provide the software you need to get set up. After you follow the specific instructions from your provider, you're set to go. *Follow these steps:*

1. Double-click the Internet icon. You see the sign in dialog box. Figure 30-1 shows the Sign In dialog box for MSN.

   If you are using another Internet Service Provider, you'll see the sign-in dialog box for that service. Follow the instructions given to you by the provider.

Figure 30-1 Enter your sign-in information.

2. If necessary, type your Member ID and password in the appropriate text boxes.

3. Click the Connect button. You are connected to the Internet, and you see the Microsoft home page.

The World at Your Fingertips

Now it's on to the fun stuff. The World Wide Web is like having a library of information and services at your fingertips. You may want to research the eating habits of Koala bears, check out a new tune from Sonia Dada, create a map to your home, or order a book. You can do all this and more. This section explains the basics of the Internet Explorer.

Understanding the Internet Explorer Screen

When you start the Internet Explorer, by default, you see the Microsoft Home page (http://www.home.microsoft.com). Before you take a look at the guts of this page (covered next), take some time to look at the available tools.

Like other applications, Internet Explorer includes a title bar, a menu bar, and a toolbar. The title bar displays the name of the current Web page. The menu bar provides access to commands for using Internet Explorer, and the toolbar provides buttons with shortcuts for frequently used commands. Table 30-1 identifies each button and provides a short description. Under the toolbar, you see the address box, which lists the address of the current page.

TABLE 30-1   Internet Explorer Toolbar Buttons

Button	Click to...
Back	Go back to the previous page you visited.
Forward	Go forward to the page a page you visited. (You can only go forward if you've used the Back button to go back.)
Stop	Stop the display of a page or the transfer of a file.
Refresh	Redisplay the current page.
Home	Display the starting page (www.home.microsoft.com).
Search	Display tools for searching the Internet. See the section "Where Do I Find Stuff On..." later in this chapter.
Favorit.	Display a list of your favorite sites. The bonus section in this chapter covers how to add sites to this list.
Print	Print the current page.
Font	Change the font.
Mail	Access mail features.

Exploring Other Internet Explorer Pages

The tools in the Internet Explorer screen help you navigate around the Web. The page itself also includes some useful features — basically the tabs at the top of the page. You can use these tabs to display other pages with information. One great page to try is the Best of the Web page (click the tab to display this page). Here you find different Web sites. You can select from several different categories including News, Business & Finance, Computers & Technology, Sports & Health, and so on. Select a category and then read a short description of any of the highlighted sites. You can jump to any of these sites by clicking the link.

 The Best of the Web picks are updated frequently. You'll see other sites of interest when you access this page.

For information about Microsoft products, click the Microsoft tab. For access to the MSN (Microsoft Network) page, try the MSN tab.

Let Your Fingers Do the Clicking

The thing about Web surfing is that you can start off looking for something legitimate like information on your competitor's product and wind up somewhere else entirely doing something like looking at pictures of Bulldogs. Part of the fun of the Internet is its unpredicatbility.

This section covers some of the different ways you can navigate using Internet Explorer.

Understanding a Typical Web Page

Before you start cruising around the Web, you should have a basic idea of how information in organized. Basically, the Web is organized into pages. Each page has a unique address or URL (uniform resource locator). For example, the following is the address for IDG Books Worldwide:

```
http://www.idgbooks.com
```

Like this page, shown in Figure 30-2, a Web page can contain text, graphics, and links to other pages. Links are usually underlined and appear in a different color. You may also find sound clips, video clips, and animations on a Web page.

Jumping from Link to Link

As mentioned, most pages include links to other sites. (And if they don't, they are pretty much a dead end.) You can go to any links simply by clicking them. You can click any of the underlined text to go to that page. Some pictures are also links; you can click the image to go to that page.

Links may take you to a related page at the same Web site or to another Web site entirely. Once at that page, you'll see other links, which you can visit. You can continue to jump from link to link until you find what you want (or at least something that distracts you enough that you forget what you were looking for!).

 TIP You can tell when your pointer is on a link because the address to that site appears in the status bar.

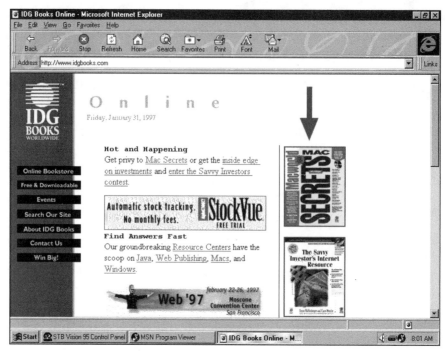

Figure 30-2 A typical Web page can include text, graphics, and links to other pages.

Typing an Address

Jumping from link to link is fun; it's a great way to explore all the varied sites you can find on the Web. It's like driving across the United States in an RV and stopping where you please. This cruising method is great if you have a lot of time, but what if you want to go somewhere directly? In that case, you can use another method to go to a page. You can type the address.

Each page has an address, called a URL (or uniform resource locator). If you know the address of the page, you can go directly there by typing the address (URL) in the Address text box. A lot of times you will see someone's address listed on a business card, on a flyer, or even in an advertisement.

To go directly to a page, follow these steps:

1. Click in the Address text box. The current address should be highlighted.

2. Type the new address. Be sure to type the entire address and get all the periods, dashes, and other characters in the right order.

3. Press Enter. That page is displayed.

See an errror message? If you type an address and get an error message, try retyping the address again. Be sure you have all the periods and backslashes in the right places.

Going Back and Forward

As you explore, you may want to retrace your steps. Internet Explorer provides a couple of methods for going back to a site you've visited:

* You can use the Back and Forward buttons in the toolbar to move back or forward a page.

* You can go to the starting page (home page) by clicking the Home button.

* You can also go back to other addresses by displaying the Address drop-down list and selecting the address you want. This list keeps track of the last several addresses you have typed.

* You can use the Go menu, shown in Figure 30-3. This menu lists the last several sites you have visited. You can also use the Back, Start Page, and Best of the Web commands to go back a page, to the home page, or to the Best of the Web page.

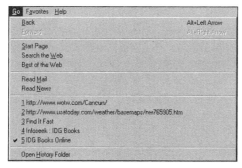

Figure 30-3   Use the Go menu to go to a previously visited site.

Stop! It's Taking Too Long

When you select a page, you may find that the Internet Explorer takes a long time to display that page. You can tell that the Internet Explorer is working because the "e" logo in the upper-right corner will be animated as the Internet Explorer searches for your page.

If you get tired of waiting or if you made a mistake and selected a page by mistake, you can stop. To do so, click the Stop button.

Where Do I Find Stuff On...

Browsing the Internet is like a treasure hunt. Sometimes you find what you want, sometimes you find something better, and sometimes you don't find a thing. If you can't get to a site via a link and you don't know the address, you can search for a topic or page of interest. Internet Explorer provides access to several different Web search tools.

The Internet Explorer provides access to several different search engines for finding information on the Internet. They all work basically the same way; you type the topic you want to find and hope for a match (or several matches). They differ in how the search results are displayed and sometimes in what is found. Some search tools also review sites and provide other directory-type tools. My advice is to try them all and see whether you simply prefer one. Also, if you try one search tool and don't find a match, try another tool. You may get different results.

Follow these steps to search for a particular topic:

1. Click the Search button. You see the Internet Searches page. You can select from several different search tools listed under the search text box. For example, you can search using Infoseek, WebCrawler, Lycos, or Excite.

2. Select the search tool you want to use.

3. In the search text box, type the word or phrase likely to be included on the page you're searching for. Be as specific as possible and use the same capitalization. The more you limit the search, the better chance you have of finding exactly what you need.

4. Click the Search button. You can jump to any of the sites shown in the search results by clicking the site you want.

SIDE TRIP

OTHER HANDY SEARCH PAGE STUFF

In addition to providing access to several search tools, Internet Explorer also provides links to several directories on the search page. You can, for instance, use the links under Phone Numbers & Addresses to look up 800 numbers, business numbers, zip codes, and area codes. Scroll further down the page, and you'll find links for Living, Financial Calculators, Business & Finance, Travel, Writer's Reference, News, Sports & Health, and Entertainment. Don't forget to try these handy resources as well when you are searching.

Page Tricks

O nce you find the page, you can simply read it and then move on. Or you may want to save or print the page. You can do the following:

* To print the page, select File → Print or click the Print button. Click the OK button in the Print dialog box.

* To save a copy of the text, select File → Save As File. In the Save As dialog box, select a folder for the page and then type a filename. (Only the text is saved; any graphics are not saved.)

* If the page contains a lot of information and you can't find what you are looking for, you can search the page for a certain word or phrase. To do so, select Edit → Find (on this page). Type the word or phrase you want to find and then click the Find Next button.

* To copy text from a page, select the text you want to copy. Then select Edit → Copy. Move to the document where you want to paste the text and select Edit → Paste.

* If you can't read the text very well, you may want to make the font bigger. To do so, click the Font button in the toolbar. Or select View→ Fonts. From the submenu, select the size you want: Largest, Large, Medium, Small, Smallest.

Good Bye!

W hen you are finished using the Internet, you should shut down the Internet Explorer and also log off from the Internet Service Provider. To close Internet Explorer, click the Close button.

To sign off with your Internet Service Provider, follow their log-off procedures. For example, to close MSN, click the Close button in the MSN Central window or right-click the MSN icon in the status bar and select Sign Out. When MSN prompts you to confirm that you want to sign out, click the Yes button.

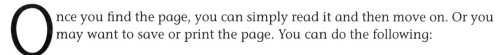

BONUS

Customizing Internet Explorer

Find a site that you like a lot, but don't want to remember or jot down those impossible addresses? Well, you can use a couple of shortcuts for keeping track of your favorite places. You can add them to your Favorites folder. Or you can create shortcuts to a site on your Windows desktop. This bonus section covers these two tips.

Save and Go to Favorite Places

You may have journeyed long and hard to get to the page of your choice. How can you be sure that you can get back? Leave a trail of bread crumbs? When you find a site you think you might visit often, you can add the page to your favorite places folder. You can then easily go to any of the places in this folder.

To add a site to your favorite places folder, follow these steps:

1. Display the page you want to add to your favorites.

2. Select ` Favorites ` → ` Add To Favorites `. You see the Add to Favorites dialog box (see Figure 30-4).

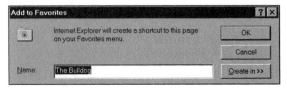

Figure 30-4   Select a name and folder for your favorite page.

3. In the Name text box, type a name for this page.

4. If you want to place the page in a different folder, click the Create in button and select the folder to use.

5. Click the OK button.

To go to a favorite page, follow these steps:

1. Select ` Favorites `. At the bottom, you see listed the folders and favorite pages you have added.

2. If you placed the page in a folder, select that folder and then select the page from the submenu that appears. If you did not place the page in a folder, simply select the page from the Favorites menu. That page is displayed.

Create a Shortcut

You can access favorite places from the Internet. But what if you want access to the place from outside the Internet? Say from your desktop. In that case, you can create a shortcut icon. When you double-click the icon, Windows 95 starts the Internet Explorer and takes you to that page.

To create a shortcut, follow these steps:

1. Display the page.

2. Select File → Create Shortcut . You see a message stating that a shortcut will be added to the desktop.

3. Click the OK button. A shortcut is added to your desktop. You can double-click this shortcut icon to log onto the Internet and go directly to this site.

As the Web increasingly becomes a mode of commerce, individuals and businesses will need to carve out their own unique places on it to stay competitive. What makes a good Web site is debated every day, but for many, having a presence — any presence — is a must. The previous chapter provided you with information that will be the foundation for working with your own Web pages. Ready?

Untangling the Web

As you learned in Chapter 30, the Internet and World Wide Web provide an easy means to accessing thousands of pages of information, products, questions, and answers. Publishing on the Web has two parts — designing your Web pages, and getting them onto the Internet. Because the second part can involve a variety of methods, this chapter focuses on the first part, with some suggestions for getting your pages on the Web.

Web sites begin with a *home page*, which acts as the welcoming page and usually provides some kind of table of contents to other pages on the site. Web pages consist of text, graphics, lines, and tables to provide the information the company, organization, or individual wishes to convey. All of them contain *hyperlinks*, "hot spots" on the page, usually indicated by a graphic, a button, or colored, underlined text. Hyperlinks allow the reader to jump to other areas of the page or to another page with a single click. The mouse pointer changes to a pointing finger over any link, indicating you can click there to make the jump.

Web pages are written in HTML — HyperText Markup Language — which provides "tags" or codes that the browser converts into the formatting you actually see on the Web page. Figure 31-1 provides an example, the Rocky Mountain Chocolate Factory's Web page.

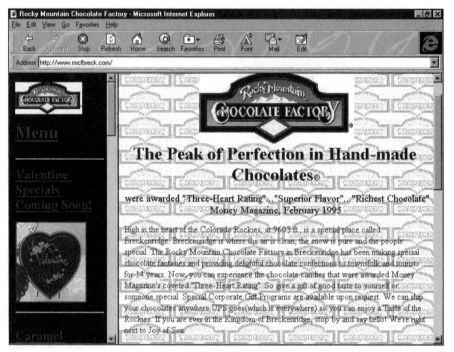

Figure 31-1 The Rocky Mountain Chocolate Factory's home page shows many typical features of Web pages.

The great news is that you don't need to learn HTML to design eye-catching Web pages. Word 97 comes with built-in Web authoring tools. You create your Web page using familiar Word features and then ask Word to convert the document into an HTML document that you can view using your browser. Note that this chapter concentrates on designing Web pages, with a brief section on the steps to getting your page on the Web. For more information on setting up shop on the Internet and World Wide Web, check with your local bookseller or Internet provider.

REUSE, RECYCLE

You can save an existing Word file as an HTML document. This can save a lot of time if you have a document that contains a lot of information you want on your site. However, check the *can* and *cannot* lists in the next section to find out what may or may not convert.

To convert an existing document:

1. Open the document you wish to convert.

2. Click File → Save as HTML .

Type a name for the document and then click <u>S</u>ave. Word saves the document in HTML format and displays it in Onlin<u>e</u> Layout view. You can edit it as you would other Web documents.

Exploring Design Restrictions

Because of the unique nature of HTML, there are certain things you can and cannot do when it comes to formatting your Web page. Generally speaking, the following restrictions apply:

You *can* use:

✳ Varying fonts and font sizes. Sizes can range from 9 to 36 point.

✳ Bold, underline, and italics

✳ Justification, such as left, center, right

✳ Graphics, which convert to GIF format, unless they are originally in JPEG (.jpg) format, in which case they will remain in this format

✳ Horizontal lines to separate sections on a page

✳ Tables, though some table formatting (such as border colors and styles) will not convert. Keep in mind, however, that some Web browsers do not support tables and will display the information in unpredictable ways.

You *cannot* use:

✳ Such character formats as all caps, small caps, double strikethrough, shadow, and outline

✳ Drawing objects such as text boxes and shapes. They will not convert.

✳ Margin settings. If you wish to increase or decrease the width of text, place it in a table.

✳ Paragraph and page borders

✳ Page numbering

- ✳ Headers and footers

- ✳ Footnotes and endnotes

- ✳ Columns (newspaper or parallel). Use tables to get a column effect. However, again keep in mind that some Web browsers do not support tables and will display the information in unpredictable ways.

Designing Your Page

Now that you have a sense of what formatting and other restrictions you face, you can look at some different design and layout considerations. It pays to try to determine your content and basic layout ahead of time. Most of the suggestions that follow are basic desktop publishing guidelines. Visit several Web sites to see how others have designed Web pages, and consider reading up on Web page design or taking a class to help you with the initial development of your site.

What do I hope to accomplish with my Web site? Are you trying to sell a product or service or merely conveying information? You will set up your site differently depending on your purpose.

What image am I trying to convey? If you're trying to advertise your legal services for writing wills, humorous cartoons and flashy graphics may not be appropriate. Try to select graphics and other elements that complement your image.

How should I use graphics? This can be tough. Graphics add a lot to the aesthetic appeal of a Web site and can also serve as hyperlinks to other pages. However, too many graphics can create a cluttered, disorganized look that will confuse and frustrate visitors. Use graphics sparingly to enhance your text and message, not take the place of it. Also, as indicated above, graphics should reflect the tone and mood of your Web site — select or create appropriate images! Also, consider that some visitors will have slower connections and may have to wait for all your graphics to display.

How many pages will my Web site contain? If your Web site will be fairly short, consider using a single document, with your hyperlinks taking the reader to other parts of the same document. Otherwise, if your site will contain a lot of information, consider breaking it into separate documents and linking between them.

How should I break up my text? Look at the different topics you want to cover and determine how you can best separate them, either by using horizontal lines and graphics or by placing them in separate documents. Visitors to your site will have an easier time when you break up pages with graphics, lines, lists, and "white space" (empty areas). Too much text without a break can turn visitors off, costing you an opportunity to share your information.

Spinning Your Own Web

Once you have a sense of your Web page design, you're ready to begin creating. Web pages generally contain several basic elements: a title, a brief description, a table of contents or other list of what your site contains, and graphics and lines to help add appeal to your site. You will look at all of these throughout the chapter.

Word comes with several Web authoring tools that make it easy for you to create attractive, informative Web pages, without having to know one HTML tag or command. Let's check to make sure you have these tools available. *Follow these steps:*

1. Start Microsoft Word.

2. Click `File` → `New`.

3. Check to see if you have a Web Pages tab in the New dialog box. If you don't, continue with "Installing Web Authoring Tools." If you do, keep the New dialog box open and skip to "Using the Web Page Wizard."

Installing Web Authoring Tools

You must select the Web authoring tools when you first install Microsoft Office. If you didn't see the Web Pages tab in the New dialog box in Microsoft Word, you can install these tools now. *Follow these steps:*

1. Close any Microsoft programs currently running.

2. Make sure the setup disk or CD is in the drive.

3. On the Windows task bar, click Start and then point to Settings and click Control Panel.

4. Double-click the Add/Remove Programs icon to display the Add/Remove Programs Properties dialog box.

5. Click Install to display the Install Program from Floppy Disk or CD ROM dialog box and then click Next. Setup displays the Run Installation Program dialog box.

6. Check to see that SETUP.EXE is in the Command line for the installation program text box and then click Finish. Setup displays the Microsoft Office 97 Setup dialog box.

7. Click Add/Remove to display the Microsoft Office 97 - Maintenance dialog box (see Figure 31-2).

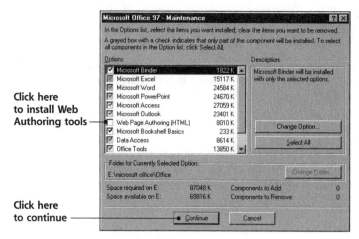

Click here to install Web Authoring tools

Click here to continue

Figure 31-2 Install the Web Page Authoring tools here.

8. Click Web Page Authoring (HTML) in the list and then click Continue.

9. When Setup indicates a successful installation, click OK and then close the Control Panel window.

Using the Web Page Wizard

Microsoft Word's Web Page Wizard takes you through a series of dialog boxes to help you create the basic look for your Web page. You can then add and format text; add bulleted lists, horizontal lines, and graphics; and insert hyperlinks. *Follow these steps to use the Wizard to create a Web page using Word:*

1. With the New dialog box open, select the Web Pages tab and then double-click Web Page Wizard. Word opens a sample Web page document and then displays the first dialog box for the Web Page Wizard, asking what type of Web page you'd like to create. For purposes of this chapter, we'll use the default — Simple Layout.

FEATURE FOCUS The Web Page Wizard and the Web Pages tab are new in Office 97.

2. With Simple Layout selected, click Next. Word displays the next Web Page Wizard dialog box, asking you to select a visual style (see Figure 31-3).

Preview the selected style in the document   ┌Select the desired style

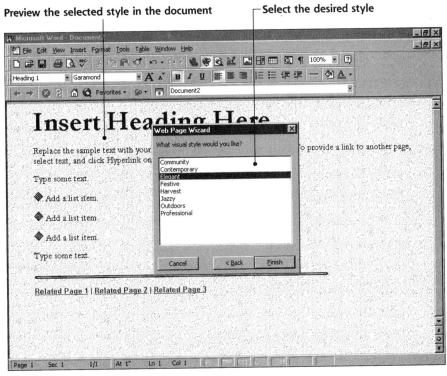

Figure 31-3 Select the style that best conveys your message.

3. Select one of the visual styles in the list.

TIP **If you wait a few seconds, Word will display a sample of your selection behind the Web Page Wizard dialog box in the document window.**

4. Click Finish. Word applies your selection to the sample document and displays sample text in various areas of the Web page (see Figure 31-4). When you create a Web document, Word automatically displays it in Online Layout view.

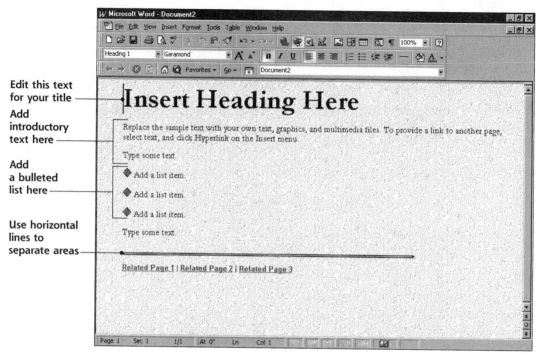

Edit this text for your title

Add introductory text here

Add a bulleted list here

Use horizontal lines to separate areas

Figure 31-4 Word displays a sample Web page document.

A Word to the Web

As you can see, the sample page provides clues for you to type information and let you see a simple Web page layout. To format the title, Word uses the Heading 1 style, which is Times New Roman, bold, 36 point. For any subheadings you wish to use, Word has included six levels, naming the styles H1, H2, H3, H4, H5, and H6. The styles use Times New Roman bold, starting with H1 at 24 point. Each subsequent style drops the point size. H2 is Times New Roman bold 18 point, H3 is Times New Roman bold 14 point, and the remaining styles drop the point size by 2, with H6 using Times New Roman bold 8 point.

Some fonts may appear different to a visitor whose browser doesn't support those particular fonts.

Other styles format such elements as an address block, a hyperlink, and a definition list. Throughout this chapter you will work with the existing layout as well as make changes, using some of these styles to suit your own needs. First, you will add a title and introductory text.

Adding and Formatting Text

The first thing you'll want to do is add a heading, or title, to your page. The title is often the first thing a visitor sees when he or she views your Web site, and it should convey who you are and what you do immediately. It could be something as simple as the name of your company or a "Welcome to..." type of heading. Make it short and to the point. *Follow these steps to add and format text:*

1. Make sure the insertion point is blinking on the first character of the sample title — "Insert Heading Here."

2. Double-click OVR on the Status Bar to turn Overtype on and type the text for your own title or heading. You can also select the heading and type the new text.

3. To change the alignment, make sure the insertion point is inside the heading and then click ▤ on the Formatting toolbar to center the heading or ▤ to right-justify it.

   Select the introductory paragraphs below the title and type your own introduction, explaining your purpose and offering any history you want visitors to know.

Working with Bulleted Lists

Use a bulleted list to provide a quick overview of information or, if the bulleted list appears on the first page of a Web site, consider using it as your table of contents for the site. If you use it as a table of contents, you can add hyperlinks to other areas of your site. For more information on hyperlinks, see "Inserting Hyperlinks" in this chapter.

Word usually provides a sample bulleted list in the Web document. If you like the location of this bulleted list, you can merely select the sample text and replace it with your own. To add another bulleted item, position the insertion point after all the text in the last item and then press Enter. Word automatically inserts another bullet and positions the insertion point for the text. *However, if you wish to start from scratch with a bulleted list, follow these steps:*

1. Position the insertion point in the location for your bulleted list.

2. Click Format → Bullets and Numbering. Word displays the Bullets and Numbering dialog box (Figure 31-5).

Figure 31-5 The Bullets and Numbering dialog box.

3. Make sure the Bulleted tab is selected.

4. Choose a bullet style from the Bulleted tab and click OK. You can also click More, select the bullet from the list, and click Insert. This style remains in effect for all bulleted lists until you change it.

5. Type the text for the first bulleted item and then press Enter.

6. Type the text for the next bulleted item and then press Enter.

7. Repeat step 6 for all items you wish to include.

Web bullets are actually small graphics. If you want to change the bullet style, you must delete each bullet individually, select all bulleted items, and follow steps 2 through 4 above.

8. Click OK.

Jazzing Up Your Page

Though having only text makes your pages load and scroll faster, it can get pretty boring for the visitor. Adding horizontal lines to break up sections and graphics to enhance your message make reading the page easier and more pleasurable. You can even make a graphic a link to another page.

Adding a Line

As I mentioned before, horizontal lines can help separate sections of your pages to make them more readable. When you select a Web page style using the Web Page Wizard, Word selects a default line style that complements the overall theme of the page. To use this style, click ▬. You can also use a basic recessed line or choose from a variety of fancy and eye-catching line styles. *To add a line, follow these steps:*

1. Position the insertion point in the location for the line.

2. Click Insert → Horizontal Line . Word displays the Horizontal Line dialog box (see Figure 31-6).

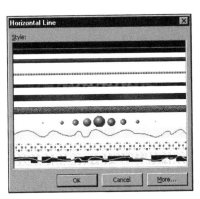

Figure 31-6 Select a line style.

3. Select the desired line style and click OK. You can also click More in the Horizontal Line dialog box, select the line from the list, and click Insert. The style you've selected becomes the default line style until you select another line style.

TIP If you selected More, Word displays a list of lines by filename. To see a sample of the line before you insert it, click ▦ to turn Preview on. Once you select a line style, you can add additional lines of the same style by clicking ▬ on the Formatting toolbar.

SIDE TRIP

WHAT'S YOUR LINE?

Except for the default line style, which produces the thin gray line, any line you select becomes a figure in the document. If you know how to use other drawing programs, you can create your own line and insert it through the Horizontal Line command. To do this, create the line in your drawing program of choice, saving it as a GIF or JPG (JPEG) image in the \microsoft office\clipart\lines folder. When you choose the Horizontal Line command from the Insert menu and click More, your new line will be listed along with the existing lines and you can insert it into your document.

Working with Graphics

One of the most exciting elements you can add to a Web page is a graphic. Graphics enhance the text and provide visual interest. You can use graphics as hyperlinks as well, allowing the visitor to jump to another page by clicking the graphic.

In order for an image to display on the Web, it must be in either GIF (CompuServe's Graphics Interchange Format) or JPEG (Joint Photographic Expert Group) format. However, when you insert a graphic into your Web document, Word will automatically convert it to display in a browser.

INSERTING A GRAPHIC

Your first step in using graphics is to go back to one of the design questions I asked early in the chapter — how should I use graphics? First and foremost, select or create *appropriate* graphics. If you have a light, humorous Web site, cartoons and irreverent pictures can help convey your message. If you are trying to sell a serious service or product, consider this when selecting your graphics. Second, remember to use graphics sparingly. They should enhance your text, but too many will make your pages look cluttered and confusing.

Graphics should enhance your text; too many will make your pages look cluttered and confusing.

To insert a graphic, follow these steps:

1. Position the insertion point in the location for the graphic.

2. Click `Insert` → `Picture` → `From File` or click 🖼 on the Standard toolbar.

3. If you haven't saved the document up to this point, Word will display a message box, obliging you to save before you can continue. Word then displays the Insert Picture dialog box.

4. Locate and display the folder containing the graphic you wish to insert.

5. Select the graphic filename and then click Insert or double-click the filename.

 WEB PATH If you want access to additional pictures, you can access Microsoft's Web site for pictures by clicking Insert → Picture → Browse Web Art Pages. You can also explore it separately at

`http://www.microsoft.com/word/artresources.htm.`

Follow the instructions for downloading images to your computer.

MOVING AND SIZING A GRAPHIC

Once you've inserted a graphic, you may want to increase or decrease its size, or move it to a new location. If you've worked with graphics in Word previously, you will recognize these techniques:

* To move a graphic, simply click and drag it to the new location.
* To resize a graphic, click it once to select it and display the sizing handles (see Figure 31-7) and then use one of the following options:

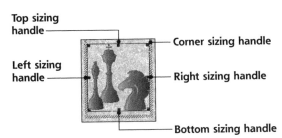

Figure 31-7 Use the sizing handles to resize a graphic.

* To increase or decrease the width, click and drag the left or right sizing handle.
* To increase or decrease the height, click and drag the top or bottom sizing handle.
* To increase or decrease the graphic proportionally (width and height at the same time), click and drag one of the corner sizing handles.

ADDING A PICTURE PLACEHOLDER

When you are designing your Web page, you need to allow for visitors who may not have a state-of-the-art browser and/or a fast connection. Some of them may not have the capability of viewing graphics or will choose to view your pages as "text only" so that they can scroll through them more quickly. To prepare for such visitors, you can include text that visitors will see if they cannot view the graphic in their browsers. This is called a *picture placeholder*. If you don't include text, visitors' browsers will usually insert some kind of placeholder that gives no indication of the nature of the image. *To add a picture placeholder, follow these steps:*

1. Right-click the graphic to display the shortcut menu and then select Format Picture, or select the graphic and choose `Format` → `Picture`. Word displays the Picture dialog box.

2. Select the Settings tab.

3. Under Picture placeholder, type the text you wish to display if visitors don't display your graphic in the text box.

4. Click OK.

Inserting Hyperlinks

One of the most important and vital parts of your Web document is its hyperlinks. These links allow visitors to jump around your document to those locations that interest them most. As I mentioned before, you can use text (which appears in a different color than your body text and is underlined) or graphics to provide links to other parts of your document (see Figure 31-8). You can also link to other documents. Creating links is a two-step process. First, you must create the file and/or bookmark to which you wish to link. (A *bookmark* is a piece of text or a location that you name so that you can refer to it later.) Second, you must link the source to the file or bookmark.

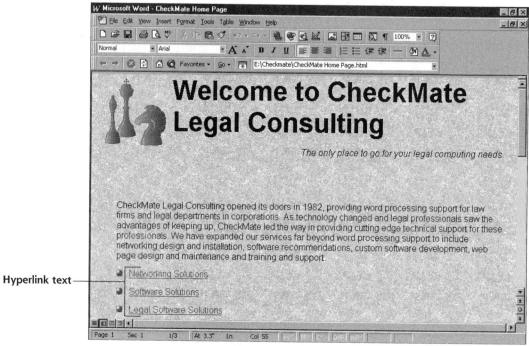

Hyperlink text —

Figure 31-8 Hyperlinks indicate jumps to other places.

Creating a Bookmark

Before you can create a link, you must have something to link to. Most often you will want to link to a specific topic in a document, even if you are linking between documents. A *bookmark* allows you to mark the topic or area of the document with a name so that you can link it by name to another section. *To create a bookmark, follow these steps:*

1. Display the text or area to which you wish to link. For example, if you have a section in the document called "Training and Support," display the section so that you can see the heading.

2. Position the insertion point in the location you wish visitors to land when they jump to this area.

3. Click **Insert** → **Bookmark** to display the Bookmark dialog box.

4. Type the name you wish to give this location in the <u>B</u>ookmark name text box and then click <u>A</u>dd. Note that you cannot use spaces in bookmark names.

5. Repeat these steps for all sections and topics to which you wish to have links.

TIP **If you want to link to another document, open that document and create the necessary bookmarks. You can then indicate the document name and bookmark in the source document when you create the link.**

Creating Links

Once you've named all your bookmarks, you can refer to them in hyperlinks. You can also link to existing files as well as Web sites, using the site's URL (uniform resource locator). The URL is the address, which begins with *http:. Follow these steps to link text or graphics to other areas of your Web site or to other files or sites:*

1. Select the text or graphic you wish to link. See the Tip and the Caution at the end of this section for hints on selecting a hyperlink element.

2. Click ![icon] on the Standard toolbar or click **Insert** → **Hyperlink** . Word displays the Hyperlink dialog box (see Figure 31-9).

Indicate link to the other document or Web page on the Internet ⎯⎯⎯

Indicate the bookmark name here ⎯⎯⎯

Click here to select from a list of bookmarks

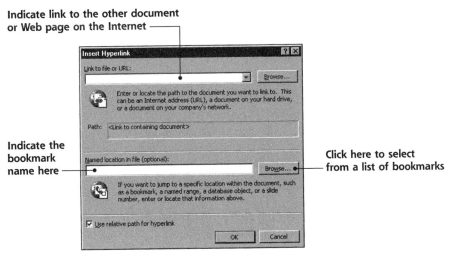

Figure 31-9 Link your text or graphic to a file and/or bookmark.

3. If you want to jump to another document or Web site, indicate the filename or URL in the Link to file or URL text box. You can also click Browse to locate and select the filename.

4. To indicate a bookmark in the document, type the name of the bookmark in the Name location in file text box or click Browse next to the text box to see a list of bookmark names, select the one you need, and click OK.

5. Click OK to accept the link. If you selected text for the link, Word changes the selected text to the default Hyperlink style, which is based on the Normal style for your document.

TIP Select a generous amount of text for your hyperlink. The more text you select, the easier it will be for the visitor to click and jump. However, if the text is within a paragraph, make sure you select only the text that logically describes the section they will jump to. For example, if you have a sentence that reads "We have trained, certified professionals providing all our training and support," two logical links would be *certified professionals* and *training and support*.

Avoid including the bullet in your selection, as this can cause unexpected graphic display results.

Viewing Your Page

Once you've got a start on your Web pages, it's a good idea to view them in your browser to make sure things will appear as you've designed them. Also, if you have access to other browsers, it's a good idea to view your Web pages in these to see what adjustments you may have to make to accommodate visitors who don't use the Internet Explorer.

Note that this section assumes that you have already installed Internet Explorer or another browser. If you haven't, please refer to Chapter 30 for more information about using a browser, before continuing.

To see how the form will appear in your Web browser:

1. Click [icon]. If you haven't saved the document, Word will ask you to save before continuing. Once the document is saved, your default Web browser will start, without connecting to the Internet. Once the browser is open, it will load your Web document into the browser window. (see Figure 31-10).

You must save the document each time you modify it before you can view it in the browser.

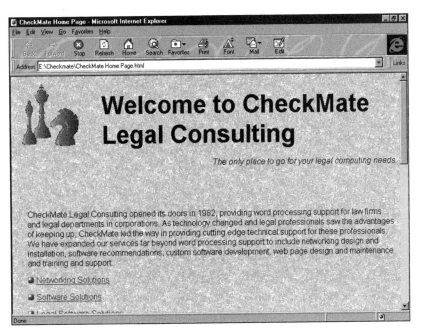

Figure 31-10 The fictitious CheckMate Legal Consulting home page is displayed in the Internet Explorer.

2. Scroll through your Web page(s) to check for display problems and other design issues.

3. Close your browser when you're finished.

Bright Lights, Big Site

When you are ready to publish your pages on the Web, you have two options. You can set up your own Web server, or you can contact your ISP (Internet Service Provider) for information on renting space on its server. The second option is usually more cost effective for individuals and smaller companies because you don't have to perform any of the hardware and software maintenance or incur the cost of higher transmission rates and other startup and ongoing expenses. If you aren't connected to the Internet and don't have an ISP, talk to friends and colleagues for recommendations.

Microsoft Office Professional comes with a Web Publishing Wizard that helps guide you through the steps of publishing your pages on the Web. However, you must have all of the following information to use the Wizard successfully:

* All files and folders you wish to publish

* The name of your ISP (and the phone number if you connect by modem) if you are not maintaining your own Web server

* The folder on the server that will contain the files (check with your ISP)
* The URL used to access your files through a browser
* The protocol necessary to upload the files to the Web (check with your ISP for details on the various protocols)

Installing the Web Publishing Wizard

Before you publish your pages to the Web, install the Web Publishing Wizard to guide you through the necessary steps for successfully getting your documents where they belong. *Follow these steps to install the Wizard:*

1. Make sure your Microsoft Office Professional 97 CD is in the drive and then display the folders and files on your CD-ROM drive using Windows Explorer.

2. Double-click the ValuPack folder to display its contents.

3. Double-click the Webpost folder and then double-click the Webpost icon. You'll see the Web Publishing Wizard End-User Licensing Agreement dialog box.

4. Click <u>Y</u>es to accept the agreement and continue. When the installation program has copied all files successfully, it displays a message about how to use the wizard.

5. Click OK to continue.

Using the Web Publishing Wizard

Once you've installed the Web Publishing Wizard, you can use it immediately. *Just follow these steps:*

1. On the desktop, click `Start` → `Programs` → `Accessories` → `Internet Tools` → `Web Publishing Wizard` (see Figure 31-11).

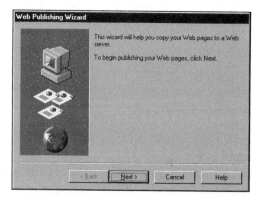

Figure 31-11 The Web Publishing Wizard.

2. Follow the instructions in each dialog box.

BONUS

Designing a Web Page Form

I f you've spent time browsing Web sites, you may have noticed that many of them have fill-in-the-blank forms. These forms allow you to enter information that the owner of the site can use for a variety of purposes. Some forms get you on a mailing list; others allow you to order a product or service. If you would like feedback from visitors or have a product or service to sell, you can add a form to your site (see Figure 31-12). Word makes it easy to create a form as part of an existing Web page or as a separate document. In this section, you use the Web Page Wizard to select and create a Feedback form as a separate document.

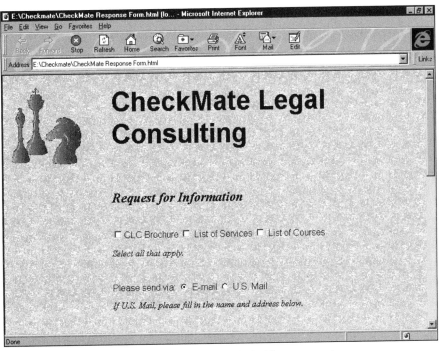

Figure 31-12   A feedback form has been included in our sample page.

Creating a Feedback Form

If you've worked with forms in Word before, or if you've worked with forms and reports in Access, you know that forms consist of *controls*. Controls are the elements on the form where users can select options or type text. Controls include option buttons, check boxes, drop-down lists, and text boxes. You will use the Web Page Wizard to create a basic feedback form and then display the form in

Form Design mode so that you can make changes to it. *Follow these steps to create a feedback form:*

1. With Word running, click File → New .

2. Select the Web Pages tab and then double-click Web Page Wizard.

3. Select Form - Feedback in the list and then click Next.

4. Select a visual style for the form (preferably one that matches the style for all your Web pages) and then click Finish. Word displays a sample feedback form in a new document window.

Modifying a Form

Modifying a sample form is not as simple as modifying the sample Web page. You have not only text to work with but a variety of items such as text boxes and option buttons. To work with these, you will need to use Form Design mode.

SWITCHING TO FORM DESIGN MODE

Before you can modify the form structure, you must switch to Form Design mode. In this mode, you can change the text for controls, increase or decrease the width of text boxes, and add or remove controls. Here's how to switch modes:

✳ Click View → Form Design Mode or click ⬚. Word changes the form appearance slightly and displays the Control toolbar (see Figure 31-13). Word sets up the controls for the form in table cells. Depending on how dark the background is, you may need to look closely to see the lines.

TIP   If you don't see the Control toolbox, click View → Toolbars → Control Toolbox.

EDITING OPTION BUTTON TEXT

When Word creates the sample form, it inserts sample text for three option buttons. You can replace the text to represent the options for your own form. Later you will learn how to delete controls such as option buttons or insert additional ones.

To replace option button text, merely select the text you wish to change and type the new text.

RESIZING TEXT BOXES

If a sample text box doesn't provide enough space for a response, or if it is much too large for the response, you can resize it. *Follow these steps:*

1. Select the text box you wish to resize. Word displays the sizing handles (see Figure 31-14).

Indicates the top of the form ─┐   Control toolbox ─┐

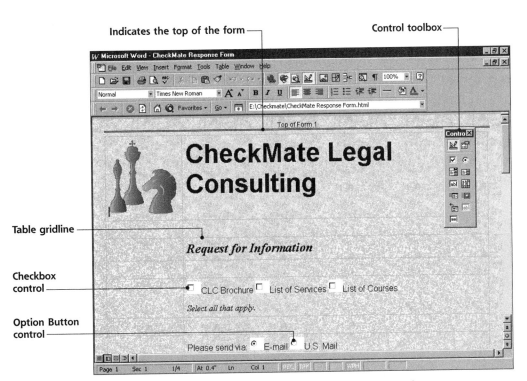

Table gridline ─────────

Checkbox control ───

Option Button control ───

Figure 31-13 A feedback form appears in Form Design mode.

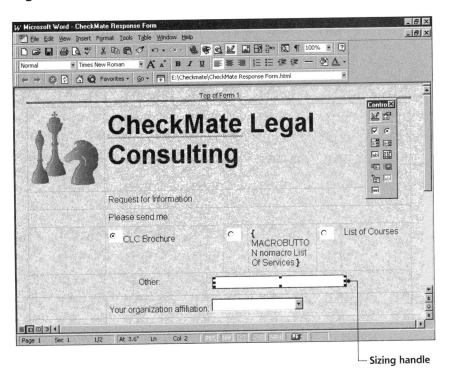

─ Sizing handle

Figure 31-14 Use sizing handles to adjust text boxes.

2. Use one of the following methods to resize your text box:

  ✳ To change the box height, drag the top or bottom sizing handle.

  ✳ To change the box width, drag the left or right sizing handle.

  ✳ To change the box height and width, drag a corner sizing handle.

DELETING EXISTING CONTROLS

It's easy to remove a control — an option button, a text box, or whatever — if you don't need it. You can also remove text or field codes you no longer need. *Just follow these steps:*

1. While in Form Design mode, select the text or control you wish to remove.

2. Press the Delete key.

TIP Adding controls can become tricky when you need to work with the Properties dialog box and set different options. Before you begin adding controls, click Help → Contents and Index. Choose the Index tab, type **form element**, and then click Display. Review these concepts carefully and then add controls using the Control toolbox. Note that, if the Control toolbox is not displayed, you should choose View → Toolbars → Control Toolbox.

SAVING AND VIEWING THE FORM

Once you've made all the changes you want, you can return to normal document view by clicking 🖫 on the Control toolbox. If the Control toolbox is not displayed, click 🖫 on the Standard toolbar. To save the form, click 🖫 and click OK. To see how the form will appear in your Web browser, click 🔍.

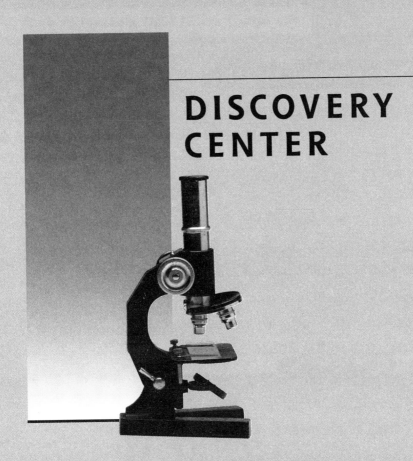

DISCOVERY CENTER

In this section, you'll discover many of the important steps for how to accomplish tasks in Office 97. The Discovery Center serves as a handy reference to the most important tasks in the chapters. These quick summaries include page references referring you back to the chapters if you need more information.

CHAPTER 1

How to Size a Window (page 15)

Do any of the following:

* To resize the window, put the pointer on a window edge and drag.
* To minimize a window, click ⬛. The window is displayed as a taskbar button.
* To maximize a window, click ⬛.
* To restore a window, click ⬛.

How to Move a Window (page 17)

1. Put the mouse pointer on the title bar.
2. Drag the window to the location you want.

How to Arrange Windows (page 17)

1. Right-click a blank area of the taskbar.
2. Select the arrangement you want.

How to Close a Window (page 18)

* Click ⬛.

How to Get Help Using the Table of Contents (page 19)

1. Click the Start button and then select ⬛ Help ⬛.

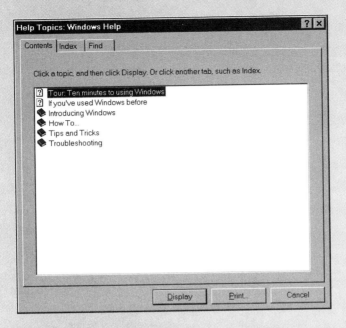

2. Double-click the topic you want.

3. Continue to double-click on subtopics until you see a help topic.

4. Double-click the help topic to new information about your question.

5. Close the window by clicking ⊠.

How to Shut Down Windows (page 24)

1. Click the Start button.

2. Select Shut Down.

3. Click the Yes button.

CHAPTER 2

How to Select a Menu Command (page 31)

1. Click the name of the menu you want to open.

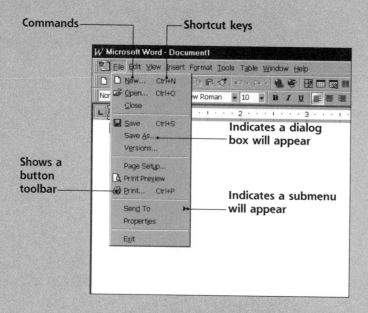

Commands

Shortcut keys

Indicates a dialog box will appear

Indicates a submenu will appear

Shows a button toolbar

2. Click the command you want to execute.

3. If you see a submenu, select the command you want from this menu. If you see a dialog box, select the dialog box options you want and then click the OK button.

How to Make a Selection in a Dialog Box (page 32)

Element	To Select	Do This...
Save	TAB	Click the tab name to display the options for that tab.
☑	CHECK BOX	Click in the check box to check (turn on) or uncheck (turn off) the option.
⊙	OPTION BUTTON	Click in the option button to turn on (appears darkened) or off (blank).
	TEXT BOX	Click in the text box and then type the entry. If the text box already contains an entry, drag across it to select the entry and then press Delete.
10 ⬍	SPIN BOX	Type an entry in the spin box. Or click the spin arrows to scroll through the text box values.
Size: 16 / 10 11 12 14 16	LIST BOX	Click the item you want in the list.

Element	To Select	Do This...
Word Document (*.doc) [▼]	DROP-DOWN LIST BOX	Click the down arrow next to the item to display other selections. Then click the item you want.
OK	COMMAND BUTTON	Click the OK command button to confirm and carry out the command. Click the Cancel button to cancel the command.

How to Get Help with the Office Assistant (page 34)

1. Click the Office Assistant. If the Office Assistant is not displayed, click ▣.
2. Type what you want to do and then click the Search button.
3. Click the topic you want.
4. Review the help information and then click the Close button to close the help window.

How to Exit an Application (page 38)

1. Save all open documents.
2. Select File → Exit.

CHAPTER 3

How to Save a Document (page 42)

1. Select File → Save or click ▣.

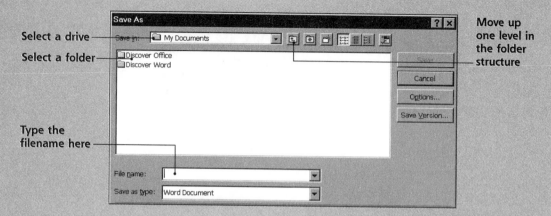

Select a drive

Select a folder

Type the
filename here

Move up
one level in
the folder
structure

2. If this is the first time you are saving a document, type a name.

3. Select a folder.

4. Click the Save button.

How to Close a Document (page 44)

1. Save the document.

2. Click the Close button in the document window or select [File] → [Close].

How to Open a Document (page 45)

1. Select [File] → [Open].

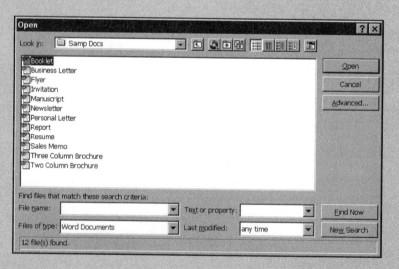

2. Open the drive and folder that contains the document. Use the Look in drop-down list to change drives and ⬆ to move up to a higher folder.

3. When you see the file listed, double-click it.

How to Create a New Document (page 46)

1. Click ▢ to create a document based on the default template.

   Or

   Select `File` → `New`.

2. Select the template you want to use.

3. Click the OK button.

How to Preview a Document (page 47)

✳ Select `File` → `Print Preview` or click ▣.

How to Print a Document (page 48)

1. Select `File` → `Print` or click ▣.

2. Make any changes to the print options.

3. Click the OK button.

CHAPTER 4

How to Create a New Folder (page 55)

1. In the Save As dialog box, click ▣.

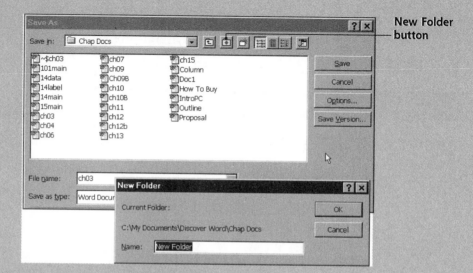

New Folder button

2. Type the name for the new folder.

3. Click the OK button.

How to Add a Folder to the Favorite List (page 56)

1. In the Save As or Open dialog box, select the folder you want to add to the list.

2. Click 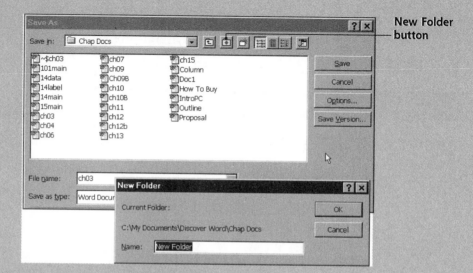.

How to Open a Favorite Folder (page 57)

1. In the Save As or Open dialog box, click .

2. Select the favorite folder you want to open.

How to Delete a File (page 58)

1. In the Open or Save As dialog box, right-click the file you want to delete.

2. Select Delete .

3. Click the Yes button.

How to Undelete a File (page 59)

1. Go to the Windows desktop.
2. Double-click the Recycle Bin icon.
3. Right-click the file you want to undelete.
4. Select Restore.
5. Click the Close button.

How to Rename a File (page 61)

1. In the Open or Save As dialog box, right-click the file you want to rename.
2. Select Rename.
3. Type a new name and press Enter.

How to Copy a File to Another Folder (page 62)

1. In the Open or Save As dialog box, right-click the file you want to copy.
2. Select Copy.
3. Change to the folder where you want to place the file.
4. Right-click a blank area of the folder and file list.
5. Select Paste.

CHAPTER 5

How to Insert a Page Break (page 74)

✳ Press Ctrl+Enter.

How to Move Around Using the Mouse (page 75)

1. Move the mouse pointer to where you want to place the insertion point.
2. Click the mouse button.

How To Move Around Using the Keyboard (page 75)

Press any of the following keys:

←	Move left one character
→	Move right one character
↑	Move up one line
↓	Move down one line
Home	Move to the beginning of the line
End	Move to the end of the line
Ctrl + Home	Move to the top of the document
Ctrl + End	Move to the end of the document

CHAPTER 6

How to Select Text with the Keyboard (page 83)

1. Move the insertion point to the start of the text.

2. Hold down the Shift key and use the movement keys to select the text you want.

3. Release the Shift key.

How to Delete Text (page 83)

1. Select the text you want to delete.

2. Press the Delete key.

How to Move Text (page 84)

1. Select the text you want to move.

2. Select Edit → Cut or click ✂.

3. Move to where you want to paste the text.

4. Select Edit → Paste or click 📋.

How to Copy Text (page 86)

1. Select the text you want to copy.
2. Select ⟨ Edit ⟩→⟨ Copy ⟩ or click 🗐.
3. Move to where you want to paste the text.
4. Select ⟨ Edit ⟩→⟨ Paste ⟩ or click 🗐.

How to Find Text (page 87)

1. Select ⟨ Edit ⟩→⟨ Find ⟩.
2. Enter the text you want to find.
3. Click the Find Next button.

How to Replace Text (page 89)

1. Select ⟨ Edit ⟩→⟨ Replace ⟩.
2. Enter the text you want to replace.
3. Enter the text you want to use as the replacement.
4. Click the Find Next button.
5. Word moves to the first match and highlights it. To make this replacement, click the Replace button. To make all replacements, click the Replace All button.

How to Check the Spelling of the Entire Document (page 95)

1. Select ⟨ Tools ⟩→⟨ Spelling and Grammar ⟩ or click 🗐.

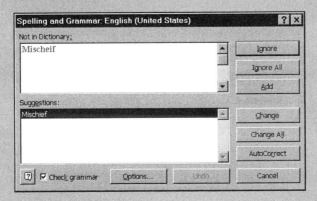

2. To skip this occurrence but stop on the next one, click the Ignore button. To skip all occurrences of this word, click the Ignore All button.

3. To replace the word with one of the suggested spellings, click the spelling in the Suggestions list. Click the Change button to change this occurrence. Click the Change All button to replace all occurrences of the word.

4. If none of the replacements are correct, correct the error by editing the word or phrase in the Not in Dictionary: list box. Then click the Change button.

5. Click the Add button to add the word to the dictionary.

6. If you want to add the error and its correction to the AutoCorrect list, click the AutoCorrect button.

CHAPTER 7

How to Change the Look of Text (page 103)

1. Select the text you want to change.

2. Do any of the following:

   For **bold** text, click [B].

   For *italic* text, click [I].

   For underlined text, click [U].

   To change the font, click the down arrow next to [Times New Roman ▼] and click the font you want to use.

   To change the font size, click the down arrow next to [10 ▼] and click the font size you want.

   To change the text color, click the down arrow next to [A] and click the color you want.

   To highlight text, click the down arrow next to [✎] and click the color you want.

How to Align a Paragraph (Center, Left, Right) (page 106)

1. Click within the paragraph you want to change.

2. To center the text, click [≡].

   To left-align text, click [≡].

   To right-align text, click [≡].

   To justify text, click [≡].

How to Indent Text (page 109)

1. To indent a single paragraph, click within it. To indent several paragraphs, select the paragraphs you want to indent.

2. To indent text, click 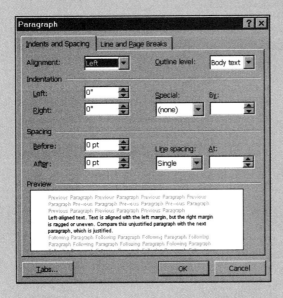.

   To unindent text, click 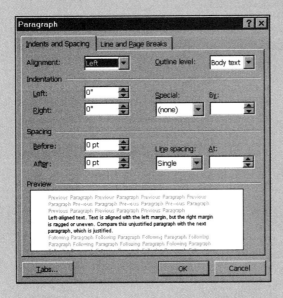.

How to Change Line Spacing (page 111)

1. To change the spacing in a single paragraph, click within it. To change the spacing in several paragraphs, select the paragraphs you want to indent.

2. Select **Format** → **Paragraph**.

3. If necessary, click the Indents and Spacing tab.

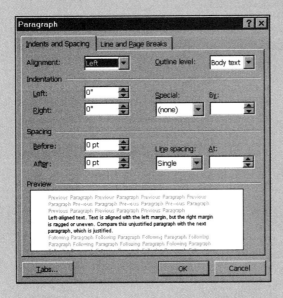

4. Display the Line spacing drop-down list.

5. Click the spacing you want.

How to Add a Border to a Paragraph (page 115)

1. To add a border to a single paragraph, click within it. To add a border to several paragraphs, select the paragraphs you want to add a border to.

2. Click the down arrow next to ▢ ▾.

3. Click the border placement you want.

How to Create a Bulleted or Numbered List (pages 117, 118)

1. Select the paragraphs to which you want to apply formatting. Follow step 2 to insert bullets or step 3 to insert a numbered list.

2. To insert bullets, click ⊞.

3. To insert a numbered list, click ⊞.

CHAPTER 8

How to Set Margins (page 124)

1. Select File → Page Setup.

2. Click the Margins tab.

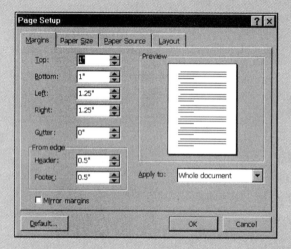

3. Press Tab to move to and highlight the margin you want to change. Type the new value. Do this for each margin you want to change.

4. Click the OK button.

How to Number Pages (page 128)

1. Select Insert → Page Numbers.

2. Display the Position drop-down list box and select Top of Page (Header) or Bottom of Page (Footer).

3. Display the <u>A</u>lignment drop-down list and select the alignment of the page number.

4. To skip a page number on the first page, uncheck the <u>S</u>how number on first page check box.

5. Click the OK button.

How to Create a Header or Footer (page 129)

1. Select `View` → `Header and Footer`.

2. To create a footer, click the Switch Between Header and Footer button.

3. Type the text for the header or footer. Use the toolbar buttons to insert special information:

   🗓 Date

   🕐 Time

   🔳 Page number

4. Make any formatting changes to the text.

5. Click the Close button.

How to Use a Template (page 136)

1. Select `File` → `New`.

2. Click the tab for the document type you want to create.

3. Click the template you want to use.

4. Click the OK button.

5. Click the text you need to replace and type the actual text. Do this for each section of text that needs to be completed.

6. Save and print the document.

CHAPTER 9

How to Set Up a Table (page 142)

1. Click 🔳.

2. Drag across the number of rows and columns you want to include in the table.

How to Enter Data in a Table (page 144)

1. Click within the cell.
2. Type the entry.
3. Press Tab to move to the next cell.

How to Select Part of a Table (page 145)

Do any of the following:

* To select text within a table, drag across the text.
* To select a row, put the insertion point within the row and then select `Table` → `Select Row`.
* To select a column, put the insertion point within the column and then select `Table` → `Select Column`.
* To select the table, put the insertion point within the table and then select `Table` → `Select Table`.

How to Add a Row or Column (page 145)

1. Select the row or column where you want the new row.
2. To insert a row, select `Table` → `Insert Rows`.
3. To insert a column, select `Table` → `Insert Columns`.

How to Delete a Row or Column (page 146)

1. Select the row or column you want to delete.
2. To delete a row, select `Table` → `Delete Rows`.
3. To delete a column, select `Table` → `Delete Columns`.

How to Delete the Entire Table (page 146)

1. Select the table using `Table` → `Select Table`.
2. Select `Table` → `Delete Rows`.

How to Insert a Clip Art Image (page 153)

1. Select `Insert` → `Picture` → `Clip Art`.
2. Click the category you want to view.
3. Click the image you want to insert.
4. Click the Insert button.

How to Insert an AutoShape (page 156)

1. Select `Insert` → `Picture` → `AutoShapes`.

2. Click the shape type that you want.
3. Click the shape you want.
4. Click and drag within the document area to draw the shape.

How to Move or Resize an Object (page 157)

1. Select the object you want to move or resize by clicking it.
2. To move, drag the object to a new location.

   To resize, drag one of the selection handles.

CHAPTER 10

How to Start the Mail Merge Process (page 165)

1. Start with a blank document on screen.
2. Select `Tools` → `Mail Merge`.
3. Under Main document, click the Create button and click Form Letters.
4. Click the Active Window button.

1. Click Get Data in the Mail Merge Helper dialog box.

2. Click Create Data Source.

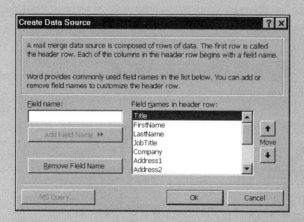

3. To remove a field, select it and click the Remove Field Name button.

4. To add a field, type the field name and click the Add Field Name button.

5. When you are finished adding or removing fields, click the OK button.

6. In the Save As dialog box, change to the drive and folder for saving this file. Type the filename and click the Save button.

7. Click the Edit Data Source button.

8. Type the information for the first field and press Tab. Do this for each field.

9. When you have finished, click the Add New button.

10. Follow steps 8–9 for each record you want to add.

11. When you have completed all the records, click the OK button.

1. In the main document window, type the text you want the letter to include.

2. When you get to a spot where you want to insert variable information (such as the name and address), click the Insert Merge Field button.

3. Click the field you want to insert.

4. Continue typing and inserting fields until you complete the document.

5. Select the File → Save command.

6. Change to the drive and folder in which to save the file. Type the filename and click the Save button.

How to Merge the Two Documents (page 170)

1. Select Tools → Mail Merge .

2. Click the Merge button.

3. To merge all records to a new document and skip blank lines, click the Merge button.

4. Print the letters by selecting File → Print .

CHAPTER 11

How to Select a Cell with the Mouse (page 187)

✳ Click the cell you want to select.

How To Select a Range with the Mouse (page 189)

1. Click the first cell in the range.

2. Hold down the mouse button and drag across the cells you want to select.

How to Enter Text (page 191)

1. Select the cell you want.

2. Type the text, up to 32,000 characters in a cell.

3. Press Enter.

How to Enter Numbers (page 192)

1. Select the cell.
2. Type the number. To type a negative number, precede the number with a minus sign or enclose the number in parentheses.
3. Press Enter.

How to Enter Dates (page 193)

1. Select the cell you want.
2. Type the date using one of these formats:

   1/4 (assumes the current year)

   1/4/97 or 01/04/97

   1-Apr (assumes the current year)

   1-Apr-97 or 01-Apr-97

   Apr-97 or April-97 (assumes the first of the month)

   April 1, 1997
3. Press Enter.

How to Enter Times (page 194)

1. Select the cell you want.
2. Type the time using one of these formats:

   13:30

   1:30 PM

   13:30:55

   1:30:55 PM

   30:55.7
3. Press Enter.

CHAPTER 12

How to Create a Formula (page 204)

1. Select the cell that will contain the formula.
2. Type an equal sign (=).
3. Point to the first cell you want to include in the formula.
4. Type an operator.
5. Point to the next cell you want.
6. Continue typing operators and selecting cells until the formula is complete.
7. Press Enter.

How to Use AutoSum (page 207)

1. Select the cell that you want to contain the sum formula.
2. Click $\boxed{\Sigma}$.
3. If necessary, select the correct range to sum.
4. Press Enter.

How to Insert a Function (page 209)

1. Select the cell you want to contain the function.
2. Select $\boxed{\text{Insert}} \rightarrow \boxed{\text{Function}}$ or click $\boxed{f_x}$.
3. Click the function category you want.
4. Click the function you want.
5. Click the OK button.

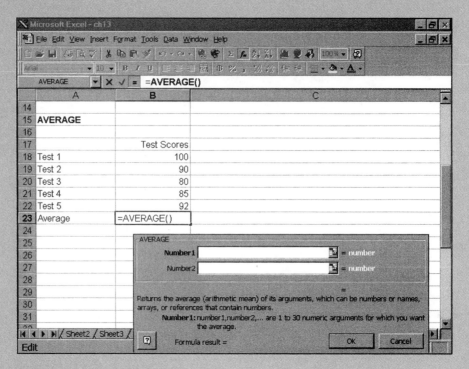

6. Enter values for each of the arguments by clicking a cell, selecting a range, typing the reference, or typing a value.

7. Press Enter or click the OK button.

How to Copy a Formula (page 215)

1. Select the cell that contains the formula you want to copy.

2. Select [Edit] → [Copy] or click [🖹].

3. Select the cell or range where you want to copy the formula.

4. Select [Edit] → [Paste], click [🖹], or press Enter.

How to Fill a Formula (page 215)

1. Select the cell that contains the formula you want to fill.

2. Drag the fill handle across the range you want to fill.

CHAPTER 13

How to Move Data (page 220)

1. Select the cell or range you want to move.
2. Select Edit → Cut or click ✄.
3. Select the cell at the upper-left corner of where you want the pasted cells.
4. Press Enter, select Edit → Paste, or click 📋.

How to Copy Data (page 221)

1. Select the cell or range you want to copy.
2. Select Edit → Copy or click ✄.
3. Select where you want to place the copy.
4. Press Enter, select Edit → Paste, or click 📋.

How to Insert Another Worksheet (page 224)

✱ Select Insert → Worksheet.

How to Rename a Worksheet (page 224)

1. Double-click the sheet tab of the sheet you want to rename.
2. Type a new name and press Enter.

How to Insert a Column or a Row (page 226)

1. Select the cell, column, or row where you want to make the insertion.
2. To insert a cell, select Insert → Cells. Select how to shift existing data and click OK.
3. To insert a row, select Insert → Rows.
4. To insert a column, select Insert → Columns.

How to Remove Cells, Columns, or Rows (pages 227, 228)

1. Select the cell, range, column(s), or row(s) you want to delete.

2. Select [Edit] → [Delete].

3. If you selected a cell or a range, select how to handle existing data and click OK.

CHAPTER 14

How to Align Data within Cells (page 237)

1. Select the cell or range you want to change.

2. To center the range, click ▤.

3. To align the range with the right edge of the cell, click ▤.

4. To align the range with the left edge of the cell, click ▤.

How to Add A Border to Cells (page 242)

1. Select the range that you want to border.

2. Click the down arrow next to ▤.

3. Click the button that represents the border style and placement you want.

CHAPTER 15

How to Change the Margins (page 250)

1. Select [File] → [Page Setup].

2. Click the Margins tab.

3. Click in the margin text box you want to change: Top, Bottom, Left, Right, Header, or Footer.

4. Type the new value or use the spin arrows to enter the value.

How to Set Sheet Options (page 253)

1. Select [File] → [Page Setup].

2. Click the Sheet tab.

3. Select the options you want.

4. Click the OK button.

How to Check and Adjust Page Breaks (page 257)

1. Select View → Page Break Preview.

2. If the dialog box telling you about setting page breaks appears, close it by clicking the OK button.

3. If you want to make a change to any of the breaks, click and drag to set a new page break.

4. To return to Normal view, select View → Normal.

CHAPTER 16

How to Create a Chart (page 264)

1. Select the range that you want to chart.

2. Select Insert → Chart or click ▥.

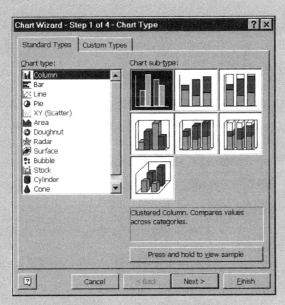

3. Select the type of chart you want to create.

4. Select the chart subtype you want and click Next.

5. Confirm the correct range is selected or select the range to chart. Select whether rows or columns are charted. Click the Next button.

6. Make any changes to any of the chart options tabs and then click the Next button.

7. Select where to place the chart and click the Finish button.

How to Move a Chart on the Worksheet (page 269)

1. Click the chart to select it.
2. Drag the chart to a new location.

How to Resize a Chart on the Worksheet (page 269)

1. Click the chart to select it.
2. Drag one of the selection handles.

How to Delete a Chart on the Worksheet (page 269)

1. Click the chart to select it.
2. Press Delete.

How to Delete a Chart on a Separate Sheet (page 269)

1. Right-click the sheet tab.
2. Select [Delete].
3. Confirm the deletion by clicking the OK button.

How To Change the Chart Type (page 270)

1. If the chart is on the worksheet, click the chart once to select the entire chart object. If the chart is on a separate sheet, click that sheet tab to display the chart.
2. Select [Chart] → [Chart Type].
3. Select the chart type and subtype and click OK.

CHAPTER 17

How to Enter Data Using the Data Form (page 282)

1. Put the pointer within the data list you have set up.

2. Select Data → Form .

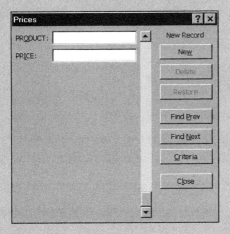

3. Type the entry for the first field and press Tab. Do this for each field in the record.

4. To add the new record and display a blank form, click the New button.

5. Complete the next record.

6. When you have finished entering data, click the Close button.

How to Delete a Data Record Using the Data Form (page 283)

1. Select Data → Form .

2. Click the scroll arrows to display the record you want to delete.

3. Click the Delete button and then confirm the deletion by clicking the OK button.

4. When you have finished making changes, click the Close button to close the data form.

How to Find Data Using the Data Form (page 284)

1. Select Data → Form .

2. Click the Criteria button.

3. Move to the field on which you want to search.

4. Type what you want to find.

5. Click the Find Next button.

How to Filter Data (page 286)

1. Select `Data` → `Filter` → `AutoFilter`.

2. Move to the column heading for the column on which you want to filter.

3. Display the filter list and select how you want to filter the data.

CHAPTER 18

How to Create a New Presentation (page 299)

1. Start PowerPoint.

2. Select one of the choices shown to choose how you want to create the new presentation: using the AutoContent wizard, a template, or a blank presentation. Click the OK button.

3. If you selected AutoContent, make the selections for each step of the wizard. Click the Next button to move through the dialog boxes. Click the Finish button when you are done.

   If you selected template, select the template you want to use and then click the OK button.

   If you selected blank, you are ready to add slides.

How to Add a Slide To a Presentation (page 304)

1. Click the New Slide command in the Common Tasks toolbar, click , or select `Insert` → `New Slide`.

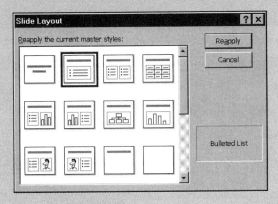

2. Select the slide layout you want to add and click the OK button.

How to Create a Chart (page 306)

1. Add a new slide that includes a chart and then double-click the Chart icon.

Or select Insert → Chart or click 📊 to add a chart to an existing slide.

2. Replace the sample data with your own data. To select a cell for editing, click it or use the arrow keys. Type the new entry and press Enter.

3. When the data are complete, click back on the slide.

How to Create an Organization Chart (page 309)

1. Add a new slide that includes an organization chart and then double-click the Org Chart icon.

Or select Insert → Picture → Organization Chart to add a chart to an existing slide.

2. Type the name for the top-level position and press Enter.

3. Type a title for this position and press Enter.

4. If you want, type an optional comment and press Enter. Type a second comment.

5. Click the next organization box and follow the same steps to add the name, title, and optional comments for each box.

6. Add any other boxes to the organization chart.

7. Click back on the slide when you have finished.

How to Insert a Clip Art Image (page 311)

1. Add a new slide that includes a picture and then double-click the Clip Art icon.

   Or select [Insert] → [Picture] → [Clip Art] to add a clip art image to an existing slide.

2. In the category list, click the category you want to view.

3. Click the image you want to insert.

4. Click the Insert button.

CHAPTER 19

How to Move Around in a Presentation (page 316)

1. Click the up scroll arrow to display the preceding slide.

2. Click the down scroll arrow to display the next slide.

How to Try Another View (page 317)

* Click   To change to...
  ▭   Slide view
  ▤   Outline view
  ▦   Slide Sorter view
  ▦   Notes Page view
  �±   Slide Show

How to Change the Order of Slides (page 323)

1. Click the Slide Sorter View icon.

2. Click the slide you want to move.

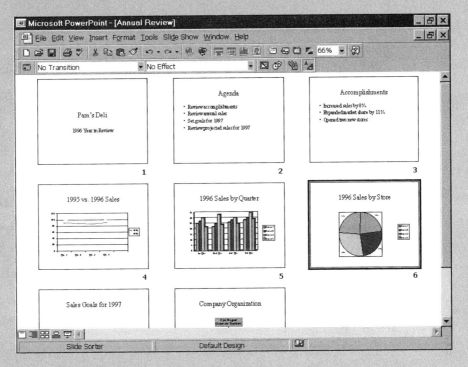

3. Hold down the mouse button and drag the slide to the new location. Release the mouse button.

How to Move Something on the Slide (page 323)

1. Click the object once to select it.
2. Put the mouse pointer within the object.
3. Drag the object to a new location.

How to Resize an Object on the Slide (page 323)

1. Click the object once to select it.
2. Drag one of the selection handles.

How to Delete a Slide (page 323)

1. In Slide Sorter View, select the slide you want to delete.
2. Press the Delete key.

CHAPTER 20

How to Change the Slide Layout (page 331)

1. Select ⎡Format⎤ → ⎡Slide Layout⎤, or click 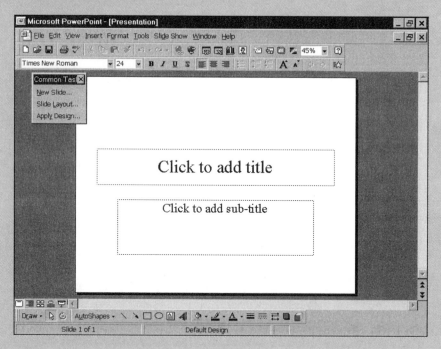, or select Slide Layout from the Common Tasks toolbar.

2. Click the layout you want and then click the OK button.

How to Change the Look of a Chart (page 334)

1. Double-click the chart object.
2. Select ⎡Chart⎤ → ⎡Chart Options⎤.
3. Click the tab you want and make any changes.
4. When you have finished making changes, click the OK button.
5. Click back on the slide.

How to Change the Look of an Organization Chart (page 335)

1. Double-click the organization chart.
2. Select the box you want to modify.
3. Use the Styles menu to select how the boxes are arranged.

4. Use the Text menu to select the font, color, and alignment of the text.

5. Use the Boxes menu to select a color, shadow, border style, border color, or border line style for the boxes.

6. Use the Lines menu to change the thickness, style, and color of the lines that connect the boxes.

7. When you have finished making changes, click the Close button for the application. When prompted to update the slide, click Yes.

How to Apply a Design (page 338)

1. Select `Format` → `Apply Design`, click 🖾, or select Apply Design in the Common Tasks toolbar.

2. Select the design you want to use.

3. Click the Apply button to apply these changes to the presentation.

CHAPTER 21

How to Create a Database Using the Database Wizard (page 350)

1. If you just started Access, choose Database Wizard under Create a New Database Using. Or, if Access is already running, select `File` → `New`.

2. Make sure Blank Database is selected on the General tab and then click OK.

3. Type a name for your database in the File name text box and then click Create.

How to Create a Table Using the Table Wizard (page 352)

1. With the Database window displayed, select the Tables tab and click New.

2. Select Table Wizard from the list and click OK.

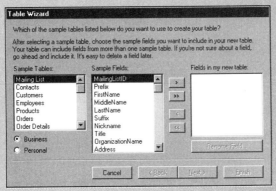

3. Select Business or Personal.

4. Select a sample table.

5. Select the desired field. —

6. Click the left-arrow button to insert the selected fields.

7. Type a name for your table and then click <u>N</u>ext.

8. Click <u>F</u>inish to begin entering data in table Datasheet view.

How to Enter Records into a Table (page 356)

* Press Tab to move to the next empty field, and then type the information for the field.

How to Create a New Table and Define Its Relationship (page 357)

1. From the Database window, select the Table tab and click <u>N</u>ew. Or if you have a table open, click 🔲.

2. Select Table Wizard and then click OK.

3. Select the options for your table, as under the earlier heading "How to Create a Table Using the Table Wizard," and then click <u>N</u>ext.

4. Type a name for the table and then click <u>N</u>ext.

5. Click Relationships, select the desired option, and click OK.

6. Click <u>N</u>ext and then <u>F</u>inish.

7. Enter data and then save the table.

CHAPTER 22

How to Add a New Record (page 362)

1. Select one of following options to add a record:
   * From the last field in the last record, press Tab.
   * Click ▸* on the Table Datasheet toolbar or next to the record number box at the bottom of the table window.
   * Select [Insert]→[Ne<u>w</u> Record].

2. Once you've added a new record, type the information for the new record.

How to Modify a Record (page 363)

1. In the Database window, select the Tables tab.

2. Select the table containing the record you wish to modify and click OK.

3. Click in the field you wish to change and make your changes.

How to Adjust Column Width (page 367)

1. If you aren't currently using Datasheet view, click the [⊞▾] button on the toolbar or choose [View]→[Datasheet View].

2. Point to the right or left edge of the column you wish to adjust until you see the pointer change to a sizing pointer.

3. Click and drag right or left to increase or decrease the column width.

How to Move a Column or Field (page 368)

1. If you aren't currently using Datasheet view, click the [⊞] button on the toolbar or choose [View]→[Datasheet View].

2. Select the column you wish to move by clicking the field selector.

3. Point to the selected column and click. A white vertical line appears to the left of the column, and a move box attaches to the pointer.

4. Drag the column to the new location.

How to Find Data (page 372)

1. If you aren't currently using Datasheet view, click the [⊞] button on the toolbar or choose [View]→[Datasheet View].

2. Select the column containing the data you wish to find by clicking the field selector.

3. Click [🔍] or click [Edit]→[Find].

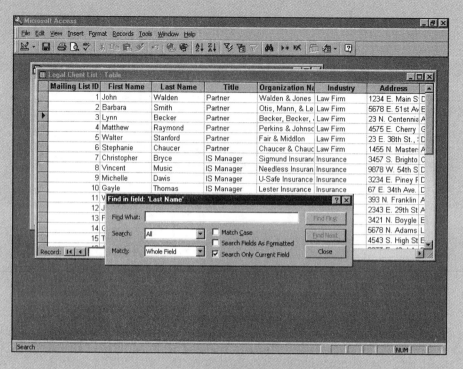

4. Type the information for which you wish to search in the Find What text box.

5. Set any other options in the Find dialog box.

6. Click Find First or Find Next.

7. Click Close when finished.

How to Sort Data (page 374)

1. If you aren't currently using Datasheet view, click the ▦ button on the toolbar or choose │ View │ → │ Datasheet View │.

2. Select the column by which you wish to sort or position the insertion point in the column.

3. Click ▤ to sort the data in ascending order or click ▤ to sort the data in descending order.

CHAPTER 23

How to Create an AutoForm (page 381)

1. Select the Tables tab in the Database window.

2. Select the table on which you wish to base the form.

3. Click ⊞ or click | Insert | → | AutoForm |.

How to Find and Modify a Record (page 382)

1. Position the insertion point in the field you wish to search. For example, if you want to search for "Friendly Felines, Inc.," position the insertion point in the Company Name field.

2. Click 🔍 on the toolbar or click | Edit | → | Find |. Access displays the Find dialog box.

3. Type the information you wish to locate in the Find What text box.

4. Set any other options in the Find dialog box.

5. Click Find First or Find Next.

6. Click Close to close the Find dialog box when you've reached the correct record.

7. Make any desired changes to the record you've located.

How to Add a New Record (page 383)

1. Click ▶* on the Table Datasheet toolbar or click | Insert | → | New Record |.

2. Type the information for the first field and then press Tab and repeat.

How to Delete a Record (page 384)

1. With the Form open, display the record you wish to delete.

2. Click ✖ or click | Edit | → | Delete Record |.

3. Click Yes to confirm the deletion.

How to Switch between Views (page 384)

1. From Form view, click the arrow next to the View button on the toolbar.
2. Click Design View, Form View, or Datasheet View to switch to the appropriate view.

How to Select and Resize Controls (page 386)

1. Click the control you wish to resize.
2. Use one of these three methods to resize the control:
   * Click and drag the top or bottom sizing handle to change box height.
   * Click and drag the left or right sizing handle to change box width.
   * Click and drag a corner sizing handle to change both height and width.

How to Move a Text Box or Label Separately (page 388)

1. Select the control containing the text box or label you wish to move.
2. Point to the move handle for the text box or label until you see the move pointer (pointing finger), and then drag the text box or label to the new location.

CHAPTER 24

How to Create an AutoReport (page 394)

1. In the Database window, select the Tables tab.
2. Select the table on which you wish to base the report.
3. Click the New Object arrow and select AutoReport or click `Insert` → `AutoReport`.

1. In the Database window, click the Tables tab.

2. Select the table on which you wish to base your report, and then click the New Object arrow and choose Report or click Insert → Report.

3. Select Report Wizard in the list and then click OK.

4. Double-click each field you wish to appear in the report and then click Next.

5. If you wish to group your records, select the field by which you wish to group them. If you select more than one, indicate which field Access should use first using the Priority arrow buttons.

6. Click Next.

7. Indicate which field or fields you wish to sort by (for instance, by last name or by company name). Use the Ascending/Descending button to indicate the order in which Access should sort.

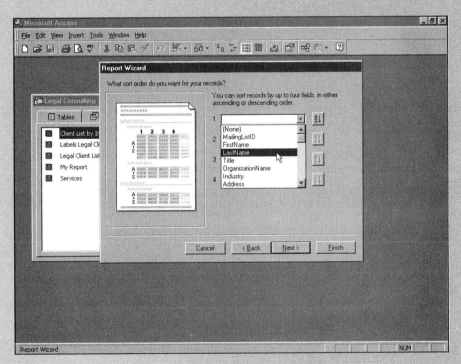

8. Click Next.

9. Make your layout selections and then click Next.

10. Select the desired style and then click Next.

11. Type a name for the report and then click Finish.

How to Move a Control in Report Design View (page 402)

1. Select the control you wish to move.
2. Drag the control to the new location.

How to Resize Controls in Report Design View (page 403)

Click the control you wish to move and then use one of these methods to resize the control:

* Click and drag the top or bottom sizing handle to change box height.
* Click and drag the left or right sizing handle to change box width.
* Click and drag a corner sizing handle to change box width and height.

How to Delete a Control in Report Design View (page 404)

1. Select the control(s) you wish to delete.
2. Press the Delete key.

CHAPTER 25

How to Select the Outlook Group (page 420)

* Click [Outlook].

How to Select the Mail Group (page 421)

* Click [Mail].

How to Select the Other Group (page 421)

* Click [Other].

How to Sort a List (page 422)

* Click the column heading for the field you want to sort on.

How to Change Your View (page 423)

✳ On the toolbar, select a view from the Current View list box.

How to Enter a Name in the Address Book (page 424)

1. Be sure you are in a mail list (the Inbox or Sent Items, for example).
2. On the toolbar, click 🔳.
3. In the Show names from the list box, select Personal Address Book.
4. In the dialog box toolbar, click 🔳.
5. Double-click the type of e-mail address you want to add.
6. Enter an e-mail address and other information in the Properties dialog box.
7. Click OK.
8. Click the X close box to close the Address Book dialog box.

CHAPTER 26

How to Create a Message (page 428)

1. On the toolbar, click 🔳.
2. In the Message dialog box, click the To button.
3. In the Select Names dialog box, double-click the name of the person you want to send the message to.
4. Click OK.
5. Type a subject line in the Subject box.
6. Type your message in the large box in the lower half of the Message dialog box.
7. Click 🔳 Send.

How to Open a Message (page 430)

✳ In a mail pile (such as Inbox), double-click the message you want to open.

How to Reply to a Message You Receive (page 431)

1. Open the message you want to reply to.
2. Click ⟨Reply⟩.
3. Type your reply in the large message box, either above or within the original text.
4. Click ⟨Send⟩.

How to Send an Attached File (page 433)

1. Create the message.
2. On the toolbar, click ⟨📎⟩.
3. Navigate to the file you want to send in the same way that you'd navigate to a file you want to open. Double-click the filename.
4. Finish the message and click ⟨Send⟩.

How to Open a File Someone Sends You (page 434)

✳ Double-click the icon that appears in the message text (the icon will have a filename beneath it).

How to Create a Hyperlink to a Web Page (page 435)

✳ In the body of the message, type the Web site address, beginning with **http://**.

CHAPTER 27

How to Create a New Contact (page 439)

1. In the Outlook bar, click the Contacts icon, ⟨📇 Contacts⟩.
2. On the toolbar, click ⟨📇 ▾⟩.
3. On the General tab, fill in information for the contact.
4. Click ⟨💾 Save and Close⟩.

How to Delete a Contact (page 443)

1. Select the contact or contacts you want to delete.
2. Right-click a selected contact.
3. Click Delete.

How to Open a Contact (page 443)

＊ Double-click the contact you want to open.

How to Update Contact Information (page 443)

1. Open the contact you want to edit by double-clicking it.
2. Add or change information.
3. Click ⊞ Save and Close.

How to Change Your Calendar View (page 446)

＊ On the toolbar, select a different view in the Current View list box.

In Day/Week/Month view, click the Day, Week, or Month button on the toolbar.

How to Make an Appointment (page 447)

1. On the Outlook bar, click the Calendar icon, ⊞.
2. On the toolbar, click ⊞▾.
3. Type a subject and a location.
4. Enter Start and End dates and times.
5. Click ⊞ Save and Close.

How to Create an Event (page 451)

1. In Calendar, select `Calendar` → `New Event`.
2. Type a subject and a location, and fill in other details.
3. Select Start and End dates.
4. Click `💾 Save and Close`.

CHAPTER 28

How to Create a Task (page 456)

1. On the Outlook bar, click the Tasks icon, `📋`.
2. On the toolbar, click `☑ ▾`.
3. Type a subject.
4. Select a due date and a start date, if any.
5. Fill in any other information you want to include.
6. Click `💾 Save and Close`.

How to Set Up Automatic Journal Entries (page 459)

1. Select `Tools` → `Options`.
2. Click the Journal tab.
3. Click check boxes for items you want to record automatically.
4. Click check boxes for contacts you want to enter activities for automatically.
5. Click check boxes for programs whose files you want to record automatically.
6. Click OK.

How to Enter Activities Manually (page 461)

1. Open the Outlook item you want to enter in Journal.
2. Select `Tools` → `Record in Journal`.
3. Click the Start Timer button to start recording elapsed time.
4. When you finish working on the item, click `💾 Save and Close`.

How to Create a Note (page 466)

1. In the Outlook bar, click the Notes icon, .
2. On the toolbar, click 🖺 ▾.
3. Type your note.

CHAPTER 29

How to Link Data (page 477)

1. Use the taskbar to move to the document that contains the data you want to link.
2. Select the data you want to link.
3. Select **Edit** → **Copy** .
4. Use the taskbar to move to the application where you want to place the linked data.
5. Move the insertion point to where you want to paste the data.
6. Select **Edit** → **Paste Special** .

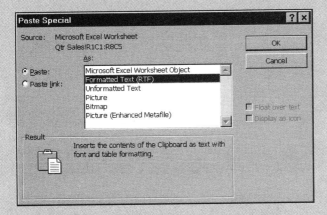

7. Select the Paste link option.
8. Select what you want the object pasted as.
9. Click the OK button.

How to Embed Data (page 479)

1. Use the taskbar to move to the document that contains the data you want to embed.

2. Select the data you want to embed.

3. Select $\boxed{\text{Edit}} \rightarrow \boxed{\text{Copy}}$.

4. Use the taskbar to move to the application where you want to place the data.

5. Move the insertion point to where you want to paste the data.

6. Select $\boxed{\text{Edit}} \rightarrow \boxed{\text{Paste Special}}$.

7. Select Paste.

8. Select the object. The name of the object will vary depending on what you copied.

9. Click the OK button.

How to Save a File as Another File Type (page 490)

1. Select $\boxed{\text{File}} \rightarrow \boxed{\text{Save As}}$.

2. Display the Save as type drop-down list and select the file type.

3. Select the folder and drive where you want to save the new file.

4. Type a filename in the File name text box.

5. Click Save.

CHAPTER 30

How to Get Connected (page 502)

1. Double-click the Internet icon on the desktop.

2. Enter the sign-in information (usually your member ID and password).

3. Click the Connect button.

How to Go to a Particular Address (page 506)

1. Click in the Address text box.

2. Type the new address.

3. Press Enter.

How to Search for a Site (page 508)

1. Click the Search button.

2. Select the search tool you want to use.

3. In the search text box, type the word or phrase likely to be included on the page.

4. Click the Search button on the screen.

How to Work with Web Pages (page 509)

* To print the page, select File → Print or click the Print button. Click the OK button in the Print dialog box.

* To save a copy of the text, select File → Save As File. In the Save As dialog box, select a folder for the page and then type a filename.

* To search for text on a page, select Edit → Find (on this page). Type the word or phrase you want to find and then click the Find Next button.

* To copy text from a page, select the text you want to copy. Then select Edit → Copy. Move to the document where you want to paste the text and select Edit → Paste.

CHAPTER 31

How to Use the Web Page Wizard (page 518)

1. With Microsoft Word running, click File → New.

2. Select the Web Pages tab, and then double-click the Web Page Wizard.

3. Select a layout and then click Next.

4. Select a visual style and then click Finish.

How to Add and Format Text (page 521)

1. Select sample text and type your own replacement text.
2. To change alignment, select the text to align and then click the appropriate justification button on the Formatting toolbar:
   * ⊞ Left
   * ⊞ Right
   * ⊞ Center

How to Work with Bulleted Lists (page 521)

1. Position the insertion point in the location for the list.
2. Click ⊞ on the Formatting toolbar.
3. Type the text for the bulleted item and then press Enter.

How to Add a Line (page 523)

1. Position the insertion point in the location for the line.
2. Click ◥.

How to Insert a Graphic (page 524)

1. Position the insertion point in the location for the graphic.
2. Click ⊞ on the Standard toolbar.
3. Locate and display the folder containing the graphic you wish to insert.
4. Select the graphic filename and then click Insert, or double-click the filename.

How to Add a Picture Placeholder (page 525)

1. Right-click the graphic to display the shortcut menu and then select Format Picture, or choose ⎡ Format ⎤ → ⎡ Picture ⎤.
2. Select the Settings tab.
3. In the Picture placeholder text box, type the text you wish to be displayed if visitors don't display your graphic.
4. Click OK.

How to Create a Link (page 527)

1. Select the text or graphic you wish to link.

2. Click 🖋 on the Standard toolbar or click [Insert] → [Hyperlink].

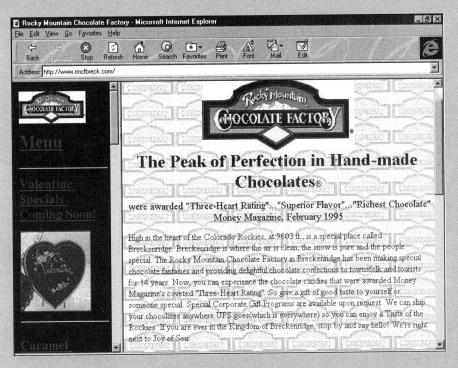

3. In the Link to file or URL text box, enter the name of the document you wish to link to.

4. Next to the Named location in file text box, click Browse to see a list of bookmarks and select the one you need.

5. Click OK when finished.

How to Test Your Page (page 528)

1. Click 🔍.

2. Scroll through your Web page(s) to check for display problems.

3. Close your browser when you have finished.

VISUAL INDEX

Word Documents

Manuscript

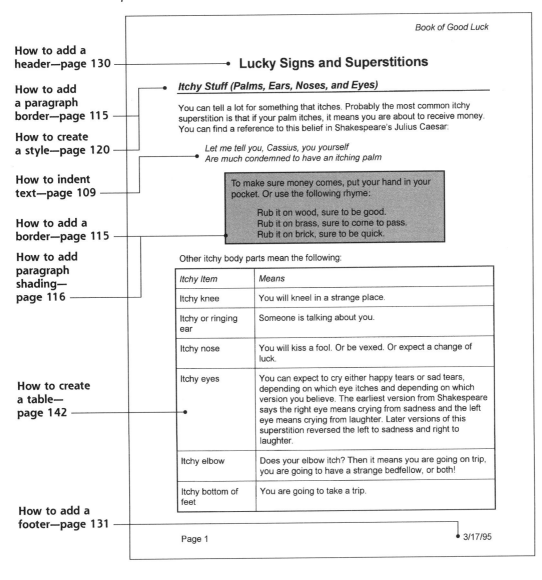

How to add a header—page 130

How to add a paragraph border—page 115

How to create a style—page 120

How to indent text—page 109

How to add a border—page 115

How to add paragraph shading—page 116

How to create a table—page 142

How to add a footer—page 131

Book of Good Luck

Lucky Signs and Superstitions

Itchy Stuff (Palms, Ears, Noses, and Eyes)

You can tell a lot for something that itches. Probably the most common itchy superstition is that if your palm itches, it means you are about to receive money. You can find a reference to this belief in Shakespeare's Julius Caesar:

Let me tell you, Cassius, you yourself
Are much condemned to have an itching palm

To make sure money comes, put your hand in your pocket. Or use the following rhyme:

Rub it on wood, sure to be good.
Rub it on brass, sure to come to pass.
Rub it on brick, sure to be quick.

Other itchy body parts mean the following:

Itchy Item	Means
Itchy knee	You will kneel in a strange place.
Itchy or ringing ear	Someone is talking about you.
Itchy nose	You will kiss a fool. Or be vexed. Or expect a change of luck.
Itchy eyes	You can expect to cry either happy tears or sad tears, depending on which eye itches and depending on which version you believe. The earliest version from Shakespeare says the right eye means crying from sadness and the left eye means crying from laughter. Later versions of this superstition reversed the left to sadness and right to laughter.
Itchy elbow	Does your elbow itch? Then it means you are going on trip, you are going to have a strange bedfellow, or both!
Itchy bottom of feet	You are going to take a trip.

Page 1

3/17/95

Personal Letter

How to
center text—
page 107

How to make
text italic—
page 103

How to indent
paragraphs—
page 109

How to add
a border—
page 115

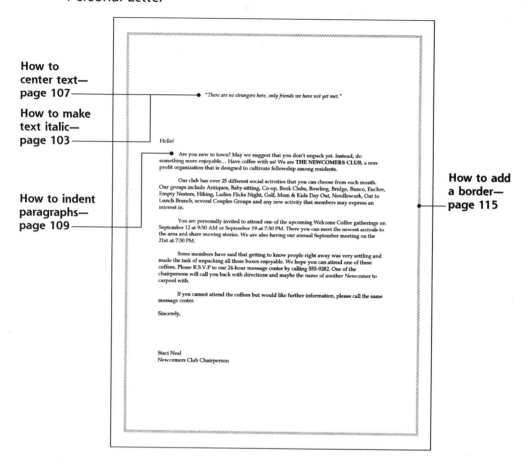

"There are no strangers here, only friends we have not yet met."

Hello!

Are you new to town? May we suggest that you don't unpack yet. Instead, do something more enjoyable... Have coffee with us! We are **THE NEWCOMERS CLUB**, a non-profit organization that is designed to cultivate fellowship among residents.

Our club has over 25 different social activities that you can choose from each month. Our groups include Antiques, Baby-sitting, Co-op, Book Clubs, Bowling, Bridge, Bunco, Euchre, Empty Nesters, Hiking, Ladies Flicks Night, Golf, Mom & Kids Day Out, Needlework, Out to Lunch Brunch, several Couples Groups and any new activity that members may express an interest in.

You are personally invited to attend one of the upcoming Welcome Coffee gatherings on September 12 at 9:30 AM or September 19 at 7:30 PM. There you can meet the newest arrivals to the area and share moving stories. We are also having our annual September meeting on the 21st at 7:30 PM.

Some members have said that getting to know people right away was very settling and made the task of unpacking all those boxes enjoyable. We hope you can attend one of these coffees. Please R.S.V.P to our 24-hour message center by calling 555-9282. One of the chairpersons will call you back with directions and maybe the name of another Newcomer to carpool with.

If you cannot attend the coffees but would like further information, please call the same message center.

Sincerely,

Staci Neal
Newcomers Club Chairperson

Report

How to create
a header—
page 130

How to
center text—
page 107

How to make
text bold—
page 103

How to change
the font size—
page 103

How to create
a bulleted list—
page 117

How to insert
an Excel
worksheet—
page 480

How to insert
an Excel chart—
page 481

How to create
a footer—
page 131

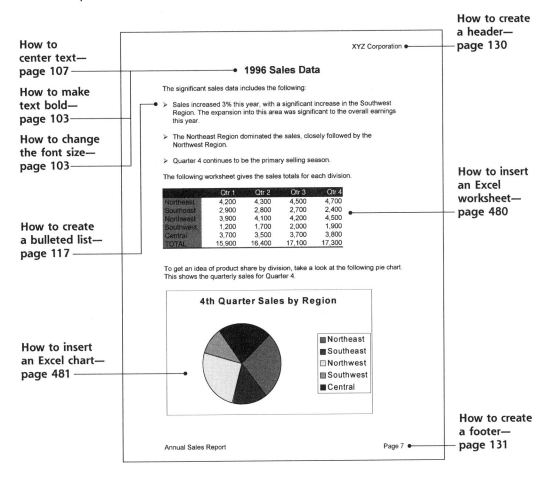

XYZ Corporation

1996 Sales Data

The significant sales data includes the following:

➢ Sales increased 3% this year, with a significant increase in the Southwest Region. The expansion into this area was significant to the overall earnings this year.

➢ The Northeast Region dominated the sales, closely followed by the Northwest Region.

➢ Quarter 4 continues to be the primary selling season.

The following worksheet gives the sales totals for each division.

	Qtr 1	Qtr 2	Qtr 3	Qtr 4
Northeast	4,200	4,300	4,500	4,700
Southeast	2,900	2,800	2,700	2,400
Northwest	3,900	4,100	4,200	4,500
Southwest	1,200	1,700	2,000	1,900
Central	3,700	3,500	3,700	3,800
TOTAL	15,900	16,400	17,100	17,300

To get an idea of product share by division, take a look at the following pie chart. This shows the quarterly sales for Quarter 4.

4th Quarter Sales by Region

- Northeast
- Southeast
- Northwest
- Southwest
- Central

Annual Sales Report

Page 7

Three-Column Brochure

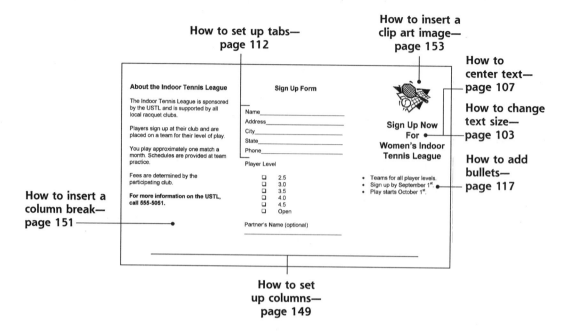

How to set up tabs—page 112

How to insert a clip art image—page 153

How to center text—page 107

How to change text size—page 103

How to add bullets—page 117

How to insert a column break—page 151

How to set up columns—page 149

Excel Documents

Monthly Sales Report

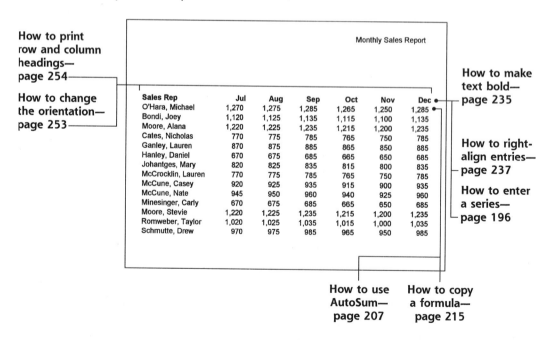

How to print row and column headings—page 254

How to change the orientation—page 253

How to make text bold—page 235

How to right-align entries—page 237

How to enter a series—page 196

How to use AutoSum—page 207

How to copy a formula—page 215

Project Tracking Sheet

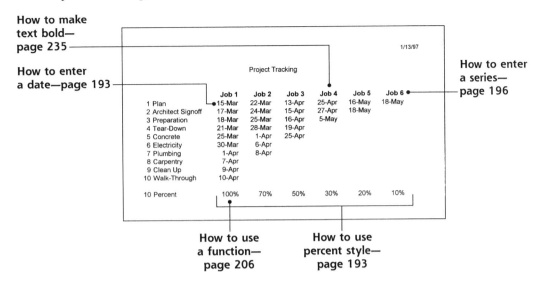

How to make text bold—page 235

How to enter a date—page 193

How to enter a series—page 196

How to use a function—page 206

How to use percent style—page 193

Quarterly Sales Report

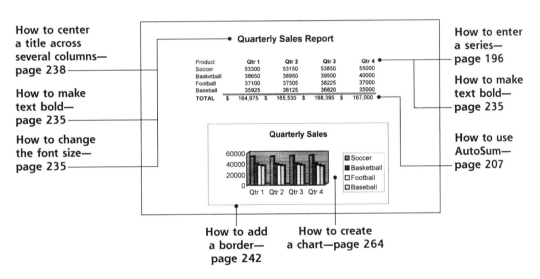

How to center a title across several columns—page 238

How to make text bold—page 235

How to change the font size—page 235

How to enter a series—page 196

How to make text bold—page 235

How to use AutoSum—page 207

How to add a border—page 242

How to create a chart—page 264

PowerPoint Presentations

Organization Chart

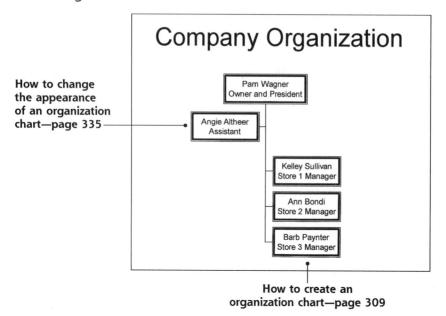

How to change
the appearance
of an organization
chart—page 335

How to create an
organization chart—page 309

Title Slide

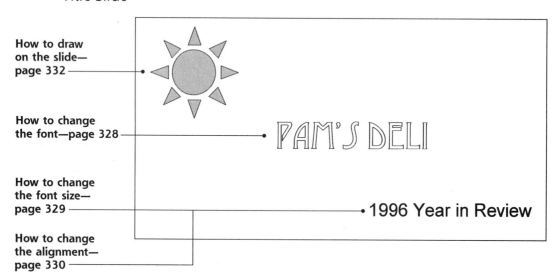

How to draw
on the slide—
page 332

How to change
the font—page 328

How to change
the font size—
page 329

How to change
the alignment—
page 330

Access Documents

Form

How to change the look of text—page 389

How to move a text box
or label separately—page 388

How to increase the
width of a form—page 386

How to add
a title—
page 389

How to select
and resize
controls—
page 386

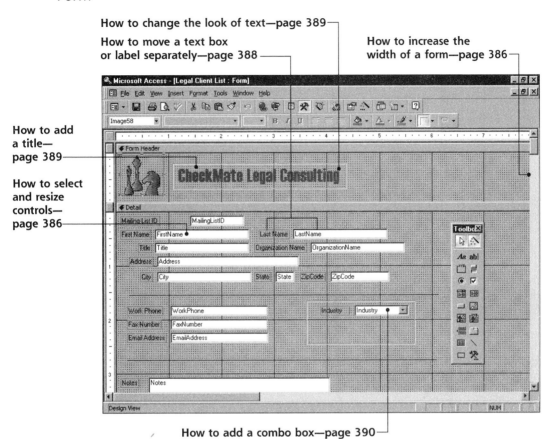

How to add a combo box—page 390

Report

How to save a report—page 398

How to resize a control—page 386

How to change the look of controls— page 405

How to move a control— page 402

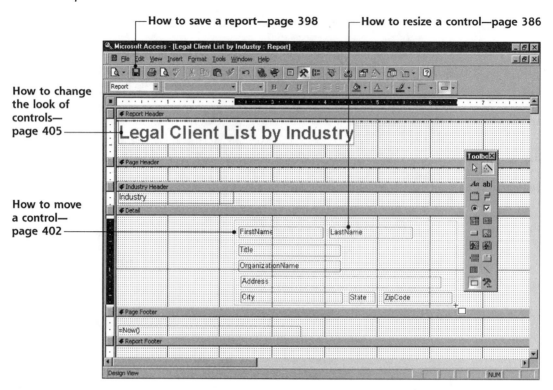

Table

How to insert rows–
page 370

How to remove rows–
page 371

How to delete a field–
page 404

How to select a data type–
page 371

How to move
a column–
page 368

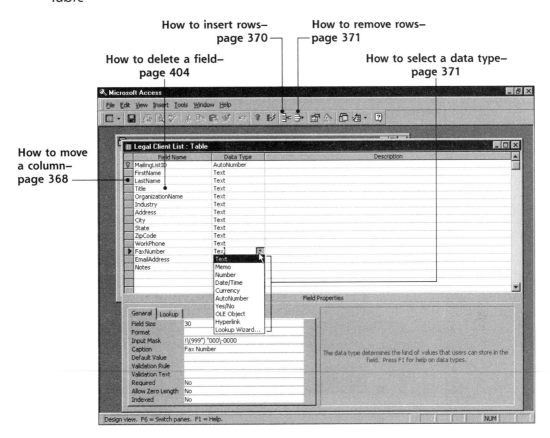

Outlook Screens

Calendar (Daily View)

How to
create a new
appointment—
page 447

How to change
your view—
page 446

How to change
the calendar scope—
page 446

How to show
a different
month—
page 446

How to open
Calendar—
page 420

How to set
or clear a
reminder—
page 449

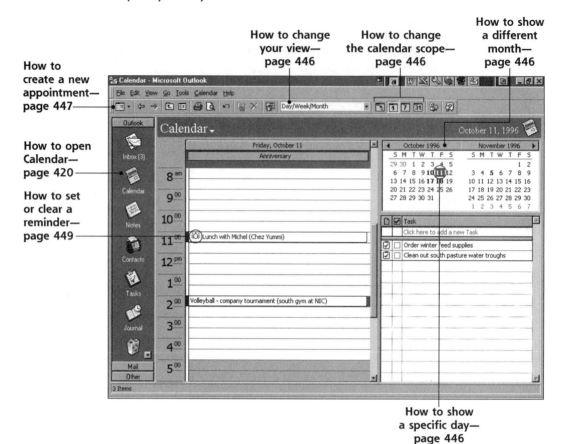

How to show
a specific day—
page 446

E-Mail Message

How to send a message— page 429

How to address a message— page 428

How to title a message— page 429

How to send a file— page 433

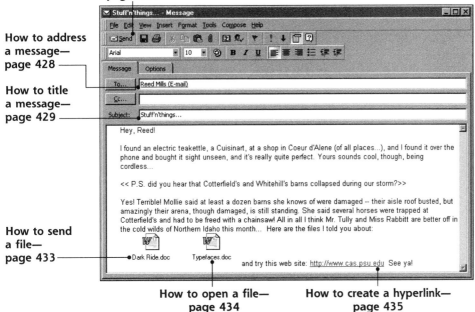

How to open a file— page 434

How to create a hyperlink— page 435

Inbox

How to change your view—
page 423

How to Enter
a name in the
Personal Address Book—
page 424

How to create
a new message—
page 428

How to sort a list—
page 422

How to open
the Inbox—
page 421

How to select
the Mail group—
page 421

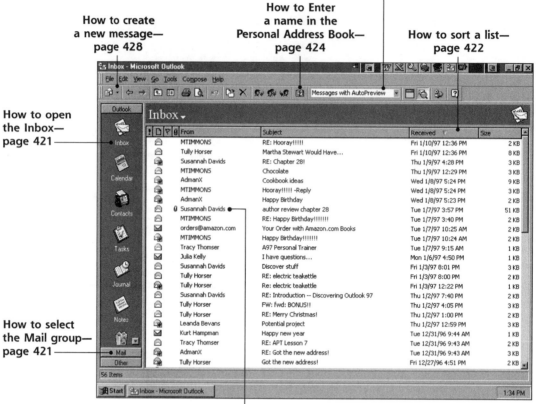

How to open a message—
page 430

Web Publishing Document

Web Page

How to add a picture placeholder—page 525

How to add and format text—page 521

How to view your web page—page 528

How to insert a graphic—page 524

How to work with bulleted lists—page 521

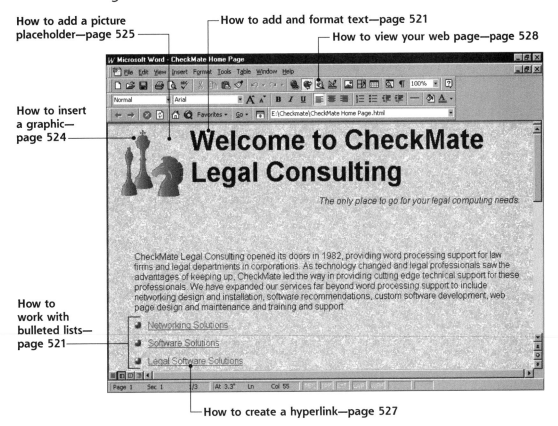

How to create a hyperlink—page 527

TROUBLESHOOTING GUIDE

his guide is designed to answer some of the most common problems that people encounter when using Microsoft Office. It follows the general order of the book, one section for each part and each Office application.

Windows and Document Problems

My desktop looks different than the ones in this book.
You can customize what icons appear on your desktop. For instance, you can add icons to programs, folders, or files you use frequently. You should see a few common icons though — including the My Computer icon, the Recycle Bin icon, and perhaps icons for the Internet or Microsoft Network.

You can also move icons around on the desktop, change the fonts, and use a wallpaper or background pattern for the desktop. Chapter 1 briefly covers some of the customizing changes you can make. For additional information, use the Help command in the Start menu.

I don't see the taskbar.
By default, the taskbar should appear at the bottom of the desktop, but you can move it to a different spot. To move the taskbar, put the pointer on a blank area (not on a button). Then drag the taskbar to the spot you want.

You can also hide the taskbar by right-clicking a blank area and selecting Properties. Check the Auto hide button and then click the OK button. When the taskbar is hidden, you can display it by putting the mouse pointer at the bottom of the screen.

Word Problems

I can't move past a certain spot in the document.
The end of the document is marked by a short horizontal line. You cannot move past this spot. If you try to click beyond this spot, nothing happens.

I see dots in between each word, arrows, plus some other weird mark at the end of each paragraph.

You can choose to display paragraph marks and space marks in your document. These elements do not print. To turn them on, click the Show/Hide [pm] button. To turn them off, click this button again.

Text started disappearing when I started typing.

Word normally is in Insert mode; that is, new text is inserted when you type. You can also use Overtype mode. In this mode, text is overwritten as you type. You may accidentally have switched to Overtype mode by pressing the Insert key on the keyboard. If you see OVR in the status bar, press the Insert key again to return to Insert mode.

Text wasn't inserted in the right spot when I started typing.

Remember that the insertion point indicates where text will be added, and the mouse pointer indicates where a mouse click will take effect. They can be in two different spots. If you point to the spot where you want to add text but don't click to move the insertion point, you don't move the insertion point. Be sure to point and click.

I thought I was selecting text, but somehow the text got moved.

If you select text, release the mouse button, and try to drag the text to extend the selection, Word thinks you want to move the selected text. This feature is called drag-and-drop editing. If you see a different mouse pointer (a box with an arrow), you know that you are moving text. You can undo the move by clicking the Undo button.

If you have this same problem a lot, you may want to turn off drag-and-drop editing. To do so, open the Tools menu and select the Options command. Click the Edit tab. Uncheck the Drag-and-drop text editing check box.

I see red squiggly lines under some words.

Word automatically checks your spelling as you type. If a word is underlined with a red, curvy line, it means Word thinks the word is misspelled. You can see alternative spellings for that word by right-clicking it and then selecting the correct spelling. See Chapter 4 for more help on checking spelling.

I see green squiggly lines under some words and phrases.

Word also automatically checks the grammar in your document. Word uses a green, curvy underline to point out what it thinks are grammatical errors. You can display suggested corrections by right-clicking the highlighted word or phrase. For more information on checking grammar, see Chapter 6,

My text looks really small (or really big), but I haven't changed the font.

If you have not made a change to the font size but text looks really big or really small, you probably have zoomed the document. Open the View menu, select the Zoom command, and check the zoom percentage. The normal zoom is 100 percent. You can also use the Zoom Control button in the toolbar.

My paragraph formatting changed unexpectedly.

The formatting for a paragraph is stored with the paragraph mark. Each time you press Enter, the paragraph options for that paragraph are carried down to the next paragraph. And if you delete the paragraph marker, the paragraph takes on the formatting of the following paragraph.

If something bizarre happens, try undoing the change using Edit → Undo. If you have trouble visualizing where the paragraph marks appear, you can display them by clicking the Show/Hide [pm] button.

I created a bulleted list, but now I can't get rid of the bullets.

When you press Enter within a bulleted list, Word adds another list item. To turn off bullets, click the Bullets button again.

I can't delete a number from the numbered list.

If you create a numbered list, Word adds the numbers automatically. You cannot delete them. To turn off the numbers, click the Numbering button again.

Word starts making formatting changes without my having selected any command.

Word's AutoFormat feature makes some formatting corrections as you type. For example, if you type an asterisk and press Tab, Word creates a bulleted list. To review or change which formatting changes are made, use the Tools → AutoCorrect command. Check the AutoFormat As You Type tab and make any changes.

I can't see the header (or footer) I created.

In Normal view, you won't see your headers or footers. To view these items, change to Page Layout view or Print Preview.

I can't delete a table.

Deleting a table is tricky. You can't just drag across it and press the Delete key. Doing so deletes all the entries but leaves the table grid. *To delete the table, follow these steps:*

1. Select the table using the **Table** → **Select Table** command.

2. Open the **Table** menu and select the **Delete Rows** command.

Most of the Table commands are unavailable.

To access the Table commands, you must be within a table. Put the insertion point within the table and try again.

I inserted a picture, but I can't see my text.

Depending on the type of picture, Word handles the text and picture differently. Sometimes the picture appears right on top of the text. Sometimes the text flows around the picture — usually part on top and bottom, but nothing on the sides of the picture. *To control how the text flows around the picture, follow these steps:*

1. In Page Layout view, click the object you want to change.

2. Open the ⬚ **Format** ⬚ menu and select the ⬚ **AutoShape** ⬚ command for shapes you've drawn or the ⬚ **Object** ⬚ command for clip art images. You see the Format Object (or AutoShape) dialog box.

3. Select the Wrapping tab. You see the different options you can use for text wrapping.

4. Select the wrapping style you want. You can select Square, Tight, Through, None, or Top & Bottom. The pictures of each option are pretty self-explanatory.

5. For Square, Tight, and Through, select where you want to wrap to: Both sides, Left, Right, or Largest side. Again, the picture in the dialog box give you a good idea of the effects of each option.

6. Click the OK button. Word wraps the text accordingly.

My picture moves around.

By default, Word moves the picture with the text. (That is, the text where the insertion point was when you inserted the picture.) *If you don't want the picture to move, you can change this option by following these steps:*

1. Click the object you want to change.

2. Open the ⬚ **Format** ⬚ menu and select the ⬚ **AutoShape** ⬚ command for shapes you've drawn or the ⬚ **Object** ⬚ command for clip art images. You see the Format Object (or AutoShape) dialog box.

3. Select the Position tab.

4. Uncheck the Move object with text check box.

5. Click the OK button.

My mail merge didn't work.

If a mail merge didn't work as expected, check the following:

✳ Be sure your main document includes the appropriate merge fields to insert the data. If not, edit the main document and insert the fields. See Chapter 10 for information on editing a main document.

* If you need to edit the data source, display the Mail Merge Helper dialog box and click the E_dit button under the Data source. Select the filename and then make any changes, as described in Chapter 10,

* The main document and data source must be associated. If that association is lost, you can tell Word which data source to use. In the Mail Merge Helper dialog box, click the G_et Data button and select O_pen Data Source. Select the data source file.

Excel Problems

I typed something, but it didn't go into the cell I wanted.

Remember that the active cell is indicated by the thick border. By scrolling the worksheet, you don't change the active cell. Be sure to point and click the cell you want. Then type your entry.

Part of one of my entries is missing. I see only the first part.

If you enter an entry that is longer than the column width, it spills over to the next cell. If that cell contains data, the entry is truncated or shortened. The cell still contains the entire entry, but you can see only the first part of it. You need to adjust the column width as covered in Chapter 14.

I entered a date, but it looks like a number.

The cell you are entering the date into may have been formatted with a different number format. Change the number format to the date format you want to use. See Chapter 14 for more information on date formats.

I see "###" in a cell.

If you change the column width and make it too small, you see number signs (###). You need to make the column wider, as covered in Chapter 14.

I see "1E+08" in a cell.

If you enter a number that is too big to display in a cell, Excel displays it using scientific notation. You can widen the column, as covered in Chapter 14.

I created a formula, but I don't see the results.

If you see the actual formula in the cell, you probably forgot to type an equal sign to start the formula. Edit the entry and insert the equal (=) sign. Press Enter.

I see "#REF" in a cell.

If you see this error message, it means that you have deleted a cell referenced in the formula. Edit the formula and correct the missing reference.

I see "#NAME?" in a cell.

If you type a function incorrectly, you see this error message. Instead of typing the function, use the Function Wizard to insert the function.

I don't see my headers or footers.

In normal view, you won't see headers or footers. To preview the headers or footers, use File → Print Preview.

I tried to do a fill, but all I got was the same number over and over.

If you want to fill a series of numbers, you have to enter the first two starting numbers, which set the pattern. Then select these two numbers and drag the fill handle. If you just select and drag one number, you get that number repeated.

I am creating a function, but I can't see the cell.

When you create a function using the Function Wizard, Excel displays the formula palette below the formula bar. If this obscures your view of the cells you want to use, drag the palette out of the way.

When I try to type in a cell, I see an error message saying the worksheet is protected.

You can turn on worksheet protection so that cells cannot be edited or deleted. If you see this message, it means protection is on. Use the Tools → Protection → Unprotect Sheet command to turn off the protection.

PowerPoint Problems

I added a chart (organization chart, clip art image), but it's right on top of the text on my chart.

When you add an object to a slide, it is placed right in the center. To integrate the object with existing slide content, you may need to move or resize the object. To move the object, select it. Then put the pointer within the object and click and drag. To resize the object, select the object and then put the pointer on a selection handle. Click and drag to resize.

I tried animating text, but nothing happened.

You won't see the animations on the slide. You see the animations only when you display the slide show.

I'm trying to type regular text, but I keep getting bulleted text.

If you are adding text to a bulleted text area, you'll get bullets. You can remove the bullets by clicking the Bullets button.

I updated the color scheme, but some items were not updated.

If you individually make a formatting change to a slide — for instance, change the colors of boxes in an organization chart or change the font — these changes override any overall presentation changes like color schemes. It's a good idea to make any overall changes first and then tweak individual slides.

Access Problems

When I open an existing database, the Database window doesn't display on my screen, so I can't work with my data.

Somehow you've selected the Startup option to hide the Database window. To unhide the current database but not subsequent databases, choose Window → Unhide. If you want to make sure the Database window always appears when you open an existing database, choose Tools → Startup to display the Startup dialog box. Select the Display Database Window check box and then choose OK.

I pressed Ctrl + End to move to the last field, last record in Datasheet view, but it kept me in the field I was currently in.

To use certain keystrokes to move around a table, you must use *navigation mode*. To activate this mode, press Tab, Shift+Tab, or the Up or Down arrow keys. Once you're in navigation mode, you can move to the end or beginning of a record, to the first or last record, and to other locations using the keyboard. For more information on these navigation techniques, see Table 22-1 in Chapter 22.

I want to change the number in a field, but when I select it and start typing, Access beeps at me and won't make the change.

The field is a specific type of field, such as a Counter field or a Calculated field. These fields are dependent on a calculation or expression to obtain the resulting data, so you cannot edit them.

I moved to one of the last fields in my table, and now I can only see the first few fields and the last few fields.

It sounds as if the first few field columns are frozen. Access indicates frozen columns by placing a dark vertical line next to the rightmost frozen column. To unfreeze columns, choose Format → Unfreeze All Columns.

I created a form for an existing table. When I tried to use it, the form was completely empty. Where's my data?

When you use a form, you may not see data for any of several reasons. First, you may not have bound the form to your underlying data. To check this, display the form in Design view and then click the Properties button on the toolbar or choose View → Properties to display the property sheet for the form. With the All tab displayed, check to see that the table containing the data is in the Record Source property box. If it isn't, select a record source in the list.

If you see the data source in the Properties dialog box, it's possible that the underlying table doesn't contain any data. Open the table to make sure it does have data. If your form is bound to a query, the query may come up empty as a result of the criteria you entered. For more on Queries, see the Bonus section in Chapter 22.

When I select a value from the list in my combo box, Access changes to this value for all records, not just the current record.

Access changed the value for all records because the control is not bound to a specific field. To bind the combo box control to a particular field in your data source, display the form in Design view and then select the combo box. Click the Properties button on the toolbar or choose View → Properties to display the property sheet for the form. Display the All or Data tab and then click in the Control Source text box. Use the arrow button to display a list of fields for the underlying table or query and then select the field name to which you wish to bind the control. Close the Properties dialog box.

Outlook Problems

Outlook problems are grouped under the different Outlook applets: E-mail, Contacts, Notes, and Tasks.

PROBLEMS WITH SENDING AND RECEIVING MESSAGES

E-mail I receive opens in Word, but I want it to open in Outlook.

E-mail is opening in Word because you have Wordmail installed and Outlook is using it as the e-mail editor. (I agree, I don't much care for it either, but when you remove it, you'll lose some messaging capabilities that are provided by Word 97, such as AutoCorrect, automatic spell-checking and highlighter.)

To remove Wordmail (and make Outlook open messages in an Outlook message window):

1. Click the Start button on the taskbar.

2. Point to Settings, and click Control Panel.

3. Double-click Add/Remove Programs.

4. Pop your Outlook or Office 97 CD into the CD-ROM drive.

5. Click Office 97 (or Outlook).

6. Click Install/Remove.

7. Select Microsoft Word.

8. Click the Change Details button.

9. Clear the Wordmail check box.

10. Click Finish.

I can't use the Check For New Mail command — Outlook makes me use the Check For New Mail On command instead.

You must tell Outlook which service you want it to use on a regular basis (so that you can use the Check For New Mail On command on those rare occasions when you want to use a different service).

Select Tools → Options and click the E-mail tab, under Check For New Mail On, click the check boxes for the services you want checked automatically and click OK.

I can't see all of my messages.

Your view may be filtered — if the words "Filter Applied" appear in the Folder banner, then there is a filter applied. To remove a filter, select View → Filter, click Clear All, and then click OK.

If you are missing old messages, they may have been AutoArchived. To learn how to retrieve archived items, ask the Office Assistant for help.

How can I send messages in plain text?

Sending messages in plain text is easy. *Just follow these steps:*

1. In Contacts, open the contact you want to send plain text messages to.

2. In the E-mail box, double-click the e-mail address.

3. Clear the Always send to this recipient in Microsoft Exchange Rich-Text Format check box.

4. Click OK.

PROBLEMS WITH CONTACTS

I can't find a name in the Select Names dialog box.

The Select Names dialog box can contain several address books, and the name you want may be in a different address book. In the dialog box, click another address book in the Show names from the box.

Names of my Contacts don't show up when I try to address an e-mail message.

Contacts with no e-mail address entered won't show up in the Select Names dialog box. Open the contact and enter an e-mail address for it, and it'll show up when you select Contacts as an address book for new e-mail messages.

PROBLEMS WITH NOTES

I can't see all of my open notes — I see only one.

The open notes are probably layered on top of one another; drag the note you see off to the side to uncover the note beneath it, and then keep dragging notes off the top of the note pile until they've all been uncovered.

PROBLEMS WITH TASKS

I've lost my TaskPad.
If you've been playing with resizing the Calendar elements, the TaskPad may have been squeezed out. To make the TaskPad reappear, resize Calendar elements smaller to make room for it, or maximize the Outlook window to show more.

I can't move my tasks up or down in the task list.
If tasks are sorted or grouped, you cannot move them up or down in the task list. You'll need to remove sorting or grouping, as follows:

* ✳ To remove sorting, select <u>V</u>iew → So<u>r</u>t and click Clear All.
* ✳ To remove grouping, select <u>V</u>iew → <u>G</u>roup By and click Clear All.

Problems with Publishing Documents on the Web

I don't see the Web page authoring tools on my menu.
The Web authoring features are part of the Web Page templates and wizard. They are also available if you convert an existing document to HTML. You know the features are available because the toolbars and menu change to reflect the tools you'll need to work with your Web pages. To use a Web template or wizard, choose <u>F</u>ile → <u>N</u>ew. Select the Web Pages tab and then select the desired template or wizard. Note: If you don't see the Web Pages tab, the Web pages features may not be installed. You may need to run Setup again and select Web page authoring components. For more information, see "Installing Web Authoring Tools" in Chapter 31.

I created several Web pages, and now I can't find them.
Word saves your Web documents with .HTML or .HTM extensions. When you display the Open dialog box, use the down arrow for the Files of type box and select All Files or HTML files.

I opened my Web page document and see a lot of brackets and codes. Where's my stuff?
If you see such things as ⟨HTML⟩, ⟨HEAD⟩, or ⟨B⟩ in your document instead of the content of your Web page, you may be using the HTML Source view option, which shows the actual HTML source code instead of the formatting and text of the Web Page. You'll also notice that certain menu options and toolbar buttons are not available in this view.

Check the Web Page toolbar to see if you have a large button on the far left side that says Exit HTML <u>S</u>ource. If so, click this button or click <u>V</u>iew → HTML <u>S</u>ource. If you don't see this button or if selecting HTML <u>S</u>ource from the <u>V</u>iew menu doesn't correct the problem, you may have opened a file that is in HTML format but doesn't use one of the extensions Word recognizes. To make sure

Word will convert the document, you can have Word display the Convert File dialog box. Click Tools → Options and then click the General tab. Click the Confirm conversion at Open check box and choose OK. Close the file, and then reopen it. When Word displays the Convert File dialog box, select HTML Document and choose OK.

I wanted to replace the bullets for a list in my Web document, but when I do, it adds the new bullets and leaves the old bullets in place.

The bullets Word uses for bulleted lists in Web documents are actually small graphic images. When you create a bulleted list, Word inserts these bullets as images separate from their associated text. To replace them, you must delete each bullet and then apply a new bullet style.

I want to edit the text of a hyperlink, but whenever I try to click to position the insertion point, Word jumps to the linked location.

Since the hyperlinks are active, Word will always jump to the linked location if you click a hyperlink. To position the insertion point in hyperlink text, click somewhere near the text that there is no hyperlink and then use the arrow keys to move the insertion point to the desired location.

I get an error message when I click a hyperlink.

This usually means you have removed or renamed the destination of the hyperlink. To check that the location is correct, right-click the hyperlink and then click Hyperlink → Edit Hyperlink from the shortcut menu to display the Edit Hyperlink dialog box. If you're linking to a file, make sure the path and filename are correct; if you're linking to a bookmark in the document, check to make sure it is spelled as you've spelled it in the bookmark name.

GLOSSARY

absolute reference — A reference in an Excel formula that is not adjusted if you move or copy the cell. Instead, the reference remains fixed.

annotation — In a reply or a forwarded message, text that the recipient types into the message text before sending it on as a reply or forwarded message.

applet — An Outlook miniprogram, such as Tasks or Calendar.

appointment — An activity you schedule in the Outlook Calendar.

area chart — A type of chart the emphasizes change over time.

ascending order — Lowest to highest, such as A to Z and 1 to 10.

attachment — A complete file or item that is sent with an e-mail message or stored with an Outlook item such as a task or journal entry.

AutoCalculate — An Excel feature that enables you to select a range and see a total (or other function) in the status bar.

AutoComplete — An Excel feature that you can use as a shortcut to making several instances of the same entry in a column. If you start typing the entry, Excel displays any entry in that column that starts with those same characters. You can press Enter to have Excel complete the entry for you.

AutoContent — A method for creating a PowerPoint presentation. You can select the type of presentation, and PowerPoint creates a presentation with sample slides and sample data. You can then replace the sample data with your own.

AutoCorrect — An Office feature that automatically corrects certain misspellings and typographical errors.

AutoCreate — An Outlook feature that allows you to create a new and different item by dragging and dropping one item onto the icon for a different type of item (for example, creating a task by dragging an e-mail message onto the Tasks icon).

AutoDate — An Outlook feature that inserts the correct date by interpreting descriptive text that you type, such as "tomorrow" or "next Thursday."

AutoFill — An Excel feature that you can use to enter a series of dates, numbers, or text items.

AutoFilter — An Excel feature you can use on data lists to show only certain values.

AutoForm — An Access feature that allows you to create a basic form to enter or modify data.

AutoFormat — An Office feature that automatically makes formatting changes to your document.

AutoLayout — One of several selections of PowerPoint slide layouts. The layout determines the placement and style of objects on a slide.

AutoName — An Outlook feature that looks up a name (or partial name) you type in the address section of a message and inserts the correct spelling and e-mail address for the name.

AutoPreview — An Outlook feature that displays the first three lines of a message in a table view.

AutoReport — An Access feature that allows you to create a basic report to display data in printed form.

AutoShape — A Word feature that enables you to draw simple shapes, such as circles, rectangles, boxes, stars, banners, and arrows, in a document.

AutoSum — A shortcut for entering and creating a SUM function.

AutoText — A Word feature that makes it easy to insert commonly used text (word, phrases, sentences, paragraphs) into your document quickly and without typing the entire entry.

axes — The two dimensions of the grid along which a chart is graphed.

bar chart — A type of chart most useful for comparing individual items.

bcc (blind copy) — A copy of an e-mail message that you send; recipients don't know who else has received a copy of a message if that copy was designated as blind.

binary file — A file created in a program such as Microsoft Word, Excel, or Access; these files contain far more information than the characters you see typed on the page.

bookmark — A spot in a document or selection of text that you name so that you can easily refer or go to that spot.

browser — A program you use to display and navigate among World Wide Web pages. Microsoft Internet Explorer is a browser.

button — A small icon included in a toolbar. Each button is a shortcut to a commonly used command or feature.

Calendar — An Outlook applet for scheduling your appointments, events, and meetings.

Card view — A view of Contacts in Outlook in which each contact's information is displayed in a business-card layout.

category — A field that identifies a file or an item so that you can find it easily by filtering or grouping; categories are information that you apply, rather than being an inherent part of an item or file.

cc — Copy; when you send an e-mail message, you can send cc (copies) to other recipients.

cell — The intersection of a column and a row in an Excel worksheet or a Word table.

character style — A set of formatting options that is applied to text. This type of style can include changes to the font, the size, the style, the color, or any other text attribute.

chart — A graph of numeric data. You can create charts in Excel and PowerPoint.

clip art — Artwork created by someone else that you are free to use in your document.

color scheme — The set of colors used for slides in a PowerPoint presentation.

column chart — A type of chart that shows data changes over time as well as comparing items.

combo box — A control you can add to a form that provides a list of options from which the user can select.

comma style — A number style that uses a comma to separate thousands — for example, "9,999.99."

comment — A note added to a cell in an Excel worksheet.

Contacts — An Outlook applet for recording names, phone numbers, addresses, home page sites, and other information about your associates and acquaintances.

controls — Text boxes, buttons, rectangles, graphics, and other elements on a form or report that make it easier to enter data or present the data in a more readable or aesthetically pleasing manner.

controls, bound — Controls tied to a specific field in an underlying table.

controls, calculated — Controls that can provide totals and other information that requires calculations.

controls, unbound — Controls that are *not* tied to a particular field in an underlying table. Use them to enter data or to enhance form or report design.

currency style — A number style that uses a comma to separate thousands and includes a dollar sign — for instance, "$9,999.99."

customize — To make changes to the default options so that a feature works the way you want.

data — Information you enter into a database.

database — A collection of information or data.

datasheet — A view of your Access data in columnar form.

data source — One of two documents needed for a mail merge. The data source includes the list of variable information (such as a list of names and addresses) that you want to merge with the main document to create personalized letters.

default — The option that is automatically selected and used by a program unless you make a change.

Deleted Items — An Outlook folder that contains items you delete from Outlook applets; to delete items from your hard drive, you must delete them from the Deleted Items folder.

Desktop — The screen you see when you start Windows. The desktop includes some icons that you can use to start using your computer. For instance, use the My Computer icon to browse through the contents of your system. You can also customize the desktop and place other shortcut icons to programs, files, or folders that you often use.

dialog box — A window that appears onscreen when you select any of certain commands and that prompts you for additional information about how to carry out that command.

drag-and-drop editing — The capability to move or copy text, objects, or cells by simply selecting the item and then dragging it.

dynaset — The resulting data that meet the criteria set in an Access query.

e-mail (also E-mail) — Short for electronic mail. Messages sent via a network or modem to other users.

e-mail message — An electronic letter or package.

event — An activity that you schedule in the Outlook Calendar that lasts at least 24 hours.

expression — In Access, the information you type in the Criteria cell of a query.

field — In Outlook, a particular type of information, such as Last Name or City or Phone Number; in a table view, a field is displayed as a column; in a card view, a field is displayed as a labeled box in the card. In Access, an individual piece of information within a record. The last name of a particular individual is one field and the address for that same individual is a second field. Each column in an Access table identifies a field.

field name — In Access, the unique "label" for each field. In Datasheet view, it would appear as a column heading.

file — An individual document, such as an Excel spreadsheet, an Access database, or a Word document, that you create or save with a unique filename.

file tree — A "map" of your computer files such as you see in Windows Explorer or the My Computer window.

fill — In Excel, a feature that enables you to quickly enter a series of numbers, dates, or text items in a range.

folder — A division of your hard disk. Each folder has a name, and folders can be stored inside other folders. You can set up folders for the different types of documents you create. A directory or subdirectory.

folder banner — The horizontal bar below the Outlook toolbars; the folder banner displays the name of the applet or folder you have open.

font — A set of characters in a particular typeface.

font size — The type size of a font. Fonts are measured in points, and there are 72 points to an inch.

font style — An attribute, such as italic or bold, applied to a font.

footer — Text or graphics that are printed at the bottom of each page in a document.

form — In Access, a fill-in-the-blank view for entering data.

form, feedback — In Access, a fill-in-the-blank form you can create for a Web site that allows visitors to respond electronically.

format — To change the appearance of text, paragraphs, pages, graphics, and so on.

formula — A mathematical equation entered in an Excel worksheet.

formula bar — The bar under the toolbar in Excel, where you see the cell reference and the contents of the current cell.

formula palette — A dialog box that is displayed when you are editing or creating a formula or function in Excel. You can use the palette to work on the function.

forward — To send to someone else a message you've received.

FTP (file transfer protocol) — The Internet standard for transferring files from one computer to another.

function — A predefined formula that you can use to perform complex calculations such as figuring a loan amount, calculating the return on an investment, and so on.

header — Text or graphics that are printed at the top of each page in a document.

HTML — The formatting language used to set up documents for the World Wide Web. Stands for HyperText Markup Language.

hyperlink — A link (usually in colored, underlined text) that you can click to jump to a file, a location in a file, a page on the World Wide Web, or a page on another network.

icon — Little pictures used to represent programs, files, printers, applets, and other elements in Windows.

Inbox — An Outlook applet for receiving your e-mail messages.

insertion point — An onscreen indicator that looks like a flashing vertical line. This line indicates where new text will be inserted if you start typing.

Internet — A worldwide network of networks — commercial, educational, organizational, government, and personal networks. You can go to any site on the network if you have a modem and an Internet account.

Internet Explorer — A Microsoft program designed for browsing the Word Wide Web.

Internet Service Provider (ISP) — A private enterprise that provides a server through which you can connect to the Internet (also called *Local Service Provider* and *Mail Service*).

intranet — A network within a company or organization that is set up and uses the same method for displaying contents and navigating as the Internet.

item — An individual applet entity, such as an e-mail message or a task or a journal entry or a contact.

Journal — An Outlook applet for recording your activities as you complete them.

journal entry — Information about an activity that you have recorded in Journal.

justified text — A text alignment. Instead of having an uneven right margin, space is added between words to keep the right margin even.

label — A tag or heading on a form or report that is not tied to a particular field.

landscape orientation — A page layout where text is printed across the long side of the page.

legend — Part of a chart that identifies what each series represents.

line chart — A type of chart that shows trends.

Local Service Provider — See *Internet Service Provider.*

macro — A set of stored Word commands and instructions that you can play back with one command.

mail folder — A folder that stores e-mail messages in Outlook, such as Inbox, Outbox, and Sent Items.

mail merge — A type of operation used to create personalized letters from two sources: a main document and a data source. Also known as form letters.

mail service — See *Internet Service Provider.*

main document — In a mail merge, the document that contains the text you want to include in each letter as well as the merge fields that insert the variable information.

margin — The space left around each edge of the page.

merge field — A special type of code used in mail merge documents to tell Word when to insert variable information, such as a name or address, in a document.

Microsoft Network (MSN) — Microsoft's online service you can use to get current news, do research, chat with other uses, exchange messages, download files, connect to the Internet, and so on.

My Computer — An icon that appears on the desktop that you can use to browse through the drives on your system and access your printer drivers and Control Panel. When seen in the Outlook bar, this icon opens a window to the top of your file tree.

navigation buttons — Arrow buttons at the bottom of a Datasheet, Form, or Report view window that allow you to move from record to record or page to page depending on the view.

newsgroup — An Internet discussion group dedicated to a specific topic. You can post your own messages for others to review and comment on, and you can review other posted messages.

noncontiguous range — In Excel, a group of cells that are not next to each other.

Notes — An Outlook applet for creating little reminder notes that look like paper sticky notes.

number format — The way numbers are displayed in a worksheet.

object — Elements that make up a database as a whole, such as a table, form, or report.

operators — In an Excel formula, the sign for the mathematical operation you want to perform — +, –, *, and so on.

Outbox — An Outlook applet for holding e-mail messages that are ready to be sent; when you dial up your mail service, whatever is in the Outbox gets mailed.

Outlook bar — The vertical bar on the left side of the Outlook window; the Outlook bar contains icons for Outlook applets and folders.

Outlook bar group — A group of icons displayed in the Outlook bar, such as the Mail group, the Outlook group, and the Other group; display a group by clicking the button for that group.

page — Printed output.

paragraph style — A set of formatting options that is applied to the paragraph. This type of style can include alignment changes, indents, borders, shading, and other paragraph formats.

percent style — A number style that formats the number as a percent. For instance, .1 would be displayed as "10%."

Personal Address Book — An Outlook address book that is separate from Contacts, although it stores similar information (name, address, phone numbers, e-mail address, and so on). In a Personal Address Book you can create Personal Distribution Lists (which cannot be created in Contacts).

picture placeholder — A feature you can use when creating Web pages to describe a picture for a visitor who may be unable or unwilling to view the graphic image itself.

pie chart — A type of chart that shows how the part relates to the whole.

portrait orientation — A page layout where text is printed down the long side of the page.

query — The process of selecting and/or manipulating data based on specific criteria.

range — A selection of cells. A range can be several cells, an entire row, an entire column, or the entire worksheet.

range name — A descriptive name used for a range or cell. For instance, you can name a range TOTAL rather than A1:A5.

recipient — The person who receives a message.

record — A collection of related information, such as the name, address, city, state, and zip of a particular company or individual. Each row in an Access table is a record.

recurring task — A task that shows up on your task list at regular intervals, such as once a week or once a month, whether or not you complete the previous occurrence of the task.

Recycle Bin — Where files are placed when you delete them. If you delete a file by accident, you may be able to retrieve it from the Recycle Bin. The desktop includes an icon for the Recycle Bin so that you can view its contents.

regenerating task — A task that shows up on your task list again each time you complete the previous occurrence of the task.

relational database — In the case of Access, a database in which you can store information in different *tables*. Each table can contain different information that *relates* to information in other tables.

relative reference — A reference in a formula that is adjusted to the relative location when copied or moved.

reminder — A visual message and/or sound that appears or plays to remind you of an impending appointment.

reply — Return a message to its sender along with your notes and replies to their message.

report — The presentation of data in a logical, readable format, usually designed to be printed.

ruler — An on-screen formatting tool you can use to set indents or tabs.

scroll bars — Strips along the right and bottom of the window that show you your relative position in the document. You can click a scroll arrow to scroll in that direction or drag the scroll box up or down to scroll through a document.

sender — The person who sends an e-mail message.

sent items — E-mail messages, task requests, and meeting requests that have been sent.

shortcut icon — An icon that provides access to a program, document, applet, or file and opens the program, document, applet, or file when clicked or double-clicked. You can place shortcut icons on the desktop or in the Start menu.

shortcut menu — A menu that displays commonly used commands related to the selected object. To display a shortcut menu, right-click the object you want to modify.

slide — One of the individual pieces that make up a PowerPoint presentation.

slide objects — Items such as charts, clip art images, tables, and text boxes that you can add to a PowerPoint slide.

slide show — An on-screen display of your PowerPoint presentation.

sort button — A column heading in a table view; click to sort the items according to that field; click again to sort the items according to that field but in the opposite order.

sorting — A method of listing items — for example in alphabetical order.

speaker notes — Printed pages that include each slide in a presentation as well as any notes for the presenter.

Start button — The first button in the taskbar. You can use this button to start programs, find a file, or get help.

status bar — The bar along the bottom of the screen that gives you information, such as the page number and insertion point position, about the current document.

style — A set of formatting options applied to text or worksheet cells.

tab — A notch at the top of a dialog box that contains more than one page of options. You can select the tab you want to view those options.

table — The layout of an Access database file, consisting of rows and columns as well as a collection of information stored in fields (columns) and records (rows).

table view — A view type in which items are displayed in rows and columns.

taskbar — The bar that appears along the bottom of the screen at all times. Each program that is running is represented by a button in the taskbar. You can use the taskbar to switch to a different program or window.

task list — A list of things that need to be done, stored in Tasks.

TaskPad — A miniature task list that appears in Calendar.

Tasks — An Outlook applet for creating a to-do list.

template — A document that may include text, styles, formatting, AutoText entries, and macros set up for your use.

text box — A box in a form or report that can contain data entered by the user or visitor to a Web site.

thesaurus — A Word feature that enables you to look up synonyms for words in your document.

thumbnail month — The small month picture, also called a Date Navigator, in Outlook Calendar and in various dialog boxes; you click a date on the picture to insert the date in a box or to display the calendar for that date.

Timeline view — A view in which items are displayed on a timeline according to when they occurred.

title bar — The bar that appears along the top of a window and displays the program name and document name.

toolbar — An on-screen row of buttons. Each button is a shortcut to a commonly used command or feature.

transition — A visual effect used to display the next slide in a presentation.

URL (Uniform Resource Locator) — An Internet or World Wide Web address. The address usually has a format similar to this address for the Microsoft home page on the World Wide Web: http://www.microsoft.com.

view — An Outlook display of all the items in an applet or folder.

Web — See *World Wide Web*.

wildcard — A character that stands in for other characters, usually in a search, to increase the chances of having a match.

Windows Explorer — A file management program that displays folders and files in a hierarchical structure. You can use this program to move, copy, delete, and view the files and folders on your system.

wizard — An automated template that prompts you to make selections and enter text to create a document.

word wrap — A Word feature that automatically wraps words when they reach the end of a line. You don't need to press Enter to end one line and start the next.

workbook — The set of Excel worksheets saved and stored together as one file. All worksheets in the workbook are saved together.

worksheet — A grid of columns and rows where you enter your data in Excel. Each workbook has three worksheets by default, but you can add and delete worksheets as needed.

World Wide Web — Part of the Internet. Information on the World Wide Web is published as pages, and the pages can include text, graphics, sounds, animations, videos, and links to other pages. You move from page to page by clicking the links.

WWW — See *World Wide Web*.

Zoom — To enlarge the display of the document.

INDEX

C

(continued)

(continued)

inserting worksheets, 224

menu bar, 3

navigating worksheets, 3

quick way to enter formulas, 215

ranges, 189–191

rearranging worksheets, 219–223

removing cells, rows, or columns, 227–228

renaming worksheets, 224

rows, 3

shortcuts for entering data, 195–198

spell–checking worksheet, 228–229

spreadsheet templates, 259–260

Standard toolbar, 182–183

starting, 3, 179–180

title bar, 3

toolbars, 3, 182

values, 191–194

workbooks, 182

worksheets, 3, 181–182, 185–189

Exit (Alt+F4) keyboard shortcut, 38

exiting

Access, 7

Excel, 4

Internet Explorer, 509

Outlook, 8

PowerPoint, 5

programs, 38

Word, 2

Explorer, renaming databases, 360

Expression Builder, 411–412

expression operators, 377

expressions, 411

F

FACCT (Foundation for Accountability), 178

favorite folders, 56–58

Favorites → Add To Favorites command, 510

Fax Wizard, 49–50

faxing documents, 49–50

feedback form, 531–534

fields, 280, 351, 353

adding to tables, 370–371

deleting, 283, 353

deleting from tables, 371–372

freezing names, 281–282

inserting, 353

moving, 402

moving in tables, 371–372

moving on form with label, 387

navigation mode, 363–364

File menu, 31

File New Database dialog box, 350

File → Close command, 44

File → Create Shortcut command, 511

File → Exit command, 38

File → New command, 47, 134, 137, 139, 259, 303

File → New Database command, 47, 358

File → Open command, 45, 57, 59, 61–66

File → Page Setup command, 124, 126–127, 251, 253, 255–256

File → Preview command, 48

File → Print Area → Clear Print Area command, 258

File → Print Area → Set Print Area command, 258

File → Print command, 48, 172, 176, 343, 397

File → Print Preview command, 125, 249–250

(continued)

home pages, 513–514

Hopey, Chris, 346

Horizontal Line dialog box, 523

HTML (HyperText Markup Language), 514

Word file as document, 514

Hyperlink dialog box, 527–528

hyperlinks, 435–436, 514, 526–528

I

icons, 12–14, 17

identifiers, 411

IDG Books Worldwide site, 505

IF function, 215

Import and Export Wizard, 490–491

importing data into Access, 496–498

Inbox, 420–422

Inbox Setup Wizard, 416–417

indenting text, 108–110

information management, 7–8

Insert dialog box, 226

Insert File dialog box, 434

Insert mode, 78

Insert Picture dialog box, 155–156

Insert → Auto Form command, 381

Insert → AutoReport command, 395

Insert → AutoSignature command, 437

Insert → AutoText command, 79–80

Insert → AutoText → AutoText command, 80

Insert → Bookmark command, 527

Insert → Break command, 74, 151

Insert → Cells command, 226

Insert → Chart command, 264, 332

Insert → Columns command, 226

Insert → Comment command, 231

Insert → Edit Comment command, 232

Insert → Function command, 209

Insert → Horizontal Line command, 523

Insert → Hyperlink command, 527

Insert → Name → Create command, 231

Insert → Name → Define command, 230

Insert → New Record command, 384

Insert → New Slide command, 304, 324

Insert → Page Break command, 258

Insert → Page Numbers command, 128

Insert → Picture command, 153, 155–156, 276

Insert → Picture → Browse Web Art Pages command, 524

Insert → Picture → Clip Art command, 311, 332

Insert → Picture → From File command, 524

Insert → Picture → Organization Chart command, 309

Insert → Picture → Organizational Chart command, 332

Insert → Remove Page Break command, 258

Insert → Report command, 399

Insert → Rows command, 226

Insert → Text Box, 161

Insert → Text Box command, 332

Insert → Worksheet command, 224

inserting

cells, rows, or columns, 225–226

worksheets, 224

insertion point, 73–75
installing
    Web authoring tools, 516, 517
    Web Publishing Wizard, 530
Internet, 499
    costs, 502
    getting connected to, 501–503
    icon for, 13
    Internet service provider, 501–502
    modems, 501
    phone line, 501
    searching for topics, 508
    what you can do on, 500
    who owns it, 502
Internet Explorer, 499
    canceling action, 507
    customizing, 510–511
    desktop shortcut, 511
    exiting, 509
    favorite places, 510–511
    going directly to page, 506
    manipulating pages, 509
    navigating Web, 504
    retracing steps, 507
    screen, 504–505
    searching for topics, 508
    toolbar, 504
    typing address, 506
    Web sites, 504–505
Internet service provider, 416,
        501–502
Italic (Ctrl+I) keyboard shortcuts, 103,
    405
italic text, 103, 329

J

Journal applet, 421
    deleting entries, 461

manually entering document,
        463–464
    manually entering item, 461–463
    manually recording activities,
        464–465
    opening entries, 461
Journal Entry dialog box, 461–465
Justify Text (Ctrl+J) keyboard
    shortcuts, 107

K

keyboard
    command selection, 31–32
    moving insertion point, 75
    selecting cell, 187–188
    selecting ranges, 190
    selecting text, 83
keyboard shortcuts, 34
    ↓ (Down One Cell), 3, 187
    ↓ (Down One Row), 363–364
    ↓ (One Character Down), 75
    ← (Left One Cell), 187
    ← (One Character Left), 75
    ← (Previous Character), 364
    ← (Previous Field), 364
    → (Next Field), 364
    → (One Character Right), 75
    → (Right One Cell), 3, 187
    ↑ (Next Character), 364
    ↑ (One Character Up), 75
    ↑ (Up One Cell), 187
    ↑ (Up One Row), 363–364
    Alt (Menu Bar), 31
    Alt+F4 (Exit), 38
    Alt+PgDn (Right One Screen), 187
    Alt+PgUp (Left One Screen), 188
    Ctrl+1 (Single Spacing), 110
    Ctrl+2 (Double Spacing), 110

N

(continued)

Percent format, 240
rounding, 212
scientific notation, 193
totaling, 207

O

objects, 349
Office Assistant (?), 34–35
One Character Down (↓) keyboard
 shortcuts, 75
One Character Left (←) keyboard
 shortcuts, 75
One Character Right (→) keyboard
 shortcuts, 75
One Character Up (↑) keyboard
 shortcuts, 75
One Paragraph Down (Ctrl+↓)
 keyboard shortcuts, 75
One Paragraph Up (Ctrl+↑) keyboard
 shortcuts, 75
One Screen Dn (PgDn) keyboard
 shortcut, 75
One Screen Up (PgUp) keyboard
 shortcut, 75
One Word Left (Ctrl+←) keyboard
 shortcuts, 75
One Word Right (Ctrl+→) keyboard
 shortcuts, 75
one–to–many relationship, 356–357
online help, 19–23
Online Layout view, 518
Open command, 39, 40
Open Data Source dialog box, 175,
 485
Open dialog box, 45, 360
 Add to Favorites button, 57
 Cancel button, 66

changing how files are listed, 54–55
Commands and Settings button,
 64–66
Details button, 54
File name option, 64–66
Find Now button, 64–66
Last modified option, 66
List button, 54
Look in Favorites button, 57
Preview button, 55
Properties button, 55
Text or property options, 65
Open Office Document command, 46
Open Office Document dialog box, 46
opening documents, 45–46
operators, 200–201, 411
option buttons, 32
Options dialog box, 33
 Calendar tab, 453
 Check grammar as you type
  option, 93
 Check spelling as you type option,
  93
 Custom Lists tab, 198
 E–mail tab, 417
 Formulas check box, 216
 General tab, 236
 Gridlines option, 235
 Journal tab, 459–460
 Save tab, 44
 Size list, 236
 Standard font drop–down list, 236
 View tab, 216, 235
organizational charts, 309–311
 adding boxes, 322
 adding to slides, 332
 deleting boxes, 321

(continued)

(continued)

(continued)

(continued)

(continued)

(continued)